LET THE CREDIT GO

By J. Rives Childs
RELIQUES OF THE RIVES (1929)
BEFORE THE CURTAIN FALLS (1932)
GERMAN MILITARY CIPHERS (1935)
THE PAGEANT OF PERSIA (1936,
under pen name of Henry Filmer)
ESCAPE TO CAIRO (1938,
under pen name of Henry Filmer)
AMERICAN FOREIGN SERVICE (1948)
RESTIF DE LA BRETONNE (1949,
in French)
CASANOVIANA (1956)
CASANOVA: A BIOGRAPHY BASED
ON NEW DOCUMENTS (1961)
DIPLOMATIC AND LITERARY QUESTS (1963)
COLLECTOR'S QUEST: THE CORRESPONDENCE
OF HENRY MILLER AND J. RIVES CHILDS,
1947–65 (1967, *edited
by Richard Clement Wood*)
FOREIGN SERVICE FAREWELL: MY YEARS
IN THE NEAR EAST (1969)
VIGNETTES (1977)
CASANOVA:
DIE GROSSE BIOGRAPHIE
(1977, *in German*)

Let the Credit Go

THE AUTOBIOGRAPHY OF

J. RIVES CHILDS

THE K.S. GINIGER COMPANY, INC.
PUBLISHERS
NEW YORK

LET THE CREDIT GO

Copyright © 1983 by J. Rives Childs. All rights reserved, including the right to reproduce this book or portions thereof by any means, electronic or mechanical, including photocopying, recording or any information storage and retrieval system, without permission in writing from the publisher. All inquiries should be addressed to The K.S. Giniger Company, Inc., 235 Park Avenue South, New York City 10003. This book is manufactured in the United States of America.

Designed by Rose Jacobowitz

LIBRARY OF CONGRESS CATALOGING IN PUBLICATION DATA

Childs, J. Rives (James Rives), 1893–
  Let the credit go.

  Includes index.
  1. Childs, J. Rives (James Rives), 1893– 2. Ambassadors——United States——Biography. 3. United States——Foreign relations——20th century. I. Title.
E748.C5245A35   1983   327.2′092′4 [B]   83-81351
  ISBN 0-8119-0516-0

Distributed by
Frederick Fell Publishers, Inc.
386 Park Avenue South
New York City 10016

Ah, take the Cash, and let the Credit go,
Nor heed the rumble of a distant Drum!

Edward FitzGerald,
The Rubáiyát of Omar Khayyám

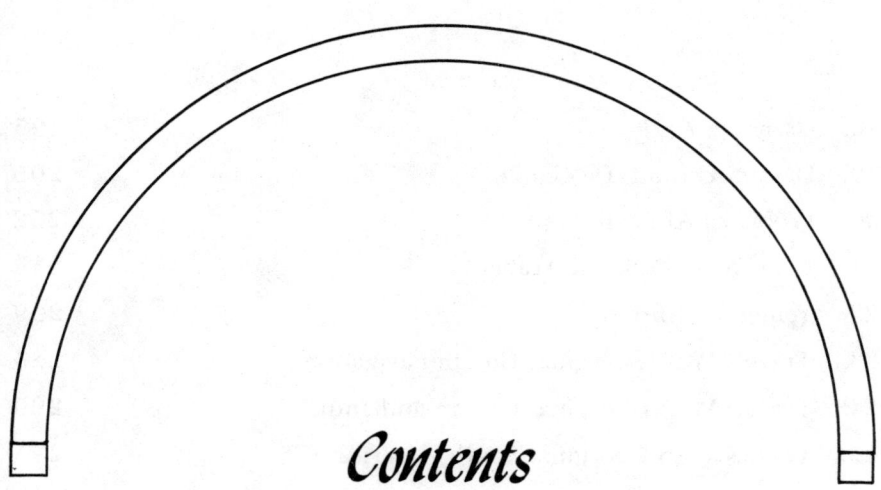

Contents

1.	Early Days	1
2.	Harvard, France and Lawrenceville	13
3.	Soldiering in France	24
4.	Paris and Yugoslavia	40
5.	Washington Correspondent	51
6.	Russia After the Revolution	59
7.	Consul in Jerusalem	80
8.	Assignment in Romania	92
9.	Posting to Cairo	98
10.	The Charm of Persia	104
11.	Two Revolutions: Egypt and Spain	109
12.	Wartime Policy in North Africa	121
13.	Assignment to Tangier	133
14.	Probing French, Spanish and German Intentions	143
15.	Diplomatic Relations in North Africa	152
16.	Wartime Intrigue in Morocco	174
17.	Attitudes Toward Allied Invasion	184

18.	*Operation Torch*	195
19.	Darlan, Giraud, De Gaulle	205
20.	Problems After *Torch*	222
21.	Four Years in Saudi Arabia	235
22.	Yemen and Ethiopia	269
23.	Travels With Georgina: Circumnavigation	286
24.	Travels With Georgina: Ceylon and India	290
25.	Travels With Georgina: South America	295
26.	Travels With Georgina: Cape Town to Cairo	298
27.	Travels With Georgina: Greece and the Islands	300
28.	Travels With Georgina: Mexico and Some of the U.S.	304
29.	Travels With Georgina: The Other Side of the World	310
30.	Travels With Georgina: England, Scotland, Ireland and France	314
	Epilogue	321
	Index	327

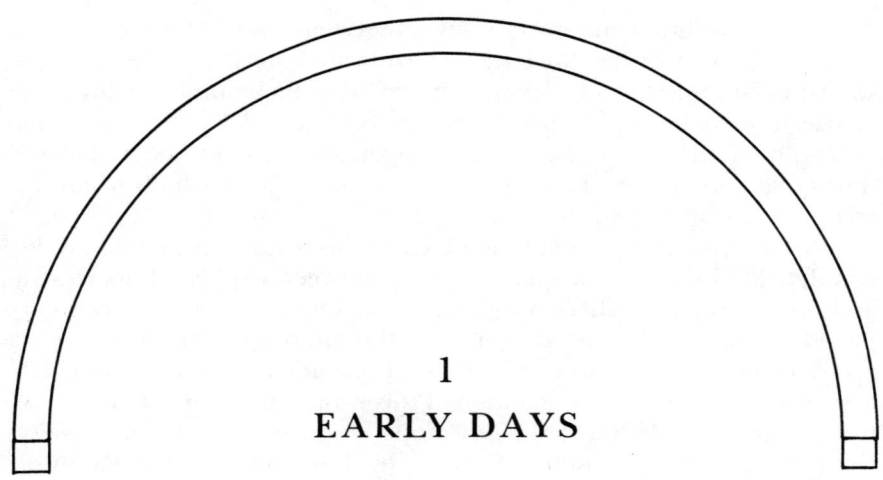

1
EARLY DAYS

My parents were both Virginians and second cousins. My father, John William Childs (1845–1930), was the son of Reverend John Wesley Childs, born in Calvert County, Maryland, in 1801, of a family residing since 1665 in Cecil County. An earlier John Child was known to have been in Queen Anne Parish, Prince George County, in 1742; his son, Gabriel, removed to Calvert County and later to Fairfax County, Virginia. The latter's grandson, John, was one of the earliest Methodist ministers in Maryland, protégé of the famous Bishop Asbury.

My mother, Lucy Howard Brown (1858–1947), was of no less distinguished antecedents by virtue of her descent from fourteen members of the Virginia House of Burgesses. She was a daughter of James Leftwich Brown of Lynchburg, first president of the Franklin Literary Society at Randolph-Macon College, of which he was a graduate; later he attended the University of Virginia. He married Mary Virginia Early, daughter of Bishop John Early, one of the founders of Randolph-Macon, and his wife Elizabeth Browne Rives.

My grandfather died before my father was five years old; his widow made a home for her family at Gravel Hill, Buckingham County, Virginia, where the Buckingham Female Institute was situated and her children might have the benefit of the educational advantages of that college. She obtained permission for my father to attend the Institute, along with several other youngsters from the neighborhood.

When war broke out in 1861, my father volunteered his services in a company known as the Buckingham Institute Guards, organized by a Captain Garland Haynes. Upon their arrival in Richmond, fearing that, on account of his small size, he might be rejected by the mustering officer, my father arranged with a stranger, some six feet tall and about thirty-five years of age, to answer to the name of John Childs when the company was mustered in.

After initial assignment as a guard of the prisons in Richmond, he was detailed in 1864 as a special courier between the War Department and the Army of Northern Virginia. At the end of the war, he contemplated moving west. To assist him in this he sought and obtained a testimonial letter from General Lee, then president of Washington College in Lexington. But he abandoned this project to enter the service of the Consolidated Railway Express Company as agent in Lynchburg, later being made superintendent. He held this post until the formation by him of a company for the buying of raw leaf tobacco, which was cured and exported abroad. While furthering the export trade of this firm, he visited England, Ireland, Scotland, France, Belgium and Holland about 1880.

About 1888, he abandoned the tobacco business and entered the real estate business at Buena Vista, Virginia, to take advantage of a boom in land values there. Upon its collapse, he returned to Lynchburg, where, at about the same time, that city's Traders Bank, of which he was a director, failed. All of the directors except himself and a colleague had recourse to bankruptcy, with the result that he spent the best part of his life discharging the financial obligations he had incurred as bank director.

My mother had graduated first in her class from the Lynchburg High School and later took special courses at Randolph-Macon Woman's College and Cornell University. She had been left an orphan at the age of fourteen with no resources, as her father had converted his real estate holdings during the war into Confederate bonds, which had become worthless. She had been obliged to enter the public school system as a teacher at the age of sixteen, two years after her father's death. In 1886 she was appointed the first woman principal in the city. Upon her marriage in 1890, she retired from teaching. I was born in 1893.

In 1898, a year of crisis in the financial affairs of my father, my mother turned to Superintendent of Schools Ned Glass, brother of Congressman Carter Glass, both friends of the family.

"Ned," she said, "I must have a job again as teacher."

"Lucy, I am sorry, but we have no vacancy except in the colored schools, and I can't offer you that, as no white woman has ever served in Lynchburg as a teacher of Negroes."

"Well, I am going to be the first, and you are going to be the first to appoint me."

"But, Lucy, I can't. What do you think your friends would say?"

"I am not interested in what they would have to say. There is nothing but silly prejudice which stands in my way, and you are going to let down the bars for me."

She was one of the most strong-minded persons I have ever known, and she was all the more so when she was convinced of the rightness of her cause.

Of course, she obtained the post, becoming one of the first southern women of any social standing to instruct colored children. In 1901, she was reappointed a principal, and she continued without interruption in that position until her retirement in 1926 at the age of sixty-eight.

As for my father, if any one trait was characteristic of him, it was his sense of honor. In the home or out of it, I never heard him raise his voice. When I once spoke disrespectfully to my mother in my childhood, he called me quietly to account. "Son, you mustn't speak that way to a lady, and least of all to your mother." He never had to readmonish me.

My earliest memories are of a home on Cabell Street, to which the family had moved from Madison Street. There we had a beautiful young female boarder of fifteen or sixteen years of age who enticed me into her bed, where she was accustomed to take a nap in the afternoon, and, by her endearments, aroused my first erotic emotions.

When I was older, we moved to a new home on Washington Street on Diamond Hill. It was here that I frequented the entrancing shop of Mrs. Bragassa, filled with children's toys, including such elaborate ones as hook-and-ladder wagons and other fanciful contraptions which were beyond my parents' means. I found it difficult to understand why these couldn't be offered me when some of my companions obtained them so readily.

I found the world a most mysterious affair which constantly presented aspects that defied my understanding. Having presented myself at a nearby grocery store on an errand for my mother, I asked for the articles she desired and told the clerk to "charge the objects to my mother."

"But who is your mother, son?" I was asked.

The question quite startled me, and I found it beyond my comprehension that everyone did not know who my mother was.

The shopkeeper at length came to my aid. "Tell me her name, son," he coaxed me reassuringly.

I relaxed and murmured, "Mrs. Childs," while still puzzled why he should have to rely on me for information I thought was in the possession of everyone.

It was one of the great milestones in my adjustment to the world. Others followed slowly, one by one.

At the public school which I had begun to attend, there was great excitement over the absence of the janitor, Joe Higginbottom, a black man. People were pointing to the nearby home of an attractive young white woman. When we had the unaccustomed visit of the police, who were closeted with the principal, we had the feeling that something strange was afoot. The grown-ups didn't wish to discuss it with us. Some of it came out slowly and piecemeal, and much of it remained a mystery. From the little we learned, Joe had entered the home of the lovely young woman, and had abused her and cut her throat. We never understood why. Joe had fled to Candler's Mountain but was pursued by bloodhounds, captured and put in jail. Weeks later, he was tried and executed, and we were given another janitor. It was only years later that we learned he had raped our young friend, but to many of us this was still a mystery.

When I perceived at an early age that my parents were unable to afford the possessions I coveted, in particular a bicycle, I cast about for means by which I might acquire such things. My attention was one day attracted to the newsboys waiting outside the *Daily Advance*, an afternoon newspaper, to obtain papers for sale on the street or for distribution to their subscribers. The impulse came over me to line up with the others and to try my hand. I cautiously acquired half a dozen copies and rushed with the other boys to find purchasers. My father's office was nearby and I had the misfortune of encountering him soon afterward on the street. When he caught sight of me, he was visibly upset; in fact, I had rarely seen him quite so disturbed. He told me to get rid of the papers and then to go home and await him there.

Sometime later, he returned home, where he found both my mother and me. He informed her in some indignation—as much as he ever permitted himself—of how he had found me hawking the *Daily Advance* as any boy of the most common origin. In his opinion it was quite unbecoming for anyone of good family to so demean himself.

My mother only smiled and stated that in her opinion there was nothing demeaning in honest work; she thought that while it might be an innovation for her son to be the first of a reputable family to sell newspapers on the streets, it would inculcate in me a sense of self-reliance, and she was in favor of my continuing. As usual, my father gracefully yielded to the assertion of my mother's good sense. Soon afterward, I organized a regular news route, comprising more than a hundred subscribers, which yielded me a sufficient income to acquire such useful possessions as a bicycle and other coveted objects to add to my contentment.

Before entering college, I had been attacked by the wanderlust, a passion which has never left me, even in old age, when I continue to respond to its urge. My first response was to accompany a boy of my age who had acquired a bicycle, as I had, with the profits from a newspaper route. We set out for quite a short excursion—a half day's run to Danville, about sixty miles distant, where we planned to see our local professional baseball team in competition with Danville. The two idols of our team were Bill Bentley, catcher, and Young Kirkpatrick, who played shortstop with consummate ability except for an occasional error. We found the team in a local poolroom in Danville. One of the great moments of my life was when Kirkpatrick invited me to join them in a game.

A more extended tour was made with a neighbor of my age, Wheeler Buckingham. At that time, the only paved road of importance in the state was the toll road in the valley, extending from Roanoke to the vicinity of Harper's Ferry, West Virginia. We set out by way of Buena Vista and Lexington. The scenery afforded by the Blue Ridge mountain range was impressively beautiful. Automobiles were a rarity and were only encountered occasionally. The most imposing car we saw was one transporting Congressman Carter Glass and members of his family from Lynchburg to Washington.

I shall always recall the abrupt descent of the road from the hill overlooking Harper's Ferry into a valley alongside a river. We were agog with excitement, for it was our first excursion outside of Virginia. On returning, we left the toll road to visit my uncle and aunt and their half-dozen children, my first cousins, in their stately and commodious brick dwelling alongside the majestic Shenandoah River. Thoughtless as we were at our age, we had not taken the pains to give notice of our prospective arrival; but we were nonetheless warmly welcomed with typical Virginia hospitality and provided with beds for our overnight stay. The unusual trip we had made provoked cries of admiration from our auditors and transformed us into the unaccustomed roles of amateur actors in a play of our devising. There was simplicity to life in those days—now gone forever, more's the pity.

I was just past sixteen when I matriculated at the Virginia Military Institute at Lexington. Having been brought up on the martial and heroic deeds of Generals Lee and Jackson, I longed to emulate them to the fanfare of military bands. I had obtained an alternate appointment to West Point, and while awaiting the time set for my appearance to take the prescribed examination, I thought it well to prepare myself at the next most important military school in the country. My mother would have preferred that I attend Randolph-Macon College, which specialized in the humanities and was founded by her grandfather in 1830, but she was not one to interpose herself to assert her preference. She used to say it was my life I had to live and not hers.

It was not long before I regretted my choice, although out of pride I did not let my dissatisfaction become known. The severely regimented discipline was quite antipathetic to my character. I was appointed to share a room in barracks with two other cadets, one a fellow townsman and the other a stranger from Louisiana. We slept on army cots and marched to and from classes in military formation, as well as to the mess where we took our meals and where, as new cadets—or "rats," as we were called—we were not permitted to converse at table except to reply to questions put to us by the older cadets.

We quickly learned that local hazing was the severest of any college. Whenever an upperclassman was crossed in any way or was actuated by some caprice, we were invited to his room and our backsides beaten with wooden cot rounds or, more frequently, with the flat side of a bayonet. A rat who was so imprudent as not to obey the orders given him by an upperclassman was beaten unmercifully without any interference by the Institute's authorities, who closed their eyes to the hazing. A rat who resisted and struck an upperclassman was once invited to pass to the gymnasium, where a score of third classmen were lined up to take on the recalcitrant rat and engage him singly in a fight with bare fists. If the rat knocked out his adversary, he was at once replaced by another third classman, and the fighting was continued until the rat's face was like so much dough. It was common knowledge that an appreciable percentage of the cadet corps were brutes and bullies whose families had entered them at V.M.I. to be rendered manageable. One of the reasons my mother had been unwilling for me to attend that institution was owing to the treatment accorded a relative, who had been hung out of a window head down, suspended by a rope until he had lost consciousness from the rush of blood to his head. He had been rescued just in time to spare him from permanent brain injury.

I have been told that since then severe restrictions have been placed on the hazing of plebes following the beating up of a rat with the sharp edge of a bayonet. One such incident occurred while I was a cadet, resulting in the expulsion of the responsible upperclassman by decision of the cadet corps.

The hazing never disturbed me as much as the severity of the discipline, which I compared to that in a prison. Every year a score or more of new students would run away when exacerbated beyond endurance. I wonder sometimes how I stuck it out for two years in the face of such an oppressive regime. Certainly the two years I spent there were the unhappiest of my life.

EARLY DAYS

The end for me was when I succumbed, with forty or fifty fellow students, to an attack of typhoid fever. Rumor had it that a student, to end classes at least temporarily, had connected the water system with that of the sewage.

At the end of my hospitalization, I went home for some days' convalescence and announced to my parents that I was through, that I would rather dig ditches than submit any longer to what I had endured.

I applied for admission to the University of Virginia and to Randolph-Macon. As Virginia was less liberal in the credits it would allow me, I chose Randolph-Macon, and entered in the spring of 1911. I was graduated with a Bachelor of Arts degree the following year. There I could breathe at last and find happiness again. My younger brother, Wesley, had preceded me to Ashland and, thanks to him, I was invited to join a fraternity. I entered with joy into the extramural activities of the College, learning how to speak on my feet in the debates at Franklin Hall, contributing to the *Randolph-Macon Monthly* and applying myself to creative writing, to which I had long aspired. What an unalloyed joy I found under inspiring professors of Shakespeare, English literature, and history! The nightmares which had assailed me at V.M.I. gradually disappeared.

As the end of my studies at Ashland approached, I became more and more concerned with my future after graduation. I was interested in writing and was encouraged in this ambition by the acceptance of my articles for publication in the *Randolph-Macon Monthly* and by my election to the literary fraternity Sigma Upsilon. If I desired to write I must find a medium to achieve that end, and it was this goal that persuaded me to seek a post as a reporter. I communicated this desire to the editor of the Baltimore *Sun*, and I received a favorable reply proposing that, upon the conclusion of the Democratic National Convention, which had convened in 1912 in Baltimore, I come there for an interview. Before the adjournment of the convention, however, I received another letter regretting that for the present there were no vacancies.

An impulse persuaded me to proceed notwithstanding. The mother of a classmate had offered me a room for a nominal sum. I had not been an occupant more than a few days before I came upon an advertisement in the Baltimore *American* for reporters for that newspaper. I presented myself forthwith to the city editor and, after a brief interview, was told to report the next morning for a first assignment.

When I appeared, I was presented to a number of my colleagues, including Burroughs Noel, a fellow Lynchburger. I was shown a large folio volume where the daily assignments were inscribed. Mine was to interview a local physician whose passion was sports, and to obtain his views on the forthcoming Olympic Games.

I set out on my quest and found the young physician quite receptive. We discussed the Olympic Games for a full half hour or more and I returned to the office quite satisfied with what I had accomplished. I found an unoccupied typewriter and proceeded to type close to a thousand words, which I deposited in the incoming basket of the day editor. To my gratification it duly appeared in its entirety in the *American* the following morning and I was complimented by Burroughs and one or two others on my promising debut. It was not long before I had fallen quite easily into the routine of the work, and this continued throughout the summer. I was subjected to something of a shock, however, when I was instructed to report to the real estate editor. He was about to go on leave, and I was to replace him temporarily. For my initiation I was taken on a tour of his contacts in real estate. I found it duller than dishwater. Fortunately, for me the time was approaching when I was scheduled to report to the small Victoria High School in Charlotte County, of which I was to take charge. Before I was to assume the disagreeable task of reporting on real estate developments, I threw my hand in and left for home to await the fast approaching date when I was due to report for my teaching duties.

After my graduation from college, I had determined to teach for a year or two to help defray my expenses at Harvard. I applied for, obtained and accepted a position in a remote section of Charlotte County, Virginia, at the princely salary of sixty dollars a month. Two weeks after signing the contract, I was offered a similar post in a small urban center at a salary of seventy-five dollars.

I went home and announced to my father that I was not going to Charlotte County, because I had been offered a much more lucrative post.

"Son, you are not going to do that," my father announced in quiet, firm tones.

"But why, Father?"

"Because you have given your word and it would be ignoble to break it."

Until that moment, I had attached little importance to such niceties, but my father's counsel happily fixed for me for all time the sacredness of one's given word. Such were the immutable principles of the Old South and, perhaps to a lesser extent, elsewhere; alas, they are now slowly being eroded.

Even before I assumed my new duties, I recognized, from an advance survey I had made, that what faced me was a lonely situation. The family with whom I was to board was comprised of quite plain country folks—a tobacco farmer, his young wife, and their two young boys in their early teens. My routine was early laid out for me. Upon concluding my teaching about three o'clock, I returned to my room and read until dinnertime and continued after dinner until a late hour; this pattern was interrupted only by three games of checkers following the evening meal, in which the head of the household was almost invariably the winner. I brought from home periodically full sets of Dickens, Scott, Bulwer-Lytton, Balzac, Molière, Thackeray, Jane Austen and other classics, which I read conscientiously from beginning to end, to the astonished bewilderment of the farmer and his wife, who found it quite inconceivable how I could be so devoted to the cultivation of my mind.

To vary my routine I took an occasional walk through the fields. Unfortunately, there was not a soul within miles who shared any of my intellectual pursuits or tastes. Due to the absence of paved roads, I had to cycle to Pamplin, from where I might follow the Norfolk & Western right-of-way (in the form of a cinder track alongside the railway) into Lynchburg. I kept an alert ear open for the whistle of an approaching train. The only other danger I ran was the traversing of a rather long railroad bridge on the outskirts of Lynchburg. Here I had to dismount from my bicycle and carry it over the ties for a distance of several hundred yards. If the worst had ever come to the worst (which it never did), I would have been obliged to ditch my bicycle and cling to the extremity of one of the ties until the train passed.

Despite my nonconformist character and the many eyebrows raised at my undue predilection for books, I was gratified upon receiving an invitation from the school board to return for another year. I had other plans, however. For the purpose of broadening my mind, I had my eyes set on an engagement for the summer with the United States Geological Survey in the Far West, and entry into Harvard for a master of arts degree in the autumn. To realize the first objective, I had sought the help of Congressman Carter Glass. It was promptly forthcoming in the form of a notice of my appointment to a U.S. Geological Survey party being formed in Montpelier, Idaho. As I learned after my arrival, we would proceed by easy stages to the hills overlooking Freedom, Wyoming, where we would erect tents for temporary quarters which would be shifted as the survey proceeded. At last at I would have a glimpse of that Far West, which was fast receding into the limbo of time, before the great romance it represented had disappeared forever.

I chose to proceed on my way by the longest possible route, so I bought a ticket on the Southern Railway from Lynchburg to New Orleans, where I would have to change to the Southern Pacific as far as Amarillo and thence go north to Denver, Cheyenne, and Montpelier. I had bought myself a sporting shepherd's plaid suit and broad western felt hat. It was my first introduction to the West, and I flattened my nose against the window a good part of the way not to miss any of the entrancingly colorful scenes and people, so different from those in the East.

Montpelier was reached on a Sunday in the early afternoon and, to my relief, the chief of our party was on the platform to greet me. He was a man of few words and was, besides, very deaf. In consequence, communication was so difficult that little rapport was established between us. The other three members of the group were encountered upon reaching the Montpelier Hotel, which was to be our temporary home until we left a few days later in a covered wagon with our riding horses.

The other three included Bud Serruys of Miles City, Montana, who became my boon companion. He was about my age and came from an aristocratic Belgian family. There was also Slim, a gaunt Mormon of about thirty years, who was charged with looking after our horses; he was slow of speech and always spoke in measured words. The only time he had been out of Idaho and Montana was when he had traveled as a Mormon missionary to the southeastern part of the country. The final member of our group was a young Mormon from Montpelier; his name escapes me, but he had a rubicund face that reflected perpetual joviality. Despite the differences in our backgrounds, or perhaps because of them, we lived a friendly, compatible life together.

Bud and I and the middle-aged leader of the survey rose early every morning and, after a wholesome breakfast, were off on horseback for our day's work. We carried lunch with us and returned late in the afternoon for supper, usually tired and ready for a deep sleep. We rarely encountered anyone in the hills or out. It was a healthy life in which we breathed pure mountain air and usually passed the nights in dreamless sleep.

Since, for me, being without books was an impossible privation, I carried a few odd volumes of Hazlitt's essays and George Borrow's delightful works in the Everyman Library for reading on weekends or at night when the spirit moved me. Slim could not conceal his astonishment at my addiction to reading, which was quite outside his ken. I am not sure that he had learned to read; if he had, it was very cursory and confined to the Mormon Bible. As the Mormons are indefatigable proselytizers, he sought to induce me to have a look at their holy book; but a glance, for politeness' sake, did not inspire a repetition.

On Sundays we took turns riding some twenty miles to the nearest post office, an isolated wooden building in the center of nowhere. My first expedition nearly ended in disaster. I lost my way, as the roads were unmarked, and found myself, after exceeding the mileage I should have covered, within sight of a strange settlement in the distance, which convinced me that I had failed to take the turning to the right to lead me to the post office I was seeking. After retracing my way, I found the turning I should have taken and, at length, the post office itself.

As I was late, I did not linger after obtaining our mail but turned around and started to gallop to our camp. I had gone only a few miles when my horse stepped into a gopher hole and I went flying over his head. As I landed unsteadily on my feet, I had only one thought in mind—not to lose hold of the reins. Fortunately, I clung to them and at length brought the horse to a stop.

I very stealthily climbed on his back and made my way home, which I reached in the late afternoon. That was perhaps my greatest adventure in the West and it taught me the lesson of prudence in my future sorties.

The brief sojourn I made in the as yet unspoiled West left an ineffaceable impression which has remained with me. It was amazing that we could journey for hours and encounter anyone but rarely. When this happened, we exchanged with pleasure the news and details about each other. Nothing could be friendlier than those chance encounters which enlivened one's isolated life. There was an openness and friendliness that warmed the heart, wholly unlike anything ever encountered in the relatively crowded East, where disguises seemed necessary to survival. Here people had recovered their true natures and were untainted by make-believe. It was a revelation which uplifted and transformed one.

It was a wrenching experience to tear oneself away from the unsophisticated and transparently genuine existence so close to nature and man's undisguised character. I have never forgotten those imposing Tetons and the great distances our visions encompassed owing to the extraordinary purity of the air. I returned by car twenty years later to introduce my mother and wife to those enchanting scenes, of a grandeur and majesty that almost defy description. It gave us an added sense of the privilege life had bestowed upon us.

At the end of the summer, Slim drove me in our wagon to Afton, Wyoming, some miles across the valley. There I took a stagecoach headed for Montpelier, Idaho, where I would board a train for the East. Parting is always a trial and it was especially so now, as we knew it was most unlikely that we would ever see one another again.

The stagecoach had among its passengers a comely young Mormon matron, en route to Salt Lake City, who intended to enter her ancestors as Mormons in that sect's archives. She spent some hours during the journey endeavoring to convert me to the Mormon faith. I was only able to deter her from that fruitless objective by disclosing that my ancestors included three Methodist ministers of the Gospel, which precluded me from being faithless to their memory. She only abandoned her struggle as we entered Montpelier many miles and hours later.

On arriving, I learned there was a public dance that evening. So much time had elapsed since I was last in a real community that I decided to look in on the festivity, but I was ill at ease and did not remain long. In those days I suffered greatly from shyness, which I did not succeed in overcoming for many years, until I was in my fifties and had gained greater poise.

I had my first sexual experience, at the age of about fourteen, with the white maid in our home. When I entered Virginia Military Institute early in 1909 to spend two miserable years, I found sexual relief with prostitutes once or twice. Later, while a student at Randolph-Macon in Ashland, I visited one of the innumerable houses of prostitution in Richmond and found a most attractive inmate who told me she had been a student at the Virginia Seminary in Buena Vista. I shuddered when she told me this, for it was obvious she had only recently entered her profession and with little thought of where it would lead her.

I had a strong prejudice against debauching a girl. At an early age, when I was growing up in Lynchburg, a neighbor asked my mother to let me spend the night in her home as a protection for her and two young girl relatives who were visiting her. The room I was given was not far from theirs, and I could overhear their laughter and giggling, as if they would welcome a visit from me. I was terribly tempted, as their door had been left open, a seeming invitation to join them in bed. But in the end I resisted the great temptation, as it would have been a heinous abuse of the trust reposed in me.

A few years later, in 1915, when I was in Colorado Springs, a young friend invited me to spend the night with him and two attractive young girls with whom he had made a tryst at a temporarily unoccupied house. He and I went to bed in separate rooms, each occupied by one of the girls. To my dismay, I found my attractive companion to be a virgin, which caused me to suspend my attempted lovemaking, despite the initial insistence of my partner that I consummate her violation. I have committed many sins, but the debauching of a virgin is not one of them.

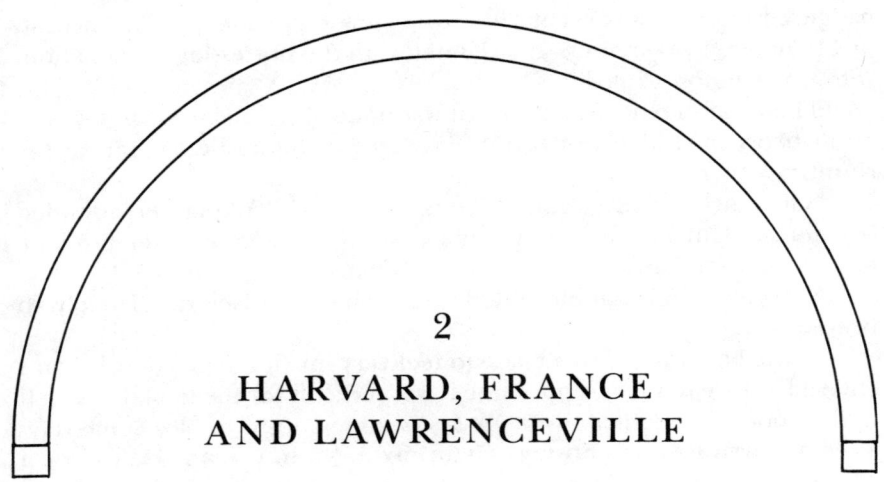

2
HARVARD, FRANCE AND LAWRENCEVILLE

*M*y farseeing mother was the motive force persuading me to enter the Graduate School of Arts and Science at Harvard in further pursuit of my education. Her argument was that I had come in close contact with only a very restricted section of America, and that my horizon would be widened by sojourning in New England and continuing my studies under professors representing an elite.

When I matriculated, the Dean remarked that I would no doubt find the standards appreciably higher than those to which I had been accustomed in the South, and that the acquisition of the Master of Arts degree might require two years of study rather than the customary one. I took his warning with the lightness of youth, but of course he proved to be right. As it turned out, it was a blessing, I profited more from my second year than from the first.

At that time the main dining-room facilities were in Memorial Hall, where I was assigned to a large table that seated about twenty, including both undergraduate and graduate students. I was the only Southerner; there was one foreigner, who was Chinese. Some fifty years later I learned that he was T.V. Soong, a member of one of the most famous families in China, brother of Madame Sun Yat-sen and later distinguished minister of finance. He rarely entered into the general conversation at the table; the most arresting occasion was when, after hearing me badgered more or less regularly by the New Englanders for my accent, he broke out, to everyone's amazement, with the protesting exclamation: "Stop picking on Childs."

The general reaction was that it was none of his business, as it was an affair between students of two traditionally antagonistic sections of the country.

"Oh, but it *is* my affair," Soong protested. "My father attended Vanderbilt University and became a southern sympathizer, and he taught me to be one."

Everyone was dumbfounded; after that, I was left relatively in peace.

In the beginning I was made to feel very much an outsider. When I entered a store to make a purchase it was difficult for me to make myself understood. The loneliness at first was almost unbearable. Some days after my arrival, I was on my way to my room in Conant Hall when I passed a student wearing the pin of my fraternity, Phi Delta Theta. I stopped to greet him and to exchange the fraternity grip. He was Don Neiswanger of Kansas. He later married and settled in New Haven, where he became acquainted with Ed Burgess, a close friend of mine at Randolph-Macon. Thirty years later, when I was named ambassador to Saudi Arabia and a photograph of me dining with King Ibn Saud was widely disseminated, they both wrote to congratulate me.

To my joy, I learned that there were a considerable number of Phi Delts at Harvard united in an alumni club which met every month for dinner. Through it some of my closest friendships were formed, including one of the dearest in my life, with Bryant King Vann of Gadsden, Alabama.

I visited him sometime later in his home and met his parents—his father, a dentist, and his mother, dazzling in her beauty, who worshiped B.K. and coveted for him an intellectual career as statesman or writer. In appearance he was a young Galahad; he was the soul of honor. He argued with me that he intended first to make a fortune; that accomplished, he would consecrate himself to a life of high and unselfish accomplishments. I insisted that it would never work, as any connection with Mammon would undermine his high resolves.

In 1940, I saw him for the last time in the home he had made in Atlanta, married to an heiress and practicing dentistry in his father's footsteps. It was obvious that his father had persuaded him he was needed as an assistant and B.K. had succumbed, sacrificing his marked superior intellectual talents and the ambitions his devoted mother had entertained for him. She died fairly early in life, and I have always thought that it was perhaps from acute disappointment at the turn her son's life, of such great promise, had taken. I have never ceased to grieve for what he might have accomplished and failed to realize.

While nearing the end of a four-year tour of duty at the State Department, I drove my wife and mother to Florida and, on our return, we passed through Atlanta to greet B.K. When we called on him at his office in town, he insisted on our spending the night at his home in the suburbs. From the moment we met, after so many years of separation, we never ceased our verbal exchanges. At breakfast I inquired whether he had preserved our literary bible, Page's *British Poets of the Nineteenth Century*. He excused himself and returned shortly holding it high in the air. I turned the pages to one of our favorites, Tennyson's *Ulysses* and the lines:

> I cannot rest from travel; I will drink
> Life to the lees . . .

and we recited it in unison, as we had so many times in the past, through:

> Death closes all: but something ere the end,
> Some work of noble note, may yet be done,
> Not unbecoming men that strove with Gods.

I could not help wondering whether these last lines were applicable still to B.K., but it was not for me to judge. It was saddening to part from him, all the more so since we were never to meet again. He died not many years later; I never learned when or under what circumstances.

The one family of Boston bluebloods I met was through B.K.'s mother. They were the Greens, and they frequently included me in their invitations. It was on one such occasion that B.K. and I met the actor Otis Skinner, then playing in a Boston theater, with his young daughter Cornelia. When she learned I was from Lynchburg she sought news of an admirer, Bland Terry, one of the handsomest young men in the city. Sixty years later, in 1977, I learned, through a mutual acquaintance I had met in Beaulieu, that Miss Skinner was alive and still remembered our meeting. Two years later, before we had time to renew personal contact, she died.

On my first arrival at Harvard, contemplating what courses I would take, I took counsel with Burroughs Noel, who was at the Law School. Burroughs insisted that I should not be influenced necessarily by the subject of the course, but more particularly by the reputation of the professor. But for his advice I might have gone sadly astray. As it was, I chose two outstanding professors, George Lyman Kittredge and Irving Babbitt—the one a world-famous authority on Shakespeare who taught twenty-four of the plays in two successive years; the other, one of the leading professors of comparative literature, whose classic subject was Rousseau and romanticism. At that time I contemplated devoting myself to teaching. The war and its consequences upset all my calculations, and I ended up by spending thirty years in the American Foreign Service. The courses I had chosen to specialize in, comparative literature and English, could not have been less practical for the career I had chosen to follow; on the other hand, they served me well by broadening me culturally in a way which could not have better furthered my intellectual development and made me a citizen of the world rather than a bureaucratic functionary. My passion for Shakespeare, first cultivated in me by my mother and, later, President Robert Blackwell of Randolph-Macon College, never left me. From 1960, in my retirement at Nice, until my return to Virginia in 1973, I spent a week or more every year attending five or six performances of Shakespeare's plays at Stratford-on-Avon. The Bard of Avon and Anton Chekhov have been my two supreme literary loves, with a few lesser luminaries following in the rear, including Schopenhauer, Brecht, Kafka, Casanova, Henry Miller, and Persian and English eighteenth-century poets.

I decided to spend the summer, between my first and second years at Harvard, in Kansas City, Missouri. To defray expenses and acquaint myself with trade, I wanted to become a book salesman and applied for employment as a salesman of *Dr. Eliot's Five-Foot Shelf of Books*. By return post, it was proposed by the New York office of the publishers that I proceed to Kansas City, which I had mentioned as one of my preferred locations, and report to the sales office manager there.

I began work on a commission basis, and was provided with a list of people who had indicated their interest from a display advertisement of the books in question. It was not long before I was able to make certain profitable generalizations to assist me in winnowing the most receptive prospects from the least promising. I soon discovered that teachers and doctors were the most interested, while lawyers and successful business executives were the least receptive. An exception were self-made businessmen. They were eager for self-improvement. In general, the wealthier and more successful were the least interested.

In the beginning I had no difficulty defraying expenses and earning a surplus; but, toward the end, my penchant for female society and the company of attractive young women of the city gradually reduced my income.

My temporary undoing was a stunning brunette, Aline Waite. Of the women I have known, she was one of the most outstanding in beauty and charm. I saw her for the first time when frequenting one of the open-air dance pavilions in Swope Park, where music was supplied by the orchestra of Arthur Pryor. I used to go there with one or two friends to worship Aline from afar. She was a superb dancer, dressed with exquisite taste, and confined her dancing to the small group who accompanied her. Cutting-in dancing was not then favored, and I would not have dreamed of incurring a rebuff by requesting a dance.

This was how matters stood when a young man of my acquaintance invited me to accompany him on a blind date with his girlfriend. I accepted and, to my astonishment, found that I was paired off with the girl of my dreams at Swope Park, whom I had worshiped these many days with no expectation of ever meeting her. Aline and I took to one another to such a degree that we were virtually inseparable. My work as a salesman went by the board, while she saw no one else but me until my return to Harvard in September.

My disillusionment came when her mother wrote me that Aline had run away and married a local businessman. There must have been disillusionment on both sides, for the next news was a message from her mother that the marriage had been dissolved and that Aline had returned home to her mother. Both of them then moved to Chicago, where Aline began to dance in nightclubs.

Two of my closest friends at Harvard were Al Jennings, who was to accompany me to France in 1915, and H.K. Dennis, two or three years my senior, who had entered the Graduate School after studying at Brown and Princeton, earned his Ph.D. in sociology, and went on to teach at the University of Illinois at Urbana.

Dennis' end could not have been more tragic. He married after he left Harvard. Both he and his wife and their two infant children perished in a storm while in a pleasure boat on the lake outside Urbana. I was abroad and only learned of the tragedy long afterward from our fraternity magazine. I could not bring myself to make contact with his surviving brothers, whom I had never known and of whose whereabouts I had no knowledge. Even after more than half a century it is painful to dwell upon the memory of a character so noble and so full of promise.

Probably no event in history has had such convulsive repercussions on the world as the First World War. It is certain that life will never be the same again on this planet. The extent of the loss in lives and in accumulated wealth staggers the imagination. It seems inconceivable that men in their right minds could have committed themselves to waste so profligate that it defies the imagination. The end is not yet in sight, nor is it ever likely to be.

On my return to Harvard the main topic of conversation was the war; it was to remain so for four years. John Reed, a Harvard graduate, returned from the Eastern Front in Russia as a correspondent to give us an inside view of the conflict. He had not yet written his electrifying account of the Soviet Revolution in *Ten Days that Shook the World*. His talk stirred our thirst for like adventures.

When my friend Al Jennings and I heard that volunteers were being sought by the newly formed American Ambulance Corps to serve with the French Army in France, we sought out the organizer in Boston and signed up to make our way to France after commencement to join the Corps.

A day in June, 1915, found Al and me at the Seamen's Church Institute in New York preparing to sign up on a British horse boat, the S.S. *Luceric,* bound for Saint-Nazaire.

Upon our arrival in France, after Al and I had surreptitiously jumped ship, we boarded the third-class compartment of an overnight train for Paris. When it came to a halt as dawn was breaking, Al asked the name of the station. *"Sortie,"* I replied, thus revealing my rudimentary knowledge of French and provoking an outburst of laughter from Al. Years were to elapse before I was perfectly at home in that language; curiously enough, Russian was much more easily acquired.

On arrival at the Quai d'Orsay station, as we entered the Place de la Concorde, I asked our taxi driver to stop. I was trembling with excitement, overcome by the incomparable vistas exposed to our sight. I was so moved that I knelt down and kissed the ground before we continued to our destination, the American Hospital in Neuilly, which would be our headquarters until we received our assignments.

La Chapelle was the station at which we received the wounded. A call would come in the dead of night that a trainload of wounded was expected. We would be awakened and drive our ambulances to meet the train. Dashing about the first-aid station would be a dozen or more aristocratic young Frenchwomen, smartly attired in their nursing costumes, preparing to receive and succor the wounded. The train would pull in slowly and we would enter with our stretchers. Lying in bunks were the living wrecks which the trenches had disgorged: legless and armless men, men blinded in one eye or both. After some days and nights of this, I began to ask myself: how long will this slaughter continue? Will it never cease? Will it continue until the end of time?

In my spare time I roamed the streets of Paris, intoxicated with the city's beauty and history. I bowed my head at the tomb of Napoleon and dropped a tear at the tomb of Heine in the cemetery of Montmartre and before the tomb of De Musset, under a weeping willow, in Père Lachaise. Then I was ordered to the College of Juilly, some twenty miles distant, a part of which had been temporarily allocated as a hospital and to which we transported the wounded from Compiègne, thirty-five miles away. There we could hear the rumble of the front-line guns and an occasional bomb dropped from a German airplane.

Quite close by, near Champ Fleury, was the abandoned headquarters of General Von Kluck; it was an admirable situation for a headquarters staff, commanding as it did a vast range of the adjacent countryside. There was nothing of value left and the rooms were stripped bare of furniture, all save one, which contained—of all things imaginable on the modern world's most fateful battlefield—a billiard table.

Before leaving Harvard, I had answered an advertisement in the Boston *Transcript* for a tutor for the young son of parents residing in Alton, Illinois, who were planning to spend the winter in Colorado Springs. In an interview with them, I had agreed to meet them in Alton upon my return from France early in October.

As September approached, while I was still in Juilly, I booked passage on the S.S. *Rochambeau* sailing from Bordeaux, which would arrive in New York in time for me to spend a week with my parents and reach Alton early in October as I had agreed.

Upon arriving in Alton, I found, to my dismay, that the young man I had been engaged to tutor was mentally deficient, but it was then too late for me to withdraw. There was nothing to do but make the best of a disagreeable situation, however unpleasant it might be. I had still an undischarged debt to my mother, who had borrowed funds for my expenses at Harvard. It would be two years or more before this was liquidated, after two years' service as an army officer from 1917 to 1919.

It was while residing in the Alton Hotel that I came upon a picture of Aline Waite in the rotogravure Sunday section of the Chicago *Tribune*. It showed her in a rather seductive pose stretched out in a scanty costume on a lion skin, and the caption announced that she was appearing in a well-known Chicago nightclub. I immediately wrote to her mother and was soon in receipt of a letter from Aline herself. It was arranged that she would come for a weekend to nearby St. Louis and would stay with a relative. It worked out perfectly. We dined in a restaurant and after dinner went for a walk in a nearby darkened park, where we could be at ease. I was due to accompany my employer very shortly to Colorado Springs, so it was many months before I saw her again, in Chicago. I was as madly infatuated as ever, but we could see no prospects, as my means were as yet insufficient to support a wife.

As disappointed as I had been with my tutorial charge, I was more than recompensed by the many charms of Colorado Springs. I soon made many friends among a select society, some of them attracted to the locality for their health. Julian Allen, of Newport and Paris, whose close friendship I had formed in the Ambulance Corps at Juilly, gave me an introduction to his charming sister. Through my fraternity brothers at Colorado College I met, among others, Warner Carson, son of one of the partners of Carson, Pirie, and Scott of Chicago, who became a dear friend until his untimely death in his prime; and Leonora Nichols, daughter of a well-known American painter. When I was teaching at Lawrenceville School the following year, Leonora came for a weekend to attend a prom. When I escorted her home to Bronxville, I proposed to her on the train, which provoked her into immoderate laughter. I lost touch with her for forty years; then, at a cocktail party in New York, I was informed that she was living in New York, still unmarried. I rushed around to have a glimpse of her, and she briefly reviewed her madcap life since we had parted. She later moved to Charlottesville and we have corresponded, but fate has consistently stood in the way of our meeting, as if bent on thwarting us through sheer caprice.

Aside from making the acquaintance of Leonora in Colorado Springs and that of the most popular young hostess there, a Miss Burns, daughter of one of the local millionaires, the most notable event of my stay probably was to see the year 1913 out and Prohibition in at the Broadmoor Hotel, with a group including Warner Carson and other young bloods. Before midnight, we had ordered sufficient drinks served at our table to last us until well after dawn. It was a notable historic celebration.

At Warner's urging I had written to Lawrenceville School in New Jersey regarding the possibility of acceptance for the teaching staff. I was informed that I could not be considered in the absence of a personal interview and that there was no provision for defraying my personal travel expenses. I decided to risk the expenditure and, after obtaining permission for a week's absence, entrained for the nearest station to the school. Happily, I passed the tests and was offered the post of assistant master, to teach English and French with lodging in Griswold House, at a salary of one thousand dollars a year.

On my way East in June 1916, I accepted an invitation to spend a week at the home of Warner Carson in Evanston, Illinois. We startled the natives when we escorted the dashing Aline to one of the dances at the Evanston Country Club. Women had not then attained the freedom in dress they enjoy now, when no distinction is made between the attire of actresses and correct *jeunes filles*. Our appearance at the Club, with Aline in a dress which caused all the stodgy chaperones, arrayed in seats overlooking the dance floor like so many sentinels of proper behavior, to lift their lorgnettes in perfectly marshaled unison, was a sight for sore eyes. The young bloods assailed Warner for an introduction to her, while the more prosaic young ladies present ground their teeth in rage. When Warner told them I was on my way to Lawrenceville School to teach, they looked upon me with a new respect.

These few days were my last contacts with Aline, more's the pity. Our correspondence petered out in the knowledge that we were at a dead end. I would give much to know what became of one of the most fascinating women I have ever known. A few years ago I was seated in the lounge of a hotel in Milan when I saw a woman enter with a small party of Americans. Her resemblance to Aline was so striking that I was tempted to approach her and inquire if she were a daughter or close relative of my old love, but I never did; I couldn't bear to be disappointed.

When I reached Lawrenceville in September, I found a throng of students and teachers assembled in front of the famous Jigger Shop greeting one another. I joined the group and was at length accosted by one of them. He gave me a searching look and, mistaking me for a student, remarked, "In what form are you?" I laughed unceremoniously and thanked him for the compliment. "I am a new assistant master," I answered, to his obvious discomfiture.

My youthful appearance (I had just passed twenty-three) caused me no embarrassment but, on the contrary, tended to make the students more at ease with me. We had very entertaining and instructive visiting lecturers of some prominence, including Cosmo Hamilton, a scholarly Englishman with a high sense of humor. He told us the story of one of his compatriots who had come out of Buckingham Palace in civilian clothes to be greeted by an officious lady and offered a white feather. He accepted it with a profound bow. Withdrawing from the pocket of his jacket a Victoria Cross, he said to her with a smile, "It is the second time I have been decorated today."

Lowell Thomas, at that time an instructor at Princeton, was one of the obscurer lecturers who paraded his as yet slender accomplishments. He spoke about a journey to Alaska and, when he concluded, I turned to a friend alongside and said, "He is the sort who could extract blood from a turnip," referring to the highly dramatic tone of his talk, from which one might have concluded that he was describing not Alaska but a voyage to the North Pole. He was later to indulge in like histrionics when advertising Lawrence of Arabia.[1]

For Easter, 1917, I took a train to visit my parents in Lynchburg and stopped off in Washington on April 5, on the off chance that I might gain admittance to Congress, which was considering President Wilson's message to a joint session of the Senate and House asking for a declaration of war against Germany for its depredations against American shipping.

The Germans were Huns who crucified babies and cut off the hands of unoffending Belgians, while the Turks were infidels and, besides, were massacring innocent Armenians of our own Christian faith. Russia was going under and the time had come for decisive action.

I made my way to the Capitol, which was thronged by people seeking admittance to the House gallery. It was obviously impossible to gain access to a congressman I knew well, Carter Glass, to obtain a card admitting me to the debate in progress. I was determined to sit in on the drama. To that end I cornered an attendant and offered him five dollars to obtain a seat. He suggested that for the moment it was impossible, but if I returned in the afternoon he would have the card of someone who had vacated a place. It was thus that I gained admittance to dramatic hours which have seared themselves in my memory.

I listened, enraptured by the patriotic periods that welled their sonorous way from successive speakers on the floor below.

America's honor had been touched . . . A great and holy principle was involved . . . Friendly nations beyond the Atlantic were engaged in a death grapple for the defense of ideals which the United States held dear . . . America could not hesitate to make the choice implicit in the preservation of its very existence.

There were many such perorations; then a wiry, sallow-faced man was given recognition by the Speaker, an insignificant blur in a sea of deeply moved humanity. My neighbor whispered that it was Meyer London, the only Socialist in Congress.

In a brief allocution, he offered the reasons that prevented him from supporting the resolution before the House. The war, he said, was one between imperialist governments dictated by the interests of capitalists. It was a war for the markets of the world, for the exploitation of colonial peoples, and it would serve in no respect the interests of the common man. In arraying itself alongside the Allied governments, the United States would not serve the interests of democracy or the rights of man which were being cynically flouted in India, Egypt and Africa. In this great and solemn hour, it behooved men not to be influenced by passion, for the judgment of events would be inexorable. For America to join a war fought between antagonists for commercial advantages was egregious folly, which only meant the destruction of innocent lives and the accumulation of the toil of past centuries. And then he raised his frail arm and, bent with the recognition of the hopelessness of his appeal before the flood of oratory which had preceded him, he cried: "Beware, gentlemen, lest the war and its consequences prove that your system bears in itself the seeds of its own destruction."

It was after midnight before the calling of the roll.

At the sound of her name, Edith Rankin, the first congresswoman, raised herself slowly and, as if in great pain and in a pathetic and scarcely audible voice, stated that she desired to explain her negative vote, that as a woman she could not cast her vote in favor of a war. She, one lone woman, I reflected, was speaking in the name of fifty-five million women of America, a voice as futile as the waves of the sea.

It was after three o'clock in the morning when I left the Capitol and made my way up Pennsylvania Avenue to a chop suey joint on Fourteenth Street for the first food I had had since noon of the previous day.

The proceedings had filled me with excitement comparable to that aroused by a tragedy of Shakespeare. I was tingling all over. I dismissed the appeals of London and Rankin as quite lacking in relevance. This was no time to question the patriotic impulses of the nation; I was eager to get into the fight. A newsboy entered the restaurant with an armful of newspapers.

"CONGRESS PASSES WAR RESOLUTION," the headlines read.
"NATION GIRDS ITS STRENGTH IN SUPREME TEST AGAINST TEUTON HORDES."

NOTES

[1] It is now generally agreed by British historians that Lawrence owed his fame to the largely false buildup of Lowell Thomas, himself deceived.

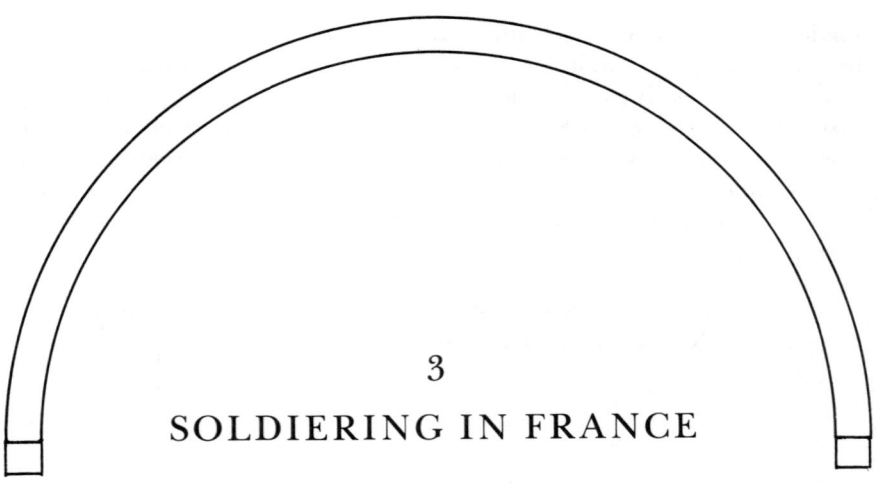

3
SOLDIERING IN FRANCE

A few weeks before our entry into the war, I had communicated with the War Department and asked to be enrolled in one of the officer training camps which were projected. In reply, I was requested to present myself before a board of examiners at Princeton. There I was given a physical and some days later was directed to report to one of the first officer training camps being organized just across the Potomac from Washington at Fort Myer. There, I found myself one of many volunteers from the adjacent Eastern Seaboard who were put to work drilling under West Point graduates of the rank of captain and attending lectures on warfare and its tactics. I was in C Company, commanded by Captain Barnes, a strict disciplinarian.

As we were only a stone's throw from Washington, our drilling attracted many young women from that city. They were quite agreeable to talk with before and after the formal parade which terminated our daily exercises. It was thus that we met numerous attractive young women from excellent families, some of whom were sufficiently hospitable to invite us to their homes. Others were of quite a different milieu and frequented certain disreputable hotels between Fourteenth Street and Union Station. They plied their trade by tipping the bellboys to conduct to their rooms those of us seeking female companions amenable to fulfilling our unconventional ends. It was my ill luck, upon my one and only visit, to encounter a novice wearing, to my discomfiture, the pin of my fraternity. In explanation, she confided that she had met a soldier by chance in her hometown of Baltimore and had been persuaded to accompany him to Washington on his way to France.

Something about her frank, straightforward recital aroused my compassion for her as a distressed and bewildered human being. I sat up half the night endeavoring to persuade her to return to her home and husband. She protested that she would never return to the hideous drudgery of her life and the ceaseless nagging of a husband ten years her elder who cared nothing for going out in the evenings to dance or to a movie but only for making money.

There was no reasoning with her; she obviously possessed only a grade-school education and had no appreciation of the gravity of her step. I pictured to her the years of possible misery and degradation ahead, the inevitable diseases and deadening of the senses from alcohol and drugs; she only turned up her nose and invited me to jump into bed with her.

I shook my head. There was something intolerable in the situation. There was the fraternity pin which she wore, the sole prerogative of wives, fiancées or mothers. There was a pang of conscience standing in the way; the knowledge that she was a novice held me back from becoming an instrument of her possible ruin. I shrank also from a shameless exploitation of her body and spent the night in a chair, leaving with her a recompense for her company before parting.

After we had been in training a few weeks, one or two of the men in my company, discouraged about their prospects of being commissioned in the infantry, decided to respond to a call for volunteers for the Air Corps. Stimulated by a sense of adventure, which had attracted me from childhood, I decided to present myself for the test. The initial one was administered by a physician. Weeks elapsed without any notice to us concerning the results. One or two of those who had taken the test decided to visit the physician who had examined us to ascertain what had happened to our examination papers. Upon inquiry, it was found that we had all passed, but the forms attesting this had been lodged in the back of the drawer in which they had been placed. I accepted this as an occult sign from on high and abandoned all thought of an Air Corps career, to such an extent that it was not until a quarter of a century later, in 1943, that, to keep a professional engagement, I was obliged to enter an airplane. From that moment I have spent my life in planes, with no concern despite several close calls.

On August 15, 1917, I was commissioned a second lieutenant of infantry and assigned to the 159th Brigade, 80th Division, at Camp Lee, Virginia, a few miles outside Petersburg. I had hoped that, by reason of my service in France and knowledge of French, I would have merited a higher rank. Captain Barnes explained that I had been late at too many formations, which I had to admit had been occasioned by lingering too long with visiting members of the fair sex.

However, to my gratification, I was selected by Major General Farnsworth, commanding officer of the 159th Brigade, as one of his aides. In the hope of an assignment to military intelligence, I had requested the intervention of Senator Martin; it came through very shortly in an assignment to the Army War College, seat of military intelligence. General Farnsworth agreed to release me temporarily for the time I would be absent.

Among those I found reporting for duty at the War College were Lee Sellers, John Graham and Robert Gilmore, of my age. Our lecturers included Captain Herbert O. Yardley, who had been in the Communications Division of the State Department and had become so absorbed in the work of encoding telegrams to diplomatic and consular establishments of the government abroad that he had applied himself to the study of cryptography in order to break other governments' codes and cipher messages.

I found Yardley's lectures fascinating. When he announced that Pershing's headquarters in France had requested that four officers be given urgent training in this work and sent to France to serve in G2A6, the branch of intelligence concerned with such work, and asked for volunteers, I immediately volunteered, as did Gilmore, Graham and Sellers. At this time, there was an abysmal dearth of such experts—so much so that the Army was obliged to have recourse to a private citizen, an eccentric millionaire living in Geneva, Illinois, named George Fabyan, who had conducted experiments in perpetual motion and was engaged in research to prove from a cipher that Bacon wrote Shakespeare. The latter project included William Friedman and his fiancée. It bordered on the theories of madmen, but it illustrates to what desperate straits the government was reduced in its search for code and cipher officers. When Friedman and I later became warm friends, I asked Friedman how anyone as intelligent as he could be involved in such idiocies. He shrugged his shoulders and remarked, "We all have to eat, don't we?" He later became one of the world's greatest cryptographers and was voted a gift of one hundred thousand dollars by Congress for a cipher machine perfected by him.

After the instruction received at Geneva, we were ordered to General Headquarters in France and reported on December 11, 1917, to the port of embarkation—Hoboken, New Jersey—for our transportation. Graham and Sellers were the first to embark, which brought them to Chaumont in France in the first contingent. Bob Gilmore and I left, after two weeks' delay, on December 26. We lost our convoy and put into

Halifax, where we remained for three days awaiting another convoy that never arrived. Finally we put out to sea alone, heading far north to elude German submarines. Most of us spent our time in the bar playing seven-up or blackjack. We reached Liverpool on the morning of January 17, 1918. More than three weeks had elapsed since our departure and our food stocks had been so reduced tht we had been put on short rations. To our dismay, we were informed that Britain had food stocks for only ten days owing to shipping losses from submarines, so we were forbidden to purchase any food while in England. We entrained for Southampton, where we arrived in mist and rain, and marched out of town to the barracks provided us. Some soup and bread and potatoes were awaiting us along with blankets, but no beds.

Bob and I, having passed a wretched night wrapped in our blankets on the floor of the barracks and half-starved, determined to walk into town in the hope of finding more food. The manager of the first hotel we reached was apologetic, but he had strict orders to serve no American servicemen. Several British officers in the hall vented their indignation. "What? These men have come to aid us and you treat them so scurvily. It's an outrage. Give them a private room and serve them some food." Then we walked back to camp and ate another breakfast there.

A few hours later we crossed the Channel to Havre, where there was more rain and more mud. On a lofty hill overlooking the city, we were received by two British officers, attached to a camp, who set off with a group to find us accommodations. We overwhelmed them with questions. The elder officer, turning to his companion, remarked in a flash of wistful understanding: "You are so like we were four years ago. Do you remember, Lionel, how eager we were in 1914 to reach France, to get into the show, to be a part of it all? After you have been out a bit it won't seem the same. You will see only the muck and you will wonder when it will end. It's bloody easy for those blighters back home to talk of fighting until we get to Berlin and about smashing the Boches until they crawl on their knees, but let them come out here and live like swine and die like bloody stuck pigs. Oh! it's easy for them to make their fine speeches in Parliament and be patriotic in Albert Hall, but it's damned hard to see a pal have his brains spattered in your eyes and be struck in the belly by a mangled arm blown from the shoulder of your orderly by a high-explosive shell. A hell of a lot you will care then about rushing into this bloody business."

Blois was the concentration center for officers unfit for service in France and detached officers awaiting orders. So Gilmore and I and others had been ordered to Blois. It was fairly free of American officers when we arrived on January 18 and, in consequence, we were billeted at the select Hôtel de France. Two days later, after retiring to bed, we heard a forceful knocking on the door, which was flung open to admit a major of the regular army. He surveyed the luxurious room, gave me a supercilious glance, and ordered me to clear out immediately. "This is too damned good for reserve officers. Who the hell do you think you are anyway?"

Bob and I gathered our things together and took our departure in silence. The entrance hall below was thronged with reserve officers evicted to make way for an unscheduled influx of regulars. A billeting officer was assigning us rooms in various private homes.

"Let's go to the Coq d'Or on the hill," I said to Bob, "and get rooms before everything is filled. I am not going to spend half the night finding a place to sleep at this hour." The Coq d'Or was a cheery second-class hotel to which we had been introduced the previous evening by two charming French girls from a hairdressing shop who were intent on extending to Americans traditional French hospitality.

A day or two later we received definitive orders to report to GHQ at Chaumont by way of Tours. There, Bob and I were unable to resist the blandishments of two charming young girls, Juliette and Rose, encountered at the station on our arrival from Blois, who easily persuaded us to break our journey for a couple of days; we justified this as a means of improving our knowledge of the French language and customs. On resuming our journey a day or two later, we bade them a tender farewell and promised to look them up at their home in Paris. It was several months before I could keep my promise, while returning through Paris from an official mission to London. Juliette was awaiting me impatiently in lodgings in Auteuil, after confiding to me by correspondence that my visit could not have been better timed, as the American general who was now her protector had to absent himself on an official mission. That was fine, but fate was determined to thwart us. It was an evening when the Big Berthas had been massed to bombard Paris; we had hardly gone to bed before the shells and bombs began falling. Juliette grabbed my arm to accompany her to the underground shelter, but I had been so exhausted by the train journey from London that I very ungallantly begged to be excused that I might indulge an irresistible need for sleep. So I gave myself to Orpheus and not to Juliette, more's the pity. The worst of it was that she never forgave my offense to her pride and she disappeared at dawn without any farewell or ever replying to my letters of regret and urgings that I be permitted to make amends.

It was late in January before Bob and I reported to the gloomy stone barracks at Chaumont which had been transformed into offices for Pershing's headquarters staff. Our section, G2A6, was a separate ground-floor building to the rear.

When Bob and I made our belated appearance, Lee Sellers rushed

SOLDIERING IN FRANCE   29

up, drew me aside and cautioned me that, when reporting to Captain Berthold, executive officer in charge in the absence of Colonel Moorman, I should give careful heed to what might be said but to evidence no surprise or offer any comments. A few moments later, we were ushered into Berthold's office.

He shook hands warmly and singled me out for his particular attention. "We are fortunate in having you join us, Lieutenant Childs. We have heard a great deal about your ability in cipher work and I believe Colonel Moorman intends to turn that section over to you. Get yourself well settled and let me know what you need."

It was all very disconcerting, but I kept my mouth shut as I had been warned by Sellers to do. At lunchtime, when Lee, John, Bob and I foregathered at the mess the two first-named had established, the mystery was revealed. On arrival of the first two, there had been marked impatience manifested at the delay in my appearance. Their curiosity excited, Lee had examined in the filing cabinets correspondence which had to do with us. It included an application from a Childs in New York State who represented himself as an excellent cryptographer, who had addressed GHQ and offered his services in cipher work. GHQ requested the War Department to commission Childs and send him to France. When word was received that I was on my way, it was assumed that I was him. It was to this error that I owed my assignment in charge of the Cipher Bureau.

The advance units of the A.E.F. had landed in France some eight months before and a high-powered radio receiving station had been set up to intercept enemy radio communications. A great volume of intercepted code and cipher messages of the enemy had accumulated, but not one cipher message had been read. The instructions in cryptography we had received in Washington and Geneva, Illinois, had been confined to the simple systems employed by Latin American countries; the War Department was uninformed on German systems when we arrived in Chaumont.

Two weeks after my arrival, Colonel Moorman, head of G2A6, returned and sent for me. He expressed great satisfaction with my addition to his staff and the report Berthold had given him of the intensive application I had given my work. I had the feeling that it would be well for me to make a graceful exit from the false position in which I found myself. I explained that whatever work I had done had been quite unproductive of any positive results. Moorman cut me short by announcing that he entertained no illusions as to the possibility of quick results, that he would be quite satisfied by my patient endeavors, and that he did not intend to be misled by any excessive modesty on my part into failing to recognize natural ability.

On our arrival in Chaumont, Bob Gilmore and I had been assigned living quarters in a readily accessible private home of the La Tour family, comprising a grandmother, mother and a young daughter. The breadwinner was a locomotive engineer whom we never saw. Bob and I had comfortable rooms where we were served a typical French breakfast, which I liked so well that I guarded my preference for it for the rest of my life. Our lunch and dinner were taken at a military mess comprising six or eight fellow officers. An infallible principle we were enjoined to respect, so top secret was our activity, was that of avoiding any discussion of our G2A6 work.

After I had been laid up with flu for a week or ten days, I returned briefly to iron out a few difficulties my staff had encountered. I was much amused when, on my return, Colonel Moorman commended me as an ideal executive in that, while I was bedridden, my work had gone on uninterruptedly.

When word was received that Friedman was shortly joining our ranks, everyone assumed that he would replace me. It happened that, just before his arrival, I solved a cipher key, adding a third method of solution of the ADFGX cipher to the two uncovered by the French agent Painvin. As a result, Moorman sent for me. "I had intended to replace you with Friedman and make you his assistant, but you have demonstrated so strikingly your capacity these days that, in fairness to you, I have decided to leave you in charge of the Cipher Bureau and to assign Friedman to code work." I was certain the decision would be a disappointment to Friedman. I was all the more careful to avoid the subject with him; good soldier that he was, he never expressed any resentment.

It was very soon after my arrival in Chaumont and assignment to G2A6 that I had the good fortune to meet Parker Hitt, American military pioneer in cryptography, then a captain of infantry and author, in 1916, of *Hitt's Manual*, published by the Army's Service Schools at Fort Leavenworth, Kansas. Despite all my searching, the only other cryptographic works I was able to uncover were A. de Grandpre's, *Cryptographique pratique* (Paris, 1905), which I found in Paris in January 1918, and *German Military Terms and Abbreviations* (British General Staff, General Headquarters, July 1918), presented to me by the British. In passing through Chaumont, Hitt had looked in on Moorman after a visit to the code compilation section nearby. He had been so appalled by the simplicity of the American trench code that he had passed directly to Moorman to express his dismay and to discuss with him how the facts might be brought home to the general staff. To that end, Moorman and Hitt proposed that I be relieved temporarily of my work on German ciphers and concentrate, in agreement with the chief of the code compilation section, on an attempt to decode a series of messages to be prepared in the American trench code. It had been agreed that any successful decoding of trench code messages would be more impressive if made by one less familiar with decoding than I was.

These details having been agreed upon, a series of messages were set up and confided to me to demonstrate how rapidly they might yield to the decoding by such a neophyte as I. The only aid given me was one clerical assistant to prepare tables of frequency.

At this distance in time, it is not easy to explain how I succeeded in reading the code messages within twenty-four hours, to the consternation of the code section and the great satisfaction of Colonel Moorman and Captain Hitt. The American trench code was replaced as soon as humanly possible and my reputation spread like a prairie fire.

It was thus that, to my bewilderment, I found myself, within a couple of weeks of reporting for duty in Chaumont, cloaked in a mantle of renown as one who had broken the American trench code and was indirectly responsible for so exposing its weaknesses that the new code devised was, relatively speaking, immune to being read easily by the enemy.

Another contribution to my credit was to have persuaded both the French and British to agree to the exchange of whatever cipher solutions we might solve in future. It seems strange that such a procedure had never commended itself to our allies previously. To preserve the knowledge from the enemy, the information was mimeographed and communicated by special courier.

It was late in February or early March that Captain Powell arrived from the War Department to acquaint himself with the code and cipher work of the British and French intelligence sections. He had come first to confer with Colonel Moorman. To my astonishment, Moorman sent for me to meet Powell and inform me that I was to accompany Powell on his get-acquainted mission to British and French Intelligence so that I might better serve as liaison officer.

The Cipher Bureau of the British War Office in London was as carefully guarded a secret as could be devised. It was situated in one of the mansions at the end of the Burlington Arcade. When we knocked, the door was opened by a man in civilian clothes who took our cards and ushered us into a parlor. A little later we were conducted upstairs; there we were locked in a room until the appearance of Hay's assistant, who led the way to Hay. I had frequent occasions to visit London thereafter, but the routine never varied.

I was a week in London endeavoring to learn what I could from the British, but most of it was Greek. I did bring away the key to the Für God system of German ciphers used between Von Todenwart, commanding a detachment at Misratah in Tripoli, and Berlin. The former's mission was to spread disaffection against the Allies on the part of the Arab population. Moorman had gained the notion that these messages, which were being intercepted by Chaumont, were of capital importance, and I had spent most of my time endeavoring to find the key, without success. To my chagrin, Hay informed me that they were of secondary importance and that he would be happy to furnish me with the twenty-two substitution alphabets employed in their encipherment. I had the impression that the British had quickly fathomed my rudimentary knowledge and, not disposed to lose any of their precious time, they had conveyed to me the least important German ciphers with which they had had to deal and ones which might be most easily comprehended by me. Later, with my advancing knowledge, they became far more communicative.

When I reported to the French War Office in Paris on March 5, 1918, I found a much more cooperative atmosphere. Work in German ciphers was headed by Captain Georges Painvin, nine years my senior and one of the greatest cipher experts that the war produced. I was in his office when the first messages in one of the most difficult cipher systems ever devised passed over his desk. He brought one over to me, running his hand through his hair in perplexity. It read:

KR v ZS CHI 82 AFADG FXGFG AGGFF DADFX FFGFD GFXXA
DGAGA FFGGD FADFA AGZDG AADAX AFDAG DGAXG
GDXGD AZFAD AFXGX AX

The letters ZS represented the German "sending station," and KR the number of letters contained in the message.

There had been widespread rumors of a contemplated major offensive by the Germans in the spring, with redoubled energy on the part of the Allied cipher bureaus to gain all possible information which might be forthcoming from their decipherment.

There had been a perceptive lull for some weeks in the use of ciphers on the Western Front by the Germans, with principal reliance on the use of codes. These, however, lacked security because of the danger of the code book falling into the hands of the enemy. On the other hand, a cipher may be changed daily, while a code book is not so readily replaced.

The introduction of a new cipher system on the entire Western Front was a plain indication of the imminent launching of the long-anticipated offensive; it burst in all its fury on March 21.

That the messages being intercepted were cipher and not code was plain to any competent cryptographer. If code had been involved, groups would have been of an invariable number of letters, but the messages in question consisted of variable groups whose only common denominator was two. Every message possessed two invariable factors: an even number of letters and only the letters A, D, F, G and X.

Here were two incontrovertible facts on which deductions might be safely based, and to the analytical mind of Painvin they were suggestive of one inescapable conclusion: there was only one possible means by which five letters of the alphabet might be arranged to represent the normal twenty-six.

A solution of the cipher should then be possible by separating the enciphered letters into groups of two and applying the test of frequency. This was not encouraging, suggesting that multiple alphabets had been employed and that a system of simple substitution, followed by a system of transposition of the letters, had taken place. The possible use of multiple alphabets was rejected; accordingly, there was no doubt that, after a substitution of the letters, these had been transposed and that a solution would involve the discovery first of the system of transposition and thereafter of the alphabet employed.

However invulnerable such a system, the keys of which changed daily on the Western Front, must have appeared to the German General Staff, it eventually proved capable of solution; Painvin developed two methods, and I a third. My method was simplicity itself. It was to seek messages with columns of identical numbers of letters. The matching of these would disclose the correct position of the columns; once that was determined, the yielding of the correct German letters was easily established.

The most important information touching on German-Turkish relations was revealed in a message sent by General Kress von Kressenstein from Tiflis on August 3, 1918, to the German Foreign Office through the German ambassador in Moscow:

> His Excellency Helferich, Moscow, for Foreign Office:
>
> According to unconfirmed reports, Baku has been taken by the Turks. German officers and soldiers have not taken part in either the earlier or present operations of the Turks in Azerbaijan. Several days ago I visited Enver Passha in Elizabethpol and received positive assurances that Baku would not be attacked without orders from his high command, but for sanitary reasons he would improve his position. To make the Turkish advance more difficult, I have placed obstacles in the way of every shipment of munitions from Baku via Tiflis up to the present time.   Kress

The message had been enciphered in a system so elementary that I solved it within an hour after its receipt from our wireless station at Chaumont. A few days later, I was working on a series of messages in the

ADFGX system from Berlin to Kressenstein. Here is the deciphered text of one dated August 8 from Berlin to Kress:

> The cipher message prepared by General von Kress was solved here at once. Its further use in operations is forbidden.

I, too, had solved the cipher of Kress with ease; moreover, I had solved the cipher of the chief of German intelligence, believed by the Germans to be indecipherable.

I had to go to London again in July to confer with Major Hay, and to visit Captain Hitchings and MacGregor at Le Touquet in France. This time I stopped in London at the Washington Inn, established for American officers. It was Sunday and, in the dining room, there was only one table occupied. I joined it and had hardly done so before another American in the uniform of a newspaper correspondent asked permission to take a seat. He explained that he had just come from an assignment in the Near East, in Arabia, where he had made the acquaintance of a very remarkable young English officer from whom he had obtained an extraordinary story which resembled a tale out of the Arabian nights. It was about a man named Lawrence who had had extraordinary adventures. The newcomer gave his own name as Lowell Thomas.

Two or three years later, I had occasion to return to London and found Thomas' name emblazoned in lights at a theater in Piccadilly heralding a talk on the now famous Lawrence of Arabia to which thousands were flocking. It was Thomas who had announced his discovery of Lawrence a few years previous and who became, in a sense, his creator. Without Thomas, it is doubtful if the world would ever have heard of Lawrence, a master showman. During the four years I later spent in Saudi Arabia as ambassador, I never heard Lawrence's name mentioned. St. John Philby's, yes—as the personification of modesty.

In recent years there had been an accumulating reevaluation of Lawrence, led off by Aldington and followed by Knightley and Simpson in *The Secret Lives of Lawrence of Arabia*. A reviewer of the latter, George Fraser, in the Paris edition of the *Herald-Tribune* of April 3, 1970, had this to say: "It has been suggested that his exploits were less than heroic ... that he was, among other things, a liar, a sexual deviate, a betrayer, a lunatic, an unscrupulous and cynical intriguer, an exhibitionist of intolerable conceit, and an imposter."

I was walking back to my work at Chaumont when I heard my name called. It was Fritz, whom I had last seen at Harvard in 1914. He had been waiting for a train to take him back to the front after a few days leave and had decided to walk into town when he saw me. He was not like his old ebullient self; he seemed depressed and troubled. I threw discretion to the winds and slapped him on the back. "Come, Fritz, what has gotten you down? Tell me what it is." He seemed touched by the concern expressed in my voice.

It was as if I had opened a safety valve, as the words flowed from him. "I have had a horrible experience," he whispered. "I can't get over it. It's preying on my mind. There was a wonderful chap in our division. Someone like B.K., the same love of poetry, graduate of Princeton, high ideals. I ran into him a few days ago, back of the line; he was on horseback. We stopped to exchange a few words, the last time I saw him. After the last attack I applied for leave and, on my way out, I passed a few wooden crosses just set up. Something induced me to stop and read the names and I suddenly saw that of my friend Phil Sellers."

"With blond hair, about six feet, went to Princeton?"

Fritz was staring at me, nodding his head.

"Why, his brother Lee has a room next to mine. We must go and find him and break the news; he has not had a word."

Fritz gave me a despairing glance, and before I could restrain him he had fled. I never saw him again or heard from him; for all I know, he too may be lying under a cross in an American cemetery which visitors idly pass by today, glancing from one name to another with no notion of the ideals which animated the boys who sleep eternally under those long, unvarying rows of crosses, of the emotions which moved them, of their dreams and aspirations, of dreams which would remain forever unrealized and unfulfilled.

In one respect an armistice existed between the Allies and the Central Powers from the outbreak of hostilities until their close. By tacit agreement, no effort was made on either side to interfere with the other's sending or receiving wireless stations. The famous ADFGX later underwent the addition of the letter V, making possible thirty-six squares and the use of all twenty-six letters of the alphabet as well as the numerals zero to nine. Its use became extended over the Eastern Front, including Russia, the Balkans and Asia Minor. On the Eastern Front the same key was employed for three successive days, instead of only one, as on the Western Front.

On November 2, 1918, I was able to reconstruct within an hour and a half the keys of the ADFGVX cipher on the Eastern Front and to read, in consequence, all messages exchanged on that front on November 1, 2 and 3. In particular, on November 3 I read one from General Von Mackensen to the German High Command, the most important message deciphered by us during the war, of which the following is a translation:

To the Higher Command

 Review of the situation: up to date it has had to be reckoned with that the enemy will attempt a crossing of Danube with the forces assembling at Lom-Palanka and vicinity of Rustchuk, with the object of cutting the railroad communication between Orsova and Craiova, and to strike forward on Bucharest.

 Since November 1, 1918, however, it appears that the Serbian armies, together with three French divisions, are engaged in an advance toward Belgrade–Semendria, and the intended attack at Vidin and Lom-Palanka seems to have been abandoned.

 It is therefore extremely probable that the Serbian armies, reinforced by the French, intend to cross the Danube at Belgrade–Semendria and march into southern Hungary, while the French army marching up south of Svistov and Rustchuk retains the task of directing an offensive toward Bucharest. In conjunction with this operation, it is not impossible that Romanian forces from Moldavia will enter Transylvania through the Tolgyes, Gyimes, and Oiros passes, thereby threatening the lines of communication in the rear of the army of occupation which have up to now as a result

(part missing)

is threatened with attack, and the further occupation of Wallachia, as laid down in order of Headquarters Staff 2 IA, N.R. 11116 OP, is useless, and in view of the stocks on hand of munitions, provisions and coal cannot be carried out. In case a general armistice cannot be expected in the immediate future, it is proposed that the army of occupation be withdrawn from Romania at once and start the march to Upper Silesia through the I-Army. Approval is requested.

K.M.   1 A GR-OP

 Every available German translator of G2A6 had been pressed into service and, as soon as we had a complete English text, I was told to rush it into Colonel Woods, executive officer of the assistant chief of staff.

 As Woods read it, his eyes fairly popping, his glance fell on my insignia of rank as a second lieutenant. "What the bloody hell is the matter with Moorman," he exclaimed "that you have not been promoted long ago?"

 "Colonel Moorman has informed me that he doesn't believe in the promotion of reserve officers."

 "He doesn't, eh? Well, I am going to see that justice is done by your promotion, which you should have had months ago."

 With that, Woods rushed out of the room with the telegram, returning a few moments later to announce that it had been transmitted urgently by airplane to the Supreme War Council. The next day a plain text message was intercepted from the Austro-Hungarian and Italian Front outlining the Austro-Hungarian peace proposals, which included the right of transit of the German Army in Romania across Austro-Hungarian territory. The significance of this condition might have been lost on the Allies had Von Mackensen's hopeless situation not been revealed.

Several weeks after the close of the war, in a call on Painvin at the Ministry of War, he remarked that he had the unpleasant duty to inform me that my chief, Colonel Moorman, had been awarded the Legion of Honor, adding with a wry smile: "In the tradition of almost all armies, it was for work performed by a subordinate, meaning yourself."

I informed him that I had been disillusioned with medals. That attitude had come about fairly recently, as a result of a conversation I had overheard in a compartment of a French train containing British officers returning to the front after home leave in England. One of the officers recounted with great glee what had happened when a request had been received from the French for a list of officers and men who merited the award of the French Croix de Guerre for their conduct in a recent engagement with the enemy. A list was carefully drawn up and, after it had been communicated to and acknowledged by the French, it was discovered to everyone's confusion that the list in question was one of officers and men who had answered sick call. It was obvious the list could not be recalled without loss of face. And so it was the sick and the lame who responded to a roll call and were solemnly decorated with a medal for bravery.

With the armistice on November 11, 1918, Yardley and I suddenly found ourselves with no more ciphers or codes to be solved. Our one source of distraction were the clandestine dance halls which sprang up suddenly. Out of respect to the war dead they were banned by the police, but new premises were opened with but little opposition on the part of an indulgent authority.

Early in 1919, Yardley was instructed to report to Italy for a highly secret mission, so secret that he did not choose to confide the subject to me. The first I learned of it was when an American colonel telephoned me from the Gare de Lyon in great agitation.

"Lieutenant," he said, "I wish to make it plain that I had no reason to suspect there were any highly secret papers in the briefcase which Captain Yardley left at the interrogation desk at the Gare de Lyon before taking the train here for Rome. You understand me, don't you?" he pleaded, as if he were addressing a superior officer.

I assured him that I understood it perfectly without attempting to tell him that I myself was not acquainted in any way with the secret papers the colonel had found on opening the briefcase.

"You must inform Captain Yardley," he insisted, "that I was obliged to open the briefcase to determine to whom it belonged. Please make this plain to Yardley, as I would not have him believe it was through idle curiosity that I opened the briefcase. Is that understood?"

I assured him that it was and that I would make this quite clear to Yardley. He seemed to be profoundly relieved and repeated over and over again his great thanks.

I telegraphed Yardley at once at the embassy in Rome to report that his briefcase was being sent to him by special messenger, and I had a reply from Yardley assuring me of his appreciation. He never once alluded to the incident in any correspondence with me or in any conversation upon his return. I concluded that it was too embarrassing for him to do so, and I knew better than to interrogate him on the subject. I left it at that.

After Yardley and I had returned to the United States we saw less and less of each other. At the instance of the War Department he had established an office in New York City to work on a Japanese code, which he broke. When Secretary of War Stimson learned of this, he ordered the work to cease and Yardley had to find other means of earning his living. One of these was the writing of The American Black Chamber, which had a certain success. He sent me a copy inscribed: "To J. Rives Childs / Le Painvin of the A.E.F. / In Memory of the Days / in Paris /. Cordially / Herbert O. Yardley / Worthington, Indiana / Oct. 11, 1931."

It was many years later, after my retirement to Nice, I learned that my friend George Painvin had established himself with his wife a half-hour drive from Nice at Monte Carlo. When I telephoned him, our warm friendship was quickly renewed. Here in translation is one of the last letters he wrote me, on November 27, 1978 from Paris:

> My very dear friend: Your charming happy New Year wishes have brought with them the warmth of your friendship which have been for me a very great comfort. I also will never forget you.
>
> I think very often of the years which brought us together. It was first your entry, as lieutenant in the American Army, into my office in the rue St. Dominique in 1918, when I was attempting to solve the problem which the Germans had presented to us with their ADFGX cipher.
>
> Then followed the moments when you gave us the pleasure, to my wife and myself, to come to our home to share our family meal . . .
>
> Then the years passed and I did not know what had become of you.
>
> In March, 1962, we had the joy to learn that you were living in Nice. We arranged a meeting and I still recall today the happiness that our two families had in finding ourselves in your home. I shall never forget

the long conversations we had. It was thus that I learned of the evolution of your career, which began with exceptional success in cryptology . . . and continued to develop brilliantly in diplomacy and in literature.

These times, already far removed, have left imperishable memories engraved forever in my souvenirs.

Last year I had the great blow to lose my wife. She would have been happy, if she had lived, to join with me to share the affectionate words which I address to you, dear and very great friend, and to assure you that I also will never forget you.

4
PARIS AND YUGOSLAVIA

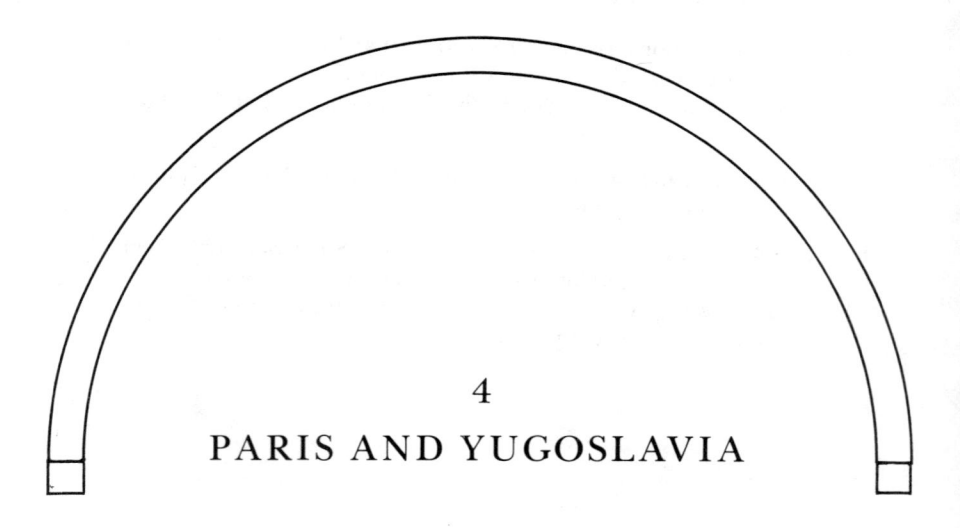

A week or two after the armistice, I had a telephone call from Paris. It was Herbert Yardley, who informed me that he had been assigned as chief of radio intelligence at the Paris Peace Conference on the staff of General Marlborough Churchill and asked if I would care to serve as his assistant. My orders came through a few days later and I joined him at the Hotel Crillon with offices in the building alongside. With a special allowance for living expenses, I suddenly found myself with an income in excess of five thousand dollars. It would be another twenty years before it would be matched.

Paris was dance mad in those days, a reaction to the incomparable tragedy of war. Out of respect for the dead the government had forbidden public dancing, but in the temper of the times it was no easier to enforce than Prohibition was some years later in the United States.

The "dancings" were usually aristocratic premises resembling private dwellings. They included the ultra-smart five-o'clock dancing around the corner from the Place de l'Étoile on the Avenue d'Iéna, crowded for the most part with South Americans, kept women of bankers, editors, deputies, an occasional well-known French aviator whose tunic was covered with medals, a sprinkling of girls from the stage and the smartest of Parisian cocottes. Then there were two on the Left Bank: one in the Rue de la Pompe, another in the Eiffel Tower district. There was another, near the Opéra, with long divans at opposite ends of the room, frequented by ballet girls and young French artists, with a free and easy bohemian atmosphere which became one of our favorites. There was yet another off the Champs-Élysées, a rather noisy and vulgar place where the girls who solicited in the promenades of the Folies-Bergère and the Casino went after the theater, and, as might have been supposed, expanded the oppressive atmosphere of a bawdy house. We came in time to know them all, more so than the general run of Americans in Paris; when one was closed, word of its new address was passed on to its habitués. They were irresponsible days, a mad reaction to four years of senseless slaughter, begotten of an inability to find any reason in our lives or to relate our experiences with life's former expectations.

Yardley and I grew tired of the Crillon and, to have greater contact with the French, decided to try out a French *pension*. We found one not far from the Étoile, but it did not live up to expectations. One day, after lunch, we were looking for a taxi when we caught sight of two attractive young Frenchwomen on the point of entering the only one in sight. Observing that my curiosity was reciprocated, I hastened forward, noting as I did that the taxi driver had been admonished to wait. I explained our predicament to two sympathetic auditors—one dark-complexioned, thin and vivacious, the other a languid blonde of fuller proportions—and asked if we might be permitted to join them if they were passing by the Crillon.

On our way, we learned that the dark-haired minx, named Jacqueline, had been trained for the ballet, and her friend, Suzanne, was in the chorus of the Casino de Paris. From this time forward, Yardley and Jacqueline were to become inseparable until his return to the States a few months later. She so integrated herself as a comrade with Yardley's friends and interests that she found us our own apartment where we might be more at ease. As a result, we were soon installed in ideal living quarters on the third floor of Rue Gustave Zéde 18, in Passy, an aristocratic section, with the privacy and comfort we sought. It comprised four bedrooms, two salons and a dining room, the three last divided by French doors which could be opened up to form a commodious dance floor. We had no difficulty in finding two other fellow officers at the Crillon: Emmett Kilpatrick of Uniontown, Alabama, forever bubbling over with irrepressible spirits; and a somewhat more subdued character, Frank Moseley. It was also thanks to Jacqueline that we found an excellent cook, who had once served the president of the Argentine as a domestic.

Through hospitable French organizations, we were soon the recipients of daily invitations from distinguished French families to lunches, dinners, teas and cocktail parties. To make some return, we organized two "at homes" on Thursdays and Sundays, strictly apportioned between our bohemian friends and members of society. Music was provided by an American jazz orchestra comprising musicians from the headquarters forces of Rue Tilsitt, while a buffet supper was furnished from the Crillon at little, if any, expense to us.

Many years have passed since the events I am recounting, but they have not dimmed the memory of Jacqueline, her kindness and her exceptional charm. They were days of singular freshness of spirit such as I have seldom known—free of all pettiness and of rare elevation, without a care in the world, veritable halcyon days and nights, on the order, as it seemed to me at the time, of the comradely spirit of *The Three Musketeers* or of Robin Hood and his Merry Men, with our Jacqueline a simulacrum of Maid Marian. They were never again to be recaptured, unique as they were and infinitely precious.

Young Sam Untermeyer, whom I had known at Chaumont, came by one day on leave and looking for company. He was unfamiliar with Paris and anxious to try out some of the restaurants for which France was famous. If it would be agreeable to me, he proposed that I be his cicerone while he was a visitor and introduce him to the very best. I laughed and told him that I did not have that kind of money. He protested that he did and that I could accept his footing the bill as only a fair exchange for my expert knowledge. He was so insistent, and I was so fond of Sam, that I ended up giving in to his persuasiveness.

We started out with one of the most renowned restaurants, which has since disappeared, in the vicinity of the Chamber of Deputies. I recall it perfectly and, more particularly, the "tab" for our lunch, which totaled the equivalent of twenty-eight dollars, an enormous sum for a meal for two in those days, including an aperitif, a fine wine and brandy. Other restaurants we sampled were Larue, Maxim's, Voisin (perhaps the most reputed), Le Grand Vatel (now a self-service restaurant) and others, many of which have since disappeared.

One of our most memorable of many social evenings began with a dinner to which Yardley and I had been invited on New Year's Eve, 1918, by a young American banker and his wife who lived on fashionable Avenue Foch. Toward midnight, our hosts proposed that we accompany them to what might be one of the most entertaining private parties in all of Paris; they had been invited by the Mumms to their château a short distance from the city. When we arrived, it was evident that many other revelers, having a festive evening with guests at their respective homes, had been similarly moved, as we, to converge on the Mumms. On our arrival we found our newly elected host standing at the head of the marble entry stairway, flanked by two flunkies in knee breeches, endeavoring to bring some order into the sea of invaders intruding upon the other several hundred guests. With admirable imperturbability, he extended most cordial greetings to everyone. He had but one request to make—that only those who had received formal invitations should proceed to the sit-down supper for two hundred on the second floor. The others would be served buffet. Yardley and I stood in a protected alcove to observe the ensuing mad scramble, resembling nothing so much as a raging sea. Only after it had subsided did we endeavor to make our way to the buffet. From a waiter we learned that some three thousand bottles of champagne had been opened for the two thousand or more present. The most amusing aspect of it all was apparent as we took our departure in the light of dawn. Drawn up in the courtyard were several ambulances into which guests, on stretchers and in various stages of intoxication, were being solicitously placed after having been tagged with their names and addresses for delivery to their homes.

The life we were leading began, after a time, to pall. Kilpatrick was the first to leave—to join the Estonian Army with the rank of captain, to which he had aspired since entering the American Army so he could match the rank his father had held in the Confederate Army. Yardley had left for the United States to join his wife, but he had not freed the office space so that I might be left undisturbed.

Two or three weeks later, the personnel officer of the Peace Conference, on an inspection tour, found me, to his surprise, at my desk. The jig was up. I was told to report to the Army for orders home. I had the temerity to plead for a few days' leeway so that I might seek another post which would keep me in Europe. With a wry face, he granted me three days' grace. I had heard that the American Relief Administration in Paris was recruiting staff for operations in Eastern Europe. I sought out the address given and was directed to the personnel officer, a Mr. Peden. That sounded encouraging, as I had taught two young brothers of that name at Lawrenceville School.

When I found Mr. Peden, I raised the question of his parentage, mentioning the two "exceptional young men of his name" from Texas whom I had taught. Were they, by any chance, related to him? He smiled. "My sons, no less," he replied.

Once we had exhausted that subject, he asked where I would like to be stationed by the Relief Administration. The Balkans were remote and romantic; I suggested Yugoslavia and had my Army orders in a day or two.

I had to take leave of a young, intelligent and attractive French girl who spoke perfect English and held a responsible position. It was a most painful task. We had met shortly after my arrival when I was dining with Yardley in a restaurant adjacent to the Opéra Comique. My back was to the fair young lady, but I had an excellent view of her reflection in a mirror. Happily, her escort was facing her with his back to me. I took a menu and wrote across the back in large letters my name and address and held it so she could see. It was soon after my arrival, when I was still living at the Crillon. Her reaction was a furtive smile from which anything might have been deduced. I had not long to wait. The next morning I had a telephone call. A mellifluous voice, in a provocative, teasing tone, asked if I were the bold young man who had introduced himself the previous evening on a restaurant bill of fare. Was that not a somewhat unconventional manner of approaching a young lady of irreproachable character?

I did not find the moment propitious to tell her of an even less conventional means I had chosen before joining the Army in France to establish contact, after my arrival, with French *jeunes filles*. I had drafted an announcement I had mailed from Virginia to *La Vie Parisienne* reading, as near as I can now recollect: *Jeune officier Américain désire entrer en correspondence avec jeune fille française, belle et cultivée. Écrivez avec photo: Lt. J.R. Childs, Lynchburg, Va., U.S.A."*

The immediate sequel was an agitated letter from my mother saying that the postmaster, an old friend, had telephoned her that his office was in receipt of some five hundred letters from France, all addressed to her son in different feminine handwriting, and had inquired as to what disposition of them she desired him to make.

To gain time, my mother suggested they be sent to her home. There, still perplexed and concluding that it was another prank of mine which she was unable to fathom, but preserving her loyalty to me, she determined to form several packets and readdress them to my APO designation. The avalanche descended on me some little time later. I quailed at the idea of opening and sorting them. Instead, I invited Gilmore, Sellers and Graham to join me at dinner in a Chaumont restaurant. Once they were there, I divided the letters into four piles and suggested they proceed to the task of opening and reading the letters and depositing the most interesting ones in the center of the table. They fell to with a vengeance, broken only by occasional peals of laughter or appropriate remarks. When the work of examination was terminated, I gathered up the center pile and spent some days examining the missives.

One letter stood out above all the others, one of the most brilliant letters I had ever read, from a young girl obviously of excellent family and highly educated; she was mistress of a pen which reduced my missive, with gentle irony, to proportions more in keeping with her keen perceptions. I long kept the letter to savor the wit, with its nuances, which had gone into its composition. It eventually disappeared from my papers deposited in the attic of my Virginia home, how or under what circumstances is a mystery. In the end she wrote through a friend to say that, regretfully, she was obliged to renounce corresponding or seeing me for the time being; if the opportunity presented itself, she would let me know. I wrote to her intermediary to plead my cause, but to no avail. It was a mystery which I could not penetrate and which now will never be divined, but it represented one of my supreme disappointments.

I was left with many names and addresses of correspondents in Paris, but none as compelling as my exasperating shrinking violet, alas. In any case, I was never lacking in companions to whom I might turn for company. One was a talented actress somewhat older than I, and there were working girls who were amusing for an evening, but none was in any way comparable to the phantom who had presented herself, not suspecting that I was in France, and had retreated in dismay upon discovering the truth. I would have given much to have met her for even a few precious moments; she was one of the most richly endowed personalities among the women I have known, and all the more provocative for fleeing in such agitation in reaction to my overtures. Another acquaintance was a beautifully groomed and attractive woman, also slightly older than I, whom I met at a *thé dansant* at one of the diplomatic establishments. We took to one another at once and went out together quite often, as she was fond of dancing, a distraction not shared by her husband. When I left Paris, she presented me with a French collection of classic poems with a warm dedication. Two years later, when I was married in Leningrad, I was so concerned to destroy all records of my past entangling alliances that I ripped from the book the page with her dedication.

It is probably out of these considerations that, although I possess a fantastic memory, the name of the French girl I met in the restaurant adjacent to the Opéra Comique and who remained my close friend until I returned to the United States temporarily in 1919, has vanished from my memory and resists all efforts at resurrection. All that I recall of our last communication was a letter from her from England that a suitor, an ex-major in the British Army, was pressing her to marry him; she would do so only if I did not. I decided the preferable course, however ungallant, was not to answer, leaving her to draw the obvious conclusion.

I left Paris with great regret. Military Intelligence had offered to have me appointed to the military staff of the embassy with one single objective—to induce a good friend, a French officer, to let me have an important report on cryptography which he had written and shown me. I found it repulsive to exploit a friendship and turned it down in favor of the military orders I had been awaiting assigning me to the American Relief Administration in Yugoslavia.

I took a train for Trieste on the great adventure which railway travel then represented after the widespread damage occasioned by the war. One set out never knowing what the day would bring. I finally reached my immediate destination via Venice and a steamer to Trieste. There I obtained rail accommodations through wartorn land once part of the Austro-Hungarian Empire. When we reached the Danube, the bridge giving access to Serbia had been gutted, making it necessary to resort to a ferry. On the opposite shore was Belgrade.

Upon reporting to the ARA, I was informed that I was being assigned to Saloniki in charge of child-feeding in Macedonia; three assistants were to take up quarters in Monastir, Skoplje and Nish, while my task would be a roving one. As rail communications had been severed between Belgrade and the south, arrangements had been made for me to accompany a British hospital unit which was making its way down the Danube by a Serbian steamer to Prazovo, thence by rail to Kragujevac, where we would be met by British lorries to transport us over the mountain to Nish, and again by rail to Saloniki. A journey normally of one day was to take us almost a week.

Several hours east of Belgrade, the river cut through the overtowering crags of the Hungarian and Serbian mountains. We observed the ruins of a Roman fortress at the entrance to the Serbian shore, along with a road built by the cohorts of the Emperor Trajan, with an inscription left by him still visible in the rocks.

At Prazovo a train was awaiting us; it consisted of seventeen coaches, of which fifteen were freight cars for third-class passengers and two were prewar third-class carriages converted into first class by simply painting "first" over "third." Glass in the windows had long since disappeared, replaced by rough boards. At Kragujevac we were obliged to spend the night. My interpreter accompanied me to a pharmacy to purchase some medicine I needed. It was almost denuded of furniture and fixtures and sadly depleted of stock. A kindly faced Serbian pharmacist informed us that the Bulgarians had stripped him of almost all he possessed, but if all went well at the Peace Conference he hoped to receive some reparation. He was delighted to hear I was an American, from a country whose President Wilson had awakened the world to a new sense of justice. When I inquired the price of my medicine, he shook his head. "I cannot ask money of an American from the land of Wilson," he said.

We passed the night in a dingy, run-down hotel. At breakfast the next morning, a waiter, unshaven and in threadbare clothes, pressed into my hands a package of cigarettes, asking me to accept it as his thank offering for Wilson and America. It awakened the memory of Wilson's entry into Paris down the Champs-Élysées and of the thunderous cries of men and women alike in welcoming him; most of them were weeping uncontrollably, overcome by emotion, in one of the greatest displays of reverence I had ever witnessed. When friends arriving from America informed me that we would most likely not ratify the Treaty of Versailles or enter the League of Nations, I refused to believe that our sacrifices in men and treasures had gone for naught and would lead inevitably to a second World War more cruel and devastating than the first. It was inconceivable that we should be so lacking in elementary intelligence. But our foreign policy since that time seems to me, from my Foreign Service experiences, to have been for the most part one long succession of misguided decisions and squandered opportunities.

It was in Yugoslavia that I began to realize so forcefully the unique place Wilson had earned for us in the hearts and esteem of the world's masses.

There are few more colorful regions in the world than the Balkan states, with their wild, rugged crags and broad amalgam of peoples. This was particularly true of Macedonia and of Skoplje, with Christian Serbs in European dress alongside Moslems in red fezzes and turbans, Albanians in white skullcaps and Montenegrins in their distinctive headgear. The red crown of the Montenegrin cap represents the bloodshed in the battle of Kossovo on June 13, 1389, when Serbia was subjected to Turkish domination; five gold threads represent the centuries which have since elapsed; while the black brimless band signalizes mourning for that day.

To take stock of the district's needs, Milt Lockwood, one of my deputies, and I toured some of the wildest parts in a Model T Ford, proceeding along the Albanian border through Djakovica to Petch. It was a dangerous country where the most visible inhabitants comprised roving bands of *comitadjis*—a term embracing both bandits and vigilantes. The only signs of life were Serbian patrols, in which each man had a gun and cartridge belt slung over the shoulder, a pistol dangling from the waist and a knife protruding from each boot. "Armed to the boots" would have been a more fitting description than "armed to the teeth."

At Djakovica we lunched with officers of the local garrison and the principal officials who had met us five miles outside the town. Lunch had hardly been terminated before we were conducted to dinner in the home of our host, Alan Bey. The only women present were those who served us. Their nonparticipation was in accordance with Moslem custom, introduced by the Turks and prevalent throughout the Near East.

The hospitality extended us as Americans was but a prelude to that showered upon us wherever we went. Upon halting the following day at the ancient monastery of Detchani in the mountains, we were shown its manuscript treasures. As we expressed particular admiration for one on vellum, the priest, before he could be restrained, tore out two pages of the precious manuscript for us as a souvenir token of Serbian admiration for Wilson.

When we reached Petch, a guard of honor was mounted outside the home in which we were lodged and orderlies accompanied us wherever we went. We had to abandon our desire to purchase some souvenirs when we found that merchants of the town had received orders not to accept payment.

The evening before our departure, we were the honored guests at a banquet attended by some sixty of the leading local dignitaries. For the first time in the history of Petch, to mark the special character of the occasion, senior representatives of the four local faiths—Greek Orthodox, Roman Catholic, Moslem and Jewish—took their seats together. At the end of the meal, the Greek Orthodox priest, with his glass in his hand, approached the Moslem mullah and, raising it, said: "In drinking to the health of President Wilson and the United States in the presence of these two Americans whose country we are assembled to honor, let us bury our differences and proclaim our union as brothers."

Every eye was turned on the Moslem. He hesitated an instant before he rose. "Friends, my religion forbids fermented drink. As a holy man, I should set an example. There comes, however, perhaps once in a lifetime, an occasion when observance of the letter of the law may become a greater offense than its transgression." He paused to take hold of the untouched glass of wine beside his plate. "I therefore drink with you on this unique occasion, in honor of a country to whose ideals we pay homage, in this fraternal association."

It was as if he had pressed a button to set off a detonation. The outpouring of applause was deafening. Men and women embraced one another. Many wept unashamedly in the fervor of their emotions; others shouted and pranced around the floor. It was a long while before calm was restored. When some semblance of order was regained with the conclusion of dinner, Lockwood and I were seized and borne on the shoulders of the stoutest men through the streets to our lodgings.

We were awed and overcome by this manifestation of love and admiration for our country. We were moved by the depth of it and its unprecedented expression; and, at the same time, we were shaken at the thought of the disillusionment which might follow our failure to live up to its expectations.

Notwithstanding the satisfaction offered by my work of saving lives rather than taking them, as well as an appeal that I continue until the spring, I was becoming impatient to take up a definite career. In September I submitted my resignation and, upon its acceptance, pursued by my perpetual wanderlust, I wrote my own orders for passage on a French vessel bound for Constantinople. Once there, I spent two or three days with an excellent English guide exploring one of the most fascinating cities in the world, set like a diadem in its resplendent setting astride the Bosphorus and the Sea of Marmora. There I boarded a coastal vessel into the Black Sea to the port of Constanta from whence, after an overnight stay in a luxurious hotel, I made my way by train to gay Bucharest, capital of Romania and known then as "the Paris of the Balkans," where every café housed a hauntingly sobbing gypsy orchestra whose strains tore at one's heartstrings.

On finally reaching Paris, I was shocked by its drab contrast with the ebullient city I had left in April. Its inhabitants resembled nothing so much as men and women, unsmiling and bleary-eyed, emerging from a prolonged debauch with no further taste for dissipation. I telephoned to one former friend after another; with few exceptions, they were in the country. I reported without regret to American military headquarters.

The officer in charge frowned as he examined my papers. "You have taken one hell of a time to report in after the receipt of your orders . . . And how is it that you had to go to Constantinople from Saloniki, which is to the east and not the west?"

I murmured something about the widespread disorganization in the wake of the war and the difficulty of obtaining transport. He apparently saw no useful purpose in challenging me. He was about to stamp new orders to get me out to Brest, principal embarkation port for the States, without further delay, when I remarked that I had been at the Peace Conference and had made many friends among both Americans and French and would like two or three days to look them up.

At first I thought he would have a seizure. He began to splutter in astonishment at my bravado, but it tapered off. "I can only admire your gall. I'll give you three days, not an hour more."

In a way, the three days were superfluous. I might as well have been hunting partridges in the center of Paris. I finally found one friend who had been demobilized in Paris and had set himself up in business selling typewriters, then in great demand. I was relieved when my three days of grace expired. The next three weeks were spent in a tent at Brest awaiting space on a ship. In the end, I turned up as one of thirteen in a cabin with tiers of bunks.

I had one last adventure. Some of us, to while away the time, used to meet to have a drink in one of the principal hotels, where some of the local and traveling women also congregated. Late one afternoon, I made up to one of the most attractive, who told me she had a room not far away at such and such an address. The one fly in the ointment was that she had promised to dine with an American general, but she said she would give him the slip and meet me at her room. She advised me not to be too early, as it might take a little time to shake the general.

All went well and I was admitted to her room at the time appointed. A minute or two later, there was a knock. We both lapsed into silence as she whispered, "Sh! It must be the general."

He kept vigil an inordinately long time, with a periodic knocking on the door which only ceased long after midnight. It was no doubt his tenacity in the face of the enemy which had brought him to a general's rank, but happily for me it was quite misapplied to the fair sex; here, he faced a contest in which age was hopelessly outclassed.

Following my demobilization in the United States in Ocotober 1919, I learned that I had been awarded a Yugoslavian medal for the Hoover relief work I had performed in southern Serbia at the end of the war. I attached so little importance to it that it soon disappeared. My indifference no doubt stemmed from my disappointment at failing to receive any recognition from Colonel Moorman for my success in the decipherment of the German ADFGX cipher. Painvin made light of my disappointment; it was taken for granted that the senior office garnered the credit. Some years later, in 1946, Colonel McNown, then military attaché in Cairo, was instructed by the War Department to present me with the Medal of Freedom. At first I declined the medal, but yielded when it was represented that he would be embarrassed by failure to execute the commission of the War Department. Somewhat later I learned that the medal is the highest civilian honor bestowed by the United States Government.

5
WASHINGTON CORRESPONDENT

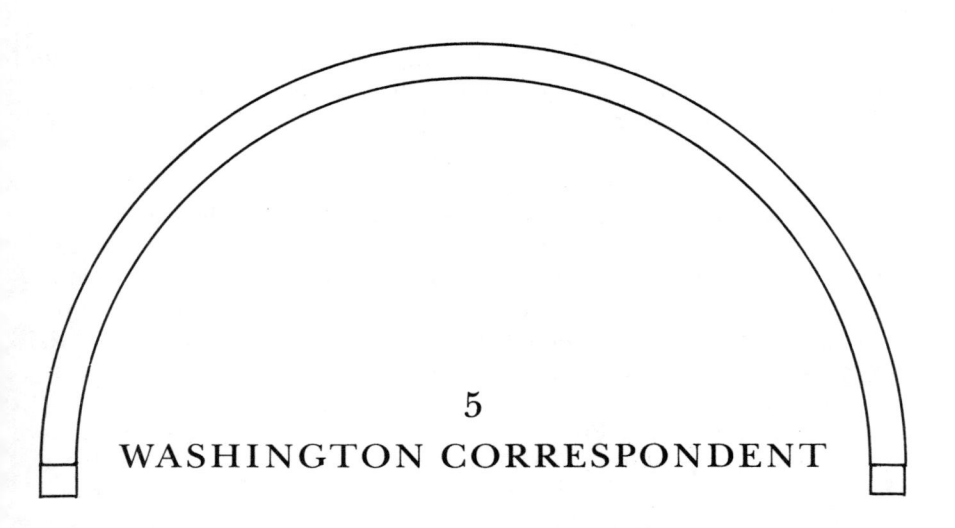

By the time my transport reached New York, I had determined to abandon any thought of taking up a teaching career in favor of the newspaper work of which I had had a first taste in 1912 as a reporter on the Baltimore *American*. What I aspired to most was creative writing, and work as a reporter seemed a more favorable preparation for that than teaching.

As I was still in uniform, my ship had no sooner docked in New York than I determined to make an initial pitch to Melville Stone, general manager of the Associated Press. I had in my possession visiting cards in Serbian, French and English for use in my relief work in Yugoslavia. Armed with such a card, which was certain to excite interest, I presented myself at the office of Mr. Stone and requested an interview. I was ushered at once into his presence.

"What can I do for you?" Stone asked me as he scrutinized my card and invited me to be seated.

I came to the point at once. "I am looking for a job."

Stone smiled pleasantly. He began by putting to me one or two searching questions. Before I realized what was happening, he had shaken my hand warmly, saying that he would communicate with Dick Probert, in charge of his Washington office, and the rest would be up to me.

When I reached Washington with a palpitating heart, Probert proved to be the least loquacious individual I had ever met; in consequence, I was left to do most of the talking. After a minimum of probing questions, he rose and told me to report to Deacon Simpson, night city editor, the next evening.

After ten days or so of delivering copy to the nearby offices of the Washington *Post* and the Washington *Star*, it came to me that I was getting nowhere very fast. I began to keep an eye on the flow of incoming overseas cables. Three from widely separated parts of the world attracted my interest a night or two later. It occurred to me that they lent themselves to a common lead. Simpson accepted with a tired air the copy I had prepared and tossed the sheets into a receptacle on a desk, with no comment other than a subdued grunt. He, too, was an unloquacious person.

The next morning Probert sent for me, to my surprise, the first attention he had paid me since I had joined his staff. I concluded that I was perhaps to be informed of the termination of my services. Instead, he greeted me with what passed, for him, as a smile; at least it wasn't a frown.

"I read your lead; it was all right." Then he added, after a pause, "but we couldn't use it." Another pause. "We are assigning you to the State Department, with Eddie Hood. He's getting along in years." He added, as an afterthought, "Keep close to him; he'll break you in."

I took leave, instinctively, on tiptoe.

I was quite elated; I had the feeling I had struck pay dirt. Subsequent events were to prove how fortunate I had been.

I was walking through Lafayette Park one morning when I encountered an acquaintance who lived in New York but came to Washington frequently on business and who was good about putting me on to newsworthy information. He was quite excited by what he had just heard by chance of a top-secret report the Red Cross had received from their representative in Riga, Colonel Ryan. The latter had contrived surreptitiously to accompany an Estonian peace commission to Moscow, where Ryan had been received clandestinely by Soviet Foreign Minister Chicherin. The importance of his report to the Red Cross was that it was the first authentic information the government had received in months from any responsible source about conditions in Soviet Russia, because we had broken relations with that government. It was certain the Red Cross would not release the report to the press. The great question was how to gain access to it.

I had a brain wave; because of my war service with military intelligence, I was well acquainted with the light echelons of its personnel. I made a beeline to the office of Colonel M. When I disclosed what I had just heard about the Ryan report, he smiled. "Would you like to see a copy?" he asked.

He disappeared without awaiting my reply and returned shortly with a copy in his hand. He excused himself and, as soon as he was gone, I had my pencil out and was copying the most striking parts. A very dramatic touch was when Chicherin led Ryan to a window with a view of Kremlin Square; as they gazed at it, the Foreign Minister, who had been a member of the czarist diplomatic staff in Paris before the Revolution, inquired wistfully, "And how is it now in Paris?"

I was still feverishly copying one of the great stories of my newspaper career when Colonel M. returned and asked, as if he did not know: "What are you doing there? I can't give permission to publish any of the text."

"But, Colonel, the American people are entitled to know what is happening in Russia." It was a classic line of the newspaper profession, but it worked.

"I suppose it is all right," the colonel observed, "but you mustn't give us as your source."

"You may count on me. I shall simply say in the opening paragraph that it has been learned of the receipt by the Red Cross, from its representative in Riga, of the first intimate glimpse of the situation in Russia, obtained by Ryan in a surreptitious visit to Moscow under cover of the Estonian peace commission."

Before he had time to change his mind, I took my leave after hurriedly making a few final notes and rushed with my story to the AP office on Pennsylvania Avenue. I said nothing to anyone as I took my place in front of a typewriter and began pounding the keys.

I had been typing about fifteen or twenty minutes when Deacon looked in my direction and growled: "What are you writing, a book? The traffic is heavy tonight and I haven't much space for you."

"You will have when you see what I have uncovered."

"You know the limit for the most sensational story?"

I knew it to be about a thousand words, or not exceeding a column, and I went on typing.

"Wait and see what I have; you will put it on the wires all right, all of it."

Simpson, as phlegmatic as he was, rose and came over to examine my manifolds. He had not read far when he snorted, "I had better send out a warning notice to expect twelve hundred words or so. It's a humdinger. I'll give it all I can." He did, and the next morning the New York *Times* spread the story in a three-column banner headline almost covering the first page.

It was the first authentic news that had come out of the Soviet Union in months. It was headlined throughout the country by almost every newspaper. The next morning there was a stampede of correspondents to Secretary Tumulty's news conference at the White House and to Secretary Colby's at the State Department. The newspapers which had been scooped on one of the most sensational stories to come out of Washington in months were unable to obtain any repudiation of it, to their discomfiture. What most rankled was that the story had been broken by a greenhorn such as me. My salary was increased by five dollars weekly. I didn't dare show my face at Military Intelligence for some days until the excitement subsided. When it was over and I called on Colonel M, he congratulated me on how it had been handled. Not the slightest suspicion fell on military intelligence as the source of the information. With confidence in me thus established, the doors were open and I was allowed to read the weekly summary of reports received from military attachés abroad. I was permitted to use my own judgment on the material I might use without embarrassment to the government. With such a grapevine at my disposition, I never lacked for interesting foreign news.

With the establishment of such a flow of information on foreign affairs, Probert decided to transfer me to cover the White House. On account of President Wilson's illness, there was almost a complete dearth of any domestic news emanating from the President or Secretary Tumulty. In those days there were only four or five regular reporters stationed at the White House. They included Frank Lamb of the Washington *Post,* representatives of the Washington *Star,* and the International News Service, Raymond Clapper of the United Press, and me.

Some time later, I was standing outside the pressroom when I observed one of the junior staff of Secretary Tumulty making his way across the entry. On a sudden impulse, I approached and entered into conversation with him. A natural question to put to him was the state of health of the President and when he thought Mr. Wilson would be able to resume his normal activities. He looked at me as if not hearing me right. "But don't you realize that President Wilson has been so incapacitated that it is quite unlikely he will ever be able to resume a normal life?"

The fact was that Mrs. Wilson and Secretary Tumulty had raised such an impenetrable wall about the President that the public had not been able to form any idea of Wilson's physical state. Through pure chance the veil had been lifted.

When I telephoned the news in to Jim Williams, the day editor, he was incredulous. "Are you sure of the facts?" he inquired.

"I can only tell you what I was told. Of course he would never agree to be quoted."

"You are reasonably sure the story will stand up?"

"Who is in a position to refute it?"

"Very well, I'll put it on the wire, but all hell will be let loose. Your job won't be worth two cents if it doesn't stand up."

Jim was right about the reaction. The story made the first pages with banner headlines. The White House was besieged by the scooped reporters, who comprised the entire corps with one exception.

I have a dim recollection that, for this particular scoop, I was the recipient of another increase in salary; it certainly didn't do me any harm.

On the fourth of March, 1921, while preparations were being made for Wilson to accompany incoming President Warren G. Harding to the Capitol for the transfer of the presidency, Tumulty approached me and remarked, "The President wrote you a letter last night, one of the four he dictated on his last night in the White House."

"I am highly honored," I said, and then I added that, shortly after being assigned to the White House, I had written Wilson a letter expressing my profound admiration and citing the evidence which had been given me in Yugoslavia of the love and esteem in which he was held. I concluded that his present letter was a delayed reply.

Once Wilson and Harding had left the White House for the Capitol, the half-dozen White House reporters made their separate ways to join them. The corridors of the Capitol were so crowded that I found it impossible to gain admittance to the President's room. In the end, a member of the Secret Service who was inside approached the door and, catching sight of me, motioned me to approach. I did so with great alacrity and, when I found myself inside, a quick survey indicated that I was the sole newspaper correspondent destined to witness a dramatic confrontation between the President and his *bête noir*, Senator Henry Cabot Lodge.

The distinguished company gathered there included President Wilson, seated at a modest-sized table signing legislation passed during the last hours of Congress, and a group of the most notable dignitaries standing by the windows, including Mrs. Wilson, President-elect and Mrs. Harding, General John J. Pershing and Chief Justice Edward D. White, to name the most distinguished. As the noon hour approached, the door opened to disclose Henry Cabot Lodge with one of the most malevolent looks I had ever seen on the face of a man. He had made it his aim to thwart President Wilson at every turn, to ensure that the United States would not enter the League of Nations and cast its weight on the side of peace. Lodge's policy would prepare the way for the appearance of such a monster as Adolf Hitler and disrupt the world in a manner from which it has not yet recovered after almost forty years of relative peace.

I was standing a little to one side behind the President and could observe minutely every move that the two adversaries might make.

"Mr. President," Lodge began, "I have been directed by the Congress to wait on you to ascertain whether you have any further communication to make before a motion is adopted for adjournment."

There was a deathly silence as the attention of everyone in the crowded room was focused on this dramatic last encounter between the two principal protagonists in the struggle over the fateful issue of American ratification of the Treaty of Versailles and entry into the League of Nations. One man had been paralyzed in the contest, the other left to gloat in triumph over his temporarily vanquished adversary. Now they were confronting each other as if in a Shakespearean tragedy, one consumed with hate, the other surveying the figure before him with Olympian detachment and serenity.

Wilson, who in 1916 had heralded the "solemn days when all the standards of mankind are to be fully tried out," who had proclaimed on the eve of American participation in the war the need for a peace without victory, who had sensed in Paris at the opening of peace deliberations a great wind of moral force moving through the world and the utter confounding of those who would oppose themselves to that wind, glanced up at the wizened figure before him and, with a sense of historical finality, responded, "No, sir, I have no further message to communicate."

His complete mastery of himself was doubtless strengthened by the thoughts which must have been racing through his mind. He had given repeated warnings of the perils to the United States and to the world implicit in American repudiation of the Treaty of Versailles and the League of Nations. He had sensed with that gift given to prophets the hopes which the little people had placed in the United States. The will of Lodge, his party and the Senate had prevailed over the long-term interests of the nation. The President had no further communication to make; he had had his say; the rest was silence. It was for history to pay the reckoning and he had no doubt, as he had himself given warning, that it would be fateful beyond measure. The destruction wrought by the First World War would be as nothing compared to that of the war that was bound to follow.

The President had invited the half-dozen correspondents in regular attendance at the White House to join him at the private residence he had chosen on R Street. Admiral Grayson and Mrs. Wilson accompanied him there. When we had assembled, Grayson recounted a touching exchange he had had on leaving the Capitol. Grayson had instinctively addressed him as "Mr. President," when Wilson raised his hand in objection, remarking, "Just plain Woodrow Wilson now."

Once at the R Street residence, the correspondents who had accompanied him there were asked to form a line and were introduced one by one into the late President's presence. As my name was pronounced he smiled, remarking, "I wrote you a line last night."

"Yes, sir, so Secretary Tumulty told me, and I want you to know how deeply I appreciate your letter."

No one could have been more dissimilar from Wilson than the newly elected President Warren G. Harding. Several months before, Harding had spoken to a relatively small group of reporters at the National Press Club and had astounded everyone present with his disingenuousness. He began by confessing that he didn't know how he had been persuaded to become a candidate. It was his close friend Harry Daugherty who had put pressure on him. He really hadn't cared to seek the nomination. But all his life he had found it difficult to say no, so much so that his father had once said to him that it was a good thing he had not been born a girl or he would have been in a family way most of the time.

Shortly after the inauguration, I was invited with a few other correspondents to a garden party for disabled veterans at the White House. With the aim of reporting the event, I followed along behind the President as he passed from one veteran to another, most of them in wheelchairs. Harding halted by the most tragically disabled veteran, who had been blinded and deprived of both legs, and the following colloquy ensued:

"Do you like to be read to?" Harding asked.

"Not particularly," was the reply from one who appeared to have enjoyed few advantages in life.

"You might find some comfort in books," Harding continued. "There are some in which I have found great inspiration."

I pricked up my ears. The books which had inspired a President, however uncultivated, would make an interesting human interest story, more particularly from one not given as much to reading as to playing poker.

"Books which have always given me a great lift and would, I am sure, cheer you up are the Pollyana books," Harding concluded.

I scrutinized the President to make sure he was in earnest. There could be no doubt of that. He wouldn't have been so heartless, when speaking with a veteran so cruelly disabled, as to have been lacking in seriousness. I turned away, let down at the loss of a story. The Associated Press would never disseminate news tending to belittle the President.

On another occasion Albert Einstein called on the President and was held in conversation for some little time on the lawn of the White House. I wracked my brain as to what I might write to color the story which neither would be disposed to deny. I had a happy inspiration and built a story around Harding's confession of his inability to understand Einstein's theory of relativity. Harding's intellectual deficiencies did not extend to allowing him to make a fool of himself by repudiating my story. It was such a hit that it was boxed by most newspapers on the front page.

The New York *World* even made it the subject of an editorial in which I was chided for not having reported Einstein's rejoinder that he was equally unable to understand Harding's theory of "normalcy."

A few weeks after Harding's inauguration, one of the White House correspondents proposed the formation of an association of those regularly assigned there. The first dinner took place at the Arlington Hotel on May 7, 1921, with George B. Christian, Jr., Harding's secretary, as guest of honor. It would never have occurred to us to invite the President or even a member of his Cabinet. A score of correspondents were in attendance as well as some six or eight guests, most of whom were from out-of-town. The guests had thoughtfully supplied us with a case of whiskey—or it may have been two, considering the state of those present by the end of the evening.

As the evening was drawing to a close and a large part of the whiskey had been consumed, Christian was called on for a speech. According to Christian, Harding had never aspired to the office of President. Moreover, he had never expected to be elected. Now that he was occupying the White House, he was deeply disturbed by a sense of his inadequacy. Christian, in turn, expressed apprehension of his own ability to discharge his heavy responsibilities. After many repetitions he appealed to the correspondents, described as "the finest, jolliest and greatest fellows in the world," to stand by him and the President in covering up rather than exposing their shortcomings. Then he took his seat, to the obvious relief of all present.

Despite the bright promise opened up to me in my newspaper career, I had become increasingly restive by the spring of 1921. Probert, bent on retaining me in Washington by reason of the valuable contacts I had formed, was quite unreceptive to any suggestions that he support my plea for a foreign assignment.

When an opportunity arose for me to accept an offer to go to France to write a series of articles for the Belleau Wood Memorial Association, I requested a brief leave of absence for that purpose. Once abroad, I would look for an opening as foreign correspondent. It did not work out quite that way, but the end result was even more interesting.

6
RUSSIA AFTER THE REVOLUTION

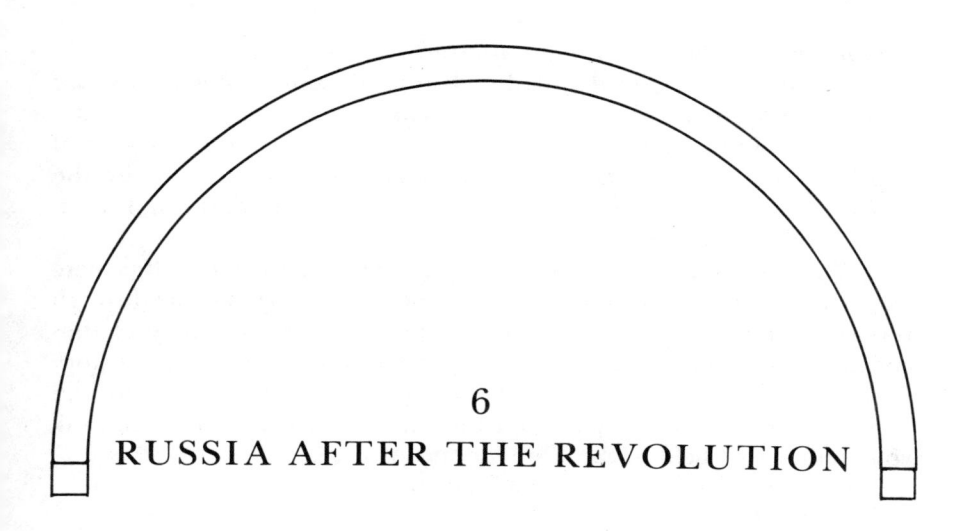

*O*ne afternoon in late July 1921, seated in a café in Château-Thierry, I was reading the Paris edition of the Chicago *Tribune* when my eye caught the announcement of an appeal made to the United States by Maxim Gorky to assist the Soviet Union during a famine afflicting that country. The appeal had been taken under advisement and was being studied by Herbert Hoover, Secretary of Commerce in the Harding administration, who had headed the American Relief Administration, which had undertaken relief work in Eastern Europe after the war. As I had been occupied with this in Yugoslavia in 1919, I telegraphed ARA's European headquarters in London offering my services. In reply, I was assured that in the event an agreement was concluded I might expect to receive my orders. These came through when I was visiting George Wythe, American commercial attaché in Vienna, a former colleague at the AP. The entire course of my life was changed by the directive I received to report to Riga, where I arrived on August 27.

There I learned of the presence of two men whose lives I had quite unconsciously affected as an AP correspondent: Emmett Kilpatrick, my former roommate in Paris, and Colonel Ryan of the Red Cross. It was only when I came face to face with Emmett that I learned how, all unknowingly, I had affected his fate.

Emmett Kilpatrick had just been released from prison under the terms of the Riga Agreement negotiated by George Lyman Brown and

Maxim Litvinov, Soviet Foreign Minister. He had spent months of solitary confinement in the dreaded Lubianka Prison in Moscow. As we talked, his eyes roved restlessly about him like those of a hunted animal.

After joining the Estonian Army, he had taken part in several engagements. When peace was concluded, he was assigned by the American Red Cross to Wrangel's White Army in southern Russia. There he had been cut off and taken prisoner.

"But, Emmett," I exclaimed, "I was an AP reporter at the State Department when a telegram from the embassy in Turkey came through reporting that you had last been seen being led off in your underclothes and that your home in the United States was unknown. I wrote a story about you saying that you were from Uniontown, Alabama, and had joined the Estonian Army to gain the rank of captain, the same rank your father had held in the Confederate Army."

Emmett's face clouded. "That's how it happened."

"How *what* happened?"

"That I was arrested and thrown into prison. You see, when I was first captured, I was under no restraint, I could go where I pleased. I asked and was allowed to see General Budenny, the famous cavalry leader. I asked what book had influenced his career the most. He only laughed and answered that he had never read a book. A little later, I was summoned before the authorities and asked why I had not stated, in the questionnaire given me to complete, my service in the Estonian Army. It was then that I was locked up."

"Goodness, Emmett, it never occurred to me that the Russians would ever see the story or that it could do you any harm."

A day or two later, I met Colonel Ryan. I mentioned that I had been responsible for according him publicity which made him, for a few days, one of the most prominent persons in the news.

"So it was you," he frowned. "It was no service to me or to the Red Cross. Your story compromised both the Red Cross and me with the Soviet Government. I had been sent here with the idea of heading a Red Cross mission to Russia, but your story cut the ground from under my feet. The irony of it is that you, the villain, are going in and I am left out."

Ryan was a colorful figure who did relief work in many countries. He died only a few years later in Persia, to which he had been drawn by his restless spirit.

Our humanitarian gesture in feeding as many as ten million Russians suffering from famine in a country with which we had no diplomatic relations but had militarily invaded seeking the overthrow of its government, is one of the most curious episodes of our history. We expended some sixty million dollars in the relief operation and saved millions of lives. It is almost completely unknown to the American public but not forgotten by the Russians we helped. On my arrival in Kiev, in 1975, when I explained to a young Russian official at the airport that I had spent almost two years with the Hoover Mission in Kazan from 1921 to 1923, his eyes lit up as he pronounced almost reverently the acronym "ARA," as the American Relief Administration was called by Americans and Russians alike. It was heartwarming to perceive that our memory was still alive, at least among some.

I arrived in Moscow in the last days of August 1921, from Riga, the capital of Latvia. As I crossed the Russian border, my mind went back to the press conferences of the Secretary of State which I had attended in Washington from 1919 to 1921. At that time the United States was obtaining most of its information about Russia from White Russian sources, which were feeding fairy stories to United States Government representatives to the effect that there were not more than one hundred serviceable locomotives and a few thousand freight cars in all of Russia and that the Soviet Government was doomed to fall within a few weeks or months. So frequent were these false predictions retailed by Secretary of State Colby that finally the profane day editor of the Associated Press began cursing over the telephone to me that the AP was "by God" tired of overthrowing the Soviet Government for the State Department and would refuse to disseminate any more predictions of a like character unless they could be attributed to a responsible source.

The railway station through which I entered the Russian capital was in indescribable confusion, filthy and run-down in appearance, filled mostly with unkempt peasants in rags. Outside there was a striking absence of life, and the depressing atmosphere given the broad avenues by this lack of human activity was accentuated by the decaying appearance of once handsome buildings, either former apartment houses or great stores, most of the latter boarded up.

In the evening the main streets were fairly well illuminated, the smaller streets not at all. At certain corners entire buildings had been shattered by artillery fire and were disintegrating. A darkened, deserted building represented what had once been the gayest café in Moscow; bare walls, a once great department store. In short, Moscow resembled, after seven years of war, revolution, civil war and foreign intervention, a city of the dead.

One indomitable man had appeared in Russia who had not lost heart; who believed, as he held counsel with destiny, that the disintegration caused by three years of war, four years of revolution and civil war, three years of blockade by foreign powers and armed intervention might still be surmounted by resolute endeavor.

He had kept faith with himself through fifty-one long years. During his exile at the turn of the century in central Siberia, he had warmed the hearts of his dispirited fellow exiles with his confident assurance that science was on the side of the workers and that there was no obstacle that could bar the progress of the all-conquering forces of human reason. Steadfast, with an invincible, inflexible will, viewing the war of 1914 as the "funeral procession of imperialism," rejecting the notion that an "imperialist war would end in a democratic peace," there came at last the moment for which he had waited and worked while spending a lifetime of poverty in shabby rooms, and often under strict surveillance. Finally, on a day in March 1917, he returned once more to Russia during the revolutionary upheaval convulsing that country, was welcomed in the Petrograd railway station in the Czar's own waiting room, was lodged in the former home of the Czar's mistress and, a few months later, took over supreme power and became master of one sixth of the surface of the earth in one of the most unparalleled political upsets in the history of the world.

Five years later, in 1922, he made one of his most important declarations, a frank avowal of the mistakes his government had made:

> Our last and most serious and most difficult task, to which we have paid until now least attention, is the building up of our economy. We have been making most of our mistakes in this particular work, which is the most important and the most difficult one. But can it be otherwise when our task itself is entirely a new one?
>
> The difficulties are immeasurable. But we are accustomed to struggle with immeasurable difficulties.
>
> We had reckoned—or perhaps it is more correct to say—we proposed with insufficient calculation to organize the production of the State and the State distribution of products according to communistic rules in a land of peasantry. We had thought to do it by the force of enthusiasm and we have failed. Life showed us our mistakes.
>
> But notwithstanding all difficulties of our strife, all sufferings of the transition period with its misfortunes, hunger and ruin, we shall not be desperate and we shall bring our deed to a victorious end.

It was the next year in Kazan that I read this in the Russian press. I can never forget the impression made on me; it was in such contrast with the ordinary declarations of those in authority. It was the first instance which had come to my knowledge of a head of government frankly confessing a mistake. It was this that convinced me that Lenin was a very great man, whatever the opinion formed of him by others.

In October 1975, I stood by the marble mausoleum enclosing the tomb of Lenin, which lies immediately outside the walls of the Kremlin.

It bears the single inscription "LENIN." Every day since it was erected, thousands of his countrymen file silently past it to pay tribute to him in an endless stream, along with many foreign visitors, not all communists. For a brief time, Stalin was given similar honorable sepulture, but all trace of this has been removed. So it is that, in all of Russia, the only memorials to Stalin are an inconspicuous statue in a museum in Tiflis, the capital of Georgia, and one somewhat more important at Gori, his birthplace in Georgia.

It is noteworthy that Stalin bears major responsibility for the reversal of Lenin's New Economic Policy—or NEP, as it was called. Catastrophic consequences followed. No less catastrophic were the savage measures of repression introduced by Stalin, which were only modified with his death.

Shortly after my return to the United States from Soviet Russia in 1923, I wrote an article on Lenin which was accepted by *Current History* magazine. But, in an endeavor to take the measure of the man, the article ran counter to the prevailing judgment of him in the United States and it was never published.

Whether we like it or not, Lenin is one of the supreme figures of modern history, and any opinions to the contrary at this late date are not likely to exercise any influence on the world's estimate of the man and of his place in history. Here is one passage from my *Current History* article:

> Five years as head of the Russian Republic have gained for Lenin a hold upon the affections of the Russian people such as no other Communist enjoys or is ever likely to possess. For the great mass of Russians have to look upon him as the Great Reconciler. When he is dead Russia, no less than the Communist Party, will mourn him and with as much if not more reason.

Had Lenin lived and had we shown more flexibility, the history of the world might well have taken a different course.

President Wilson was singularly ill-served by the representative on whom he relied, David R. Francis, the then American ambassador to Russia, whose knowledge of foreign affairs was on a par with that of the political hacks often appointed as American chiefs of mission abroad on the sole basis of financial or other services to their party. The Russian Revolution was outside any terms of reference available to Francis, a former governor of Missouri. The most apt characterization of him is that by the British journalist, Phillip Knightley. In a masterly survey, Francis is described as a "barroom politician who knew little of Russia and to whom Bolshevism was a 'foul monster.' " Francis equated one of the most fateful events of the modern world to a Central American revolution which would splutter and die. Viewing it thus, he abandoned the then capital, Leningrad, for Vologda for what he considered greater security, refusing all overtures from Lenin for the continuance of relations on even an informal basis. Nor was this his only error of judgment. He thought that if we moved troops into Russia and if American constitutional government were introduced by American bayonets and free elections proffered a people unacquainted with them, all would be for the best in this best of all possible worlds. In our ineradicable naïveté we committed the same mistake in Vietnam with disastrous results. Shall we never grow up and read aright the handwriting on the wall?

An obscure American foreign service officer, Felix Cole, serving in Archangel, was sufficiently perceptive to inform Washington on June 1, 1918, that the Russian politicians advocating intervention were discredited officeholders seeking to regain power and were more responsible even than the Communists for the collapse of Russian resistance on the battlefront. The men who ruled Russia, however badly, he presciently informed Washington, were the Bolshevik leaders. If Joseph McCarthy or Patrick Hurley or John Foster Dulles had been around, Cole would have been walking the streets in search of another job.

According to Knightley, some three hundred thousand Allied soldiers "marched into Russia to fight the Germans and stayed to fight the Red Army." These included French, British, Americans, Italians, Canadians, Australians and Japanese. There were also Poles, Greeks, Finns, Czechs, Slovaks, Estonians and Latvians. Following the Russian Revolution in March 1917, the Bolsheviks withdrew from the war but, even after the armistice with Germany in November 1918, fighting by Allied troops against the Red Army continued until there were mutinies of American, British, Canadian and French forces. As Knightley reports "some raised red flags, sang revolutionary songs, and refused to obey orders." There were few if any reports of all this in the press, and a "student today can find little reference to it in his country's history books."

Our intervention not only strengthened the Russian Communist government but sowed in Russian minds a suspicion and distrust of us which have never been eradicated. The democratic institutions we have found suitable for our own needs are a development of centuries. That they suit us is no assurance that they will have some magic property for Russia, China, Vietnam or Africa. The paradox is that we have been paranoically obsessed by a morbid fear of the so-called "menace of Russian Communism" when we should have been far more concerned with our own irrationality, which conducted us in Vietnam to the greatest military debacle in our history and is now leading us to the brink of economic disaster. It is time we ceased to be bemused by fears which have no substance and concern ourselves with life's realities.

One of my first acts on reaching Moscow was to seek out Soviet propaganda material and, in particular, documents reproducing the texts of diplomatic notes and significant declarations of policy. It was a disheartening task, for the Russians did not seem overly eager to disseminate their propaganda; in any case, it was some days before I found a shop where such material was available. Most of what I acquired has long since been lost in the course of my frequent displacements, but one or two publications have been preserved. One is a note drafted by Lenin, Radek, and Chicherin to the foreign powers shortly after the surrender of the Central Powers at the end of 1918. The note began by reviewing the Fourteen Points of Wilson and his expression of sympathy for the Soviet Republic; but, it was observed, the United States had, notwithstanding, supported the advance of Czechoslovakian troops into Russian territory.

> This was the first thing that the Working-man peasants experienced in practice from your Government and that of your Allies. And after that they experienced another thing—the invasion of the north of Russia by the troops of your Allies in which American troops participated, the occupation of Russian territory without any cause and without any declaration of war . . .

> You have promised, Mr. President, to help Russia secure full and unhindered opportunity for the adoption of her independent decision with regard to her own political development and her national policy. But in reality this assistance expressed itself in the fact that the Czechoslovak troops and soon afterward your own troops and those of your Allies attempted at Archangel, at Murmansk, in the Far East, to force upon the Russian people the government of oppressors . . .

> The acid test of the relations between the United States and Russia has not given exactly the kind of results that one would have expected after your message to Congress, Mr. President.

At the time of the dispatch of the note, Wilson had made the armistice with Germany conditional upon her withdrawal from occupied territories. As to this, the note observed:

> We are ready, Mr. President, to conclude an armistice on these conditions, and we request you to inform us as to the time when you, Mr. President, and your Allies intend to remove your troops from Murmansk, from Archangel and from Siberia . . .

> You demand the independence of Poland, Serbia, Belgium, and freedom for the peoples of Austria-Hungary . . . But strangely we do not notice in your demands any mention of freedom for Ireland, Egypt, India, or even the Philippine Islands . . .

We shall see how much longer the predatory motives of world capitalism may be disguised from the workers of the world by high-sounding words and tinkling phrases. The press of capitalist America and Great Britain and France has contrived to suppress the publication of our message . . . Time is on our side, for the audit of the imperialistic slaughter is about to take place.

The accounting, the inexorable audit of mankind, begins with the Armistice which is now concluded by the Allies with the Central Powers. We shall see how the fourteen points of Wilson will be redeemed and how much good faith attaches to the professions of capitalist statesmen.

What first impressed me in the Soviet Union was the runaway inflation, a reflection of prevailing political and economic instability. The rate of exchange of the dollar on my arrival was one million rubles; a few days later it was five million. No note of a higher denomination than five hundred rubles existed. In consequence, money circulated in packets, the contents of which no one verified; one's pockets had to be stuffed to make the most ordinary purchase.

In all of Moscow but one or two private restaurants were to be found—these for the convenience of foreigners. The population was fed in public kitchens or issued rations for home consumption. Walter Duranty, correspondent of the New York *Times,* introduced me to one of the two public restaurants. Its clientele was as heterogeneous as the table appointments; the food was excellent and the price quite moderate, not exceeding the equivalent of a dollar or so for lunch. One rubbed elbows with elegantly dressed actresses and black-marketeers in the shabbiest of clothing. This was the most fascinating aspect of life as it was then presented. If we had not been strictly enjoined by the senior staff of the Relief Administration not to take advantage of the incredibly cheap prices found in the public markets for jewelry, furs and precious objects being offered for sale by members of the formerly wealthy class to sustain themselves, fortunes could have been made. Such things as sable capes went for a pittance hardly sufficient to meet the price of a dinner. It was a topsy-turvy world.

After a few days I received my assignment as assistant supervisor of the Kazan District on the Volga. It embraced the Autonomous Tartar Republic, the Chuvash and Mahri Oblasts peopled by Russians, Tartars and Bulgars of Moslem and Christian faiths. Heading the operation was Ivar Wahren, a naturalized American of an excellent Finnish family, with an adventurous background. He had run away from home to America where he had enlisted in the Army to learn English and had risen to the rank of captain. He went ahead of us to Kazan to establish quarters. We found him some days later ensconced in a luxurious home assigned us by the local authorities, who had relegated the former owner to the basement.

I was delegated to accompany the first food train to Kazan. It comprised a private railway car the government had assigned for our use and a sleeping car for a dozen American journalists, including Floyd Gibbons, in the heyday of his brilliant career with the Chicago *Tribune,* and Walter Duranty, on the threshold of his fame.

Also with us was Colonel Arthur Lynch, representative of the many quixotic persons who were drawn to Russia. In the South African War, he had become a naturalized Boer and had commanded the Irish Brigade against the British in that conflict. Upon its conclusion, he was sentenced to death for high treason, commuted to penal servitude for life, then pardoned; he served with the British Army in the First World War and later entered Parliament as a Labor member. On our journey he would leap from the train at every stop to shout, "Long live the Soviets." He had gone through life espousing unpopular causes to dramatize himself.

Not long after our arrival, Sir Philip Gibbs, war correspondent and author, visited us in Kazan seeking evidence of the famine. We sent him with an interpreter by ship to the nearby Canton of Spassk. Upon his return, he was so deeply shaken that he asked to be excused from discussing what he had encountered until the next day when he had recovered his composure. Here is what he told us then:

> When we left the ship for the interior we stopped at the first village but could observe no sign of human activity. On entering a hut we found an entire family huddled on the floor. They had had nothing to eat for days except a mixture of grass and coarse grain. It was the same in all the other huts. Overcome with pity, I offered all the money I had on me, some millions of rubles, to the village headman. "Comrade, thank you but this cannot help us. There is no food in the village and no one with sufficient strength to send to the Volga where it might be purchased." It was brought home to me that money is of value only when it has been converted into a commodity. I might have given these peasants a million pounds sterling but it would have been of no more use than stones.

Gibbs later wrote a novel *The Middle of the Road,* based on his experiences in Russia.

It was at first contemplated that our aid would be limited exclusively to children, but this was soon found impractical and, in the end, relief was extended to all those in need. Within six or eight months, we were feeding one million people daily in the Kazan District and ten million in the whole of the famine-stricken regions. As our organization never included more than a dozen Americans in Kazan, we had to rely chiefly on volunteer Russian workers. Two Americans were quickly added to our staff—Van Arsdale Turner, who shared the inspection and supervision of the food kitchens throughout the district with me, and John Boyd, in charge of transportation. This involved the unloading of a daily train of foodstuffs routed to us from Moscow and the distribution of it in spring, summer and early fall by steamer on the Volga and Kama rivers and by horse-drawn transport to the provinces. In the winter, transport had necessarily to be by sleigh at temperatures sometimes as low as forty degrees below zero. Internal transport at that time was practically nonexistent. It speaks highly for Soviet cooperation and Boyd's able direction that transportation problems were minimal.

Some thousands of kitchens for the preparation and serving of one meal a day were organized by local committees. In the larger cities and towns every effort was made for these to be inaugurated by the American staff. By the employment of printed instructions in Russian, organization of kitchens in the provinces were left to wholly Russian committees. It was extraordinary how efficient our organization proved to be, supervised as it was by so limited a number of Americans. It spoke highly for our Russian personnel that, despite the great scarcity of local foodstuffs in the midst of a widespread famine, there never came to our attention, at least in the Kazan District, any instances of theft of the foodstuffs sent us from the United States or any abuses by the committees in the food distribution—and this when people were dying of hunger. During my stay in Kazan, I was constantly on the road, at which times I had to transport sufficient supplies of foodstuffs for my own consumption and that of those accompanying me. Not once was I ever solicited to share my food with others, nor was there any loss through theft of what I was transporting for our individual needs. The explanation of this exemplary situation is to be found in the extremely satisfactory state of our relations with the central authorities of the Tartar Republic.

We had been established in Kazan only a very few days when our first and only crisis arose. One morning our office manager and another member of the local staff were arrested, with no notification or explanation to the district supervisor as required by the Riga Agreement. It was obviously an initial test by the local Soviet authorities and one which, in the opinion of both Wahren and myself, had to be met firmly.

We agreed that a letter should be addressed by Wahren at once to Muktarov, president of the Tartar Republic, to be delivered personally by us to the authorities. Unless satisfactory explanation was furnished, justifying the arrest of our two employees, distribution of foodstuffs would be terminated within twenty-four hours. That same day, we were informed we would be received by the government.

It was a strained and gloomy evening when we met by the light of oil lamps. We left discouraged, after some hours of discussion, with no agreement, but, to our relief, our two arrested employees appeared at the office the next morning, having been given their freedom. When they requested to be relieved of their duties, we were obliged to acquiesce. It was the end of any further interference with our personnel. From that time on, our relations could not have been more satisfactory. A year later, Colonel Haskell wrote me, after I had been promoted to Wahren's place, and inquired to what I attributed the exceptional degree of confidence we enjoyed with the authorities in Kazan. I recounted how we had dealt with our first and only crisis and how, since that time, we had operated on the assumption that we could trust the local government, and they had reciprocated. Trust, I said, breeds trust, while distrust can only breed distrust. It was as simple as that.

Notwithstanding the famine, the routine of life continued in ways which never ceased to astonish us. In Kazan, then a city of some 150,000 inhabitants, there was opera every evening as well as a legitimate theater, to both of which we were given complimentary passes. We went often, particularly when we were not traveling. The first performance I attended was *Carmen*, with a remarkable Persian singer, Muktarava, in the title role. To a Russian accompanying me I expressed surprise that, in the midst of a famine, the theater would be filled. "You may be sure," was his answer, "that aside from you there is not a person present who has had a full meal today." Later we invited the principal singers to an evening supper after the performance; the way in which they went after the food convinced me.

Ten years later, when I met the Persian minister to Egypt, Jevad Khan Sineky, in Cairo and told him about hearing his compatriot Muktarava sing in Kazan, he disclosed that he had been the means of giving her her start. While Persian consul general in Baku during the war he had heard her singing in the streets and had been so impressed that he had seen that she obtained the singing lessons which made her subsequent career possible. He had lost touch with her and was delighted to have the news I gave him.

Because of my limited knowledge of Russian, I went only once to the legitimate theater in Kazan, to see an American play, *Potash and Perlmutter*. When the curtain rose on the first act, a voice near me, tinged with amusement, said, "My furniture!"

"Was it stolen?"

She smiled. "I suppose it was in a way. When the Revolution took place, my country home was requisitioned. You see some of its contents there on the stage. Why should I complain? I have a well-furnished flat here in Kazan. *Nitchevo,* it doesn't matter.

Nitchevo. No word so perfectly reflects the philosophic resignation of the Slav confronted by adversity, however severe. The Russian has been uttering it during centuries of suffering, faced by one of the severest climates in the world, under the tyranny of the czars and the oppression of such Soviet leaders as Stalin.

Nothing is more characteristic of the Russian than his attachment to cultural values even under the most difficult circumstances. I found an illustration of this in Kazan in 1921 a few weeks after my arrival, when the famine was at its height. I was quite incredulous when informed there was an interesting art exhibit in the city. Despite the bitter cold in October, I ventured out with a member of the local staff in a secondhand fur coat I had purchased from a peddler. For reasons of economy the building was unheated, and my teeth were chattering as I made the rounds of the paintings displayed. One of the local artists excited my particular interest. I was informed that he was one of Russia's most talented painters, Nicolai Fechin, and that I must be well instructed in art to have singled out his work. It was quite otherwise, I insisted; I was a complete tyro when it came to art.

My visit to the exhibit was not without interesting consequences. Having ascertained that Fechin, then forty, was interested in commissions, I sent word to him. Having a hard time to feed himself and wife and daughter, he was happy to paint my portrait in exchange for food packages. Upon my marriage to Georgina de Brylkine in Leningrad the following year, I had Fechin paint her portrait; both paintings now hang in the library of Randolph-Macon College in Ashland, Virginia.

Fechin was hesitant as to whether he should emigrate to the United States where a former patron, W. S. Stimmel, of Pittsburgh, had offered to pay his traveling expenses and guarantee him work for three years. In the end, he decided to emigrate and had no difficulty obtaining exit visas for his wife and family. I was able to obtain American visas for them. Fechin died in 1956 in Santa Monica, California.

Shortly after my arrival in Kazan, William Simson, born in Estonia, of about my age, speaking impeccable English, presented himself, having been sent by the local authorities in answer to my request for an interpreter. I took an immediate liking to him and gave him a desk in my office. He was to accompany me on every inspection trip I made. I helped to save his life on one occasion and a strong attachment was established between us. If he were a planted agent of the Soviet Government, of which there could be little doubt, we could not have been better served, as we might be satisfied that he would be honest in his reports. His presence was an important factor in ensuring the highly satisfactory relations we enjoyed with the Tartar Republic authorities.

J. Rives Childs, a portrait by Nicolai Fechin, painted in 1921, now hanging in the library at Randolph-Macon College, Ashland, Virginia.

Of Estonian origin, he had been sent to school in London by an Englishman residing in Estonia who had taken him under his wing. Unfortunately, he was not attracted to study but preferred to take employment as a valet at the Savoy Hotel. On the outbreak of the Revolution, fired with partisan fervor for the cause of the underdogs, he made his way by ship to Petrograd in pursuit of his star. When the Bolsheviks seized power, he joined the Red Army and rose rapidly in rank. In one of the periodic purges, he was arrested and summoned for interrogation with another officer, a stranger. The examiners were satisfied with his explanations and he was instructed to return to his command. What follows is in Simson's own words:

> What I have to tell you is so strange that you may find it difficult to believe, and that will not surprise me in the least. I tell it as it happened.
>
> I was suddenly seized by some unaccountable impulse which was dictating my actions quite independent of myself and to which I felt an imperative need to yield. An inner voice was dictating my speech when I spoke, hardly conscious of what I was saying. "I came here with that officer", pointing to my companion, "and I shall not leave without him."
>
> One of the interrogators asked if we were friends.
>
> "I have never laid eyes on him before we met here," I answered as everyone regarded me incredulously. A long silence ensued when I spoke again. "It is hard to explain, but I shall try. You may find it incomprehensible. I somehow feel that destiny has linked my fate with his."
>
> The judges shook their heads in bewilderment. The other officer disclaimed in turn ever having seen me before. They put a few perfunctory questions to him and, in the end, told us we were free.
>
> Some months later, I was rearrested. This time the charge was much more damaging and was one of those things which, when put under a powerful light, was far more difficult to justify, as it defied exculpatory analysis. I was lying in my cell, given over to despair and convinced that no way was open for escape, when the door was suddenly flung open. "This is it," I said to myself. A lamp was flashed in my face and I heard someone remark softly, "It can't be." I waited and then looked up. Bending over me was the officer with whom I had linked my fate. After a little while, he told me to get dressed and follow him. "I can't free you unconditionally," he informed me, "but I can see that you are exiled to Kazan." I became a translator at the radio station until appointed your interpreter.

It smacks more of a fairy story than the truth, but it was not for me to doubt it. I had experienced too many instances of being guided by an invisible hand.

In my initial inspection journeys into the interior, in addition to Simson serving as interpreter, I was accompanied by Skvartsov, secretary of the Communist Party of the Tartar Republic, until the government gained confidence in us. He was the keenly intelligent son of a priest, about my age, of inexhaustible energy. He exemplified many Leninist Bolsheviks of those days, dedicated with complete disinterestedness to the ideals of the Revolution and could not have more ably seconded me in my organization work outside Kazan. On our first journey we headed for Menzelinsk on the Kama River, a tributary of the Volga, where we convoked a meeting aboard our steamer—furnished us by the government—to form a committee for the local canton. After election of a local teacher, a member of the cooperatives and a local official, a fanatical Communist arose and denounced the choices on the grounds they were not all Communists. It was eminently fitting that the Communist disturber should have been taken firmly to task by Skvartsov. With the authority of his office, he emphasized that the ARA was a humanitarian and not a political entity, that the meeting had been properly guided in its selections by independent and not party considerations. A year later, he was transferred to Minsk and later, still in his prime, succumbed to typhus.

Early in October, we were traveling by sleigh when a violent snowstorm came up suddenly when we were endeavoring to reach our destination that evening. No landmarks were visible in the great drifts sweeping about us. Alighting from our two sleighs, we stopped to take mutual counsel. After two hours of travel from our last stop, retracing our steps would have been difficult. To remain where we were risked being frozen; to push on might result in losing our way irretrievably. I put it to Skvartsov as to what we should do. He placed his arms akimbo and looked me up and down incredulously. "You ask *me* what to do, you who have come to Russia to aid us, risking your life to do so! My dear friend, it is for *you* to make the decision, not for me; I am in your hands."

Ignoring the peril of our situation, I could not suppress a smile at the vehemence of his declaration, and admiration for his courage and unselfish disinterestedness. I proposed to go on and trust to luck. Far better to advance than retreat.

There was general agreement. After struggling with our horses for about half an hour through the ever-mounting drifts we espied, to our great relief, dim lights in the distance. It proved to be the village where we had planned to stay overnight. We sought out the most prominent dwelling and knocked. There was no sign of any occupant but, after continued knocking, an upper window was raised and a head emerged.

"Go elsewhere, you can't come in here. We have ARA stores, and no one is admitted except those connected with the distribution."

Despite our fatigue and half-frozen state, we broke into laughter, a relief from our tension. Skvartsov stepped into the breach. "We have an American representative of the ARA with us here. Let us in, we are freezing."

We were welcomed to our home for the night with profuse apologies followed by general laughter. I found it sobering that we had reached our destination as if mysteriously guided. There would be even more striking instances shortly.

I returned to Kazan convinced that the famine was even more widespread and grave than had been suspected. The presentation of these views to headquarters in Moscow prompted a request for precise details. An intensive survey was needed. I volunteered to set out on one embracing all the cantonal capitals.

Moscow proposed to send two American newspapermen, Huddleston and Varges, to accompany me early in November. We set out in three sleighs: Simson and I in one (Skvartsov could not spare the two weeks necessary), the newspapermen in a second, and our rations in a third. I equipped myself with fur-lined stockings, felt boots, a fur-lined hat, a fur coat, and still another large loose fur coat over the first. Even with such protection it was only possible to bear the intense cold of an open sleigh for an hour or two before taking refuge in a peasant home for warmth.

One would never have suspected from the outward appearance of the villages the tragedies concealed within. The first settlement at which we halted reflected the conditions to be found in all. We stopped at one hut to warm ourselves and share the samovar's hot water for the preparation of a cup of tea. The premises were quickly filled with peasants curious to meet us. As they entered they bowed toward the icon in a corner of the room, making the sign of the cross. A spokesman revealed in his hand some *lebeda,* a mixture of grass and coarse grain. "We older people may contrive to live a few months on this, but our children will die if they are not given more nourishing food. Some are now being fed in the American kitchen. Cannot all be accepted?"

The most lasting impression the Russians whom I encountered on our survey made on me was their simple dignity and heroism. In describing their wants, they spoke not as Russians or Communists but rather as members of the great family of humanity. We traveled some thousands of miles among a starving population, but not once were we molested or solicited to share the food we had with us, nor was any of it stolen. In other countries, under similar circumstances, we would have risked death.

By the time we were approaching the end of our survey, the two newspapermen had left for Moscow convinced of the magnitude of the famine. Simson was showing signs of exhaustion. Fortunately, we were in a town with a doctor. The latter confided to me that he suspected Simson had contracted spotted typhus and, if he were to be saved, I should rush him to a hospital in Kazan. The nearest railhead was twenty-four hours by sleigh. I telegraphed Kazan requesting our private railway car be sent there. We left that morning at four, stopping only at post stations to change horses. By evening I was in such a state of fatigue that I would throw myself on a bench in a post station and fall asleep instantly. The last lap was made in a rough cart driven by a girl. I was fast asleep on the straw in the cart when, on entering the suburbs of the town at the railhead in the predawn of the second day, a piercing locomotive whistle caused our horses to break into a gallop and overturn the cart, throwing my head into collision with a brick wall. Fortunately, the fur cap I wore cushioned the effect of the blow.

While we waited for our train in quarters we found, Simson was in such delirium I wondered whether he would reach Kazan alive. A single precious bottle of cognac remained to us. I unstoppered it and we quickly consumed it with no effect whatever, so great was our exhaustion after seventeen days of uninterrupted travel during which we had slept but two nights in bed, preferring, as a protection against insects, the floor of the peasants' huts where we were lodged.

My report on the conditions we had found persuaded Wahren that I should proceed to Moscow to support my account in person. In December 1921, Moscow presented an improved appearance from that of three months previous. Store fronts had been unboarded; hoarded stocks had emerged from their hiding places. The faces of people in the streets had taken on new animation; it was as if a magic wand had been waved over the city.

It was Lenin who supplied the spark. His premature death was a tragedy both for Russia and the world. Born in a family of the lesser nobility at Simbirsk, a graduate of the University of Kazan, he was steeped in both Russian and Western culture. There was no trace of vanity in him or self-glorification. A woman who sought his photograph was asked by him, "Why do you desire my picture? I am no different from other men."

I recall two instances of his compassion. One was his plea for clemency for Rose Kaplan, who had attempted to assassinate him in 1918. Another was given me by one of our staff in Kazan, Zena Galitsch, who had served as one of Lenin's secretaries. When Béla Kun, military governor of the Crimea after Wrangel's defeat, ordered the execution of ten thousand White officers and sympathizers, Lenin summoned him to Moscow. "We had civil peace within our grasp," Lenin told him, "and you, who are not even a Russian, have thrown it away. How can we promote reconciliation with the blood of these victims on our hands?"

With my task completed in Moscow, I left in our private car for Kazan. En route I was assailed by alternate chills and fever, diagnosed as typhus when I reached Kazan. I was put at once to bed. For five days I was delirious. I dreamed, during that time, that Secretary Hoover had cited my report to President Harding to support a request of Congress for additional relief. Six months later his secretary, Christian Herter, later U.S. Secretary of State, visited Kazan and confided that portions of my report had been read by Hoover at a cabinet meeting and that it had helped to obtain additional funds for Russian relief from Congress. The Associated Press telegraphed news of my critical illness home, which provoked headlines in the Lynchburg press.

To occupy myself during my slow convalescence, I began to form a collection of books on Russian numismatics and one on Russian coins. To my chagrin the first coins I purchased proved to be counterfeits, a useful lesson. In the end the coins—genuine—numbered some twenty-six hundred only matched by a collection in the Hermitage Museum in Leningrad; my books on Russian numismatics, comprising sixty-odd, were later presented to the Hoover War Library.

On the recommendation of the physicians attending me, I went to Berlin to complete my convalescence at the Hotel Adlon. I was so weak that I rarely ventured into the streets. At the end of two weeks, by reason of the runaway German inflation, my bill for room and meals totaled fifteen dollars.

The most direct route for my return to Kazan was that which I had taken to arrive, via Riga. In view of subsequent events, I chose, under urging of my psyche—the one logical explanation—to return by a most circuitous route through Copenhagen, capital of Denmark; Stockholm, capital of Sweden; Helsinki, capital of Finland; Leningrad, then capital of Soviet Russia; and thence by rail to Moscow and Kazan.

As I was still convalescing, I broke my journey for two or three days in each of these cities. In Leningrad, where we had one of our most important ARA offices, I naturally called on Herschel Walker, the director, to meet him and the other personnel. While seated in one of the larger rooms, I was attracted by the sight of a strikingly beautiful young Russian woman in one of the open cubicles. I asked to be introduced. She was Georgina de Brylkine and spoke flawless English, gained from attendance at "The Cliff" in Eastbourne; German, from studies in Dresden; and French, from her mother of French birth, as well as Russian. Her father was Paul Brylkine, an officer in the Imperial Russian Navy, as were his parental forebears before him since Peter the Great.

She had been immobilized with her mother by the Revolution, when a fortune in securities and jewelry on deposit in a bank had been seized. She had resorted to one expedient after another to live—the most recent, employment by the ARA. That evening I accompanied her and her mother to the opera and, before leaving Leningrad, had obtained her agreement to an exchange of correspondence. Within six months, on August 13, we were married in the Greek Orthodox St. Isaac's Cathedral

Georginia de Brylkine Childs, a portrait by Nicolai Fechin, painted in 1922, now hanging in the library at Randolph-Macon College.

in Leningrad, after a civil marriage ceremony some weeks previous witnessed by a Red Army soldier and a sailor.

But I am anticipating my story. I had returned to Kazan alone even after the conclusion of the civil ceremony.

In the early spring of 1922, the greatest problem confronting us was that of transport. For a period of several weeks, while awaiting the breakup of the icebound rivers, thaws and floods interrupted all distribution of food. The spur track connecting the Kazan railway station with normal steamer halts on the Volga River nearest Kazan was suddenly washed away over a section of several thousand yards. Until it was repaired, transportation between the river and the station would be interrupted, with the consequent problem of storing the trainloads of food arriving daily from Moscow.

The Soviet Commissar of Transport for the Tartar Republic informed John Boyd that the spur track could not be repaired in less than a week. When John's pleas for more rapid action came to naught, he had final recourse to Karl Schwarz, head of the Cheka. Schwarz telephoned the Commissar: "I have Comrade Boyd in my office. It is now 10 A.M. If the track is not completed by noon day after tomorrow, you will be placed under arrest for sabotage."

"We don't have the necessary labor force."

"How many do you need?"

"At least two hundred."

"You will have them in two hours. At noon, day after tomorrow, you will be Commissar of Transport or in jail."

Within thirty-six hours the first food train held up in the Kazan station crept over the restored spur to the Volga for steamer loading.

The Cheka, or Ogpu, is generally identified abroad as an instrument of political repression. In the beginning it had the much broader function of stepping into any malfunctioning economic breach susceptible of shock-troop treatment. It is possible that it was through the Cheka that the Revolution survived.

One other example. I was on an inspection trip up the Kama River to Perm. On our return, I stopped at Izhevsk and decided to proceed overland by car to Chistopol without reckoning with the appalling state of the roads. After exhausting our supply of spare tires, we limped into a small village of the Kama, where we were lucky enough to find a telegraph station. I seated myself alongside the telegrapher (having a pass which permitted this) and sent one telegram to the captain of my ship, who was awaiting us at Chistopol, directing him to come for me, and the other to the Cheka there to see to the prompt execution of my order. In less than an hour I had a reply from the Cheka that the steamer had left and would be with me in three hours.

Upon arrival, the captain found the wharf impractical for the embarkation of my car. Happily, he espied sufficient lumber alongside for construction of a temporary platform. When I awakened the next morning in my cabin, we were en route to Kazan. These were the epic days of the Revolution; there was confusion, there were famine and unprecedented misery, but the wheels turned somehow under countless expedients.

However relentless the Cheka and the Communist Party in getting things done, under the many difficulties which presented themselves, there were nevertheless, at least then, some safeguards against the abuse of authority. Once, when traveling with Skvartsov, we were informed at a posting station that no horses were immediately available. As Secretary of the Communist Party, Skvartsov threatened the head of the local Soviet with arrest unless horses were produced within an hour. Later, when we passed through the same village and requested horses, there was a mad rush to fetch them.

I was later called before a judicial authority in Kazan. The head of the village Soviet had brought charges against Skvartsov for alleged abuse of authority. Questions were put to me and taken down in writing. It was clear that, notwithstanding the influential post occupied by Skvartsov, he could be held accountable for his acts, at least in the pre-Stalin era.

After my marriage, my mother-in-law sought my counsel as to how she might transfer abroad some valuable assets she had succeeded in salvaging, including some sixty eighteenth-century gold snuffboxes. In my advice and efforts to assist her, I committed two grave errors: first, not heeding a warning, given me in a dream, of the seizure of the collection by the Russian customs; second, dispatching it, most injudiciously, in a single packet.

I was in Moscow when news was received that the pouches of the ARA courier had been opened for the first time by Soviet border authorities and the collection seized along with contraband sent in the same pouches by two other members of the ARA mission. I had no other alternative than to offer my resignation and make preparation for our departure.

Happily, my mother-in-law still had possessions of value left. Early in 1923, we packed up and proceeded to Leningrad. Paintings by Guardi, Tiepolo and Repin, as well as other objects, were granted export permits by the Fine Arts Department. I had no difficulty obtaining an exit visa for my wife. We decided to proceed to Berlin and there enlist the aid of the German Government in furthering Russian issuance of an exit visa for my mother-in-law. Our departure and journey were without incident except for the destruction of a considerable correspondence she had injudiciously conserved from her guardian, General Tatiesheff, aide to Czar Nicholas, murdered with the imperial family at Ekaterinburg. I have since regretted that I did not offer to read at least the last letters for any information that might contain of the last days of the imperial family and staff. My feeling was that it was much too dangerous to run such a risk.

7
CONSUL IN JERUSALEM

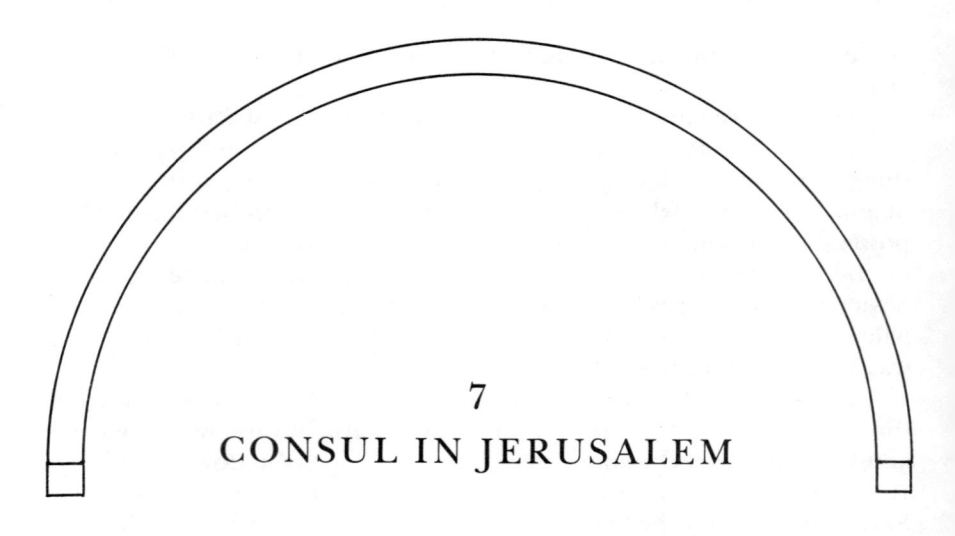

I had an offer from the *Christian Science Monitor* to be their correspondent in Russia, but for my wife it was too bohemian an existence, so that settled it. Instead, at her suggestion, I took the examination for the U.S. Foreign Service and was appointed an officer of Class VIII, or consul, instead of the usual rank of vice consul.

I had no private income. During the greater part of my service, the remuneration was so paltry and the allowances, if any, so penurious that my wife and I had difficulty making both ends meet; to have had children was out of the question. In the absence of allowances for living quarters, the best we could do in Romania was to rent an apartment in a private home to which we had access through the servants' entrance; to take advantage of home leave every two years we could afford to travel only by freighter. The expedients to which we were reduced were so amusing for employees of one of the world's richest nations that we could not resist the challenge presented by our plight.

My first assignment was as consul to Jerusalem. In 1923 there were few more interesting countries than Palestine. Two thousand years had elapsed since Jews had ruled over any part of it.

I spent the best part of my life in the Middle East, for the most part from 1923 to 1953, and, when not present in that area, from 1937 to 1941 I was serving as Palestine desk officer in the State Department. From my long and intimate acquaintance with that particular region and the Near East in general, I believe I am in a position to affirm that there is no problem in that area which is more important to the United States than that of the Arab-Jewish conflict centering about the comparatively newly created State of Israel.

The problem presents a striking dilemma for those who would weigh the scales between the two parties. It is that both have suffered appalling wrongs: the Jews, at the hands of the Nazis, impelling their search for a safe haven; the Arabs, from their dispossession to make way in Palestine for the Jews, to right a wrong for which they had no responsibility. Nor should a fundamental factor be overlooked—that Jerusalem is as much a sacred city for the Arabs as it is for Christians and Jews.

When I was posted to Palestine in 1923, it was governed, after liberation from Turkey, as a mandated territory by a British high commissioner answerable to the League of Nations. When the British were charged with this responsibility in 1922, the Jewish population of the country was only seven percent; the Arab population, close to ninety percent.

Responsibility for the turmoil provoked in Palestine following the termination of the First World War may be found almost *in toto* in the Balfour Declaration of 1917, which had the unforeseen consequence of the creation, in 1948, of the State of Israel.

The Balfour Declaration was a British wartime measure designed to rally world Jewry to the Allies' cause. Britain was fighting with its back to the wall and there was no time for searching scrutiny of legal niceties. The Declaration was a grab bag into which almost anything could be read and, as such, was to have most fateful consequences. It also expressly excluded certain specific contingencies which nevertheless came about in the end.

Let us examine this fateful instrument.

First of all, note that there is no mention in it of a Jewish state. All it contemplated was the establishment in Palestine of a "national home" for the Jewish people.

There was an all-important limiting provision that, in its fulfillment, "nothing shall be done which may prejudice the civil and religious rights of existing non-Jewish communities in Palestine," a strangely elliptical reference to the Arab majority. In short, it was a provision, if any attention was to be paid to it, which rendered completely nugatory the Declaration itself. It was the sort of double-talk which from its very inception characterized the Balfour Declaration and the Jewish National Home in Palestine. Bluntly, it constituted nothing less than a cruel deception.

From the establishment of the British mandate over Palestine in 1922 until its termination in 1948 with the creation of the State of Israel, British policy oscillated between one or the other of the two incompatible provisions of the Balfour Declaration, depending on the shifting international situation and the degree of pressure brought to bear on the British by the United States under American Zionist pressure.

Note that the primary objective of the Balfour Declaration was the promotion of Jewish immigration into Palestine. Yet this was not realizable without prejudice to the rights of the preponderant Arab population.

Not all Jews are Zionists. Rabbi Judah Magnes, a distinguished American Jew, head of the Hebrew University in Jerusalem until his death in 1948, urged a binational state for Palestine, envisaging an Arab-Jewish partnership. Had his counsel prevailed, there would be peace in the Near East. Even today voices are not wanting in continued support of this solution.

Zionist pressure on the United States Government manifested itself as early as 1917 when obtaining endorsement by President Wilson of a Jewish National Home in Palestine. There were not lacking eminent American Jews who actively opposed Zionism for one reason, amongst others, that it would distract American Jews from a full allegiance to American citizenship and its obligations.

With the end of World War I, a slow but steady trickle of Jewish immigration into Palestine passed almost unperceived. However, stimulation of an active antisemitic movement in Germany under mounting Nazi provocation in the 1920s resulted in an increased flow of Jews into Palestine, with a counterreaction on the part of Arabs, culminating in civil disturbances. These became in time such that the British Government was persuaded, in the interest of maintaining law and order, to introduce checks on Jewish immigration into Palestine.

Reaction of American Zionists was swift and quite unprecedented. The time was 1938, when I was on duty in the State Department, charged, among other duties, with serving as desk officer for Palestine.

Within a few days I was submerged by some 100,000 letters and telegrams from Zionists and Zionist sympathizers appealing for United States intervention with the British Government in opposition to any reduction of Jewish immigration into the Promised Land.

Rarely in American history had there been such a mustering of agitation, directed by a small minority, upon the United States Government to influence public policy.

Note that it involved not the general public but an ethnic minority of minuscule proportions. It was soon to become such a power that, in 1975, it could command no less than seventy United States senators to take collective action on behalf of Israel, obtain what now amounts to an annual grant by the American taxpayer of some two billion dollars to Israel, and lead a chairman of the United States Joint Chiefs of Staff to raise a protesting voice against the intermixture of such a small element in the determination of American foreign policy. It is also true that, alone among foreign nations, the bonds of Israel entitle the American taxpayer to a deduction for interest payments on his federal income tax.

Let others draw appropriate lessons. So unprecedented was the pressure brought to bear in 1938 upon the State Department by American Zionists and their sympathizers in respect of Palestine that Secretary of State Hull was moved to summon a conference on the issue. The group included Undersecretary of State Sumner Wells, Assistant Secretary Adolph Berle, legal adviser Green Hackworth, the chiefs of the Near Eastern and European divisions, and a dozen or more others.

In this distinguished company I was the most junior officer present; accordingly, I took my seat in as inconspicuous a place as I could find. I had never had occasion to exchange a word with Mr. Hull and had no reason to believe he knew me. However, when the discussion was approaching its end, to my surprise, the Secretary suddenly pointed a finger in my direction. "Can you think," he asked, "of any inducement that could be offered the Arab population for Jewish immigrants?"

I had no need to weigh my reply and I answered at once in the negative. He made no effort to challenge it but followed it at once with another question, "Why not?"

I could not ponder my reply but answered after only an instant of reflection, "Because of the attachment of every man for his own hearthstone." I have never since been able to think of a better one but I have often regretted that I did not have the courage to have preceded my reply by inquiring of the Secretary if he could think of any inducement which might be offered the native population of Tennessee to move out of that state to make way for foreign newcomers.

Press reports telegraphed from the United States to the Middle East regarding the political pressure brought to bear upon the White House gave rise to a quite new development in the Arab world, namely violent anti-American manifestations, as reported by the Associated Press from Jerusalem, on November 1, 1938. Until then, the United States had enjoyed in Palestine, Egypt, Arabia, Iraq, Lebanon, Syria, Jordan, and throughout the Moslem world a highly privileged place, enhanced by the presence in Cairo of an American University and a long respected American College in Beirut. We were looked up to as the most disinterested of all foreign powers. For one who had gone out to the Near East as early as 1919, as I had in the heyday of our universal esteem, it was tragic to observe, from the 1930s on, its progressive decline until today only the shattered shreds of it wave tattered in the breeze.

An attempt by the British Government to organize a conference in London to work out a mutual agreement between Arabs and Jews having proved fruitless, it issued a declaration, on May 17, 1939, fixing unilaterally its future policy. Jewish immigration into Palestine would be permitted until the Jewish proportion of the population of that country had risen from the then existing ratio of 28 percent to 33 1/3 percent. The government observed that the framers of the Palestine mandate "could never have intended that Palestine would be converted into a Jewish state against the will of the Arab population of the country." It was a belated admission but, nevertheless, one taking into account practical and equitable realities. The outbreak of the Second World War in 1939 suspended implementation of the new administrative measures contemplated for Palestine.

The next important development affecting Palestine was the historic meeting, on February 24, 1945, between President Roosevelt, returning from Yalta, and the aging king of Saudi Arabia, which took place on an American destroyer in the Suez Canal. His recently created kingdom in the barren wastes of the Arabian peninsula was but slowly adapting itself to the ways of the modern world. With the conclusion of agreements, in the early 1930s, with American oil interests for the exploitation of what was to prove one of the richest sources of petroleum in the world, diplomatic relations had been established between the United States and Saudi Arabia. These were destined to develop into very close ties, the closest of those with any Arab state and only disturbed by the appearance upon the scene, in 1948, of the State of Israel.

In the course of the historic meeting between President Roosevelt and the Saudi king, the former gave his personal assurance to the latter that the United States would not change its Palestine policy without full and prior consultation with both Arabs and Jews. This undertaking was reaffirmed after Roosevelt's death by his successor, President Truman, in a formal communication on April 5, 1945, to King Ibn Saud.

Four months later, in August 1945, with the ink hardly dry on the assurance given, President Truman, as an electioneering ploy and in response to Zionist pressure, requested the British to facilitate the admission into Palestine of 100,000 Jewish immigrants. A few months later, in December 1945, resolutions were passed by the United States Senate and House, under Zionist pressure, for unrestricted Jewish immigration into Palestine, limited only by the economic absorptive capacity of that country.

There are passing references to these and other broken American pledges to the Arabs in one of the most informative and reliable studies of the Arab-Israeli conflict: *The Arabs, Israelis and Kissinger* by Edward Sheehan, written under the auspices of the Center for International Affairs at Harvard University. Its bona fides are therefore impeccable, contrasting in this respect with the crass misinformation on the subject with which the media are largely littered. As Sheehan related:

Within a year President Truman was telling his ministers to the Arab states, "I'm sorry, gentlemen, but I have to answer to hundreds of thousands of people who are anxious for the success of Zionism."

Feisal never forgot what seemed to him a breach of faith . . . Following the Six-Day War of 1967 . . . President Johnson and Nixon assured Feisal they would press Israel to relinquish conquered Arab territory; nothing happened . . . In the Spring of 1972 Washington conveyed hints to Feisal that if he would help to persuade President Sadat to diminish the enormous Russian presence in Egypt, the U.S. would mount more serious pressure upon Israel . . . Sadat expelled the Russians in July of that year. But Nixon ignored this momentous action; Feisal felt humiliated and betrayed.

One of the understandable consequences was the Arab oil boycott of 1973. I was in Nice at the time and had a long-distance call from a former member of my staff who had retired in Rome. The following conversation took place:
"What do you think ot it?"
"The same as you, Paul. We had it coming to us. You can only kick a man in the backside for a certain time until he reacts."
Paul chuckled. "I wonder if we shall draw any conclusions from the lesson?"
"Very unlikely. We have been kept in such ignorance of the realities by our leaders."
"Quite, and also by the press. They have been frightened to disclose the truth on account of their advertisers."
In 1946 I was appointed by President Truman as American minister to Saudi Arabia after twenty-three years in the Foreign Service. On July 1, 1946, I presented my letter of credence in Jiddah to His Royal Highness Prince Feisal in his capacity as Foreign Minister and Viceroy of Hejaz. Dining with him that evening, he emphasized that a fair solution of the Palestine question was a matter of life or death to the Arabs, who viewed Zionist aspirations in Palestine as having the ultimate aim of swallowing up the Arab world. He said that his country and the Arab world were placing great store in the sense of justice of the United States.

In my telegram reporting these events, the first after assuming charge of the American Legation, subsequently raised to the rank of Embassy, I observed somewhat prophetically, as subsequent events would prove: "I am convinced that unless we proceed with utmost circumspection, in considering all phases of possible repercussions of Palestine question, we may raise difficulties for ourselves in this most strategic area of vital national interest which will plague United States in years to come."

In February 1947, Great Britain, as mandatory power, referred the Palestine problem to the United Nations. A United Nations Commission of Inquiry which was set up recommended, on August 31, partition of the country into Arab and Jewish states with economic union. Jerusalem would be international. These recommendations were substantially adopted by the General Assembly on November 29, at a time when Palestine comprised 1,289,000 Arabs and 679,000 Jews and when Zionist landholdings represented only 8 percent of Palestine's total area.

The preponderant Arab population expressed violent opposition and, shortly thereafter, in March 1948, fighting broke out in Palestine. The United States expressed opposition to a forcible implementation of partition and, three days later, called for declaration of a truce and further consideration of the problem by the General Assembly of the United Nations.

The Zionists, insisting that partition was binding, launched military operations to establish their state. To terrorize the Arabs, Jewish terrorists of the Irgun, a factional organization, massacred in cold blood 250 civilian inhabitants of the Arab village Beit Yasin, putting it to fire and sword. The result was that anticipated by the attackers: panic on the part of the Palestine Arabs, who fled in thousands for safety to nearby Arab countries.

Events now succeeded one another in seven-league boots. On May 14, 1948, the British Mandatory Administration ceased to exist with the withdrawal of the British High Commissioner. On the same day, the State of Israel was proclaimed in Jerusalem and at the same time recognized by President Truman.

From that time to this, there has been no peace in the Near East nor any acceptance of Israel by the Arab world.

The first reaction of the Arabs was an unsuccessful attempt on their part to invade Israel. Their repulse resulted in the flight, with them, of thousands of Arabs previously inhabiting Palestine. For thirty years these people have subsisted as homeless refugees housed in tents or given shelter in Lebanon, Syria, Iraq, Jordan and elsewhere.

In the years that followed, American newspapers, responsive to Zionist advertisers, particularly in the eastern United States where large numbers of Jews are concentrated, exercised a virtual boycott of news favorable to the Arabs. A striking example was given me by a reporter of the Lynchburg News when I visited Lynchburg on my return from Saudi Arabia in 1950. In discussing the attitude of the American press to Arab news she recalled the reaction of a Jewish resident of the city who had telephoned the *News* after publication of the photograph of an Arab child refugee to inquire whether this reflected any antisemitic attitude.

Shortly afterward, the United States Air Force invited me to visit a number of air bases where Saudi Arabian nationals were being trained under an accord with the Arabian Government by which, in return, we were granted certain facilities at their airports. My first stop was at Wichita Falls, Texas. When a reporter sought to interview me, the American general commanding the base informed me privately that he would have to telephone Washington for permission, as there had been a strict security regulation against giving out any information about the presence on the bases of Arab trainees. The reason given was to avoid any hue and cry on the part of the Zionists. Happily, a telephone call elicited approval from Washington of the disclosure by me of statements of fact concerned with American interests.

On returning from abroad in the spring of 1973, a number of my Foreign Service colleagues wrote me to express their concern at the undiminished pressure by Zionists on the shaping and control of American foreign policy in the Near East. In response, I drafted a letter on the subject which I addressed to the editor of the Washington Post in light of my long experience. When, after the lapse of some time, I had no acknowledgment and my letter remained unpublished, I addressed it to the Richmond Times-Dispatch, which promptly printed it in its entirety. My letter concluded: "there is not the least doubt in my mind, based on thirty years' experience in the Middle East, that so long as our unconditional support of Israel continues, there will be no peace in that area."

The sequence of events accorded with these expectations. In its issue of July 7, 1973, from Paris the *International Herald Tribune* reported that the traditionally strong Saudi tie with the United States "depends on the United States having a more evenhanded and just policy" in the Middle East. It was added that Saudi Arabia might be compelled to freeze its oil production because of rising Arab resentment of United States support of Israel. Three months later, Saudi Arabia followed the other Arab states in introducing a virtual embargo on the shipment of oil products to the United States.

Numerous examples may be offered of the long arm of Zionist influence in American politics and foreign policy subversive of American interests. New York Times correspondent James Reston reported, on March 24, 1974, in the Richmond Times-Dispatch that, because of Senator Fulbright's consistent opposition to the American Government's heavily weighted pro-Israeli policy, which he deemed, as chairman of the Senate Foreign Relations Committee, contrary to American interests, Zionist forces were being marshaled to defeat his reelection in Arkansas after twenty-odd years of outstanding service.

Another instance: *The Congressional Quarterly* has revealed lecture earnings of pro-Israeli senators subsidized to promote the United Jewish Appeal in the following amounts: Senator Birch Bayh, $21,500; Senator

Hubert Humphrey, $27,500; Senator Henry Jackson, $9,700; Senator Edward Muskie, $14,600; and Senator Mike Gravel, $7,200.

Another writer has calculated the "inordinate price" we have paid for the abnormal United States-Israeli relationship. In the twenty-five years from 1948 to 1973, total dollar contributions from the United States to Israel were $14.14 billions, or $4,500 for every Israeli citizen, comprising: United States Government economic aid, $1.73 billion; military assistance, $3.62 billion; private contributions, $4.49 billion; Israeli bonds subscribed, $2.05 billion; and loans, $1.45 billion.

In 1951, Israeli Prime Minister Ben-Gurion affirmed the "collective obligation of all national Zionist organizations to aid the Jewish State under all circumstances and conditions even if such an attitude clashes with their respective national authorities." In other words, the Zionists demand the allegiance of American Jews to Israel.

From a position of universal respect and goodwill we once enjoyed in the Arab world before creation of the State of Israel, we are left with no firm friends on whom we may count in that area except Israel. The immensely powerful Zionist lobby in the United States, centering its influence on the government, has bent American foreign policy from one of benevolent but essentially passive approval of the aims of the Balfour Declaration to an undistinguished defense of Israel, to the prejudice of American international interests in the Middle East, in particular our oil interests as well as the attainment of peace.

The Arabs do not expect us to cut Israel adrift but only that we maintain an even balance in our relations with these two opposing forces. We are not asked to abandon Israel or leave the country to its own devices. We are only asked to refrain from interposing our influence to give that power an unfair advantage *vis-à-vis* the Arabs. When I served in Saudi Arabia from 1946 to 1950, in a critical period of that country's evolution, I had many intimate conversations with the venerable, sagacious King Ibn Saud. A constant refrain ran through his many declarations to me—his strong desire for close, friendly relations with the United States. He and his sons who have succeeded him ask to that end only that we maintain an even keel and not favor Israel at Arab expense.

It is a fateful issue and demands the exercise by us of evenhanded justice in the preservation of fundamental American interests in a highly strategic area of our troubled world.

My brief year and a half in Palestine proved most useful to me in the relations I formed throughout my sojourn in the Near East. The British High Commissioner, Sir Herbert Samuel, had surrounded himself with outstanding British public servants such as Sir Gilbert Clayton, Chief Secretary; Sir Ronald Storrs, Governor of Jerusalem; and Sir Norman Bentwich. On a lower level were figures such as George Antonius, author of *The Arab Awakening*, published in 1939, which I had the pleasure of reviewing for the Washington Post.

I shall always remember how captivated Georgina and I were when we first made George's acquaintance at a reception given in 1924 by Sir Herbert Samuel for General Maxime Weygand, French High Commissioner for Syria and Lebanon. Shortly after, with the rapid flowering of our friendship, we made one of our first motor tours of the archaeological treasures of Jordan at Amman, Madeba, Jerash and Kerak. At Amman, in the absence of Emir Abdullah, we had our introduction to Arab hospitality at dinner offered by Emir Shaker, uncle of Abdullah, in tents overlooking ancient Philadelphia. The principal dish was a whole sheep. As a special mark of favor, our host plucked one of the eyes, which he offered to my wife. Rising to the occasion with perfect diplomatic aplomb, she slipped it into her mouth as if sheeps' eyes were a staple of her diet.

Present was Emir Adel Arslan, of a princely Druse family, who had accepted a post in Jordan, after expulsion by the French from Syria. It was the first of many subsequent instances given me in the Arab world of acceptances of government posts by Arabs in Arab countries not their birthplaces. The binding tie, as I discovered, is the Moslem faith, much as Christianity was in the Europe of the Middle Ages. I was to meet Arslan again, in Egypt in 1931, in Baghdad in 1934, and in Istanbul in 1949. Both he and George Antonius furthered my way in the Moslem world immeasurably. Through George, I was to be introduced in 1931 to the newspaper circles of Cairo, then largely controlled by the Lebanese and dominated by his father-in-law, Dr. Faris Nimr, editor of *Mokattam*. Through George and Arslan, I formed a warm friendship with an obscure Egyptian journalist, Abdul Rahman el Azzam, who became in the years ahead Secretary-General of the Arab League. Thanks to him, through his father-in-law, a chamberlain of King Ibn Saud, I had an incomparable entrée when I was appointed in 1946, first as minister, then ambassador, to the court of His Majesty King Ibn Saud, a post I was obliged to relinquish only by reason of health.

I have been asked many times which of my diplomatic posts I liked the best; I have been obliged to confess that I was attached to them all equally. If I had not found them all of consuming interest, I would have been seriously deficient as a servant of my government.

In 1931, shortly after an assignment to the legation in Cairo, I received, to my astonishment, a letter from my superior in the State Department saying that attention had been drawn to me for being unduly interested in Soviet Russia. After the initial shock, giving it the thought it deserved, I replied in the following sense. I began by confessing that I had been puzzled by the inquiry; I had always considered it a primary duty of a diplomat to follow events not only in the country to which he was assigned but also wherever they were of significance to American interests. I had served for two years in Kazan, Russia, from 1921 to 1923 as a representative of Mr. Hoover's American Relief Administration. After my departure, I had been interested in keeping myself abreast of developments in that country, particularly so far as they might affect the peace of the world. Since the rise of Hitler, I had similarly found it my duty, as a diplomatic officer of the U.S. Government, to follow as far as possible events under the Nazi regime as they might have a bearing on peace. Similarly, I had followed with great interest the Reichstag fire trial. None of these facts justified the conclusion that I was a Communist, a Nazi or an arsonist. My letter never occasioned a reply.

It may have been unanswerable.

A few months after arriving in Palestine, I was invited by the American organizers of a "Golden Rule" luncheon, given to promote greater understanding between members of the diverse faiths and communities in Jerusalem, to be the spokesman of the American community. I accepted when assured that the principal officer of the consulate had declined to be present and would not take it amiss if I spoke.

For my introduction I chose a quotation from Woodrow Wilson: "Do you covet honor? You will never gain it by serving yourself. Do you covet distinction? You will gain it only as the servant of mankind." I cited also examples of the nobility of Saladin toward his Christian foes, and that of Wilberforce in his campaign against slavery.

Almost everyone of any prominence was at the luncheon. I was the last to be called on and, as I rose, I observed the mild surprise on the part of those present. To most of them I was unknown. But my address was so well received that my wife and I were thereafter showered with invitations. Among them was one from the Storrs, who, invited us to an intimate dinner for former Prime Minister Sir Herbert Asquith on a visit to the Near East. The most interesting remark I heard him make was that he had declined High Commissioner Allenby's invitation to draft the ultimatum to the Egyptian Government following the assassination of Sir Lee Stack by Egyptian nationalists on the grounds that he was no longer a member of the British Cabinet.

My greatest error in embarking on my new Foreign Service career was my failure to adjust to the idiosyncrasies of my chief. As a result, I spent six years awaiting a first promotion. It was evened up later; between 1939 and 1945 I had no less than four promotions, but they meant much less. By that time, I didn't know from one year to another in what grade I was, they followed so swiftly. *Tant pis*. By that time worldly hope no longer mattered.

The Worldly Hope men set their Hearts upon
Turns Ashes—or it prospers; and anon
Like Snow upon the Desert's dusty Face,
Lighting a little Hour or two—is gone.

In 1973, when I pulled up stakes and left Nice for my birthplace, Lynchburg, Virginia, with the remains of my wife and mother-in-law, and ordered inscriptions for a joint tombstone, I decided I might as well include my own, and I added the above.

8
ASSIGNMENT IN ROMANIA

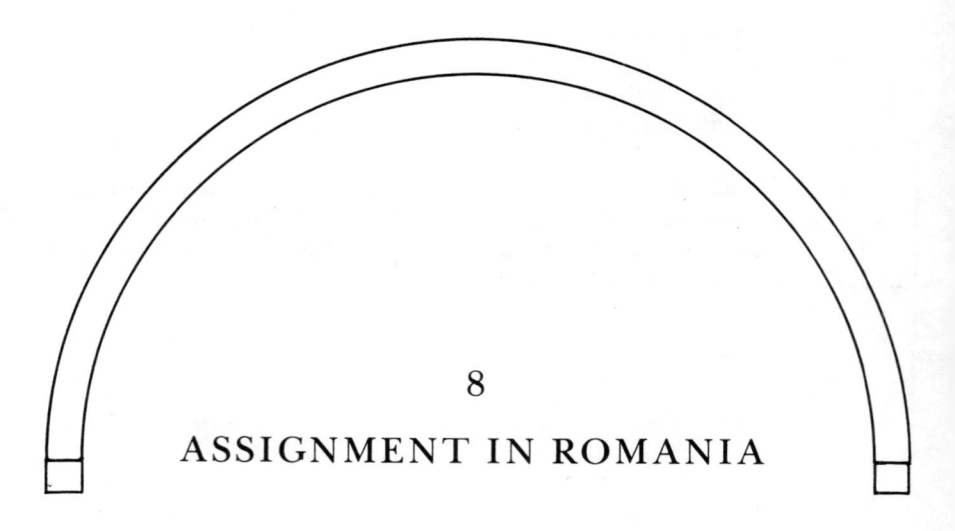

*W*e spent five years in Romania, an entrancing country whose capital, Bucharest, was known, with some justification, as the Paris of the Balkans. The official family of the consulate general was closely knit, presided over by a very understanding consul general, Eliot Palmer, and his lovely Canadian wife, Eno. There were two junior vice consuls, George Arnold and Jack MacAndrews.

Some months after arriving, I was entrusted with the economic work. As I had never had any instruction in economics, I hastily sent for the syllabus of the prestigious London School of Economics and ordered those books which seemed to offer the greatest possibility of remedying my ignorance. At that time, the Department of State followed the excellent practice of publishing, for the information of its officers, the grades accorded their economic reports. As time passed, Bucharest received an increasing number of "excellents" and "very goods", to my understandable gratification. In the end, I received a personal letter from an officer in the Department having oversight of the Bucharest consulate. It stated that the economic work had attracted increasing notice, so much so that information was desired as to where I had pursued my economic studies.

I had a hearty laugh and took great pleasure in replying that I had had no formal instruction in economics but had pursued it on my own by reading books recommended in the London School of Ecomonics syllabus. It convinced me that what one studies at college or university is of less importance than learning how to apply oneself.

It may shock the troglodytes if I mention that I did not neglect even Communist publications, in particular *International Press Correspondence*, then published in Berlin, with which I had great difficulty in placing a subscription. Its economic analyses were of outstanding quality, with due allowance for any Marxist bias.

For all its glamor, it is doubtful if there was a more corrupt country in Europe than Romania. Corruption in the government administration was such that bribery was taken for granted. When tenders were asked by one of the ministries for mechanical saws, an American firm was outraged when the contract was given not to its lowest bid but to an appreciably higher one submitted by a German firm. When the American representative complained, he was blandly informed that he should have acquainted himself with the common official Romanian practice of giving preference not to the lowest but to the highest bidder, as, the greater the sum involved, the greater the rake-off to the disbursing officer.

Even the royal family was not above dipping its hands in the public till. On the occasion of Queen Marie's visit to the United States in the late 1920s an effort in this respect was roundly checkmated by no less than an unintimidated American business manager, less impressed than her trodden-upon subjects, according to the gleeful account of one of her entourage.

The Queen proposed to visit one of the leading New York department stores in return for a consideration. To this end, she thereupon instructed her lady-in-waiting, Madame Simonne Lahovary, to communicate by telephone with the store she had chosen and make it known that Her Majesty would expect in return the customary contribution of five-thousand dollars for one of her Romanian charities. The manager, all suavity, in welcoming the great honor Her Majesty would confer on his store, explained that, as a corporation, it was governed by a board of directors and, accordingly, it would be necessary for him to have from Madame Lahovary a letter on the subject which he might submit to the board, a customary procedure in such circumstances. He was pleasantly surprised to be informed by the trusting lady-in-waiting that he would receive the letter by special messenger that day.

Upon receipt of the letter, he promptly telephoned the trusting Madame Lahovary that all arrangements would be made to receive Her Majesty with appropriate ceremony on the day and hour she might designate.

"And the check?" Mme. Lahovary inquired.

"I am sorry, but the board was not disposed to pay for her visit."

"In that case, I am sure Her Majesty will prefer to visit one of your competitors."

"I doubt that very much, as we shall have no other course than to inform the press and to make your letter available as a matter of public interest."

It is superfluous to add that the Queen had no alternative but to swallow her pride and make the visit without any recompense.

My tour of duty in Romania, from 1925 to 1930, coincided with the period of unbridled speculation that culminated in the Wall Street crash of October 1929. The economic unhealthiness of that period was plain enough. Romanian banks were paying 15 to 18 percent on time deposits; loans commanded a minimum of 39 percent, extending even to 40 percent. Yet American bankers assailed the Ministry of Finance and local banks, offering or even pleading with them to accept loans of excess American capital. Ivar Kreuger, the so-called wizard of finance, came to Bucharest to obtain the Romanian match monopoly for millions on which he would eventually default and end by blowing out his brains.

The looming disaster was strikingly prefigured in the following conversation in which I participated between the president of a local bank, Ionel Protopopescu, who, with his wife, had become our closest Romanian friends, and an American banker, Brown, from New York.

P: "Speculation on the New York Stock Exchange and your economic policies are deeply disturbing to me. There are three means available to us to discharge our debts to you: one, our exports, which your tariff policy effectively bars in large part; two, with gold, which we do not possess; and, three, through services and other invisible exports of limited scope for us."

B: "And the factories in Europe which may be transferred to the United States in payment of Europe's obligations."

P: "And their income?"

B: "May be reinvested in Europe."

P: "With Europe becoming eventually the economic vassal of America. What do you envisage for the Europeans?"

B: "Nothing simpler; wages and salaries will be paid by the American entrepreneurs."

P: "Thank you and permit me to say that your solution smacks of Alice in Wonderland economics."

B: "It is not original with me; it represents the thinking of our most conservative bankers. Forget classical economics; it cannot account for the boom on the New York Stock Exchange. We are developing new principles."

P: "I hear an ominous echo of the past: John Law and the Mississippi Bubble."

B: "Our boom is unprecedented; it is ushering in perpetual prosperity."

P: "We have heard such a siren call, luring investors to their ruin, over the centuries."

B: "My dear sir, ten, twenty years hence, I hope to meet you again to recall our conversation and to have you acknowlege that I was right."

Brown never returned to Romania. He may have been one of those who jumped out a window in Wall Street the following year. If he had returned, he would not have found Protopopescu. That banker died after the failure of his bank consequent upon the closing of the doors of the Credit Anstalt in Vienna, the slight gust of wind precipitating the collapse of the financial structure of Europe built on American sand. Had he returned in 1948, he would have found the once elegantly dressed Nina Protopopescu living in a small room with six others in what has become known as the People's Democratic Republic of Romania. It is perhaps too much to suppose that if Brown is still alive, he would agree that the folly of our political and economic policies under Harding, Coolidge and Hoover may have attributed appreciably to Europe's collapse.

In 1930 I was the guest in New York City of Percival Farquar and his charming wife, of Romanian origin. He was an international promotor, with connections all over the world, and on this particular evening he and Mrs. Farquar had assembled quite a number of prominent financial figures. As we left the dinner table, our eyes caught the headlines of an evening newspaper exposed on a table: "HOOVER SIGNS SMOOT-HAWLEY TARIFF." Although the guests were staunch Republicans, with the single exception of myself, there was not one who did not deplore approval by the President of the highest tariff wall ever erected by the United States, foreseeing as they did the disastrous repercussions it would have on the European economy and indirectly on our own. It was only a short time before Hoover was obliged to declare a moratorium on the collection of European debts to us. My mind went back to Lenin and Russia. Was the era proclaimed by Marx and Lenin approaching? Did our capitalism bear within itself the seeds of its own destruction?

Early that same year, while preparing the annual review of Romanian commerce and industry for 1929, the conviction grew within me that the Romanian economy would inevitably be threatened if the Soviet Five-Year Plan fulfilled even a part of the expectations formed of it. Of course, those were the days when few, if any, students took seriously the possibility of Russia's ever offering a challenge to the West in any field. But the facts were that some 90 percent of Romania's exports comprised lumber, livestock, wheat and oil, which were already being seriously undermined by Russia and Romania's traditional Near Eastern markets. In the general economic review I submitted to the Department of State on May 17, 1930, I wrote:

> With the conspicuous identity which exists between the export trade of

Romania and the growing volume of Russian exports of cereals, oil products and timber from neighboring Black Sea ports, the future of Romanian economic development is inevitably bound up with Russian economic development. Continued expansion of Russian exports of commodities upon which the Romanian trade balance is so completely dependent may have far-reaching consequences in the distinguishment of which no prophetic insight is needed.

Hardly four months elapsed before Virgile Madgearu, Romanian Minister of Commerce, appeared before a League of Nations Assembly in Geneva on September 22, 1930, to plead for a preferential European tariff for Romanian products as "a matter of life and death." In support of his request, he pointed out that, as a result of the reemergence of Russia in world markets, Romanian exports had declined in 1929 by 20 percent. The country was being threatened with economic disaster.

I was beginning to suspect that the economic squeeze might extend to a political one. On returning to the United States in 1930 for a new assignment, I observed aboard ship a good friend Leahu, Romanian consul in Chicago and nephew of Prime Minister Jules Maniu, busy studying German. I suggested that he would apply himself more usefully if he were to study Russian, as Romania's fate was likely to be linked more closely with Russia than Germany. He looked at me incredulously. The truth is we were all living in a fools' paradise, some a little more than others.

Occasionally I went to Vienna as a courier for the American legation. My bible was then, as it is now, the best-informed and most objective newspaper in the world, the *Manchester Guardian Weekly*. In it I had read of the workers' flats which the socialist municipality of Vienna had built immediately after the First World War. The idea of constructing homes for workers anywhere outside Soviet Russia impressed me as so revolutionary that I was curious to visit them. I was impressed by what I saw, including the nurseries to care for children while the parents were at work, and upon my return, I conveyed an expression of my interest in what had been accomplished to the Austrian minister in Bucharest.

In my naïveté, I was far from anticipating his reaction. "It's nothing but Bolshevism," was his comment. "We taxpayers are being victimized by the socialists who are governing Vienna." My own opinion was that it was excellent insurance against the possibility of violent revolution, but it was not for me, a very junior officer, to labor the point. In Romania the signs of social disintegration were widespread; the ruling class seemed intent on digging its grave.

If our five years in Romania were difficult ones owing to our own stringent financial circumstances, they were not without other compensations. We were frequently invited by Romanian, French and American friends to accompany them on extended excursions. It was thus that we explored the extraordinarily varied regions making up Romania, including scenic and romantic Transylvania, where German colonists had settled in the Middle Ages to form Christendom's barrier against the Moslem Turks, as well as Bukovina and the Dobruja, with their mosaics of many different peoples. Gypsies everywhere added haunting music and color to one of the most variegated lands I had been privileged to know. The scene suggested that of an operetta in which colorfully attired peasants, in costumes peculiar to their particular village, moved in endless procession across the stage. Nothing could have been more representative of Romania and neighboring Hungary than the incomparable operettas of Emmerich Kalman (1882–1953), such as *Countess Maritza, The Circus Princess, The Bajadere* and many others. After I retired, I used to spend every Christmas with my wife in Vienna, where we spent the evenings at the Volksoper or Opera, preferably to hear Richard Strauss and Emmerich Kalman. It has always been a mystery to me that one seldom, if ever, hears Kalman in the United States.

A final word on Romania. Settled by Trajan's Roman soldiers, the country is a mixture of Slavs, Latins, Germans, Hungarians, Bulgarians, Turks, Greeks and Gypsies. The language is a compound of Latin, Slavic, Turkish and Greek; its culture bore a strong Byzantine stamp.

With its fertile wheat fields, the deep majestic forests of the Transylvanian Alps, and its savage grandeur peculiarly suited for the background of so macabre a tale as *Dracula*, Romania is an entrancing country. One of my most lasting and unforgetable memories of it is the drive we made through the wild mountain fastnesses of Transylvania to catch a superb view of the lofty and solitary castle of Count Dracula. It raises its head in majestic splendor from the highest peak in the mountain chain, and we gazed from the valley upon its silhouette which had held so many spellbound. There was some discussion whether we would make the ascent by car for a closer view. Someone murmured, "Oh no, it would break the spell, let us leave it as we see it."

And so we did, with never any regret.

9
POSTING TO CAIRO

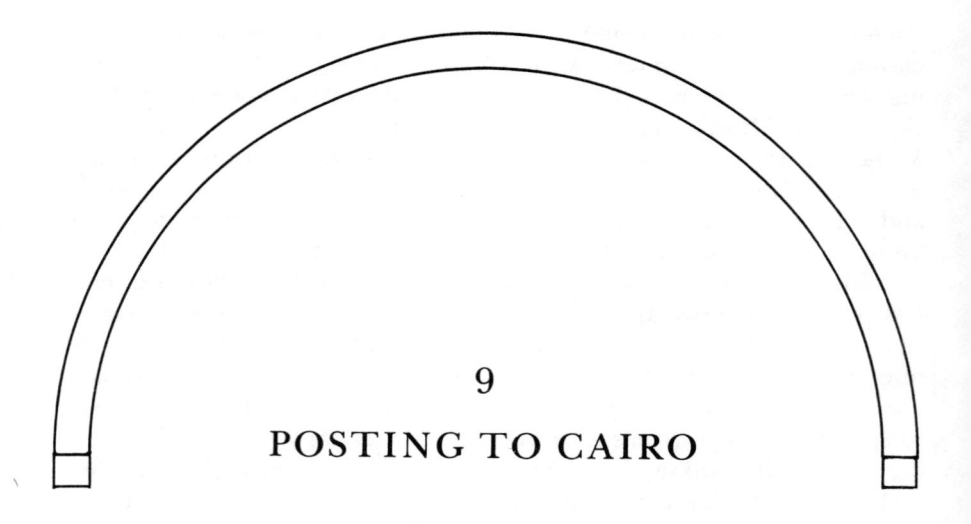

*M*y economic and political reports were no doubt responsible for my assignment in 1930 as second secretary and consul in Cairo. My mother-in-law had spent a winter in Cairo before World War I and had traveled overland under the escort of a dragoman in Palestine, Syria and Lebanon. In Cairo she had met a well-known member of the Coptic community, Bakhoum Bey, through whom we were introduced to that circle. On her side, Georgina had gone to school in England with Sherifa Kurhan, a member of the Egyptian royal family with distinguished Turkish connections. So we had no dearth of contacts with influential Egyptians and Turks.

On the way out from home by ship late in the year, an American married to an English official in the Sudan gave me most useful counsel on how to get along with the British, effective masters of Egypt: "The English will first endeavor to freeze you out. When they find they can't, they will take you in." By far, the most useful advice given me.

An Englishman in Bucharest gave me counsel on Egyptian relations which I chose to disregard: "Here you have made a practice of mixing with Romanians, which most English avoid. You will find it impossible to consort socially with Egyptains. If you do you will be ostracized."

I remarked that, if I were to learn anything of Egypt, it was more essential that I get to know the people of the country than the American or British colonies. As it turned out, apart from a few of the traditional troglodytes, we had no difficulty making our way among the high and low alike.

We arrived late in the year and were offered the hospitality of the home of George Wadsworth, first secretary of the legation, until finding an apartment in Garden City, around the corner from the legation. One of its greatest conveniences was that it had no telephone. It was not until seven years later, on my assignment to Washington, that I was obliged to yield and accept such a breach of privacy. When I made application in Alexandria, Virginia, for the installation of a telephone, I was asked for particulars of the last telephone I had had. "This is the first," I replied, "and I am not very happy about it."

The young lady taking my application flew into quite a rage: "I haven't time to jest, so give me the information."

"I am giving you the facts, so please come down to earth and accept me for what I am, an eccentric, who refuses to bend to a conformist society."

My chief in Egypt from 1930 to 1933 was William N. Jardine, who had been president of Kansas A&M College and had served in Coolidge's Cabinet as Secretary of Agriculture. If all political chiefs of mission were as agreeable as I found Jardine to be, there would be little complaint on the part of career officers. Aside from questions of agriculture, he left me full freedom in the internal direction of the legation when Wadsworth departed shortly after my arrival.

Fortunately, American problems in Egypt were relatively simple. At that time, the American colony in Egypt, not exceeding fifty, included principally professors at the American University in Cairo, archaeologists, missionaries, a few businessmen and three American judges of the Egyptian Mixed Courts. Of these, the senior was Judge Pierre Crabites of New Orleans, resident for many years in Cairo and an indispensable source of information.

If any country in the Near East has been a racial melting pot, it is Egypt. Since gaining independence, it professes to be Arab, but no country in the Arab League, of which it is a member, could be less so. Basically, the population is Hamitic, with a compound of ancient Egyptian, Sudanese and Berber blood, with an intermixture of Arabs who conquered the country in the seventh century, Greeks and Turks, the latecomers, who, for a time, made it a part of the Turkish Empire.

Early in the nineteenth century, Mohammed Ali, an Albanian, after distinguishing himself with Turkish forces in Egypt, was named governor with the title of pasha. A descendant acquired from the sultan the title of khedive. In 1881, Great Britain took the momentous step of occupying Egypt for the protection of law and order, then threatened by a nationalist uprising headed by Arabi Pasha. The real purpose was the protection of British investments, including, in particular, the Suez Canal, lifeline of the British Empire's communications with India.

From 1881 to 1914, Egypt still formed a nominal part of the Turkish Empire, even though ruled by a local dynasty under British occupation. The anomalous situation was only terminated with the declaration, in 1914, of a British protectorate over the country upon the entrance of Turkey into the war on the side of the Central Powers. In 1922, in the face of an unprecedented tide of nationalist sentiment, Britain proclaimed the independence of Egypt, subject to four reserved points. In other words, while Egypt possessed the outward façade of independence, namely a king and constitutional government, the effective ruler continued to be Great Britain.

If a king reigned, it was a British high commissioner who pulled the strings; if a prime minister ostensibly presided over the government, it was British advisers installed in most of the ministries who pulled the levers. I made it a point to cultivate their acquaintance and established warm friendships with Keown-Boyd, Director of Public Security; John Besly in Justice; Hugh-Jones in Finance; and Horace Mayne in Communications. Mayne described to me an interview he had with Sir Percy Loraine, High Commissioner. The latter summoned Mayne to account for his approval of specifications for a public tender without having consulted the commercial secretary of the residency to protect the interests of British bidders. Mayne's answer was that he was an adviser, not to the British but to the Egyptian Government, for whose interests he was responsible. I conceived profound admiration for the loyal services these British nationals gave the Egyptian Government.

It was some little while after my arrival that an incident occurred which brought home to me that the resolution I had formed to become acquainted with Egyptians had made an impression in high quarters. At a tea party in Cairo given by a British couple who had resided in the country for some years and took an independent line in receiving Egyptians, I was presented to Mohammed Mahmoud Pasha, graduate of Cambridge University, former Prime Minister and leader of the Liberal Constitutional Party. Taking my hand warmly in his, he remarked: "You need no introduction. I know all about you." Perceiving my bewilderment, he added, "You have become well known as one of the first foreign diplomats to establish social relations with Egyptians."

Our meeting occurred about 1932. I had found, on arriving in Cairo, social lines as strictly drawn between Anglo-Saxon and Egyptian communities as I had been warned they would be. I had not been slow in endeavoring to breach them. In view of my junior rank, I had never contemplated that my endeavors in this respect would excite attention. That they had was proof not only of how deep racial lines ran but also how sensitive Egyptians were to them. There could have been no more conspicuous example than the Gezira Sporting Club, most frequented social center of the British and diplomatic communities, in the very heart of the city. This great tract of land, with its golf, tennis and other facilities, was open to anyone of social standing, with the sole exception of Egyptians. By very special dispensation, half a dozen princely Egyptians were admitted. In this age, it seems incredible that such a closed society should have been perpetuated in the capital of Egypt until World War II.

In my time, only a handful of the older British residents maintained social relations with Egyptian families, and these, for the most part, were Christian Copts. The exceptions among British officials were John Besly, Grafftey-Smith and Williamson-Napier. At the time of the Ital-Ethiopian War in 1935, word went out that British Army messes, as a matter of policy, should entertain Egyptian officers. By that time, such overtures were too transparent; they amused rather than impressed the Egyptians.

What a single individual could accomplish in this regard was brought home to me by an article by Stanley Parker, editor of the *Egyptian Gazette*, the British language newspaper, on January 5, 1934, the day of our departure for Tehran, our new post in Persia. If I had become, according to Parker's overly generous estimate, "an outstanding figure in Cairo," I fear I may have raised some eyebrows in the State Department for my advanced nonconformist views. In 1930–34, the world seemed to me to be falling about our heads. With a world economic depression, the delicate economic and social fabric of Europe and the West began to be torn asunder. Hoover's moratorium on war debts, hailed as the most important event since the 1918 armistice, appeared in retrospect like fighting a forest fire with a garden hose. Hitler was consolidating his insensate power with the cold efficiency of an international gangster. There were warnings enough by the *Manchester Guardian,* and there were the storm signals of reporters William Shirer, John Gunther and Edgar Scott Mowrer. The world's indifference reflected a kind of paralysis of the will, most powerful accomplice of the Hitler regime. With the swift succession of a Spanish civil war, a mutiny in the British Fleet and suspension of the British gold standard, these and other events assumed for me an apocalyptic character portending the end of that world into which we had been born.

There was never any concealment on my part of views, formed as early as 1922 in Soviet Russia, that the latent strength of that country was being seriously underestimated by the West. When Parker asked me for an anonymous review of Calvin B. Hoover's *The Economic Life of Soviet Russia* for the April 3, 1931, issue of the *Egyptian Gazette,* I wrote of how Lenin:

enters Russia in 1917 from which he had been exiled and without funds and with only a corporal's guard of followers, seizes power by his astute grasp of the realities of the situation, and becomes master of one sixth of the earth's surface. Surrounded by armies of the victorious Great Powers he successfully frees Russia from the invaders (inclusive of the United States) and in the midst of the most indescribable economic disorganization, formulates a tentative plan for the electrification of the country, its industrialization, and the mechanization of agriculture, a plan put on paper in 1920 under his direction with the hope of its being achieved in fifteen years and is realized in ten years with an output of power stations four times that of pre-war and an industrial output double that of 1913. Declamations and embargoes have proved futile to stay the inexorable march of events in Russia.

There was a certain exaggeration on my part here in that Lenin was not without funds when he returned to Russia. What I sought to underline was that the country was making progress. That was also the opinion of some other economists more expert than I. When Paul van Zealand, an economist, later Belgian Prime Minister, visited Egypt on a financial mission in 1931 or 1932, we had long talks about the world situation. I sought his opinion of my thought that Russia might in time develop greater political freedom and we a more just economic regime. He saw Russia as far left of center, the West off center to the right, with the two destined eventually to converge. He had visited Russia and had set forth his views in a brief pamphlet in 1931, *Reflections on the Five-Year Plan*, of which he presented me a copy.

If, in my reports to the State Department, I reported developments as I saw them objectively, it was to serve rather than subvert my country. I was mindful of the counsel given me by Prentiss Gilbert, one of our most brilliant career officers, which I sought before taking the examinations for the Foreign Service: "Knowing you as I do, if you would be happy in your career, be prepared to serve cheerfully at any post to which you may be assigned and to report the truth as you see it, however disagreeable it may be to Washington."

In 1932, my wife and I, having received permission to take home leave, were on an Isthmian Line freighter from Port Said to New York at a cost of passage of forty-two dollars each, when I received a telegram from the legation in Cairo to the effect that, for reasons of economy, Foreign Service salaries had been reduced by 15 percent and all leave was to be taken without pay. My first impulse was to reply asking if we were expected to swim ashore but, on reflection, I determined to abide by my resolution to borrow money on my veteran's insurance and to purchase a car for the purpose of obtaining a close-up view of the United States, essential in the discharge of my official duties abroad. By rigid economy, we were successful in reducing travel expenses for my wife, my mother-in-law and myself, covering the eighty-five hundred miles to the West Coast and return, in the twenty-three days spent, for some seventy-five dollars each. Because of the Depression, prices were exceptionally low.

Jardine had asked me to plumb the state of public opinion and report to him on the probable outcome of the forthcoming presidential election in November. If Roosevelt won, all political chiefs of mission would have to tender their resignations. Wherever I stopped, I made it a point to remark, in order to elicit a frank reaction: "I suppose all you people are voting for Hoover."

The answer generally received, in one form or another, was: "Only those in insane asylums, mister."

A variation given by a colored porter on a train was: "If you question those in Pullman cars there is some division of opinion, but in the coaches it is overwhelmingly Democratic."

I wrote Jardine that he might as well begin packing, that Roosevelt would win by an overwhelming majority. The only contrary straws in the wind were in Reno, where the ignorant gamblers were offering two to one on Hoover, and in New York, where bankers were convinced of a Republican victory.

10
THE CHARM OF PERSIA

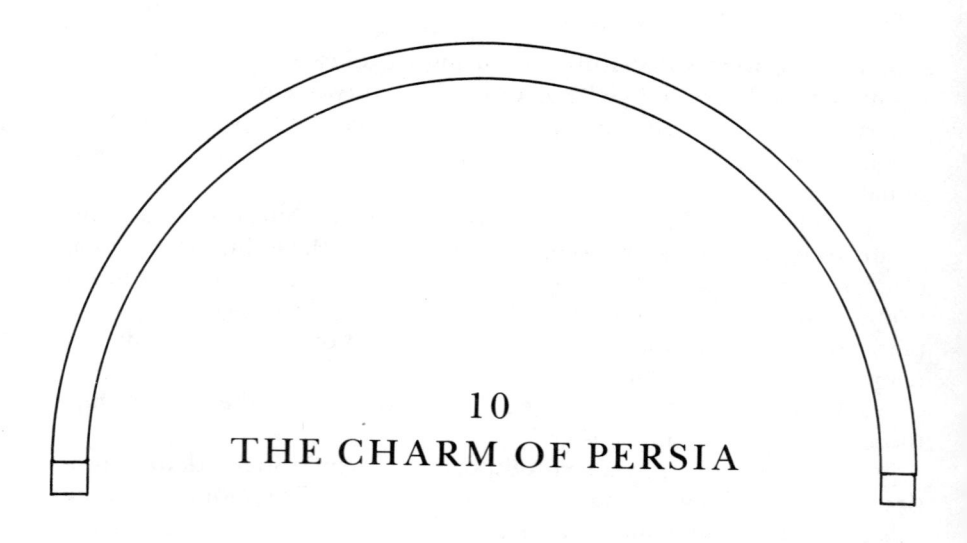

Of the more than one hundred countries I have visited in the course of my life, I know of none which matches Persia, ancient home of our Aryan Indo-European ancestors. To the solemn grandeur of its natural scenery is united a past of exceptional interest; it has contributed to the world more diverse religions than perhaps any other country: Mithraism, Manichaeism, Mazdakism, Shi'ism, Bahaism and, by no means least, Zoroastrianism, source of important elements of our Christian faith.

World literature has received a greater heritage from the Persian poets Sa'di, Hafiz and Firdausi than from any other Oriental source; the quatrains of Omar Khayyám, as translated by FitzGerald, have become an imperishable part of English literature. Many of the *Arabian Nights* are the work of Persian storytellers, and one of the most notable of the characters portrayed in that work, Haroun-al-Raschid, was born and died in Persia.

George Wadsworth, my predecessor in both Cairo and Tehran, had made the trip from Cairo by car but not in the dead of winter, as I was called upon to do. We set out in January 1934, in a secondhand car purchased from Jardine which was to give me no end of trouble with its worn tires and mechanical deficiencies. We had hardly traversed the Canal and ventured into the Sinai Peninsula before being halted by a flat tire. The jack proved defective and it was with difficulty that we succeeded in changing the tire. We passed Beersheba with a sigh of relief and stayed overnight in the hospitable home of George and Katy Antonius in Jerusalem; George had left the Department of Education to consecrate himself to *The Arab Awakening* with the patronage of Charles R. Crane, a remarkable American whose true worth is today little appreciated.

No American between the two World Wars exercised a greater influence in the Near East than he did. His first contact with that area occurred in 1918, when he was sent, at the instance of President Wilson and the Paris Peace Conference, as a member of the King-Crane Mission to look into the question of Palestine. After investigation, the mission made known its farsighted conclusion that, if the principle of self-determination was to be taken into account and the "wishes of Palestine's population to be decisive it would be necessary to limit Jewish immigration and to abandon any plan to make Palestine a Jewish State."

In the early 1920s, Crane sent an American engineer, Karl Twitchell, to Yemen and Saudi Arabia with an offer of disinterested technical assistance at Crane's expense. So impressed was the Saudi Arabian monarch by this initial American contact that, when American oil interests sought concessions of King Ibn Saud, later developed by the Arabian American Oil Company consortium, they found it desirable to use Twitchell as an intermediary. Incongruously, the man who had been indirectly more responsible than anyone else for these oil discoveries, of unparalleled proportions, never derived any financial profit from them.

But more of this and of my four years in Saudi Arabia and of the close relations I enjoyed with King Ibn Saud, one of the great men of our era, later.

We were twenty-eight days in reaching Tehran, a distance of two thousand, five hundred miles from Cairo, after being snowbound for five days at Kangavar in the mountains between Kermanshah and Hamadan and after crossing the desert at night between Damascus and Baghdad, with my wife screaming hysterically from fatigue. But all that is long ago and far away. A Persian governor, Farajollah Khan, rescued us from the primitive *chaikhani*, or teahouse, where we had found temporary lodging, and installed us in his home. Emerging from it after lunch, I was arrested by a Persian soldier who had espied on the floor of my car a revolver I carried for protection from bandits. He had never heard of the immunity of diplomats, and it was only after lengthy explanation that he released me but retained my weapon, which was eventually recovered through the Persian Foreign Office. Such incidents only added to the spice of life and were never of serious concern. Nothing is more purposeless than to worry about matters which are beyond remedy.

To travel in Persia is to view one of the world's most impressive museums. Those who rush about by air miss that intimate appreciation of the country and its people which can only be gained by personal contact. It must be done leisurely by motor, traveling with folding cots in order to be prepared to sleep out under the stars or in abandoned caravansaries which line many of the routes. It was thus that we visited that jewel of cities, Isfahan, on the route between Tehran and the south, with its exquisite bridges, palaces and mosques, resplendent remnants of the Sefavid reign of Shah Abbas, of the sixteenth and seventeenth centuries. Further south was rose-colored Shiraz, birthplace of Hafiz and Sa'di, and intervening, Persepolis, where Dr. Ernst Harzfeld was laying bare an Achaemenian palace. A visit in 331 B.C. by Alexander the Great was commemorated by burning the city in the course of a drunken orgy at the instigation of the courtesan, Thais, in retaliation for the firing of Greek temples by the Persians.

In the solid rock of the mountain range overlooking Persepolis, two tombs have been discovered which contain remains of the last Achaemenian rulers, Artaxerxes II (404–359 B.C.) and Artaxerxes III (359–358 B.C.). But of greater interest than these are the tombs and rock sculptures across the valley at what is known as Naksh-i-Rustam. Here is portrayed the early pageant of Persian history, including two fire altars of the ancient Aryan nature worship out of which Zoroastrianism developed, an Elamite rock sculpture, the rock-hewn tombs of Xerxes I, Darius the Great, Artaxerxes I (494–465 B.C.) and Darius II (424–404 B.C.). Of the four tombs, only that of Darius the Great bears an inscription in old Persian, Susian and Babylonian testifying to his faith in the new religion of Zoroaster.

With the conquest of Persia by Alexander the Great, the great Achaemenian dynasty disappeared from history after a reign of little more than two hundred years. In that brief period, a homogenous Persian character had been developed almost contemporaneously with the blossoming of a like cultural and national consciousness at Athens. In the democratic city states of Greece, nurturing full freedom of expression for the individual, there appeared, in the brief span of two hundred years, the fathers of our present civilization: Plato, Socrates, Aristotle, Herodotus, Aeschylus, Euripides, Solon and Pericles, to name but a few. Yet of the Persian civilization, contemporaneous with that of Greece, hardly one name has been preserved apart from those of its rulers.

The unrolling of the panoply of the past in Persia was one of its great fascinations. The contemporary celebration in Persia of the New Year, known to the Persians as No-Ruz, on March 21, represents a modern survival of the Aryan custom commemorating the birth of spring. From the days of Cyrus to the present, it was the custom of the king to receive his subjects on this day and to exchange presents. Doctor

Willis relates that, as late as 1867, the shah distributed gold coins in handfuls from trays offered to invited dignitaries when he received them in audience at the palace on March 21. In 1932, however, only single coins were distributed, and after that year this ancient custom was discontinued.

As little work was deputed to me by my chief in Persia, I determined to occupy myself with an exhaustive study of Soviet-Persian relations, which eventually extended to more than three hundred pages. It must have been entombed in the Department of State archives, as I never learned of the reception accorded it.

Its most important conclusion was that the struggle between communism and capitalism (or imperialism, as it was most commonly designated by the Soviets) was destined to find its most important theater in the East and that it was there rather than in Western Europe that the destiny of our world might be decided. I added that there was no reason to believe there had been any change in the Soviet conviction that the forces set in motion by Leninism might not have the convulsive repercussions in the East which Lenin had envisaged when he saw in Western domination of that area the Achilles heel of capitalism. No gift of prophecy was needed to foreshadow the future development of Soviet policy in the Middle and Far East; it was limned in Soviet doctrine so clearly that even those who ran might read. The pity was that there were so few readers.

In 1953, following my retirement from the U. S. Foreign Service, I was interviewed by a representative of *Time* magazine, from whose issue of February 16, 1953, these excerpts are taken:

> "Iran. On the basis of my studies and sojourn in Persia, I am convinced that Persia is now entering a period of chaos and anarchy... From the time of Darius and Cyrus, Persia has known only peace through a strong man... To prate of democracy to the Persians is like advocating prohibition to the denizens of hell." Childs believes that "the money we are pouring into Persia is money thrown down a drain," and that the U.S. faces "the alternative of seeing Russia take over the whole of Persia, or, if we are sufficiently farsighted, only the northern half." His urgent recommendation: "The U.S. should be prepared, if necessary, to occupy southern Persia and regain possession of [The Abadan oil refinery], preferably at the request of ... a Persian government sympathetic to the Western world." If Britain does not back the U.S., Childs says that the U.S. should act alone.
>
> "Egypt. The U.S. should strongly support Dictator Mohammed Naguib, who deserves the most unreserved backing by the Western Powers.

"Israel. We should announce to the Israelis that they cannot count upon our continued financial support unless they entertain and implement some reasonable compromise with the Arabs, including respect for the decisions of the United Nations. . .

"Morocco. I spent five years in Morocco from 1941 to 1945. . . President Roosevelt came to the Casablanca conference in January, 1943, and with the recklessness of a schoolboy told the Sultan he should assert his independence of the French. . . This was like throwing a Roman candle into a barrel of gasoline." Childs' recommendation: the U.S. should promote "greater liberty for the Moroccans, within the framework of the French Union, without inciting the Moroccans to open rebellion, which has only been to the advantage of the Communists."

Thirty years later, I find this analysis singularly apropos.

11

TWO REVOLUTIONS: EGYPT AND SPAIN

*W*ith the outbreak of the First World War and its repercussions, I had become convinced that the world into which we had been born was fast disappearing and would never be restored. I found few, however, who shared this conviction. By the end of the war, when I voiced such opinions, I was called a Bolshevik and, in consequence, thought it wiser to keep my thoughts to myself. There is nothing so unsettling to our fellowmen as the revelation of truth; they run from it as if it were the plague.

The fact that I was not jailed or ostracized was due to my strain of blood; it so happened, as I had discovered from research, that I came from distinguished ancestors. My mother had joined the Colonial Dames of Virginia by virtue of descent from sixteen pre-Revolutionary War members of the Virginia House of Burgesses. Yet there is a strain of eccentricity in Virginians, no matter what their antecedents may be.

I was now about to witness two revolutions indicative of the deeply unsettled state of the world. In Persia, my chief, through jealousy, had requested my recall. This was most agreeable to me, all the more that I was ordered to return to Cairo where I had left many friends, so many that my return resembled a homecoming.

The Italo-Ethiopian War was in its cuckoo stage. Britain was massing a large part of its Fleet in Egyptian waters while Washington, until I assumed charge, was complaining that it was receiving little or nothing from the legation in the way of reporting and analysis of local developments.

Questions uppermost at the Department of State included whether the Suez Canal would be closed to Italy, what action the British Fleet might take to impede Italy's moves, and whether Egyptian nationalists would exploit the situation to extort concessions from Britain.

I spent an evening with Nokrassy Pasha, whose ostracism by the British for his suspected involvement in Sir Lee Stack's murder in 1924 had not caused me to ignore the overtures he had made me. His services as a nationalist leader are commemorated by an imposing mausoleum in Cairo. Nokrassy was categoric in assuring me that Egyptian nationalists would take every advantage of Britain's embarrassment by Mussolini and Hitler. I spent a fruitful afternoon with one of the ablest members of the Cabinet, Abdul Wahab Pasha, with whom I had enjoyed close ties, who echoed Nokrassy's views. Not less illuminating was my extended conversation with one of the rising youthful leaders, Abdul Rahman el Azzam, in the garden of Groppi's popular café. After two hours of an exchange of views, I raised this question: "Surely the nationalists will not play the fascist part by promoting disorders to add to Britain's embarrassment in a move to extort full independence?"

Azzam's eyes twinkled. "That is precisely what we shall do in the absence of immediate British concessions. Otherwise, you will see full-scale rioting in Cairo in three weeks."

Britain miscalculated both the internal Egyptian situation as well as the international one. The British military in Egypt were generally persuaded that Mussolini had transformed Italian armed forces so effectively that British units in the Mediterranean might be no match for the new weapons the Fascists had developed. There was also the deepseated fear that, if Mussolini were checkmated, social upheavals in Italy might pave the way for communism there.

It is now clear that, if Britain had taken a firm stand, the Ethiopian adventure would have collapsed. In such a case, it is unlikely that Germany would have provoked war in 1939. In 1935, the German minister in Cairo, Von Stohrer, assured me that, if the League of Nations adopted sanctions against Italy, Germany would not dispute them. Hitler's policy was one of wait and see which way the wind might blow. When it blew hot and then cold, he took his cue and concluded he had nothing to fear from powers as irresolute as Britain and France.

My probing completed, I entrained for Alexandria to confer with the consul general there. The typing of a seventeen-page dispatch embodying my conversations and conclusions was completed as I reached my destination. In the absence of airmail, it reached William Phillips,

TWO REVOLUTIONS: EGYPT AND SPAIN

Undersecretary of State, three weeks later. That morning, Phillips had read in the New York Times of the outbreak of riots in Cairo the previous day. Phillips was handsome in his acknowledgment. I was formally commended for "the excellent manner" in which the information had been presented. It was added that "the dispatch has proved of distinct assistance to the Department in gaining an understanding of the course of developments in Egypt."

The situation in Egypt and in Ethiopia had attracted to Cairo such famous American correspondents as Floyd Gibbons, an old friend from Russian days, and Vincent (Jimmy) Sheean. I introduced Jimmy to Maria Riaz, a Romanian I had known in Bucharest, married to an Egyptian and one of the most brilliant and cultivated hostesses in Cairo, in whose salon one might find André Malraux and even Barbara Hutton.

Floyd Gibbons gave me no peace until I overcame the reluctance of Keown-Boyd, virtual Minister of the Interior, to receive him in my company at his home. I anticipated a most informative meeting but listened instead to a monologue by Floyd about his recent experience as a war correspondent in Shanghai: "I was sent to Shanghai in 1932 on the heels of the Japanese landing there. I was keeping three stenographers busy in relays when I was interrupted by the receipt of a triple priority cable from the bosses back home. I took one look at it and said: 'Well, folks, that will be all. Pack up and we'll get the next ship out of here.'

"'What's happened?'

"'Just a kidnaping, that's all: Lindbergh's baby. The most this war will get from now on will be a few paragraphs on an inside page...' That's news for you."

And that was all that came of our call on K-B, who probably was better acquainted with the Egyptian situation than anyone else in the entire country, not excepting the British high commissioner, the prime minister, or the king himself.

During the remainder of 1935 and the beginning of 1936, the local situation was moving in the direction forecast by Nokrassy and Azzam. Civil disturbances in the end assumed such proportions that Great Britain announced its willingness to grant full-fledged independence to Egypt with only one reservation, that of the right to garrison Cairo and the Suez Canal with British forces.

Following the withdrawal of British forces from Cairo to the Canal in 1951 and young King Farouk's alienation of public opinion by his corruption and irresponsibility, Egypt was effectively isolated. The way was open for the revolution of 1952 and the advent of the masses to power in the persons, successively, of Naguib, Nasser and Sadat. History had turned full circle. Colonel Arabi's revolt in 1881, which had occasioned British occupation of Egypt, had been completed by the return of the people to power. The old regime of the pashas, many of aristocratic Turkish blood, was ended.

Before 1952, there was probably no other country in the world where the social inequalities were comparable to those in Egypt. Between the masses, on the one hand, living in grinding poverty, and the pasha class, flaunting an ostentatious luxury, the gulf was stark and pitiless. Between the two wars, the pashas and numerous princely families, along with wealthy foreign residents, did not refrain from flaunting their sybaritic existence. Not a few kept open house where guests were welcome, as in Russia before the Revolution, to lunch or dine without prior invitation. Receptions for six or seven hundred people, in spacious palaces, were commonplace. Sumptuous delicacies were in abundance, including the finest wines and champagne, in proximity to an undernourished population living in filth and squalor.

Many foreigners and even some thoughtful Egyptians were alive to the injustice of it all. Yet I cannot remember ever having heard any premonition that it was a society destined shortly to disappear. It was accepted generally that no revolution was possible so long as British armed forces were present. In truth, it was but a few months after the disappearance of British armed forces from Cairo that King Farouk was swept incontinently from his throne.

Sixteen years before this, that violence erupted on July 17, 1936, at the opposite end of the Mediterranean, in Spain. Some months previous I had been stricken with diphtheria on the eve of embarking for a month's leave in Europe, the first I had had in four years. I could not but be grateful for the uncommon compassion shown me when my leave was extended to no less than five months, perhaps in recognition that my illness had been the consequence of overwork.

Attracted as I had always been to scenes of international crises, I could not resist the temptation, upon leaving the Egyptian hospital, to take ship for France in August with the idea of making my way by slow degrees to Spain.

Georgina accompanied me as far as Vitel to join her mother there, and I found our old friend Baron Henri de Malval, who persuaded me to spend a few days with him at his château near Paris. I arrived by slow stages, husbanding my strength in Paris, where I met by prearrangement Baroness Marcelle de Jouvenel, a pioneering French writer and journalist, whose acquaintance I had made in Egypt in 1930 when she was on her way to Ethiopia for her first travel book, *White, Brown and Black*. Upon hearing of my project to visit Spain, she had announced her intention to join me after having been commissioned to report the war for a well-known French publication.

When all plans had been completed, we took the most direct route for Biarritz with only one overnight stop. The second day we stopped for lunch with friends of mine, Count Michel Zogheb and his wife, a well-known French cinema star. We did not stop at Biarritz but pressed on to Hendaye, which was to be our headquarters.

Opposite Hendaye, Spanish Republican and Nationalist forces were locked in combat, the former to defend, the latter to conquer the frontier town of Irun. With my diplomatic passport, I obtained a French pass permitting entry into the frontier zone where admittance was restricted to the population resident there, journalists such as Marcelle, and others who could justify their presence.

The small Bidassoa River marked the frontier. Perched on a bluff on the French side, within reach by foot, was the village of Biratou, the outskirts of which commanded a full view, much as in a theater, of the rolling meadows on the opposite Spanish side, where forces of the two adversaries were drawn up. A road skirted the river from Behobie, just west of Hendaye, offering access to Biratou. Traversing it was not without danger as, from time to time, stray bullets whistled over or fell in its immediate vicinity. It was the sole access to Biratou by car. I asked Marcelle if she were prepared to run the risk of braving the ascent from Behobie by car to Biratou for a bird's-eye view of the fighting in progress in the valley opposite. She was plucky enough, so we threw the car into first speed and set out as fast as we might safely negotiate the rather winding road leading to Biratou perched on the heights above. In a very few mintues we were safely on the terrace of a café-restaurant offering a superb view of the desultory combat taking place hardly more than a stone's throw opposite in Spanish territory. A more perfect view of the fighting could not possibly have been found. Our vantage site resembled the loge of a theater from which we might follow the play's action. The place was full of journalists and a number of military attachés from the Madrid embassies. Shells were being lobbed intermittently from Nationalist gun emplacements within our vision on the upper slopes opposite into the valley below occupied by Republican forces in small numbers. These occupied an armored train, bearing the initials U.H.P. (Union of Proletarian Men), moving slowly back and forth on a railway spur and firing from time to time against the small groups of Nationalists scattered in the slopes above. Its intermittent character suggested a leisurely dress rehearsal more than active combat, and in this respect was typically Spanish.

At length, a half dozen of us, including Marcelle, decided to follow on foot the road by which we had reached our vantage point for a closer view of the scene beneath us centering about the locomotive. Some of us were preparing to take photographs of the engine when there was a warning burst of rifle fire and a voice in French asked who we were.

"Journalists," was the reply.

"Have you any message for us?"

"Yes, we are friends. What is your situation?"

"One of confidence and fearlessness." There was a pause followed by a request that we return to Biratou, determine the situation of the opposite side as far as that might be possible, and come back and report. As no one fancied such a task, we regained the restaurant terrace.

After lunch, the waitress advised us to return to Hendaye on foot through the fields, as the road by which we had come was too dangerous, exposed as it was to the fire of the Nationalists. I disliked the idea of abandoning my car. Marcelle proposed that we proceed in it to the edge of the village, place car seats on either side of our exposed heads and shoulders and, after waiting for a lull in the gunfire, make a dash for it over the road by which we had come. Aside from the whine of a few stray bullets which passed over our heads, we reached the international bridge between Irun and Behobie without mishap but with some relief.

Refugees were streaming across the bridge from Irun into France. One sole figure presented himself headed for the Spanish side. He was a young man, coatless and hatless, without baggage, obviously of the working class. When his passport was found in order, he began waving his arms in agitation. He brushed his lips with the back of his hand and waved toward Irun. He turned to the gendarme and asked, "Will you have a glass with me before I go?"

"I'm sorry," the gendarme answered softly, "it's against the rules."

With that, the young man, hardly more than a boy, his shirttail flapping grotesquely behind him, headed for Irun, a volunteer in the armed struggle against fascism. As we watched him, there was a long hissing noise followed by a dull thud, marking the passage of a shell which had failed to explode in Irun.

The following day, Marcelle and I went down to the docks to observe a French ship with refugees from Bilbao and entered into conversation with a young Frenchman, Jean Ehrhard, who had been teaching in Spain. He was eager to visit Barcelona to observe what was happening on the Republican side. I fell in with his proposal that we drive there in my car. It was the beginning of a warm friendship which lasted forty-odd years, despite our widely separated lives during which we met only at long intervals in Paris for a meal together. He taught for some years in Saigon and even in the United States while I was living in retirement in Nice.

Before setting out for Barcelona, we drove to the international bridge in the hope of perhaps having a look around Irun. On reaching the Spanish side of the bridge, we were halted by a Republican militiaman who barred our passage. "Irun is no place for foreigners," he said. Then, observing our disappointment, he added: "It's our place to be here. We are young and can die fighting for a cause we hold dear. We accept the risk and expect to be killed, but with you it's different."

I said to Ehrhard in English, "I see a café up there. Let's ask if we can go for a drink. If he refuses, we can slip away when he is not looking."

The militiaman turned on me a far from friendly smile. "I wouldn't do that," he observed in English. He slapped his gun. "There was a foreigner a few days ago from France. He wanted to go to San Sebastian. He didn't tell us he was one of Franco's spies. He had a Hungarian passport but couldn't speak any Hungarian, only German. Not exactly regular, was it? We have to keep a sharp eye open for all kinds. He wanted to go to the café up the street you had a longing to see. I told him he couldn't. He hung around for a while and, when he thought I wasn't looking, he slipped off in the direction of San Sebastian, but he never even reached your café." He slapped his gun once more and winked.

"You are quite a polyglot, speaking English, Spanish, French, Hungarian and German. Where did you learn English?"

He thrust his head so close to mine that I had to step back. "My friend, I have seen so much since July seventeenth that I can't remember much before then." He laid his hand on mine, revealing a ring with the hammer and sickle.

I said something about its being a Communist device. He broke into a flood of Spanish and then shifted to English. With a vehemence which startled me, he shouted as he grasped my arm: "No, it's more than that. It represents everything I live for, everything, do you understand?"

It was a spirit, as I came to learn, that animated large numbers of Spanish Republicans, particularly the youth. It was a fanaticism matched by that of the Nationalists. It was a fanaticism which was to tear Spain apart and, ultimately, the greater part of Europe.

Ehrhard and I left at dusk on the evening of September 1 and presented ourselves to the strict Spanish control at the Col de la Perche. After minute examination of every scrap of paper we possessed by heavily armed youth of both sexes, we were permitted to proceed to nearby Puigcerda, where we spent the night to await a decision whether we might continue on to Barcelona. The next morning we were again interrogated and provided with passes under the seal of the Puigcerda authorities. Even in Soviet Russia I had not encountered such careful scrutiny.

The countryside and towns we traversed presented no unusual appearance except for the notable absence of travelers and the presence of armed militiamen at the entrances and exits of towns and villages and occasionally at churches, sometimes intact and sometimes in ruins, surmounted by the black-and-red flag of the Catalonian anarchists.

On reaching Barcelona in the early afternoon, we found the streets deserted, evidence that the Civil War had introduced no change in the observance of the traditional Spanish siesta. A few hours later the city was teeming with youthful militiamen and workers. Requistioned private cars and taxis were to be seen bearing hastily painted initials—F.A.I. (Federation of Anarchists of Iberia), P.S.U.C. (Union of Socialists and Communists), and P.O.U.M. (the left-wing Trotskyites)—and filled with shouting, heavily armed youths carried away with enthusiasm for their respective causes.

Apart from the militiamen, the most striking feature of the crowds on the street was their dowdy appearance. Not a smartly dressed woman was to be seen, while the men were generally coatless and hatless. It brought back to me an image of the Moscow I had seen in 1921, except that there was no lack of merchandise in the shop windows. The brilliant night life for which the city had been notorious had disappeared, including its elegant bordellos and assignation houses, while a curfew was in force from midnight to dawn.

Our first move, once we were settled at a hotel, was to obtain passes from the proper authorities for our departure to France on the seacoast route via Gerone, Perpignan, Montpellier and Marseille. We were directed from one authority to another, ending up at the Antifascist Militia of the Popular Front. A long queue stretched ahead of us until I bethought myself of my diplomatic passport. I confided it to Ehrhard, who was fluent in Spanish, and he returned shortly with a militiaman who ushered us at once into an enormous office where a young man in uniform gave us a friendly welcome. He was about to stamp our passports when he was interrupted by a telephone call, an historic one as it proved.

"Yes, this is the head of the Antifascist Militia. What can I do for you? . . . The Italian Consul General, yes? . . . You say you have heard that an Italian subject has been arrested and shot by our militia? My dear sir, there must be some mistake; it is true that people die in Barcelona, but no one is ever shot."

Whatever the facts—and we never learned them—the incident served as a pretext for Mussolini to break off diplomatic relations with the Spanish Republic. He refused to accept the explanation that people were dying in Spain only of natural causes.

With our visas permitting us to leave the country, we decided to remain over for one or two days to obtain a better appreciation of the situation. A most interesting contact we made before leaving the headquarters office of the Antifascist Militia was a young Frenchman who belonged to that organization. In view of his friendliness, we adjourned to a nearby café. Brought up in Russia as the son of a French consular officer, he had identified himself with the revolutionary movement in

1917 in resentment at his mistreatment by the czarist police for whistling a revolutionary song of whose character he was quite ignorant. After Russia, he had participated in the abortive Hungarian and German communist revolutions and, with their failure, he had become a journalist in Paris. In the belief that a revolutionary situation was brewing in Spain, he had come to Barcelona in February.

Ehrhard asked if he were a Communist. "No. I am not. I have never been able to adjust myself to that party's discipline. Forgive the expression but, after years of revolutionary activity, I have concluded that politics is a whore *(la politique c'est une putain)*. Life would lose all its meaning for me if our struggle to improve the welfare of the working class were reduced to nothing more than a struggle for power by one faction against another."

My mind went back to the Russia I had known in 1921 to 1923. The hopes he was voicing were those I had heard from Muktarov and Skvartsov. Stalin had ground them under his heels.

Our interlocutor described for us the defense of Barcelona. On the eve of the decisive day of July 17, it was general knowledge that the Army was preparing a *coup d'état*. The one means for the defense of the city was to assemble in the streets before the military acted. At dawn on the seventeenth, when he saw people streaming out of their homes in answer to an appeal by the Popular Front, he was convinced that victory was imminent. The immediate problem was that of obtaining arms. He assembled a group of some forty workers in a truck which they drove about until coming upon a military detachment armed with rifles and machine guns.

"Upon which, we drove toward them with terrific speed, braked to a stop and, before the troops could recover from their astonishment, I shouted to them to abandon their officers and come over to us, that it would be a crime to fire on their own people. Our fate was hanging by a hair until they responded and we obtained our first arms.

"With reinforcements and arms we drove to an important square held by the Army. When I saw that a body of men had been told off to attack us, I gave orders for withdrawal down a side street. Then I ordered half my detachment to take stations in the windows of the second floor of a building and to fire only when I fired my pistol. The other half of my men were posted in the entryways of adjacent buildings. When the troops opposing us had advanced into the street, I took aim at the commander and fired six shots in rapid succession. A fusillade from my men posted at the windows threw the enemy into confusion, while the other half of my detachment rushed to attack at close range. It was all over in a few minutes. This gives you some idea of how Barcelona was recovered from the Army fascists and how the Republic was preserved."

After lunching together at Los Caracoles, we strolled on the Ramblas. Our friend pointed out a gutted church from whose belfry he and his men had been fired on in July. "When we entered the church to seize the offenders, I gave strict orders that the priests should be spared, not suspecting that they had participated in the firing. It was only when several had been seized with arms that I ordered their execution."

Visiting the Department of Agitation and Propaganda I was informed that the only foreigners in that organization or with the Popular Front were French, German anti-Nazis and Italian anti-Fascists. As we emerged again on the Ramblas, a procession was forming to honor a sixteen-year-old boy who had fallen at the front. There was no music. As the procession got under way, bearing various banners of their organization, the throngs on the street raised clenched fists in the anti-Fascist salute.

That evening, we dined at Los Caracoles in company of a group of young Frenchmen who had arrived that day from Perpignan with funds for the Spanish Popular Front. They were typical of youths who, in the United States, would have been attending sporting events, with their thoughts far removed from serious concerns. The evening was passed in a discussion of politics and the international situation on which their lives and their welfare and that of their families depended. Now, when I go through Perpignan or other European cities, my mind reverts to those earnest young men, so attractive, so full of youthful dreams.

As Ehrhard and I returned to our hotel, the tramp of many feet could be heard gathering momentum ahead of us in the darkness. We moved to one side with other pedestrians when, out of the night, there loomed, like ghosts, a body of militiamen with military packs and steel helmets. The majority were mere boys with pinched faces, the older ones with unkempt beards. Someone alongside remarked that they were troops back from Majorca after an unsuccessful attempt to regain that island for the Republic. There was not a sound as we watched them, other than the tramping of their feet and the rustle of the autumn leaves in the trees lining the Ramblas.

Where are they now? The great majority undoubtedly perished in the initial test of 1936–39 between democracy and fascism. The tragedy of it all was that the lines drawn were far from clear-cut. The fascists were on one side of the barricades and, on the other, democratic foes cheek by jowl with totalitarian Russia. It was the disunity of purpose of those supporting Republican Spain which ensured a Franco victory. I did not see this then, but I did note at the time that the struggle in Spain had far more than local importance, that it represented a fight "which may still have to be fought, perhaps in France, Great Britain and the United States unless democracy is to lie down without a struggle before political gangsterism."

We set out the next day for Nice, where Ehrhard left me and I joined my wife at Èze-sur-Mer. From there we headed for Athens to take ship for Egypt, passing by Lake Garda and Riva and thence along the Dalmatian coast through Spalato, or Split, to Dubrovnik. From the magnificent Gulf of Kotor we began the ascent into Montenegro, through Cetinje, a primitive hamlet. The country was far from reflecting the atmosphere of that Marsovia into which Franz Lehar transformed Montenegro in one of the most delightful of all operettas, *The Merry Widow*. We emerged from the mountains at Petch where seventeen years before Milt Lockwood and I had been given a moving reception as Americans. I had no desire to face our former Yugoslav friends after our failure to realize the hopes that they had expressed so confidently in 1919. We pressed on toward Athens and our destination, Egypt.

The Anglo-Egyptian treaty negotiations had temporarily stabilized the Egyptian crisis. It was possible to relax. In consequence we resumed our excursions into the desert, our greatest source of distraction. Once we took ship from Suez to Hurghada, where we drove over a little-traveled route along the Red Sea to Kosseir. From there we headed due west and, after surmounting an escarpment of savage grandeur, we arrived at the edge of the desert separating us from the Nile. We reduced the air in our tires and, taking care not to waggle the steering wheel, headed west, with no track to guide us, over what appeared to be an endless expanse of sand. Our only compass was the sun. Our main preoccupation was to keep moving as long as we were in sand. At length, after an hour or more, the verdant Nile Valley loomed on the horizon. We made for the nearest village, which was on a main road but twenty miles north of Luxor. There is a fascination in the desert to be found nowhere else in nature—the brooding loneliness, a silence of a spectral character. The loneliness is deeper than that of the sea. In the desert there is no least sound, no echo except possibly in the mind.

From time to time, we explored the world's oldest monasteries, at Wadi Natrun and at St. Anthony's, reached only by a ill-defined track near the Red Sea. The most interesting was St. Catherine's, a two-day journey by car over the Sinai Peninsula. There, the nineteenth-century scholar Konstantin von Tischendorf had found in a wastebin one of the oldest surviving manuscripts of the Bible, which he acquired for a pittance. It passed to the Czar and was later purchased by the British Museum from the Soviet Government. In 1930, Kirsopp Lake of Harvard offered ten thousand dollars for permission to photograph only the title pages of the manuscript treasures remaining in the monastery. Even the personal intervention of King Ibn Saud did not overcome the obduracy of the ecclesiastical authorities. They had never recovered emotionally from the loss, through ignorance, of their most precious manuscript.

Such was the suspicion aroused by the Lake negotiations, in which I had participated, that, when I later visited St. Catherine's, I was refused entry into the library. But I had at least some glimpse of the monastery's history when I was shown the refectory, where coats of arms of Crusaders had been carved to commemorate their stay. The outward aspect of the monastery would alone have repaid a visit. Enclosed by ancient walls, it is situated in a small oasis forming the cleft of a narrow valley. The sudden sight of it, after a long journey over the desert and stony hills of Sinai, hidden as a splotch of greenery in an otherwise barren canyon, calls to mind a deceptive mirage.

Egypt itself, with its ancient monuments and the Nile, which threads its way from central Africa to water the crops of a virtually rainless country, the graceful feluccas skimming over its waters and the stately palm trees standing along its bank, had something of a mirage-like character. A part of all this, of the desert and of life in Cairo in those days, I sought to put in a novel, half fact, entitled *Escape to Cairo*. It fell so flat when published in 1933 that I conceived an aversion for it and could only bring myself to look at it again after twenty years. When I did, I read many passages with incredulity, asking myself, "Was it I who actually wrote these?"

One quotation with a political overtone will suffice, an exchange between a Turkish diplomat, my very dear friend Sevki Pasha, one of the most perfect gentlemen I have ever known, who contributed greatly to my development, and the hero, an American. The time was 1936.

> "I admire the English. I spent five years, five very happy years in the Turkish Legation in London. The English are a great race. They have exercised a steadying influence in the world now for several centuries. Like all empires, they have now reached their apogee and are in decline. As the British Empire disintegrates—and the process of disintegration is already to be seen—the same unsettlement of forces will take place as occurred with the decline of the Roman Empire."
>
> "What world force in your view is likely to take its place?"
>
> "Who knows? America might if it were older and more mature. I see no single force capable of taking at this time the place of the British Empire. Perhaps it may represent the last great empire of the world."

This was an epitome of one lesson I had drawn from my five years in Cairo. I had drawn another from my visit to Spain—that the struggle there was a dress rehearsal for one between totalitarianism and human dignity. A third was brought home by what I had seen in Egypt and Spain—that the obtuseness of those in authority was heading us all toward disaster.

12
WARTIME POLICY IN NORTH AFRICA

*W*hen France fell and signed an armistice with Germany on June 22, 1940, the free world held its breath. Would England follow next?

I was at that time on duty in the Department of State in Washington, and responsible for our relations with Saudi Arabia, Palestine, Egypt, Libya, Cyrenaica, Tunisia and Morocco.

In those summer months of 1940, our attention was concentrated on North Africa and, in particular, on how and by what means something could be saved from the wreckage of France. By incredible obtuseness, Hitler had granted armistice terms to France leaving the French Empire, including French North Africa (Tunisia, Algeria and Morocco), free of Axis occupation and even free of any Axis controls other than the right given, under the armistice terms, to Italy to maintain a small armistice control commission in French North Africa, and to Germany to have a few port control officers.

One may only explain Hitler's obtuseness by his confidence that the war was over and that England's surrender was only a matter of weeks. There were some in the Department of State and in the War and Navy Departments who shared this view.

Contrary to the popular view and to that portion of the American press which delights in baiting the State Department and the American Foreign Service, representing them as stumbling and uninformed, the

121

Department, even before the outbreak of war, was continuously taking stock of the situation as it was likely to evolve and devising means as to how American interests might best be protected. There can perhaps be no better illustration of this than the forethought which went into the means by which French North Africa might be preserved for the Allies. This forethought, which found expression in the North African economic accord with General Weygand, paved the way for the Allied landings in North Africa on November 8, 1942.

The germ of that accord was born as early as October 1940, and by that date, if not before, there was full recognition by the United States Government of the supreme strategic importance of French North Africa to the Allies.

As early as July 1939, I was called upon, in addition to my multifarious routine duties (we were at that time only seven officers in the Near Eastern Division), to prepare for Secretary Hull an analysis of the strategic aspects of the situation in North Africa and the Mediterranean in the event of a new World War. The study was completed on August 7, 1939, slightly less than a month before the outbreak of hostilities. Most outstanding conclusions were that, in the event of a new World War, Spain would have much to lose and little to gain by supporting the Axis Powers. It was assumed, therefore, that Spain would probably remain neutral in the event of a new World War.

France was believed capable of successfully defending its North African possessions.

Italy was considered virtually invulnerable to attack in Libya, but not in a position to invade successfully either Tunisia or Egypt from Libya.

The view was expressed that the Mediterranean itself and its shores would be the seats of very important operations as soon as war broke out.

With the advent of war, the Allies could count upon being able to command Gibralter—giving access to the Mediterranean in the West—as well as the Dardanelles and the Suez Canal—giving access to the Mediterranean in the East.

The greatest difficulty to Allied freedom of communications through the Mediterranean, it was anticipated, would come in the central portion of that sea where Sicily almost touches North Africa and where Italian submarines and aircraft might render the passage of that strait extremely difficult for Allied vessels.

Finally, it was concluded that, on the strength of the known factors, Great Britain and France should be in a position to hold their own generally in the Mediterranean and North Africa and, in time, to reduce Italy by the effective weight of economic pressure, if no other.

Reviewing this analysis some thirty-five years later, little should have been altered. We were principally off in overestimating the invulnerability of Italy in Libya.

I shall never forget the reception this analysis received from the officer in military intelligence to whom I submitted it for review. After he had finished reading it, the officer observed me with concern: "This is not going to be published, is it? You are not a journalist by any chance?" The inference was that I was a newspaperman masquerading as an officer of the Department of State.

Captain Bode, in naval intelligence (who later committed suicide after he had lost two ships in the war), with whom I constantly conferred and in whose keen intelligence and mordant humor I found great delight, used to emit a growl in the best Bode tradition whenever he saw me approaching. "Some more of your pipe dreams or plain statements of fact this time?"

With the fall of France, our studies became less speculative, but we still endeavored to forecast the course of events, not always unsuccessfully.

The Battle of Britain was launched by the German Air Force in its first heavy onslaught on July 10, 1940. It reached its peak in the week ending August 17. The crux, however, according to Winston Churchill, came on September 15, "one of the decisive battles of the war."

On September 7, there was an announcement of the intention of the Vichy Government to send General Weygand to North Africa to direct French North African activities and, a month later, on October 9, General Weygand's arrival in Algeria was announced.

I was lunching that day with Wallace Murray, chief of the Division of Near Eastern Affairs; Paul Alling, assistant chief; and Harry Villard of the Division. As we came out, I remarked: "The New York *Times* reports this morning that General Weygand arrived in Algeria as delegate general of the French Government. I wonder if something couldn't be done with Weygand to hold North Africa as an outpost for us?"

Wallace Murray turned toward me and asked, "What makes you think that?" My observation had set his mind to working, and in those days it didn't let much escape it.

"I can't really say. I just have a hunch. French North Africa needs supplies and we are in a position to furnish them. That might be the wedge."

"Get to work on that right away," Wallace countered. "Let's develop the idea."

At least three other men in different parts of the world were toying with the same idea: Emmanuel Monick, secretary general of the French residency in Morocco; Leon Marchal, head of the economic section of the French residency; and David Eccles, at that time head of the British economic warfare section on the Iberian peninsula.

Let us see how these threads in time were woven together.

On August 26, Freeman Mathews, chargé d'affaires in Vichy, reported to the Department a conversation he had had with M. Monick, newly appointed secretary general of the French protectorate in Morocco. It was on the eve of the latter's departure for his new post. M. Monick stressed the desirability of closer economic relations between French Morocco and the United States, pointing out the strong independent spirit in Morocco, his own chagrin at the armistice and subsequent developments and the excellent morale of the unbeaten French colonial forces in North Africa, and suggesting that British policy toward Morocco was likely to be cooperative.

Upon Monick's arrival in Morocco, he found a sympathetic adherent to his ideas in Leon Marchal. It was decided that Marchal would proceed to Madrid and seek discreet contact with the British there.

In Madrid, Marchal had the good fortune to find a principal representative of the British Ministry of Economic Warfare, David Eccles, who had been dreaming the same dream as Monick and who did not need to be convinced of the political implications of Allied economic relations with French North Africa. The two—Marchal and Eccles—worked out the draft of a British-French Moroccan clearing agreement involving the exchange of sugar and tea for Moroccan phosphates. As this exchange could not be made directly, it was to be undertaken through a triangular trade arrangement involving Spain.

Meanwhile Monick, not content to work only through the British in Madrid, commissioned A. C. Reed, of the Socony-Vacuum Oil Company in Morocco, to proceed to Washington to pursue the subject with Jean Monnet, a former colleague in the French embassy in London who, in 1940, had joined the British Purchasing Commission in Washington. Reed was to endeavor at the same time to learn the views of the Department of State.

Before Reed's arrival and before any firm ideas had taken shape, we began to explore with officers of the Trade Agreements Division (Southworth and Ross) and officers of the International Economic Adviser's Office (Livesay, and Stinebower and others) the possibility of a limited exchange of goods with Morocco. A meeting to this end was held in the Department on October 15 with no definite decision being reached, certain skepticism concerning the value such an arrangement having already manifested itself on the part of Herbert Feis, the Economic Adviser.

While these exploratory talks were proceeding and I was preparing a memorandum entitled "The Political Implications of American-Moroccan Trade," unexpected but nonetheless welcome moral support for the views we were urging in the Near Eastern Division was given in the appearance of Arthur Reed, Monick's unofficial emissary. Reed, whom I had first met in Egypt some years previously, called at my office in the Department on October 25.

I can still recall my excitement when he set forth the object of the mission. "This is providential . . . You are manna from heaven. I am writing a paper on this very subject, trying to convince others in the Department of the soundness of the proposition, and you arrive as living proof." I had the feeling that victory was now ours in the Near Eastern Division and that our views as to the political importance of trade with Morocco would readily be accepted by the economists, buttressed as our views were by such confirmation as Reed had to give them. However, I reckoned without the conservatism of our adversaries.

Here is what Reed had to tell me: He had been sent by Monick to investigate the possibility of obtaining permission for small quantities of petroleum products to be transported from Aruba in the Dutch West Indies to French Morocco in return for the export to the United States of certain strategic minerals such as manganese, cobalt and other minerals available in Morocco. The French protectorate authorities would be unable, under the terms of the armistice with Germany, to agree to obtain navicerts for any shipments to Morocco, but General Noguès, the Resident-General, was willing to give assurances that none of the petroleum products introduced into French Morocco under the arrangement envisaged would be transshipped from that country.

Reed said that, in his opinion, the problem had a political significance transcending the relatively small amount of trade which might be involved and thereby confirmed the conclusions already independently reached by the political officers concerned with the problem in the Division of Near Eastern Affairs. He expressed the view that such an exchange of goods would tend to withdraw French Morocco from its economic tie with metropolitan France and, indirectly, the Axis.

I asked Reed if he thought the views he expressed represented those of Noguès and Monick. He replied that, of course, the French protectorate authorities could not be expected to express themselves so freely, but that he had gained the impression that they were sincerely desirous of preventing French Morocco from falling into the hands of the Axis. It was his understanding that he had been requested by Monick to come to the United States with that consideration in mind.

I asked what significance he attached to the appointment of General Weygand as Delegate-General of the Vichy Government in French North Africa. Reed offered as a reasonable hypothesis that General Weygand had been sent to Africa as a form of insurance by those in Vichy not unalterably opposed to the British, with a view to using him as a rallying point for protecting French North Africa against German absorption in the event German demands on France proved too onerous to accept.

Reed was introduced to other officials of the State Department immediately concerned with the problem and he had a number of conferences with Jean Monnet, as well as with officers of the British embassy, including in particular Helm and Marris, two of those most sympathetically disposed to what we had in view.

Out of these conversations, there developed a proposal that Reed serve as the liaison in Morocco between the British embassy in Washington and the French protectorate authorities in developing the trade arrangements proposed, and that the communication facilities of the Department should be made available to the British embassy and Reed, this owing to the obvious impossibility of direct contact between the French and British authorities. I drafted a memorandum recommending the approval of this procedure on the ground that "from our larger defense interests it is important that French Morocco should not fall into hostile hands, and anything done to bolster the morale of the authorities and people of that area and to avoid the collapse, whether economic or political, of French Morocco is all to the good."

The memorandum, approved by Wallace Murray, chief of the Near Eastern Division, on November 1, was forwarded on that date to those officers in the Department most directly concerned, namely, Harry Hawkins, Herbert Feis, Ray Atherton, Henry F. Grady and Adolph A. Berle.

Shortly thereafter when Berle, the Assistant Secretary of State, had time to study the proposal, he found it of sufficient interest to summon Wallace Murray and me to his office to discuss it. This conference may be considered an important milestone in the formulation of American policy toward a North African economic accord. It was not only the first time this policy had been examined and attention given to its implications by one of the higher executives of the Department, but out of this conference there resulted decisions which led directly to the Weygand-Murphy accord of February 26, 1941.

At this conference Berle stated his belief that the basis of using Reed, an American, as an agent for British economic exchanges with Morocco was too narrow. He asked if any objection could be perceived to the United States dealing directly on the subject with the French protectorate authorities or with General Weygand in Algeria. Murray replied that we had not suggested a broader approach in the belief that the narrower one was all that we might hope to achieve for the time being.

The ways and means of an approach were then discussed and it was agreed that two telegrams would be drafted and sent by the Department, one to Consul General Felix Cole in Algiers instructing him to approach General Weygand[1], and the other a telegram to J. C. White, American diplomatic agent in Tangier, directing him to pursue parallel conversations on the subject of the possible exchange of products with Monick, Secretary General of the French protectorate in Morocco.

In the midst of these developments, a message was received from Chargé d'Affaires Mathews in Vichy recounting a further visit he had received from Monick. The latter had proceeded from Morocco to France on business and had called on November 6 at the embassy to stress again the importance of closer economic relations between Morocco and the United States, giving it as his view that Morocco had to look toward the Atlantic for the time being. He expressed the opinion that the question of increasing Moroccan-American trade was of the greatest importance as a means of maintaining Morocco's freedom of action. He reported that he had charged Reed, of the Socony-Vacuum Oil Company, to visit the United States to investigate the possibilities of obtaining supplies of gasoline but had had no word from Reed concerning the outcome of his mission. He added that both General Weygand and General Noguès were determined not to accept any German foothold in Morocco.

The views of Monick were in striking confirmation of those set forth in my memorandum already prepared on the political implications of American-Moroccan trade, which was circulating among the officers of the Department when Mathews' account of his interview with Monick was received. As it was important to keep the latter's interest alive, we obtained the approval of Berle and Welles, the then Undersecretary of State, to the dispatch of a telegram over Secretary Hull's signature to Vichy on November 9, instructing the embassy to inform Monick that the Department had received and read with interest the account of his views and that consideration was being given to the possibility of arriving at some arrangement along the lines suggested by him. This was the first definte decision of policy on this subject by the United States Government.

In the meanwhile, following the conference among Murray, Berle and myself, we set to work drafting the necessary telegraphic instructions to our legation in Tangier and consulate general in Algiers concerning the exploratory conversations which those offices were to institute with the French protectorate authorities in Morocco on the one hand and General Weygand on the other. In support of the policy formulated in the telegrams, there was attached a more comprehensive memorandum, dated November 12, 1940, in which it was reiterated that "from our larger defense interests it is important that French Morocco should not fall into hostile hands, and anything done to bolster the morale of the authorities and people of that area and to avoid the collapse, whether economic or political, of French Morocco, would appear to be in our interest."

The telegram to Algiers was dispatched on November 13, but the telegram to Tangier was held up for some ten days or two weeks.

I was concerned at that time not only with the problems of Morocco, but also with those of a considerable number of other countries, and I had completely lost sight of the telegram when Wallace Murray remarked to me one day: "By the way, has there been any reaction from Tangier to our telegram?"

I knew to whom the telegram had been routed for approval and I was able to track it down finally in the office of Herbert Feis, head of the Division of International Economic Affairs. When the telegram was found on his desk, he announced that he had no intention of approving it.

"See here," he said to me, "I consider this to be my war, and as long as I am where I am I don't intend to approve any project or measure which I consider would prejudice the forces fighting the Axis."

I asked him if he meant to imply that the officers of the Near Eastern Division were actuated by any less spirit of devotion to our country than he, adding that the measures we were proposing to facilitate American-Moroccan trade had been framed directly with a view to preventing Morocco from falling into the Axis orbit.

Feis declined to be moved by any argument. He stated that he was wholly opposed to the idea we had advanced, that he did not believe any advantageous results could or would come of it and that he did not propose to lend his support to it in any way.

I replied that that was his prerogative, but where there was a difference of opinion on policy between different divisions of the Department, it should be resolved by an assistant secretary, the undersecretary or the secretary himself. In the present case, the policy in question had been approved by Assistant Secretary Berle. If Feis opposed the policy, he had no right to block action by holding the telegram on his desk but should attach his dissenting views to the draft and let it pass on for review by other interested officers.

Feis expressed his concurrence and stated that he had already prepared his views. They were:

> NE's memorandum on the political bearings of this matter is of great interest and its conclusions may be correct. However, I think it ought to be pointed out:
>
> That all the reports regarding the possibility of Morocco and the North African colonies giving assistance to Great Britain are conjectural and prospective.
>
> That the possibility of cooperation with Germany may be more difficult than is brought out in this analysis. . .

As a result, it was only on December 3 that the telegram to Tangier finally left the Department.

It is only fair to Feis to state that the skeptical view taken by him toward our argument that Morocco and French North Africa might best be preserved for the Allies by binding it economically to us was by no means an isolated point of view. From this time forward and to the very eve of the landings by Allied troops in French North Africa in November 1942, officers of the Treasury Department and of the Bureau of Economic Warfare, as well as Feis, not only displayed a lack of sympathy with the policy outlined, which came finally to be adopted, but even interposed obstacles to the development of trade exchanges with French North Africa in the mistaken view, wholly disproved by subsequent events, that economic aid to French North Africa meant economic aid to the Axis.

Toward the end of November or the beginning of December, rumors began to circulate in the Department that the question of an understanding between the United States and the authorities of French North Africa was to be taken out of the hands of the Department. The report was that the White House had taken an interest in the matter. A little later we learned that the President was sending Robert Murphy to French North Africa to report on the situation and to engage in direct conversations with General Weygand and other French officials there. Murphy, who was already under assignment to the embassy in Vichy as counselor, was to take up residence in Algiers to be in direct contact with Weygand.

The sequence of events would appear to have been as follows. On November 6, when Chargé d'Affaires Mathews reported his conversation with Monick, he sent at the same time a telegram to Bullitt, former ambassador to France, then in Washington, inviting the latter's particular attention to the report of Mathews' talk with Monick. As we know from Cordell Hull's *Memoirs,* Bullitt, even when ambassador to France, had been accustomed to deal more often than not directly with the President rather than the Department of State. Presumably, in line with the highly personalized diplomacy which the President favored, Bullitt went to the President and had no difficulty inducing him to approve the assignment to North Africa of one of Bullitt's old Paris protégés, Murphy, to investigate and promote the possibility of safeguarding French North Africa from the Axis. As the *Roosevelt and Hopkins* study by Robert Sherwood reveals, neither the President nor Hopkins had confidence in the professional cadres of the Department. They were persuaded that it was more desirable to work in foreign affairs outside the State Department. Bullitt's suggestion, therefore, was all the more likely to be agreeable to the President, offering as it did the opportunity to bypass the Department by dealing directly with Murphy.

It would take us too far afield to find the answer to the President's lack of confidence in the career officers of the Department and of the Foreign Service.[2] Many of Roosevelt's early friends and acquaintances in the Department and Foreign Service were from the Groton-Harvard group, whose private wealth had enabled them to enter the diplomatic service at a time when the service was denied to any American not of independent means. Until 1924, the highest salary paid an American diplomatic officer was three thousand dollars, with no allowances of any kind. Prior to 1924, therefore, the Foreign Service was of necessity made up to a large extent of dilettantes who were more interested in the social entré the service gave them in European capitals than in the little work which then fell to American diplomats. As this was an era when ambassadors and ministers were appointed almost exclusively for political considerations, the service attracted few men of ambition. The President, understandably, had no patience with the playboy type of public servant with which our diplomatic service was so largely filled before 1924. After the enactment of the Rogers Act in 1924, which opened the service to men of ability and not exclusively men of wealth, it was some little time before the deadwood which had been drawn into the service before 1924 could be eliminated. Roosevelt, however, had formed his ideas of the service from the wealthy Newport and Bar Harbor types whom he had known personally, and he had little knowledge of and failed to adjust himself to a service which by 1932 had been radically transformed, made up, as it came more and more to be, of hardworking Americans from all walks of life whose qualifications were ability rather than wealth.

While this is to a certain extent conjectural, one thing may be definitely asserted. From the end of 1940 onward, the political direction of American interests in French North Africa became less and less a matter in which the State Department had a controlling hand and more and more one with which the President personally concerned himself. As we know from Yalta and other political milestones, this was to become more and more the President's practice, namely withdrawal from dependence upon the experts of the Department and the assumption by the President personally of the political as well as the military strategy of the war. The greatest genius known to the world could not have assumed so herculean a task with any prospect of complete success.

When Murphy was preparing in Washington to proceed to French North Africa, he did not confer either with Assistant Secretary Berle or Wallace Murray, who had performed the spadework for the task for which he had been entrusted. Consequently, when it was found that

Murphy had departed without the papers that had been prepared to assist him in his undertaking, notably the memoranda to which reference has already been made, these had to be flown to Lisbon with orders to the legation there to send them if necessary by special messenger to Murphy in Algiers. Some months later, when I met him in North Africa, I asked him the reason for his not having conferred with Assistant Secretary Berle, if not with Wallace Murray, before departing on his important mission. His answer was that he was not sure as to the character of Berle's relations with Bullitt—a striking reflection of the personalized diplomacy of the administration.

As these events were taking place, my four-year period of assignment in Washington was drawing to a close. I had no notion what post in the field was in store for me. One afternoon, my chief, Wallace Murray, called me into his office to announce that the Department intended to assign me to the legation in Tangier as acting chief of the mission. J.C. White, who headed the post at the time as diplomatic agent and consul general, was being assigned as ambassador to Haiti. I was to have the title of chargé d'affaires *ad interim* and consul general, but this was later reconsidered and I went out as first secretary and consul with the title, while in charge, of chargé d'affaires *ad interim*. When I had been at my post for more than three years, an acquaintance inquired into the meaning of the abbreviation "a.i." in my title. I replied that nominally it meant "*ad interim*" but that, in this particular case, it might well be interpreted as meaning "*ad infinitum*."

Some of my friends in the Department were curious to know the reasons behind the fact that I was being sent out to undertake the responsibilities of a mission but was not being endowed with the authority which the title of diplomatic agent would have afforded me.

I have never been able to fathom why I was left in Tangier for four and a half years as chargé d'affaires *ad interim,* which must come close to setting a record for the incumbency of a post by a chargé. Some years later, when I met Kippy Tuck, the ambassador in Egypt, who had been chargé d'affaires in Vichy in 1942, he said, "I have been waiting for years to meet you to find out how you came to be assigned to Tangier for almost five years as chargé d'affaires."

I told him I had no more idea why than he. "The only possible explanation that I have yet been able to draw," I added, "is that the Department wished to conserve for Murphy a position senior to that of any officer in French North Africa, and this would have been manifestly impossible if I had been diplomatic agent and he only counselor."

Before I left for my post, Paul Alling, assistant chief of the Division, said to me: "You will find a staff in Tangier of only five or six. I think the

Department can arrange to let you have either an additional clerk or an additional vice consul, when you have had a chance to look around after your arrival and ascertain which you need the most."

From the time of my arrival, developments began to move so fast in North Africa that we not only had the clerk and vice consul but personnel began moving in in such numbers that, within another year and a half, our staff numbered sixty-five.

NOTES

[1] See Weygand, *Mémoires*. p. 483, for an account of the reaction to this telegram on the part of General Weygand.

[2] For example, reference is made to Sherwood's *Roosevelt and Hopkins* pages 115, 135, 216–27, 278, 629, 755–56, 774, 876.

13
ASSIGNMENT TO TANGIER

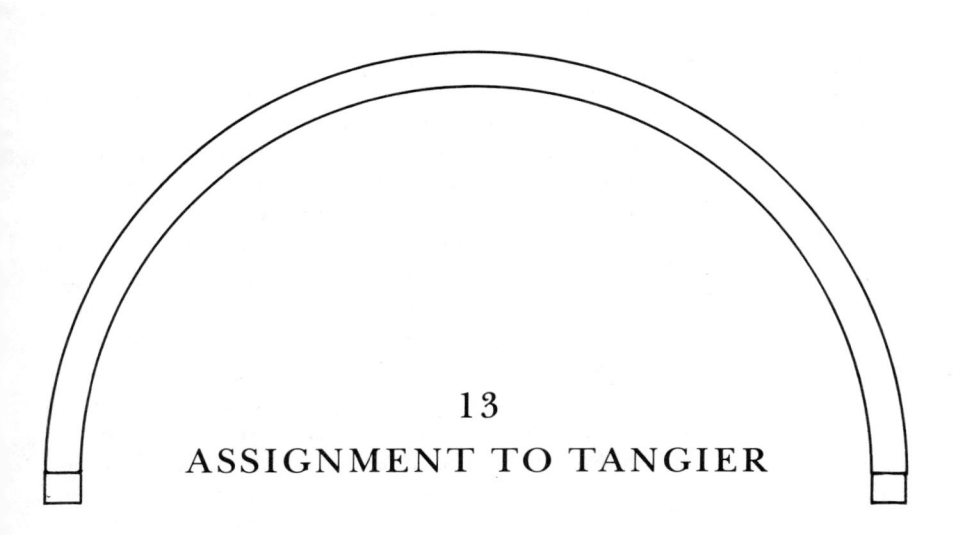

As late as the early part of this century, it was unsafe for European residents of Tangier to venture beyond the confines of the town. A Greek who did so, Perdicaris, had managed to cloak himself in the mantle of American citizenship and created an international incident when he was kidnaped by the Moorish chieftain Raisuli. The briefest note in diplomatic history, dispatched by the United States Government to the sultan, "Perdicaris alive or Raisuli dead," brought about the eventual release of Perdicaris. The note was drafted by Edwin Hood, dean of correspondents in Washington.

At the turn of this century, Morocco constituted the last rich prize remaining for distribution in Africa after the scramble of the Great Powers for colonial territory in the long era of imperialism drawing to a close at the end of the First World War. The intense rivalry among France, Great Britain and Germany which arose over the fate of Morocco was a measure of its great strategic importance.[1]

It was France that early coveted Morocco. Having acquired Algeria in the first half of the nineteenth century and Tunisia a little later, the French Republic aspired to the extension of its influence westward to embrace Morocco. Spain likewise became interested in Morocco, notably the northern coast, fronting as it did the Spanish peninsula. As for Great Britain, it had a vital interest in the fate of a country whose northern shores commanded the Straits of Gibraltar, a link in the lifeline of the British Empire.

In an effort to reconcile these international interests, a series of accords was negotiated among the interested powers in the decade immediately preceding the First World War. First in importance was the Anglo-French accord (*Entente Cordiale*) of 1904, a principal provision of which was the granting to Great Britain of a free hand in Egypt in return for a free hand for France in Morocco. One important limitation was imposed in the light of Britain's preoccupation with control of the Straits of Gibraltar. Article 7 forbade the erection of fortifications or strategic works on the Moroccan coast from Melilla to the mouth of the river Sebou, except on Spanish-owned territory (Melilla and Ceuta). Subsequent deals were made by France with Italy, providing for Italy's recognition of France's paramount rights in Morocco in return for French recognition of a free hand for Italy in Libya. Spanish approval of French aspirations in Morocco was obtained in an agreement which contemplated the cession to Spain of the northern part of Morocco as a zone of influence.

France had now cleared the decks for action with all interested powers save one—Germany. In 1905, the German Kaiser dramatically touched at Tangier in his yacht, landed and visited the German legation. There he made a resounding speech in which he recognized the sultan as an independent sovereign, asserted the principle of commercial equality for all nations in Morocco and proposed that Morocco be placed under international control.

As a consequence, a conference of powers interested in Morocco assembled at Algeciras in 1906, including representatives of Austria-Hungary, Belgium, France, Germany, Great Britain, Holland, Italy, Portugal, Russia, Spain, Sweden and the United States. From this conference there emerged the Act of Algeciras, constituting the international charter of Morocco. Although the integrity of the sultan's domains was reaffirmed in the Act, France and Spain retained the privileged political position they had carved out for themselves in Morocco. The Act affirmed the important principle of "ecomonic liberty without any inequality" for all countries, or the principle of the "open door." The United States entered a reservation that American interest was confined to an economic one and that American signature did not imply involvement in the political affairs of Morocco.

Germany continued to be dissatisfied after the Algeciras Conference with the prospect of French hegemony over Morocco and persisted in its blackmail of France. In 1911, internal disorders in Morocco led to the dispatch of French troops to Fez. Germany sought once again to shake France down. The German gunboat *Panther* was sent as a threatening gesture to Agadir, southernmost port of Morocco. For a moment it seemed as if Europe might be precipitated into a world war, with dispute over the division of the Moroccan spoils as the initial provocation. Great Britain interfered decisively, however, in Lloyd George's famous Mansion House speech. In return for the cession of almost half of the French Congo, Germany recognized, in effect, in the Franco-German Convention of 1911, France's preponderant interest in Morocco.

The way was now clear for France to legalize its position, and this was effected in the protectorate treaty concluded between France and the sultan on March 30, 1909, granting France a protectorate over Morocco and the exercise of all international responsibilities for Morocco through the French resident general, acting as minister for foreign affairs of the sultan. France concluded with Spain a convention granting a zone of influence or subprotectorate to that country in the northern part of Morocco. The convention provided for the eventual setting aside in the Spanish enclave of a special zone for Tangier under a system to be subsequently determined.

Thus, by 1912, the greater part of Morocco had come under the protection of France. A French resident general, established at Rabat, directed the affairs of Morocco on behalf of the sultan. A narrow strip in the north along the Mediterranean coast had devolved to Spain as a subprotectorate. The Spanish established a high commissioner at Tetuan, the capital, to direct the affairs of the Spanish protectorate. Here resided also the Sultan's representative for the Spanish Zone, the khalifa.

There still remained for solution the character of the Tangier zone at the extreme northwest tip of Africa, lying along the Straits of Gibraltar.

The international character of Tangier antedates by far the international rivalry displayed over Morocco. Although the Moroccan seat of government has never been in Tangier, all foreign diplomatic missions were maintained at that port from the eighteenth century until the end of World War II. In the latter part of the century, the diplomatic and consular representatives of the powers resided at Tetuan, only a few miles distant. The powers were forced to shift to Tangier when one of the foreign consuls, firing at game from the window of his house, shot and killed a Moor.

Having removed to Tangier, the consular corps began to meet to discuss questions of public health. In 1805, the sultan formally recognized their right to concern themselves with the public health of the port. In this work the American consul, first appointed to Tangier in 1791, participated with is colleagues. In 1840, the sultan issued a decree confirming the public health regulations drawn up by the consuls. These regulations became the organic act of the sanitary council. These functions were subsequently turned over to a hygienic council, which soon took on the functions of a city council. Of this council of twenty-six members, ten members were appointed directly by the foreign representatives.

The strategic significance of Tangier, lying opposite Gibraltar, had given Great Britain a particular interest in assuring itself that no great power should obtain control of the city and be afforded the opportunity to build up a counterpart to the Gibraltar fortress. It was on this account that Great Britain had insisted that France and Spain should assume the obligation not to erect any fortifications or strategic works along the northern Moroccan coast. For the same reason, the various international instruments concerning Morocco contained provisions envisaging an eventual special regime for Tangier.

Conversations were opened immediately before the First World War among Great Britain, France and Spain, looking toward the drafting of a special administrative regime for Tangier. These negotiations were interrupted with the outbreak of war and were not resumed until 1923. In 1923, a convention was concluded by Great Britain, France and Spain providing for the administration of the city of Tangier and a hinterland of restricted area under an international administration comprising a mixed court, a legislative assembly made up of representatives of the foreign and native communities, and a committee of control comprising representatives of the statutory powers, i.e., Great Britain, France and Spain, and those powers adhering to the Tangier Convention—Belgium, Portugal and the Netherlands. Italy subsequently became a statutory power in 1928, with the revision of the convention to include Italy, and Sweden later adhered to the convention, although never participating actively in the administration.

Although the United States, as early as 1787, with the conclusion of its first treaty with Morocco, had exhibited a special interest in that country, it did not accept the invitation of the powers to participate in the Tangier administration. The controlling reason was the disinclination of the United States in 1923 to become politically involved there.

A provision of the 1923 Tangier Convention was that the signatory powers would use their influence to persuade all the signatories of the Act of Algeciras to adhere to the Tangier Convention, with the exception of Germany, Austria and Hungary, which had renounced their rights and interest in Morocco in the peace treaties growing out of the First World War. The only signatory of the Act of Algeciras, other than the United States, which did not adhere to the Tangier Convention of 1923, was the U.S.S.R. Prior to 1945, no invitation was extended that power to participate in the Tangier Convention as a signatory of the Act of Algeciras, for the initial reason that Great Britain and France were not in diplomatic relations with the Soviet Union, and later for the reason that no interest was ever manifested by the Soviet Union to particiate in the administration.

Unlike other powers, the United States never relinquished its extraterritorial rights in either French or Spanish Morocco, and the failure of the United States to adhere to the Tangier Convention of 1923 ensured the maintenance of American extraterritorial rights in Tangier as well as the continued functioning of the American legation there, the only diplomatic representation remaining in Tangier after 1928. However anachronistic these rights, they ensured incalculable advantages to us in the fateful years of 1935–45.

On the eve of June 14, 1940, at the time of the collapse of France, Spanish military forces from the Spanish zone moved without warning into the international zone of Tangier with the announced purpose of insuring the neutrality of Tangier and maintaining public order.

It was not until November 3, 1940, that the Spanish military authorities in occupation of Tangier attempted any interference with the international administration. On that date, an order was published dissolving the international committee of control and the legislative assembly and proclaiming the head of the occupation troops as governor general and delegate of the Spanish high commissioner in Morocco.

For the United States, the situation was complicated by the fact that we had never recognized the Spanish protectorate in Morocco; there was all the less reason for our recognition of an act of force by Spain in Tangier.

The British Government, which had more direct interests involved, was constrained immediately following these events to conclude a provisional agreement with the Spanish Government concerning Tangier. In return for British recognition of the Spanish occupation of Tangier as an *etat de fait,* the Spanish Government guaranteed to British subjects the right freely to enter and leave Tangier "as they are at present doing." This was interpreted as relieving British subjects of the necessity of obtaining Spanish visas or of submitting to any control of their movements. This actually became of enormous benefit to us for, shortly after my arrival in Tangier, I asserted the same right for American citizens, on the ground of most-favored-nation treatment, which the Spanish were not in a position to refuse. As a result, we were able to staff the legation, preparatory to the landings, with an unrestricted number of military, air and naval personnel, as well as intelligence and counterintelligence agents, to the intense annoyance of the Axis. If we had had to depend upon Spanish visas for their assignments to Tangier, it is certain that our staff would have been reduced to a handful. Certainly it would never have been possible for the legation in Tangier to become, as it did, the center of American intelligence for French North Africa, under the direction of Colonel William A. Eddy, nominally the naval attaché, and Colonel William C. Bentley, military attaché.

While incorporating Tangier in the Spanish zone of Morocco, the Spanish Government, in the provisional agreement respecting Tangier concluded with the British Government in December 1940 and January 1941, pledged itself not to fortify Tangier. At the same time, a special economic regime for Tangier was assured. This regime, providing for the continued maintenance of a free exchange market and unhampered imports, was introduced by the Spanish administration early in 1941 and was maintained throughout the Spanish occupation of Tangier. In addition, the Spanish guaranteed to Great Britain the continued functioning of the British post office, the British Eastern Telegraph Company, and the English, French and Spanish editions of the Tangier Gazette, a British newspaper. What these assurances meant was that mail could be sent freely from Tangier to the outside world through the British post office without any Spanish or Axis censorship and, likewise, telegrams through the Eastern Telegraph Company, while a press favorable to the Allies was assured through at least one newspaper. It would be difficult to exaggerate the benefits which these concessions conferred, first upon the British and then upon ourselves, in granting the Allies in this tiny corner of Africa a site, however small and circumscribed, where we were able to build up completely undisturbed and unrestricted a propaganda and intelligence center whose network extended eventually through the whole of Morocco, Algeria and Tunisia.

Thus, at the beginning of the Second World War, Morocco had been divided into a French and a Spanish protectorate and the international zone of Tangier. Spain, seeking to extend its influence in Morocco, had taken advantage of the first weakness displayed by France to march into Tangier and incorporate that zone, to all ostensible purposes, as a part of the Spanish protectorate.

One of the great questions was whether Spain, on its own initiative or abetted by Germany, would take further advantage of French weakness and seek to extend its protectorate southward into Morocco in an area to which it had long had pretensions. An even more ominous question was whether the Axis would strike through Spain at Gibraltar and continue across the Mediterranean to establish itself in Morocco, Algeria and Tunisia, with Germany and Spain dividing Morocco, and Germany and Italy distributing Algeria and Tunisia between themselves.

The United States was now committed to the promotion of closer economic exchanges as a means of detaching Morocco from Axis influence. Disclaiming throughout its history any political interest in Morocco, the United States was compelled by contemporary events to a reexamination of American foreign policy because the political fate of Morocco would become vital to the defense of the United States.

Such was the situation that faced me as I took charge of the legation in Tangier on February 3, 1941. Happily, we possessed the almost unrivaled body of treaty rights which were to serve us well in the fateful months ahead.

When I first arrived in Tangier, after spending many years in the Near and Middle East, I realized that I would have a difficult time, as only acting head of the mission in Tangier, in obtaining due recognition. Prestige counts for far more in Moslem lands than in the West, and it was necessary for me to be zealous in claiming the respect due even the acting head of an American diplomatic establishment.

I called on the mendoub, but he made no move to return the call. After a lapse of some ten days, I sent for Mr. Abrines, the dragoman of the legation. I had evolved what I thought was a diplomatic way to bring home to the mendoub his omission to return my call, without leaving any rancor.

"Mr. Abrines," I said, "I want you to call on the mendoub and convey my deep regret that illness has prevented him from leaving the mendoubia since I saw him last."

"But, sir, the mendoub is in perfectly good health; I saw him only a day or two ago."

"Do as I tell you," I replied.

Mr. Abrines returned some little while later with a broad grin on his face. "I called and transmitted your message, just as you had directed me to do. The mendoub looked very puzzled. 'But, Mr. Abrines, I have not been ill at all.' And then he smiled. 'Go and tell the American representative that I shall be calling on him tomorrow morning.'"

I think the mendoub must have himself greatly enjoyed the telling of the story for, from that time, there was no suggestion of the want of respect toward the legation. The Arab, as well as the Moor, has a very keen sense of humor and also a very deep appreciation of personal and official dignity. They particularly appreciate a point being brought home to them, even at their expense, when it is done with a touch of humor.

The appreciation of these factors was one of the secrets of the success of the French protectorate administration over Berbers and Arabs alike.

In my relations with the Moroccan officials, I was always scrupulous to respect the obligation which the United States Government had assumed, when recognizing the French protectorate in 1917, namely, the right of the French protectorate administration to be the sole intermediary between foreigners and the maghzen (the native administration). Very early during my residence in Morocco, efforts were made on the part of Moroccan officials to establish direct contact with the legation. It was not possible, of course, for me to decline to receive such officials, but whenever I had occasion to entertain them at the legation, the French consul general in Tangier was always invited at the same time.

Other American officials not under my jurisdiction were not so scrupulous in this regard. One of the control vice consuls, who had delusions of grandeur which included that of filling the role of a second Lawrence of Arabia, spent much of his time, until he learned the error of his ways, in propaganda work among the natives.

Referring to this, I outlined to the Department of State, in September 1941, what I believed our policy should be toward the native population. It was suggested that we avoid the cultivation of relations involving internal Moroccan politics. Not only was this politic but it was an obligation we owed the French administration. The French protectorate authorities, it was pointed out, were known to be extremely sensitive on this score and they had successfully resisted the efforts of the German Armistice Commission to establish relations with the Moors. While not suggesting that our officers should refrain from all contacts with the Moorish population, it was believed they should eschew relations with those Moors known to be actively identified with the underground nationalist movement, which might tend to complicate the French maintenance of public security by encouraging the Moorish population in the belief that we were sympathetic to that movement.

In the spring of 1942, the same control officer who, I may repeat, was not under my jurisdiction, without consulting either the legation of the French authorities, established himself in Fez, a nerve center of the nationalist movement. To cloak his activities, he installed himself in the British consulate at Fez, which had been closed in 1940, and with other British consulates in Morocco, entrusted to our safekeeping. It was pretended that it was serving as an American consulate. This was one of numerous instances of a division of authority which occasioned constant embarrassment to the legation in Tangier, nominally responsible for our political relations with Morocco.

The first we heard of the development was when the diplomatic cabinet in Rabat informed Consul General Russell in Casablanca, to whom the control officer was nominally assigned, but who had no more authority over him than the legation, that General Noguès could not tolerate the use of the British consulate by us or the presence in that "nerve center of Arab nationalism" of the officer in question.

It would seem to be inconsistent with our friendly relations with both the local French and Spanish authorities for us to endeavor to undermine their position with the native population unless we had determined such a course of action would be in our interests. It was not believed in fact that such would serve our interest, but would play directly into the hands of the Axis. It might, by provoking internal disturbance, have given a pretext to the Axis to intervene in Morocco for the purpose of preserving order.

Our young Lawrence had proposed that we publicly state over the radio the necessity for the calling of another Algeciras Conference after the war to reconsider the status of Morocco. There could not have been conceived an action that was more calculated to arouse antagonism on the part of the French against us. The same officer had suggested an intensive propaganda among the Moors, for what purpose it was not clear. The Moors had from time immemorial joined in with the heaviest battalions, and this they did when we entered Morocco on November 8, 1942. This was not out of special attachment to the United States but because they respected force. Nothing would have contributed more quickly to a request from the French authorities for the removal of our control officers from Morocco than the belief that they were indulging in propaganda among the Moors to subvert French authority.

I proposed that the Department authorize me to see Noguès and to assure him that it was not the policy of the United States Government for our officers to engage in activities which might subvert the authority of the protectorate government. Instructions substantially along these lines were issued me and I was able to set Noguès' mind at rest. The British consulate in Fez was again closed and the offending officer directed to other duties.

As a result of the strong measures taken by the French protectorate authorities against the Moorish nationalist movement after World War I and the great liberty allowed this movement in the Spanish zone, consequent upon the obligation felt by Spain for Moorish aid in the Spanish Civil War, Tetuan had for long been the center of Moorish nationalism, Fez a secondary center.

During World War II, the basic aims of both the Nationalist Reform Party and the Moroccan Unity Party involved recognition that the sovereign rights of the sultan were unalterable; recognition that any protectorate over Morocco was for the purpose of protection against outside aggression and that such protection should cease when no longer justified for that purpose; an increasing share in the administration of Morocco and in the conduct of foreign affairs; and a liberal and progressive educational program.

These aims, singularly reasonable, later became more radical in scope, calling for immediate independence. Even in World War II, the National Reform Party had more advanced objectives than the Nationalist Reform Party. It advocated the attainment of world Mohammedanism, the adoption of Arabic as the official Moorish language to the exclusion of Berber, recognition of the Alouite dynasty as the sole family entitled to reign as sovereigns, and abolition of the French protectorate in the shortest possible time.

Owing perhaps to the Moorish strain in Spanish blood, there is a much more natural affinity between the Spanish and Moors than between the Moors and the French. A few years before the Second World War, Colonel Beigbeder, as Spanish high commissioner, established in Cairo a Moroccan Institute of Culture as a center for Moroccan students desirous of attending the Egyptian or Al Azher universities.

The spiritual home of Moorish nationalism was for long Egypt, and it is therefore not surprising that Egypt should have been in the forefront of those countries supporting Moorish nationalist aspirations. For long, the nationalism of the Moor was more cultural and religious than political and showed little inclination toward Pan-Arabism. In 1942, a keen observer in Morocco considered that Moorish nationalism in that year had only reached a stage of development similar to that attained by Arab nationalism before World War I. Since that time, the movement has shown progressive development, particularly under the stimulus of outside influences. I have endeavored to set forth my own experiences in dealing with the Moroccan question during the Second World War in the belief that they may offer some useful guidance in respect of the future.

It will not be easy to reconcile the views of the protecting powers with those of the large national groups. From the former, we are seeking a great defense effort entailing great domestic sacrifices. What weakens those powers must in the end weaken us. At the same time, we are faced with the necessity of taking into account the legitimate aspirations of peoples, however fanatically inspired, whose considerations of self-respect oftentimes outweigh those of security in this troubled world.

It is believed that the United States must bend every effort to effect a reconciliation between these opposing interests, for without such a reconciliation our own security interests and the peace of the world must suffer.

NOTE

[1] In the late Middle Ages, both Spain and Portugal, at one time or another, held either briefly or for long periods territorial outposts on the Moroccan coast. Portugal, in the era of its great world discoveries, set up forts and settlements at Arzila, Alcazarquivir, Safi, Mazagan, Mogador, and Agadir. Spain held the two so-called presidios of Melilla and Ceuta on the Mediterranean coast of Morocco from the fifteenth and sixteenth centuries. As Metropolitan Spanish territory they occupied the same relationship to Spain as Algeria to France. Great Britain, for a brief period in the latter part of the seventeenth century, held Tangier as a colonial possession. Britain's voluntary relinquishment of Tangier has been characterized as one of the greatest blunders of its colonial history.

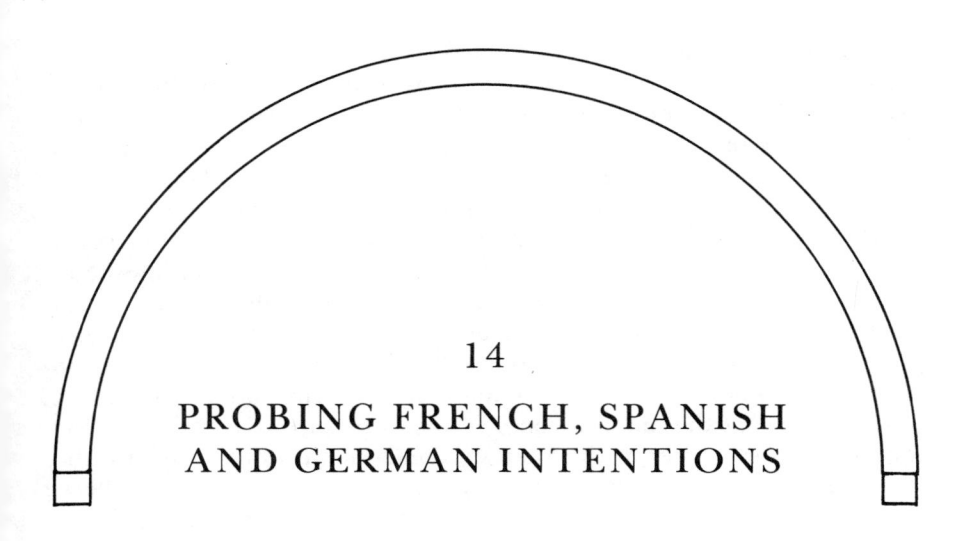

14
PROBING FRENCH, SPANISH AND GERMAN INTENTIONS

A partial answer to one of the important political questions confronting me as I assumed charge in Tangier was given in my journey, in February 1941, by car across western Spain to Algeciras from Lisbon. Before crossing the Portuguese-Spanish frontier at Badajoz we were farsighted enough to provide ourselves with foodstuffs. It was well that we did so for, as it was, my wife and I arrived in Tangier half-famished. From Badajoz, the situation became progressively worse the farther south we traveled, with an almost complete absence of potatoes and most green vegetables; a great dearth of sugar and butter and other fats; and a complete lack of white flour. At San Fernando, outside of Cadiz, where we stopped to eat, no bread whatever was available and the meat offered us was in a state of decomposition. At the deluxe Cristine Hotel in Algeciras, one of the great hotels of the world, bread was available only during two or three days in each month. Here, as in the luxury hotel in Seville at which we stopped, fellow guests took it as a matter of course when we marched to the table with supplementary foodstuffs in our hands.

Having served with the Hoover relief mission in Soviet Russia, I was well acquainted with famine conditions. While I saw no conditions in Spain comparable to those encountered in Russia, widespread malnutrition was very evident and Spain was in no position to engage in military adventures. This view was confirmed to me by David Eccles of the British embassy in Madrid when I met him in Tangier, as also by Arthur Yencken, British minister-counselor in Madrid. The latter, whom I had known in Egypt, expressed the strong belief that France would persist in its January refusal to enter the war on the side of Axis.

The second problem confronting us, that of German intentions toward Morocco, was of a more menacing character. In 1914, German representatives had been expelled from Tangier and French Morocco, although allowed to remain in Spanish Morocco. During the First World War the German legation in Tangier had been acquired as a residence for the mendoub, the sultan's representative, and since that time no official German representation had been permitted anywhere in Morocco except the Spanish zone. It was to be surmised that, with the occupation of Tangier by the Spanish, the Germans would press for the right of official representation in Tangier. As early as February 25, 1941, I expressed the view to the Department of State that it would accord well with Hitler's love of the dramatic to synchronize the return of German official representation at Tangier with the reacquisition of the former German legation.

Colonel Robert Solborg, an American intelligence agent, who rendered able services in French North Africa preparatory to the landings, gave me, on March 14, the first confirmation of this development. On that date, he had been informed by the Italian vice consul at Tetuan that a German consulate would be established in the mendoubia on March 17.

On March 15, the adjutant of Colonel Yuste, delegate in Tangier of the Spanish high commissioner in Tetuan, called on the mendoub and showed him two orders of the khalifa, the sultan's representative in the Spanish zone, one removing him from office and the other appointing the Moorish Qadi of Tangier as pasha, to act as the khalifa's representative in Tangier. The mendoub was given orders to vacate the mendoubia by ten o'clock the following morning, and he was informed he would be removed by force if necessary. The mendoub having been removed, the way was paved for the triumphal return of the Germans to Tangier after an absence of twenty-seven years.

The German consulate was soon staffed with an imposing number of German agents of every category, who developed in Tangier their main base of espionage for North Africa. The French consul in Tangier, M. Triat, expressed the view to me that the Spanish Government had apparently been forced to permit the return of the German consulate in an endeavor to placate Germany, which had been pressing Spain for collaboration along far-reached lines.

This was a threatening enough development but there was more to come, even more ominous. Under the German and Italian armistice terms with France, it was envisaged the Armistice Control Commission in North Africa would be Italian, with only a negligible German Port Commission at Casablanca.

With the failure of Hitler to bring the war to a speedy conclusion, as had been anticipated, the appointment of General Weygand to North Africa and a fuller appreciation of the importance of French North Africa, the Germans succeeded, early in 1941, in obtaining the agreement of the French to the dispatch to Morocco of a German Armistice Commission, which eventually numbered some two-hundred.

General Noguès, the French resident general, wishing to be perfectly frank with us and to take us in his confidence, told me in Rabat on April 20 that he had just received word from General Weygand that Germans, in addition to the then small Commission, were scheduled to arrive shortly in Morocco, despite energetic protests by Weygand. Noguès stated that when, a little time previous, he and Weygand had had notice of the reported reinforcement of the German Armistice Commission, they had flown to Vichy to protest and that both Darlan and Pétain had protested to the Germans. He and Weygand had returned to North Africa under the impression that no more Germans would come. To Noguès' discomfiture, he had now been informed that he might expect some one hundred additional members.

I told General Noguès that I was sure that my government would be very concerned at this development, as he was no doubt aware that any such development affecting this part of Africa was of particular concern to the defense departments of the United States Government. I then asked him what he thought were the immediate aims of the Commission in Morocco.

Noguès replied that he did not think they contemplated a German occupation of Morocco, as in Norway, for the Germans had not sent anyone worth mentioning, apart from the Armistice Commission. He had refused several requests of the Commission for German merchants to enter Morocco on the grounds that France was still at war with Germany.

I was later to be shown highly confidential correspondence between Noguès and Darlan concerning the entry into Morocco of German private citizens, including a communication from Vichy transmitting a request from the German Government, on the third of March, that Germans be given equal rights with those enjoyed by other nationals in Morocco.

In Noguès' reply on March 7, arguing against the acceptance of this request, there was cited Article 19 of the German Armistice Agreement. The point was also made that acceptance of the German request would alienate the United States and place Morocco in acute economic dependence upon Spain and Germany. This would be an intolerable situation, as it would undermine the independence of the French protectorate administration.

Upon my arrival in Tangier, I had found in Tetuan, Spanish Morocco, French Consul Claude Clarac, whom I had known in Persia five years before. He became of inestimable assistance in keeping me informed of certain developments.

Through Clarac, I now learned that, in a discussion between him and the German consul in Tetuan, the latter had observed that the substitution of additional German commissioners for the Italian Armistice Commission had been due to Germany's lack of confidence in the French administration in Morocco.

Clarac had replied that, in French Morocco, where France was faced with the problem of exercising authority over the native population, it was not possible for a third authority to share that task. It was on that account that the protectorate authorities were taking measures against any Moors having dealings with the Commission.

It was the French contention, fully supported by the Moroccan treaty statutes, that the French protectorate administration was alone authorized to deal with the sultan and the native administration. General Noguès rightly recognized that nothing was more calculated to undermine the authority of the French than direct contact between the German Armistice Commission and the native population. He was wise enough to perceive this from the beginning and, accordingly, the most stringent measures were taken against a number of Moors who, upon the arrival of the Germans, were so injudicious as to play up to the Germans by entertaining them socially. When such Moors were taken in hand by the French and banished to the south, the example set by the firmness of the French effectively resulted in the virtually complete isolation of the Germans from the native population.

Recognizing the wisdom of this policy, we were happy to give the French protectorate authorities our fullest support in the achievement of this objective.

The problem confronting the French was one which we too had to face. In Morocco, the extraterritorial regime which we enjoyed included the very singular right, which had grown up under the old treaties, to appoint from among the native population twelve protégés, for signal services rendered the United States, as well as protégés from among those Moroccan merchants who did a substantial amount of business with the United States. The effect of the nomination of such protégés by the American legation in Tangier was to remove such natives from the local jurisdiction and to place them, in all judicial matters in which they might be the defendants, under the exclusive jurisdiction of the American consular courts in Morocco.

In March or April 1941, M. du Gardier, chief of the diplomatic cabinet at Rabat, called on Willard Quincy Stanton, our consul in Casablanca, to bring to his attention the case of a well-known Moor, an American protégé, who was giving the French protectorate authorities great concern owing to his reported association with the German Armistice Commission. The call made on Consul Stanton by the chief of the diplomatic cabinet, accompanied by the French controller at Casablanca, was the first direct indication given us that the French were prepared to take a firm stand on German activities among the Moorish population. Stanton was informed that the French protectorate authorities were determined to strike hard and effectively against obvious German purpose to create unrest and disaffection among the Moors against the French. It was emphasized that if the Germans succeeded in establishing contact with American protégés among the Moors, French efforts to deal effectively with other natives might be paralyzed.

As I reported to Washington, "in view of the very critical character of the political situation at this time in Morocco affecting the security of the French protectorate and, indirectly, our own defense interests," Stanton was authorized to notify the French protectorate authorities of our decision to withdraw protection from the native in question.

It was not alone against Moors that the French authorities in Morocco moved to circumscribe as much as possible the activities of the German Armistice Commission. The most explicit orders were issued by General Noguès enjoining French officials from having any contact with the Commission outside the scope of their official mission. Measures were taken to keep all members of the Commission under strict surveillance. One or two French private individuals who interpreted "collaboration" as extending to the social entertainment of members of the Commission suddenly found themselves the subject of French judicial proceedings for dealing with the enemy. These measures were so effective that, throughout its sojourn in Morocco, the German Armistice Commission found itself isolated.

Even before these developments, with a view to strengthening the ability of the legation in Morocco to follow Spanish and German military objectives in North Africa, I had recommended, on March 5, that an American military attaché be assigned to Tangier, where we had no military staff. The first news of the acceptance of my recommendation came over a broadcast by the BBC on April 29, with the announcement that Major (afterward Colonel) William C. Bentley was being transferred from the American embassy in Rome to the legation in Tangier as military attaché.

Bentley was an able young Air Force officer who performed signal services in the period preceding the landings. His office was eventually expanded to include Major John W. Edwards and Captain Bernard Bernadoni. Some months later, in October, the Department of State requested my reaction to the possible establishment of a naval attaché's office in Tangier. I replied that there was no doubt that the appointment of an American naval attaché to Tangier would attract great attention in the area and would be disturbing to the Germans. I also expressed the opinion that it would be interpreted by many as the initial step preparatory to possible American naval action off the African coast. I added that the number of German armistice commissioners in Morocco would make it difficult for the French to raise objections. It was pointed out that, inasmuch as in extraterritorial countries the staff of a mission is a matter of concern only to the government making the appointment, any approach to the French protectorate authorities would be as a courtesy only and not as an obligation, while in the case of the Spanish it would be unnecessary and inappropriate for us to approach them on the subject in view of our nonrecognition of the Spanish position in Morocco. It was eventually decided to establish such an office, which opened early in 1942 with the arrival of Colonel William A. Eddy, a Marine officer who had given distinguished service in the First World War and who rendered most conspicuous service in Tangier, where he headed up all OSS activities in French North Africa.

With the addition of a military attaché, we were in a far better position to keep watch on military developments and to gauge the probable intentions of the Spanish and Germans.

From British sources we learned, on February 12, that Weygand had refused all British proposals for staff talks and that the British general staff was satisfied that it was impossible for Germany to move troops either by air to North Africa or by land across the Mediterranean in numbers sufficient to form an effective force.

Early in April I discussed with the French military attaché in Tangier the reported arrival of Spanish troops and matériel in the Spanish zone. He did not consider it disquieting. He said that Spanish troops in that zone numbered only 130,000, and that a considerably greater number would be necessary to launch an offensive against the French zone. Some days later I inquired of General Noguès his opinion of the Spanish threat to Morocco. He thought the Spanish would act only if pushed by Germany. He considered that possibility still a danger, however.

I said I had heard that French North Africa was very short of military matèriel. He confirmed this, adding that the British must not be impatient and that Morocco must not become a second Yugoslavia (Germany had overrun Yugoslavia on April 6–22, 1941).

Noguès informed me there were two currents of opinion in the German Armistice Commission. The economic section was not opposed to American economic aid to French North Africa, but the German military were suspicious of it. He assured me there had been no demand from the Germans for ports or bases in Morocco. He thought that the objectives of the German Armistice Commission were to survey the ground from a military point of view and to know what was going on.

He expressed the view that the ensuing months would be the most critical for Britain. He was not sure whether Hitler would make an all-out attempt to invade England, as it might be too much of a gamble for him. Noguès thought that the factor that had so far stood in the way of a German drive against the Straits of Gibraltar was the fear of provoking political upheaval in Spain.

Substance was given General Noguès' deductions in a talk which I had on May 12 with the departing Spanish minister in Tangier. Concerning the appointment of Lieutenant General Luis Orgaz as both Spanish high commissioner and as commander of Spanish forces in Spanish Morocco, it was emphasized that Orgaz was one of the most monarchically inclined officers in the Spanish Army. The minister added that everyone in Spain from Franco down was opposed to intervention in the war, as it was felt Spain needed a period of tranquility to recover from the ravages of the Civil War. However, so long as the Germans were in Hendaye, the question of what would happen to Spain was not one which the Spanish could decide of their own volition. For the present, it appeared to him the Germans were too much preoccupied with the eastern Mediterranean to bring matters to a climax in the western Mediterranean. He thought Serrano Suner, the Foreign Minister, had lost much of his influence, and stated that those who were pronounced monarchists were being placed in positions of influence, as Spain wished above all else to be allowed to work out its own destiny.

A few days later Colonel Beigbeder, former Spanish foreign minister and former high commissioner to Spanish Morocco, who had made a visit to Tetuan, sent word to me privately that he was quite satisfied that the situation in Spain was developing in accordance with the nation's interest. He added that, at a recent meeting of Spanish generals, all without exception had expressed opposition to Spain's entry into the war, as well as the passage of German troops across Spain.

In a conversation at Rabat on May 13, General Noguès expressed the view that the next four months would be the most critical in the international situation. He thought the next German military objective would be Crete (events proved him to be correct: Crete was attacked by German airborne troops on May 20, 1941) and then a push in the East. He did not expect any important developments in the western Mediterranean before the end of June.

On June 3, I reported that there was nothing to indicate any immediate military developments in Morocco. While tension had been notable as a result of developments in the eastern Mediterranean and there was a certain infiltration of Spanish troops in the Spanish zone, there was nothing which gave evidence of any contemplated offensive operations.

In further conversation with Noguès on June 9, I asked whether he was an optimist or a pessimist concerning the course of the war. He avoided a direct reply but did remark he thought the British action in Syria would have the effect of upsetting German plans in the Near East temporarily. He did not anticipate any action in French North Africa in the immediate future, as the Germans did not undertake two widely separated operations at the same time. He did not look for any decisive phase in the war in 1941.

A noticeable lessening in the tension, induced by the strengthening of the German Armistice Commission, was reported early in July. Such tension, which had begun to ease off with the German offensive against Yugoslavia, was stated as having shown since that time a continous and marked decline.

The Germans launched their offensive against Russia on June 22, 1941, and their attention was never to be diverted from that area until the fall of Berlin in 1945. While tension became less great in the western Mediterranean with their preoccupation with Russia in the east, there could be no relaxation of our vigilance.

Surveying the situation six months after my arrival, in the summer of 1941, it seemed clear that Spain, as had been foreseen as early as 1939, was in no position to enter the war but desired above all else to be left free to work out its great internal problem of recovery. Ciano's *Journal* and his diplomatic correspondence all bear this out. However, we were not in Ciano's confidence; all we had to go on at that time were stray bits of information which we were able to pick up here and there an endeavor to fit into a coherent whole.

In the belief that the war was virtually over, with the conclusion in 1940 of the German and Italian armistices with France, Hitler had let slip from his grasp two great prizes which France continued to hold, the French Fleet and French North Africa. If Hitler had moved against North Africa before directing his attention to the east, the war undoubtedly would have taken a far more difficult course for the Allies. Hitler, however, underestimated the importance of the Mediterranean and its shores until too late.

It was not too late, however, in 1941, and the great question absorbing us was whether and how Hitler might seek to recover from his mistakes in the west. Once Germany had become engaged with Yugoslavia and with Russia in the first half of 1941, it seemed as if North Africa could breathe freely for a time, but there was no assurance to this effect.

The signs available to us seemed to indicate, at the end of the summer of 1941, that Spain would not enter the armed conflict of its own volition. There was the possibility, nevertheless, that pressure from Berlin and Rome, coupled with the tempting offer from Germany of French Morocco, in whole or in part, might induce Spain to march against Gibraltar and French North Africa. We know now that such pressure was repeatedly exerted. The great art of procrastination, in which the Spanish so excel, was ably brought to bear by General Franco to withstand successfully this pressure.

The contingency of German pressure upon Spain to induce its entrance into the war was one against which we had constantly to be on our guard. It behooved us to do something more than "wait and see"; it was necessary to develop some positive policy that might effectively ensure that Spanish Morocco, at least, would not enter the war or continue to give aid and comfort to the enemy.

15

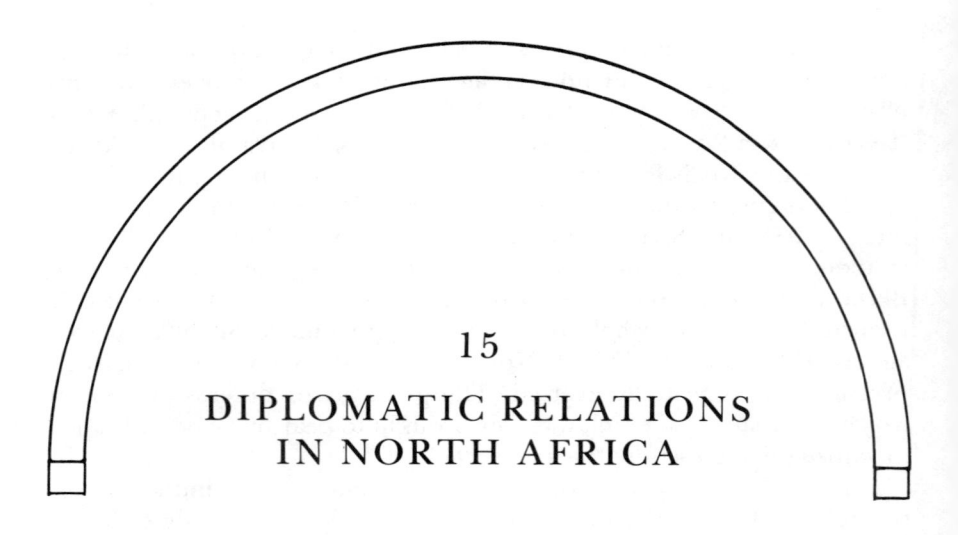

DIPLOMATIC RELATIONS IN NORTH AFRICA

The policy of our nonrecognition of the Spanish zone of Morocco and our still more frigid attitude toward the forceful seizure by the Spanish of Tangier rendered exceedingly difficult the problem of my official relations with the Spanish authorities in Tangier and the Spanish zone.

Before leaving Washington, I had sought instructions from Wallace Murray as to the attitude I was to adopt. He had suggested that I conform to the policy which had been adopted by our officers in Manchukuo toward the Japanese. I was told by the Far Eastern Division that our officers had maintained correct social relations with the Japanese but had carefully refrained from participating in any official Japanese functions.

In the Spanish Civil War, my sympathies were wholly with the Republican Spanish. I believed then, as did millions of other Americans, that the Spanish Government of Franco was a fascist and totalitarian government, which indeed it was, and that it considered its destinies entirely bound with the Axis, which indeed it did not. I was for long to remain under this last mistaken hypothesis until I discovered that the Spaniard is first, last and always a Spaniard, having an attachment to no other foreign government. If Spain had closer relations with the Axis at the beginning of the war and remained so until the fortunes of war turned against the Axis, it was because Spain felt its national interests better served by the Axis than by the Allies. It was as simple as that, but it took me quite a while to find it out.

I was helped in penetrating the Spanish character and developing remarkably close relations with the Spanish authorities by my long sojourn in the Arab world. The Spaniard is an extraordinary mixture of the Latin and the Arab. From the Arab he has acquired a profound sense of personal dignity which imparts to the lowliest peasant a noble mien. From the Arab he has inherited a high sense of honor and noblesse oblige. In common with the Arab, the Spaniard has an aversion to the formal trappings of the West and the legal abracadabra with which our legal minds have encumbered life. With the Spaniard, as with the Arab, confidence founded on personal relationship is everything.

Experience in the Arab world and the study given by me to the Spanish character were to aid me immeasurably in gaining Spanish goodwill and confidence. The beginning, however, was far from easy.

First of all, we had never recognized the Spanish zone and we were all the less disposed to recognize the unilateral action of the Spanish Government in moving into the international zone of Tangier and seeking to incorporate that zone in the Spanish protectorate. This, obviously, could not create an atmosphere of cordial relations.

Moreover, in 1941, Spain was as partial to the Axis as the United States was to the Allies, although having declared itself a nonbelligerent. Official relations, therefore, between Spanish and American representatives, while correct, could not be but strained and, on the part of Falangist-minded Spanish, even frigid.

Further, the Spanish felt themselves insecure in Tangier, while we were faced with the extremely delicate task, in an atmosphere which at times approached hostility, of maintaining unprejudiced our important treaty rights and our very special position given us by the presence of our legation in Tangier. The situation called for the exercise of tact, patience, and a high degree of firmness.

One of the first tests came within a few weeks after my arrival. A naturalized American citizen of Italian origin arrived in Tangier with his sister, an Italian, in a small boat in which they had rowed across the straits from Gibraltar. The brother was promptly arrested and spirited off to Tetuan, and the sister, although released, was warned that she and her brother would be expelled for illegal entry. Word of the situation was conveyed to me by the sister. I at once took counsel with Ernest Dempster, my invaluable coadjutor, who, although a British subject, had spent twenty-eight years in the service of the legation as legal adviser in all matters having to do with our complicated treaty relationships with Morocco. Dempster concurred that firm action was desirable. We drafted a stiff telegram to the Spanish high commissioner in Tetuan, whom I was careful to address not as high commissioner, which we did not recognize, but only by his military title. I pointed out that by virtue of the extraterritorial regime which we enjoyed in Morocco, American citizens were not subject to Spanish jurisdiction but only to the jurisdiction of American consular courts and that, if the American who had been taken in charge had committed any offense, the case could only properly be heard in such a court. I demanded, therefore, his immediate release into my custody.

The telegram obtained results, for the following day the American, who had been released in Tetuan, appeared at the legation, and I heard no more of the matter. Nor was there any further effort on the part of the Spanish authorities to contest our extraterritorial jurisdiction.

The next test came on March 21. After the removal of the mendoub, the sultan's representative in Tangier, plans were made by Spanish authorities for the ceremonial entry into Tangier of the khalifa, the Sultan's representative in Tetuan and the Spanish zone, to signalize the absorption of Tangier into that zone. The diplomatic and consular corps were invited by the Spanish to occupy a place of honor in the reviewing stand, and we were invited by the khalifa to a luncheon given by him in honor of the occasion.

I telegraphed the Department that, in accordance with the understanding reached in the Department regarding my relations with the local authorities, I did not propose to accept their invitation, as to attend such official functions would be an implicit recognition of the *status quo*. I was the only foreign official representative in Tangier absent. While my Allied colleagues continued to attend until the close of the war all such functions in Tangier, the American legation was never once represented.

I do not know whether my absence on this occasion was considered an affront by the Spanish. Whatever the reason may have been, when I and the senior member of my staff, John C. Shillock, made an informal courtesy call on the new Tangier administrator, Colonel Carvajal, we were left standing and not even offered a seat. I refused to take offense. In order to break down the wall of reserve with which the Spanish confronted us, I invited, some weeks thereafter, Colonel Carvajal and two of his assistants to dinner at the legation, acting on the old Arab principle that once one had been able to have even his enemy break bread with him, a long way has been taken toward making him one's friend. While the acceptance of my invitation had no immediate effect in breaking down the barrier which for long separated us from the Spanish, it helped at least in making our relations somewhat smoother. The fact is that, during the first year or two of my residence in Tangier, our quarantine was such that any Spaniard entering the legation on his own initiative was a marked man. As, by and large, only the Spanish Republicans were sympathetic to the Allied cause, no Spaniard, other than Spanish officials who might be the occasional recipients of American hospitality, could afford to run the risk.

Before the American landings in French Morocco in November 1942, no serious problem ever presented itself in connection with our relations with the French protectorate authorities. These relations could not have been more cordial, extending from General Noguès, the French resident general, to the most junior functionaries.

The economic accord concluded between the United States and French North Africa on February 26, 1941, by Murphy and Weygand, had, of course, created a most favorable atmosphere for the development of close friendly relations. Moreover, while the French, with the conclusion of an armistice, had withdrawn from the war, the sympathies of the overwhelming majority of Frenchmen were profoundly anti-Axis and particularly pro-American.

General Noguès himself had taken a very advanced position in June 1940, in favor of the French continuance of the war in North Africa. When word was first received by him of a possible armistice, he had sent emissaries to Pétain, urging the continuance of the struggle in Morocco, Algeria and Tunisia. Noguès' strict sense of discipline had finally brought him, but only with the greatest reluctance, to defer to the decision of Pétain.

The French resident general had had a brilliant record in the French Army. He had served for some years in the campaign of pacification of Morocco under Marshal Lyautey and had come to know the Moroccans as did few other Frenchmen. It is a great tribute to him that, during his proconsulship, which extended from 1936 to 1943, including the period when French fortunes were at their lowest ebb, no shadow of disturbance arose to affect Franco-Moroccan relations.

General Noguès, who had served on the French Supreme War Council, owed his appointment as French resident general to the Popular Front government of Léon Blum. He survived numerous changes in the French Cabinet between 1936 and 1940, weathered the storm of 1940, retained his situation unimpaired after the removal of Weygand from North Africa in 1942, and was left at his post until 1943. Breasting, as Talleyrand had once done, so many governmental changes, Noguès had come to be looked upon as a consummate opportunist. Certainly no one not possessed of the keenest political sense and capacity to maneuver adroitly could have remained in his post for so long.

Noguès was a slim, wiry type, of medium height, with the somewhat dry manner of many Frenchmen. He was most friendly to the United States. His overmastering loyalty was, of course, to France. Schooled in the tradition of Lyautey, he had one paramount passion in life: the maintenance, unimpaired, of the Moroccan tie to France. This was the mainspring of all his actions; it was the key to his conduct on all occasions.

General Orgaz, who had been captain general of Barcelona and had taken a prominent part in the Spanish Civil War, was very much of a martinet and was known as a genuine tartar. He not only remarked to my British colleague my absence at the ceremony in Tangier on May 30 but expressed himself with considerable feeling on the subject.

Before I had even learned of his displeasure, I had called on the Spanish consul in Tangier, the day after the ceremony, to express my personal regret at not being able to attend. I told him I desired, however, to make an informal call on General Orgaz at Tetuan, with the military attaché and my senior secretary, whenever it might be convenient to the high commissioner. The consul assured me that he understood our position and that he had explained it to General Orgaz. The consul, no doubt out of diplomatic considerations, thought better of disclosing to me that Orgaz was thoroughly vexed and had so expressed himself.

Before an interview with General Orgaz could be arranged, he went to Madrid, where he unburdened himself to Sir Samuel Hoare, the British ambassador, concerning what he regarded as the affront I had offered him. The British ambassador, rightly concerned with any development which tended adversely to affect the delicate relations of Britain and its partner, the United States, with the Spanish authorities, brought the matter to the attention of Alexander Weddell, the American ambassador.

I had never had occasion to make the personal acquaintance of our ambassador in Spain, whose long professional career in the American Foreign Service may have made him a good deal more dexterous in dealing with his foreign professional colleagues than a politically appointed chief of mission. I shall always be grateful for the able manner in which Ambassador Weddell turned Sir Samuel Hoare's demarche.

"I do not know our chargé d'affaires in Tangier," he observed, "but I do know that he has had some eighteen years of foreign service. If he failed to attend the ceremony over which General Orgaz presided, you may be very sure that it was neither due to a whim nor to conscious neglect, but rather was in conformity with what he regarded as in American interests."

Upon the return of General Orgaz to Spanish Morocco, an interview with him was arranged on June 18 for me and two members of my staff, Major Bentley and Secretary Shillock. He received me, if not cordially—which I had never anticipated—at least politely.

I had no success whatever when I endeavored to draw him out into a discussion of the situation in the Spanish zone or of the international situation. His noncommittal and extremely reserved attitude was in marked contrast with that of General Noguès, the French resident general, who consistently displayed great freedom in his discussions with me from the beginning of our relationship.

I remarked to Orgaz that international tension appeared to be concentrated in the eastern Mediterranean and that, as long as this was so, I thought we might look for inactivity in the western Mediterranean. I asked if he were not also of this opinion. The high commissioner replied that he really did not have an opinion on the subject.

It being obvious that I was getting nowhere very fast, I took my leave after some hour's inconsequential conversation. The ice had at least been broken; this, if nothing else, could be put down on the credit side of the ledger.

Throughout 1941, our relations with the Spanish authorities remained, if not cordial, certainly correct. So long as the fortunes of the Axis were in the ascendency, the Spanish authorities in Morocco found it prudent to maintain an attitude of reserve toward the Allies, as well as the United States, which had identified itself with the Allied cause. Such fraternization with foreigners as the Spanish authorities engaged in was with the Germans and Italians, whose support had made General Franco's victory possible.

In an effort to establish a trading position with the Spanish and to give us some leverage, thought had been given to the possible development of a program of economic aid similar to that which had been concluded for French North Africa. Monick, in Rabat, had suggested to me in April that we give earnest consideration to such a program with a view to realizing the same objectives in Spanish Morocco as we had before us in French North Africa. I had sought to prepare the ground with General Orgaz on June 18 for such an accord by inquiring of him what products Spanish Morocco needed and whether we might help in supplying them. He put an abrupt end to my feeler by replying that Spanish Morocco had no need of aid.

I came to the conclusion that, if we were unable to establish a basis of mutual aid, we might well, through our economic strength, bring some pressure to bear upon the Spanish zone to convince the authorities we were a force to be reckoned with. Accordingly, when the legation was approached by merchants in Tangier to facilitate the issuance of American export licenses for the shipment of lubricating oils, tires and tubes to Spanish Morocco, for which British permission had already been accorded, I recommended that we should be extremely slow to grant any such licenses.

This policy, accepted by the Bureau of Economic Warfare, soon had its salutary effects. Senor Propper, Spanish consul in Larache, called on me in August, serving presumably as an informal intermediary of the Spanish authorities, to raise the question of the legation's support for the facilitation of products in desperately short supply in Spanish Morocco. He remarked that I did not seem to be as sympathetic toward the promotion of such trade as I had been previously.

I recalled that when I had discussed this subject with General Orgaz and had inquired as to his needs, I had been informed that he had none. I asked Propper why, if there was indeed an interest on the part of the Spanish authorities in the matter, they did not approach the legation directly. His reply was that they could not depart so openly from Spain's autarchial economic policy and intimated at the same time that they could not risk offending Germany and Italy.

By a curious reversal of roles, the British, who had been somewhat reluctant to go along with us in economic aid for French North Africa, had shown themselves overly anxious to placate the Spanish and were anything but approving of placing restrictions on the flow of strategic items to Spanish Morocco which we had recommended.

In our renewed recommendations following Propper's visit, it was observed that it would seem the elementary part of prudence to permit only enough goods to be exported to the Spanish zone to supply the current needs of that area. So long as the Spanish zone had insufficient goods to permit accumulation of stocks, it was to the advantage of Spain to keep its contacts open with the United States and Great Britain, the only sources of supply of most necessities.

In September I saw General Orgaz again. The high commissioner was, as I had come to understand, a thorough patriot, intensely devoted to his country and to what he regarded as his duty. His immediate entourage and the Spanish diplomatic officers stationed in Tangier were in terror of him. He was a stocky man with a rather large head who listened carefully to what one said, absorbed it, but had little to say in reply. I suspected that, like so many men who display a gruff demeanor, he was at heart a sentimentalist. I determined to lay siege to him on that basis.

I stated that appeals had been made to the legation to facilitate the export of certain badly needed goods to Spanish Morocco. We would do what we could, but the needs of our own domestic economy for vital goods unfortunately precluded the freest hand in releasing many products.

I had with me one of our propaganda magazines in Spanish, showing the sky line of New York, and said I hoped he would one day have an opportunity to view that impressive spectacle. He replied that he had always cherished that dream. I said I felt sure he would be particularly interested in California, where Spanish influence was so evident, adding that in America we recognized the debt we owed to Spanish culture.

The general thanked me for the "amiable" allusion to Spain. While the Spanish had made many mistakes and had many shortcomings, he continued, they were a generous and romantic people and, wherever they had passed in the world, there remained imprints of those aspects in their character.

He seemed pleased when I observed that the civilization of the United States was not exclusively Anglo-Saxon in character but that it was an amalgam of British, French, Spanish, Italian and peoples of many other races and lands. This, it was suggested, constituted its strength and greatness.

I left him on this occasion convinced that not only had the ice been permanently broken but that the walls of reserve guarding the inner sanctum of his personality had been slightly breached.

As remarkable as it may seem, we became in the end fast friends. In 1943, when, to meet an engagement with General Mark Clark, I was obliged to fly for the first time, General Orgaz considerately sent to Seville for a special plane of American manufacture so that I might be more comfortable. In 1950, I met by chance in Venice a Spanish diplomat who had been in Tangier at the same time as I. Introducing me to his bride he remarked, to my amusement, "Here you see the only person, whether Spanish or foreign, who was ever able to get along with General Orgaz when he was in Morocco as high commissioner."

He was speaking jocularly, of course, and he may not have intended it as the compliment I interpreted it to be. I came to have great admiration for Genral Orgaz, for his rectitude, his devotion to duty and his incorruptibility. His country suffered a great loss in his death, a loss it could ill afford. I count it as one of the great privileges of my years in Morocco that I was able in the end to gain the confidence of such a man.

It was, I believe, at the end of 1943 or at the beginning of 1944 that I received a call one day from Mme. Renee Reichmann, a Jewish refugee prominent in Jewish councils in Tangier. Mme. Reichmann stated that if I could persuade General Orgaz to approve the issuance by the Spanish legation in Budapest of visas for five hundred Jewish children threatened with extermination by the Nazis in Hungary, it might well be the means of saving their lives.

I did not need an authorization from Washington to move me to undertake this humanitarian task. I saw General Orgaz and explained to him the situation. There was probably no means, I said, for these children to be transported from Hungary to Spanish Morocco, so that the question of their actual entrance into Spanish North Africa was largely an academic one. The important consideration was that the Spanish legation be authorized to grant the five hundred visas, as this would have the effect of indirectly enveloping the children with the mantle of Spanish protection and might thereby save them from the Axis incinerators.

I knew, or rather suspected, that General Orgaz had a heart of gold. He was especially gentle with children. The moment I made the request his eyes glistened. "I shall telegraph Madrid at once and give my authorization," he said. "But mind you, my accord may not be the only measure necessary. Madrid must agree to issue the necessary authorization to the legation in Budapest."

I telegraphed Ambassador Hayes in Madrid. During the years in Tangier the cooperation we had with the embassy in Madrid could not have been closer, first under Ambassador Weddell and then with Mr. Hayes and his extremely able minister-counselor, Willard Beaulac. The embassy replied that the matter would be pushed, and it was, with the result that the five hundred visas were issued.

The Jews are a persistent people and, once we had the five hundred visas, Mme. Reichmann called on me again and wondered whether we could obtain another seven hundred. I could not say no and I went again to General Orgaz. Again, he gave the authorization for visas, this time for seven hundred adults.

On the eve of my departure from Tangier in 1945, Mme. Reichmann wrote me an extremely touching letter of thanks in which she stated in part: "The International Red Cross in Budapest, not having been able to obtain German transit visas for these [1,200 persons], were able notwithstanding, thanks to the entry visas for Tangier, to obtain the release of this number of Jews from a Nazi concentration camp, put them in a house rented for the purpose which, through the authorization given for visas, was protected by the Spanish Consulate in Budapest. Thus, 1,200 innocent souls owe their lives to you."

This was not correct. They owed their lives, first of all, to Mme. Reichmann and next to General Orgaz and the Spanish authorities. The legation was only an instrument. Still, it is a comforting thought that whatever errors we may have made and however feeble our efforts may have been in one direction or another in Morocco during that period, we did play a part in one concrete accomplishment, the preservation in the midst of the mass slaughter of the years 1939–45 of the lives of seven hundred adults and five hundred children.

On the eve of Pearl Harbor, an important insight into the Spanish attitude was given me in a conversation with a fairly highly placed Spanish diplomat. He referred to the rising discontent in Germany against the terrible loses sustained by the German Army in Russia. He scouted any idea of Spain's granting any bases to the Axis so long as the eastern Mediterranean remained under Allied control. He thought that, if the British lost Suez, there might then arise the eventuality of Spanish cooperation with the Axis, inasmuch as, under such circumstances, Spain would be assured of freedom of movement in the whole Mediterranean basin. He intimated indeed that, once the Axis had gained effective control of the eastern Mediterranean, Spain would have no other course open to it than to throw in its lot with the Axis.[1]

Summing up the political and strategic situation at this time, I wrote:

> It has been generally expected that sooner or later Germany will follow up the dispatch of its Armistice Commission, now assigned to French Morocco, by a thrust toward Northwest Africa.
>
> Actual collaboration of Spain with the Axis, looking to the blockade of the western Mediterranean, would be forthcoming only in the event of a successful Axis blockade of the eastern Mediterranean. German difficulties in Russia and the failure of Germany to fulfill the boastful swashbuckling October claims of Hitler are tending for the first time to rob Germany, in the eyes of Spanish officialdom in the Spanish Zone, of the aura of invincibility which has attended for so long the martial progress of the Nazis...
>
> There are no immediate indications of any active German operations in this area.

Pearl Harbor, and the entrance of the United States into the war, brought about a noticeable easing of our relations with the Spanish in Morocco. Throwing our weight into the war made the Spanish all the more concerned about not being involved themselves.

A few days after these events, a Spanish diplomat informed me that, while considerable pressure was being brought by Germany upon Franco to enter the war, the Generalissimo would use every means possible to avoid being involved. Spain's interests, he said, dictated her abstention, although political considerations over which it had less control might involve it. It was suggested that we could help Spain maintain its nonbelligerent status by continuing to supply it. Both from this and other Spanish sources, it was clear that the desire to remain out of the war was widespread.

In a further analysis given me by the relative of a Spanish official lately returned from Madrid, it was learned that the Spanish Government itself was endeavoring to keep the country out of the war. One of the cabinet members most in favor of intervention was said to be Foreign Minister Serrano Suner. Dissatisfaction with the Falange was reported increasing. A principal leader in opposition to the Falange and to Suner's policy was identified as General Orgaz.

A few days later, Clarac, French consul in Tetuan, informed me that General Orgaz had remarked to him significantly that the new developments in the war appeared to make its outcome doubtful. The high commissioner thought Germany too occupied in Russia to attempt a German drive through Spain.

At this time, the possibility of working with General Orgaz in respect of Spanish Morocco, as we were working through General Weygand in French North Africa, began to take shape. On January 5, 1942, I telegraphed the Department of the increasingly friendly attitude of the Spanish zone authorities toward the legation and of the expression of hope by one high official that we send an American vessel to Tangier with supplies.

No intimation was given me at the time, but I learned some twenty years later, with the publication in 1963 in *Foreign Relations of the United States Diplomatic Papers 1942*, that President Roosevelt had telegraphed from New York to the Secretary of State, on January 7 of that year, expressing agreement with my suggestion about Orgaz and inquiring what could be worked out.

Clarac informed me on January 8, 1942, that he saw clear evidence at Tetuan of Suner's waning influence in Spanish foreign affairs and of the intention of Orgaz to take more and more decisive lines in the affairs of Spanish Morocco. The opinion was expressed that Orgaz desired to work in concert with French Morocco and Portugal to preserve the *status quo* in the western Mediterranean. The chief of Orgaz' military cabinet had informed Clarac that the high commissioner's sole preoccupation was Spanish interests and that he was not moved by attachment to other countries. The inference was clear that Orgaz was not bound in his sympathies, as were some Spanish officials, to Germany or Italy.

That the Department of State was giving serious consideration to the issues raised in these reports was made abundantly evident by the verbal message brought to me from Washington by Colonel William A. Eddy, who arrived on January 26, 1942, to open a naval attaché's office. The message authorized me to make overtures to General Orgaz, in my discretion, concerning the position which he might take in the event Spain and Spanish Morocco were involved in the war and to assure him of the moral and material support of the United States should he resolve to resist any Axis aggression.

Between the time of Colonel Eddy's receipt of these verbal instructions from the Department of State and his arrival in Tangier, the British forces, which had been almost at the Tunisian border in their pursuit of Rommel from Egypt, had been suddenly thrust back in one of those lightning maneuvers characteristic of Rommel. That struggle, which at one moment seemed to promise the possibility of Allied control of the whole of North Africa, had so far reversed itself in a few days that there now appeared some doubt whether Egypt might be held.

It would have been absurd, of course, under such circumstances to approach Orgaz and I accordingly telegraphed the Department that the time appeared wholly inappropriate and that we were accordingly suspending any action. At the same time, the local situation was developing more and more in a manner to lighten our apprehensions.

An important meeting which took place early in February 1942, between General Noguès and General Orgaz, permitted a frank exchange of views and an estimation of their respective interests. When I called on General Noguès two days later, he assured me of his conviction that Orgaz sincerely desired to preserve the *status quo* in the western Mediterranean. Meyrier, principal assistant to Noguès and later French ambassador to China, informed me that relations between French and Spanish Morocco had never been more cordial. Meyrier thought that Spain, and General Orgaz in particular, were indisposed to engage in any military adventures. There had been a time when Spain had been tempted by the German offer of a portion of French Morocco, but that time had passed. Spain, it was believed, now realized that in the event of a German victory all Europe, including Spain, would be completely dominated by the Nazis.

Confirmation came a month later when I called on General Orgaz to present Colonel Eddy, our naval attaché, and Orgaz stressed his desire to see peace maintained in Morocco. Colonel Eddy inquired what the position of Spanish Morocco would be if it were invaded by the Axis. To our gratification, Orgaz replied unequivocally: "We would not know the answer to that until the day itself." He then inquired what was meant by a change in foreign policy. Eddy replied he was thinking of the possibility that Madrid might join the enemies of the United States. To this, Orgaz replied with considerable emphasis: "I consider it inconceivable that Spain should ever go to war with North America."

This was a long way forward in our relations from the dark days of 1941, when we encountered a wall of Spanish reserve around us. It promptly encouraged us in April to make concrete proposals for an economic accord when I presented, in accordance with instructions from the Department, a memorandum outlining the basis for such an economic understanding. Orgaz' comment when he read it was, "This is really a step forward."

At the end of the month, he communicated with me expressing his acceptance in principle. While our proposals for an economic accord eventually fell through, a less inclusive accord governing the importation of petroleum products was concluded on July 29, 1942, with General Orgaz. Our petroleum attaché in Madrid, Walter Smith, had come to

Spanish Morocco for that purpose, and during the second interview which we had with the high commissioner, he agreed to the petroleum accord, subject to approval by the Madrid government, which was later given. The accord provided for the supply of petroleum products on the basis of 80 percent of the consumption in 1941. No products were to be employed in a manner directly or indirectly useful to the enemies of the Allied powers. There would be no accumulation of stocks. An American petroleum attaché would be assigned to the legation in Tangier to supervise the program and to cooperate with the local authorities in its control. Great satisfaction with its conclusion was expressed by General Orgaz. Upon the arrival of the first oil shipments, he wrote me: "Once more I must thank Your Excellency for the interest and diligence with which you are endeavoring to relieve the exceptional situation in which this North Africa area, which is observing the strictest neutrality, finds itself as a result of the war."

We had come far in two years in the development of our relations with the Spanish, beginning with an atmosphere of almost frigid reserve, which had thawed with time, until they had become markedly cordial. It had required infinite patience, the avoidance of any false step and the development of those economic measures at our disposal.

As I recalled to Washington when I summed up the course of events on August 31, 1942, the Spanish authorities had been distinctly cool upon my arrival, at a time when petroleum reserves were large and there were no important restrictions on the flow of supplies. I had early expressed to the Department my view (which differed radically from that of the British) that the Spanish authorities in North Africa were likely to be far less independent toward us once they had been made to feel their economic dependence on us.

It was true that the international picture had changed materially in the interval during which the policy I had recommended had been applied. It was possible, of course, that the markedly changed attitude displayed toward us by the Spanish had been due in considerable part to the worsened international position of Germany, but I expressed the view it had also been due in part to bringing home to the Spanish authorities, by our economic policy, that they were under the economic necessity of cultivating our goodwill.

Whatever the causes, we had every occasion for extreme gratification that on the eve of the Allied landings in French North Africa on November 7–8, 1942, our relations with the Spanish authorities in Spanish Morocco were not only friendly but cordial. These sentiments, which we had labored so long to develop, were to stand us in good stead on that fateful November night when Vice Admiral Hewitt flung his Western Task Force on the Atlantic beaches of Morocco.

I came to know Noguès, the French resident general, extremely well. He gave me, at an early date in our relations, his confidence. He spoke to me with great freedom and candor; I was even taken into the intimacy of his home—a rare honor paid by a Frenchman to a foreigner—and lunched with him and Mme. Noguès from time to time both in large official groups as well as tête-à-tête, where conversation could flow freely, uninhibited by the presence of others.

The principal assistants of Noguès were as cordial in their relations with me as Noguès. A great deal has been written of the collaborationist French. I never encountered one in the French protectorate administration, nor, for that matter, among the French consular officers serving in Tangier, Tetuan and Larache in Spanish Morocco. There were a few collaborators in private circles in French Morocco and there were perhaps a dozen in the French colony of some two-thousand in Tangier, but they lived apart, under the odium of their compatriots. No Frechman of any integrity would be seen with a collaborator.

Shortly after my arrival in Tangier, I had visited Rabat, seat of the French protectorate, to make the acquaintance of General Noguès and other officials. There I met for the first time Secretary General M. Monick, prime author of the North African economic accord. We established a firm and warm friendship. Monick was of enormous aid to me by his counsels. Unfortunately, he became so conspicuous to the Germans by his friendship for us that Vichy was compelled to withdraw him from Morocco in the early autumn of 1941.

Meyrier, who became French ambassador to China after the war, was another of my great supports. In the darkest days of Allied fortunes, his sympathies for us never altered and were never concealed. He and other French diplomatic officers assigned for duty at the residency, whose number included Léon Marchal, Du Gardier, Hardion, Charpentier and Montespieu, rendered invaluable aid to me in my mission.

Monick, who was well acquainted with Weygand, put great confidence in the letter's willingness to act with us at a decisive moment by throwing French North Africa into the war. Shortly after my first visit to Rabat, Monick sent word to me in March that the signing of the Murphy-Weygand accord had given Weygand an assurance about the future that he had previously lacked. Weygand, Monick observed, had felt he had let the French people down in 1940, through no fault of his own. As he had no wish to do so again, he was now acting with the greatest prudence and counseling patience. Monick thought the accord had stiffened Weygand's attitude toward Vichy, where on a recent visit he had deplored Vichy's continued yielding to German demands and had put his foot down on the sending of additional Germans to Morocco.

Two months later, in May, Monick recounted to me at Rabat a long conversation he had had with Weygand. The latter, I was told, had said that he was thinking day and night of the responsibility he would have to take and that we would take. While he could not discuss in advance those eventualities with American representatives, he was anxious to know in the most precise terms possible the help he could count on from us. The timetable of the help he might receive was as important as the help itself. Monick informed me he attached the utmost importance to his conversation with Weygand, as it was the first occasion when he had gone so far as to envisage the possibility of committing himself to taking a decisive stand under given circumstances. I considered what Monick had related to me so important that, while in his home, I wrote out what he had told me for him to check personally so there would be no possible misinterpretation in the account to be given to Washington.

The following month, Monick commented to me again on Weygand's attitude. The latter had been greatly encouraged by a personal message from Secretary Hull. Weygand, it was said, had not appreciated the role of the United States until recently. At a Council of Ministers meeting in Vichy on June 4, he had insisted that the French Government must take account of the American attitude in all its important decisions.

At the end of August, in informing me of his own recall, Monick assured me his conviction of the ultimate victory of the Allies had never once wavered. He was gratified that he had been able to do as much as he had for the Allied cause. Because of his temporizing tactics, the Germans had been unable to make any cobalt shipments from Morocco.

Monick thought Weygand had gained greatly in moral stature and commanded an influence second to Pétain, both in North Africa and France. Unfortunately, Weygand did not live up to the expectations formed of him by so many. When the Germans forced Pétain to withdraw him from North Africa at the end of 1941, he returned to France, went into seclusion and remained inactive until the end of the war.

There is no doubt that Weygand, as well as Noguès, as Clarac emphasized to me in May, displayed in North Africa the greatest suppleness in their dealings with both Vichy and the Germans. It was they and Monick who had been able to obtain the approval of Vichy to our economic accord on the argument that an exchange of good with the United States was essential to the maintenance of the French North African economy.

With the declaration of Pétain on May 19, 1941, that France proposed to follow a policy of closer collaboration with Germany, shipments from the United States under the accord were suspended.

On June 9, I had a long talk with Noguès, who stated that he and Weygand were very discontented with the status of American aid. It had been promised months previous. Relying upon our promises, he had gone to great lengths to prevent the introduction into Morocco of Germans outside of the Armistice Commission.

I asked Noguès how he could reconcile our declared policy of granting all possible aid to the Allies with the continued extension of aid to French North Africa, if that area were to be dominated by the Germans. I cited the aid given the Germans in Syria and more recently the consideration given to the granting of French African bases to the Axis.

Noguès assured me he had stood up to the Germans. Weygand had given a most solemn undertaking that the goods we made available would never go to the Germans. As to bases, he assured me he had never had any intimation from Vichy that the granting of any such to the Germans was contemplated.

In response to my observation that we were concerned at what appeared to be increased French collaboration with the Germans, Noguès remarked that he thought the word a misnomer. French policy was directed toward a softening of the armistice terms in return for certain small services.

I asked him if he thought the granting of permission to German planes to land in Syria answered that description.

He answered that what had happened in Syria was most regrettable in his view and that, moreover, it was difficult to know all the circumstances.

From this and the many other interviews I had with the resident general, I formed the firm conclusion, as I reported at the time, that Noguès was entirely sincere in his desire for cooperation with us, that he would work with us as far as might be possible under the increasingly difficult circumstances confronting him (*vis-à-vis* the Germans and Vichy), but that we had to act to give evidence that he could rely upon our backing and support.

There were many Frenchmen who deplored the policy of Vichy but who felt it their duty to remain at their posts. Of that number, there was none of my acquaintance in North Africa who was more disheartened than Clarac. In July, he called to express his bitter disillusionment over the policy of his government. He termed its statement on Indo-China "shameless" and added, "Our policy in Syria was understandable if we intended to be consistent, but this time [the policy in Indo-China] makes no sense at all."

I was later to have the greatest difficulty in persuading him to remain at his post as consul in Tetuan. He wished to go to London and join De Gaulle. It was only under my earnest persuasion and argument—if he left, his place might be filled with a collaborationist—that I succeeded in overcoming his resolution.

A very useful French contact which the legation enjoyed in Morocco was the journalist Pierre Lyautey, who, as nephew of the late marshal, had a wide entrée among both French and Moroccan officials. In September he called on me after a visit to Vichy and Madrid. At Vichy he had had an hour's conversation with Pétain. He reported that he had found a much more optimistic attitude in Vichy with regard to an ultimate victory of the Allies than he had encountered in the spring.

The marshal had questioned Lyautey at great length concerning the activities of American representatives in Morocco. Pétain, he intimated, had wished to be disabused of the suggestion that the Americans were acting as an advance guard for an Anglo-American or an American military operation or trying to stir up Morocco against the French. Lyautey had insisted that the Americans were in Morocco for no other reasons that those connected with the economic accord. He had emphasized also that the Americans were only a handful, as compared with some two-hundred Germans of the Armistice Commission. He had expressed the view that, if there were concern about American activities, there should be even more concern about the Germans.

Marshal Pétain's inquiries about the American control officers under the economic accord may well have been occasioned by German protests. Only a little while before, I had been informed by Du Gardier, chief of the diplomatic cabinet at Rabat, that he had had a call from Herr Auer of the German Armistice Commission and the latter had lost his temper completely when referring to the American control officers. He had banged the table in indignation at the presence of such a large number of American officials. Du Gardier had replied that they had a right to be in Morocco and he could not admit the propriety of the German Armistice Commission to question the performance by American consular officers of their functions.

General Noguès showed great freedom in discussing with me the progress of the war. At the end of August he informed me he had been most apprehensive four months previous that action was being prepared by the Germans in Morocco. That danger had passed and he did not believe anything to be imminent. He thought the principal effort of the Germans in Russia would be to reach the Volga and to move upon Baku by an encircling rather than frontal assault.

He was called to Vichy in September to defend his position and returned sustained, at least for the time being, in his post. I was invited to an informal lunch with him on September 29, in company with Meyrier and Hardion and our respective wives; I had never found him so amiable, almost genial. After luncheon, he drew me aside for a long talk during which he showed the greatest freedom in his references to the Germans and left no doubt as to his feelings toward them.

He had found the Germans in France in a vile frame of mind, which he interpreted as a reflection of their nervousness over the Russian campaign. They were proving most recalcitrant in their dealings with the French, including even matters of the smallest moment, and they were failing to fulfill engagements already entered into with the French. The greatest surprise to the Germans in Russia had been not the strength in matériel possessed by the Russian Army but the failure of the Soviet State to disintegrate politically.

I inquired whether there were any new developments so far as the German and Italian Armistice Commissions were concerned. He replied that they were spending their time riding about the country.

I said I had heard at Marrakesh that a Frenchwoman had been expelled from the country for drinking a bottle of champagne with a member of the Italian Armistice Commission. He replied that that was correct and that he had taken similar measures with a Frenchwoman who owned a hotel in Marrakesh, and who had been friendly with a member of the German Commission.

In November, with the recall of Weygand by Pétain, another crisis arose in our economic aid program for French North Africa. Shipments of goods under the accord were again suspended by us pending a review of the situation.

I telegraphed to the Department expressing the view that, in the light of the importance of Morocco to us, it was believed that, despite the recall of Weygand, we should continue to maintain our ties with the country if only through reduced economic aid.

General Noguès, in a talk with me on November 30, said a great fault had been committed in the loose talk which had developed about the economic accord. Reports had reached him from as far afield as Madrid that Weygand was a man of the United States. This talk had done great damage to Weygand. The announcement of the suspension of the accord, following the departure of Weygand, played directly into the hands of the Germans, as it tended to justify the German contention that the accord had a political and not exclusively economic basis. He hoped the accord would continue on the latter basis.

Early in February 1942, I saw Noguès again. He expressed the view that the Germans had lost immense strength in Russia. He doubted if they could launch a full-scale offensive again before June or July. He thought Russia had shown up wonderfully well militarily but voiced apprehension, widely held among the French leaders, of the possible danger to Europe if the Russians were too successful.

Widespread disappointment and disillusionment had been aroused among the French in Morocco by the retreat of the British in Libya. Noguès did not consider that the campaign had taken a critical turn for them. He felt, however, that they had shown weakness in their failure to dispose of Rommel's forces.

With the fall of Singapore, discouragement became even more widespread. Pierre Lyautey called on me again on March 1 and reported that a great change had taken place in French public opinion since Singapore, the escape of the three German war vessels from Brest (*Scharnhorst, Gneisenau,* and the *Prinz Eugen*) and the inconclusive British campaign in Libya. In 1940, the French, or at least French leaders, had believed a German victory inevitable. The Russian campaign. the U.S. entry into the war, and the prospect in December that all of Libya and Cirenaica might fall into British hands had persuaded many Frenchmen that an Allied victory was fairly imminent. The more recent turn of events had brought about the belief that the war could only end in a stalemate unless it were to continue for some years, with all that that would mean for the ruin of Europe.

Paradoxically, Lyautey observed, the French people were becoming more democratic than they had been at the time of the armistice. In 1940, there had been a revulsion of feeling against the Republic, but a notable reaction had now set in. There was, moreover, less and less belief in the possibility of collaboration with Germany.

Lyautey thought the world situation had changed so materially that the aspect of things had shifted also in French North Africa. In the previous autumn he had foreseen the possibility of an Allied landing in Morocco in the spring of 1942. Now, with French disillusionment, we would have to face a more prudent and reserved attitude on the part of the French.

Lyautey cautioned us against Admiral Darlan, who, he said, felt strongly that France should be in a position to exploit the peace when it came. Darlan believed the war would end in a stalemate and that France would be in an excellent bargaining position between the Allies and the Axis. We should keep a careful eye on Darlan and on the possibility of a German coup in North Africa. Noguès had pursued an extremely adroit policy, but, with Allied reverses, this policy would become more and more difficult. He added that Noguès' position was now very strong. He had encouraged the visit to North Africa of Puchey, minister of the interior, who, while a Germanophile (he was later tried and shot), was anti-Darlan. Noguès had desired to bring him to North Africa to play him off against the admiral.

Lyautey left with me the strong impression that the action of Darlan, in agreeing to furnish supplies for Rommel's forces, was not so much due to German pressure as to a desire for an Allied stalemate. The intimation was that Darlan conceived it in the French interest to bring about such an objective.

In reporting this to the Department, I suggested that a motive in Darlan's permission for supplies to be moved through Tunisia to the Germans might well have been that, had the British reached the Tunisian border, the entire Vichy position in French North Africa might have been imperiled, as it might have provoked the adherence of French North Africa to the Allies.

Another crisis in our relations with the French arose with the return of Laval, on April 15, 1942, as French prime minister. Triat, French consul in Tangier, expressed great concern over the reported news and the possible effect it might have on Franco-American relations. He did not think the change need portend any immediate shift in Morocco.

I went to Rabat to explore the situation with the residency. Noguès, as Lyautey had foreseen, had become more cautious in his expression of views, but I obtained some illuminating comments from Bernard Hardion, his chief of civil cabinet, later ambassador to Spain.

Hardion did not anticipate that the change would result in the granting of bases to the Germans in Morocco, or any advantages they did not then possess, nor were any changes in French personnel in Morocco anticipated.[2]

Laval, Hardion said, was consumed by hatred for England because he felt that power had destroyed his plans for European peace. There was also Laval's deep-seated distrust of the Russians. Hardion stated he did not have this fear which animated so many Frenchmen. He thought the world faced the greatest social revolution in its history, irrespective of the Russians, but that it would be dominated not by the Russians but by the Anglo-Saxons.

Hardion thought it was a mistake to interpret Pétain's acceptance of Laval as complete submission to Germany. The turn of events would mean a closer economic collaboration, dictated by France's imperative need to survive, but would not involve a military collaboration, not concessions of the Fleet or North Africa. He recalled that, even in 1940, Laval had opposed the granting of facilities to the Germans in North Africa, and it was unreasonable to suppose that he would be more disposed to grant them now than he was then.

Hardion saw no signs of any imminent German move in French North Africa. The French military authorities in Morocco perceived no indication of such a move.

Two months later, on June 5, I talked with Noguès at length. He said the advent of Laval to power had changed nothing. I asked him if Laval had not been brought back under German pressure.

"Indirectly, if you like," was his reply, "but the Germans are already dissatisfied with him." Noguès added that Laval now had the full confidence of the marshal in a way he did not have before, but it was Pétain who continued to exercise the chief power. Noguès did not anticipate any changes in North Africa. He stressed that Laval was, above all, a good Frenchman. When he (Noguès) had been in Vichy recently, he had been told his directives remained the same as they had before.

Regarding the international situation, he said that Russian counteroffensive appeared to have seriously upset German plans. He thought the Germans were greatly overextended in their communications. They had been obliged to double the number of their divisions in France after the St. Nazaire affair (the British commando raid), and they would be plagued with the problem of not knowing where the enemy would strike next.

During my visit to Rabat an official at the residency estimated that 80 percent of the people in Morocco were wholeheartedly for us.

In August, the battle in the eastern desert between Rommel and the British took one of its periodic turns favorable to the Germans. Clarac called on me after a visit to Rabat and reported that morale was extremely low there owing to Allied reverses, the disintegration in Vichy and the lack of support French Morocco was receiving from France. Those returning from Vichy reported a decline in the prestige of the marshal and growing loss of credit by Laval. There was a conviction that Laval might not last beyond October and would be succeeded by Deat or Doriot. In such a case the tendency toward detachment of French North Africa from France would be greatly accelerated.

Early in August, I saw Lyautey again after he had been in Paris and Vichy. In Paris he had been struck by the jealousies and divisions which existed between the various German authorities. Laval's chief support came from Abetz, but the Wehrmacht distrusted all French politicians and was of the opinion that the only way to deal with France was through a *gauleiter*. Lyautey thought the deep fissures dividing different German adminstrations would one day, at a moment of extreme tension, contribute greatly to the crack-up of Germany.

He had been greatly impressed by the extreme consideration shown for the United States by the Germans. They seemed to wish to maintain a bridge with the United States through France.

I saw Lyautey again in the latter part of October on the eve of the landings. He said opinion in France, from which he had just returned, was that Germany was finished, with a crack-up expected before the end of the winter. It was coming more and more to be felt that the total occupation of France by Germany, which was expected in the near future, was the only possible way to resolve the tragic destiny of France. Pétain's star, no less than Laval's, had set. On a recent visit to France and Germany, Auer, German consul general in Casablanca, had urged replacement of Noguès by Petri, French ambassador to Madrid.

Lyautey said that, when he left Paris, there had been general talk of the possibility of some German action at Dakar. He thought that, despite the apparent lack of German forces for an operation in French North Africa, events were contributing to that possible eventuality.

As if confirming Lyautey's prognostications, we learned that one of the principal German agents in Tangier, Hermann Goeritz, who had returned from Germany a few days previous, had applied on October 23 at the French consulate general in Tangier for a visa for Dakar, stating he wished to be the first German official to make a visit there since the war. Vichy, it was learned, had instructed the French consulate not to issue the visa "for the time being."

I think, in summing up, it is reasonable to state that our relations with the French authorities in Morocco in 1941 and 1942 until the landings could not conceivably have been more cordial. General Noguès, his associates, French Consul Clarac in Tetuan, and the staff of the French consulate general in Tangier were remarkably free in giving us information. There was never any mistaking their sympathies with the Allied cause.

Why, then, the resistance on the part of the French to our landings, which resulted in such needless loss of life?

There can, at least, be no gainsaying the fact that we could hardly have had in Morocco an atmosphere more favorable to us on November 8, 1942.

NOTES

[1] We now know from the Ciano correspondence that Franco had, in fact, committed himself to cooperation with the Axis under such circumstances.

[2] This did not prove an accurate prevision. A little later, in June, the entire staff of the French consulate general in Tangier was changed under pressure from Germans on grounds that the personnel had been too friendly with us.

16
WARTIME INTRIGUE IN MOROCCO

From 1940 to 1944 there were probably few spots on the globe where more intense espionage and counterespionage activities were concentrated than in Tangier.

Under the terms of the economic accord for French North Africa concluded between Murphy and Weygand on February 26, 1941, it was provided that the United States would have the right to exercise control of shipments to North Africa to ensure that such shipments were not improperly transshipped or misused. For that purpose, a dozen or more American private citizens with a thorough knowledge of French were commissioned by the Department of State as control vice consuls and assigned to the consulates at Casablanca, French Morocco; Algiers, Algeria; and Tunis, Tunisia. Their ostensible activity, to control shipments from the United States, was actually only a minor function; their larger objective was to collect all information of an economic and military character that might assist the United States in any other plans it might have for the area. In the beginning, the possibility was envisaged that General Weygand, with or without the concurrence of Vichy, might be persuaded to join hands with the Allies; only some time later did there emerge the more ambitious project of Allied landings on the French North African coast.

The control vice consuls were under the supervision of Robert

Murphy in Algiers. With the establishment of a military attaché's office at the legation in Tangier in the spring of 1941, I made the suggestion, agreed upon after considerable correspondence, that the military attaché might assign to the control officers specific tasks in the collection of military information.

There soon began to flow into the office of the military attaché a great mass of data which was evaluated and coordinated—an invaluable assistance to the defense departments of our government in preparation for the landings in November 1942.

With the opening of a naval attaché's office in January 1942, under the command of Colonel Willam A. Eddy, a Marine officer, who eventually had three assistants, this work grew apace. Colonel Eddy headed all activities in French North Africa of the Office of Strategic Services and played a notable part in the work preparatory to the landings.

In the summer of 1942, Colonel Eddy approached me and stated that the chief pilot at one of the points along the Moroccan coast where it was contemplated a landing would be made had offered his services to our government. The Navy Department was extremely anxious to have him come to the United States in order to provide nautical information in furtherance of the landing. To preserve the secrecy of his departure, the chief pilot was prepared to take French leave and to have his wife announce to his friends that he had deserted her and disappeared. But how to spirit him out of French Morocco to Tangier and thence to Gibraltar where he could be given transportation to the United States?

Eddy stated that, if I concurred, the assistant naval attaché, Lieutenant Frank Holcombe, and one of the control vice consuls would drive to French Morocco with a trailer carryall. The chief pilot would be met in the darkness at an isolated spot and brought to the frontier between the French and Spanish zones. Before arriving at the frontier, he would be placed in the open trailer with a tarpaulin covering him. As there was never any inspection of legation vehicles at the frontier, there was no reason to anticipate any difficulty. Once in Tangier, there were no problems involved in conveying him surreptitiously to Gibraltar by special boat from the coast in the dead of night.

Despite every precaution, the passage over the frontier came within a hair's breadth of disaster. When Holcombe and Browne, his companion, arrived at the frontier with their human cargo, they were obliged to leave the automobile and trailer to present their passports for stamping by the passport control officers.

There was suddenly tremendous barking from a dog which had sniffed the presence of the pilot in the trailer. Holcombe and Browne came out and threw rocks at the dog until they were able to remove his suspicious presence. Fortunately, none of the frontier officials took any notice and the travelers were allowed to depart without further mishap.

The chief pilot was hurried to Gibraltar and then to the United States, where he worked closely with the Navy in planning the landings. He was aboard the lead vessel which entered Moroccan waters on November 7–8, 1942, and was subsequently decorated by the United States Government for his invaluable services on that occasion.

One of my constant preoccupations, occasioned by the presence of more than a hundred German and Italian secret agents in Tangier, together with an almost equal number of Americans and British, was that of taking all practical measures to avoid any incidents between members of my staff and the Axis group.

The opening of a German consulate in Tangier brought the question to an acute stage. While the German consul sent me the usual formal communication, announcing the assumption by him of his new duties, he made no effort to call, nor were any efforts made by any members of his staff to establish relations with us. I thought it advisable to caution members of my staff against the establishment of any social contacts with the Germans.

Consul General H. Earle Russell in Casablanca informed me, in July 1941, that Herr Auer, a German diplomatic officer and member of the German Armistice Commission, had made overtures to one of the vice consuls on Russell's staff. Russell wrote me that he was in favor of a strict quarantine of the Germans and asked for my advice as to the policy to be followed.

I replied that I had already adopted such a policy and that I thought the members of his staff should be even more careful about contacts with the German Armistice Commission. Among the principal reasons given was that any such association would be looked upon with suspicion by the French. I added that any junior officer who was of the opinion that he was sufficiently experienced to match wits with a senior German diplomatic officer and to obtain useful information in the process, as the vice consul had intimated it was in his capacity to do, impressed me as being, to say the least, naïve.

After our entrance into the war, my concern became one of avoiding any incidents between members of my staff and Axis representatives which might have embarrassing consequences in our relations with the Spanish. A few months after, Lieutenant Holcombe was dining with a group of friends in an Italian restaurant. Beside them was a table which included the Italian consul general, the Duke of Badoglio, son of the marshal, and a number of other Italians. Conviviality characterized both tables.

In the course of the evening, Badoglio fancied Holcombe had made remarks offensive to Italy, with whom we were then at war, and, when the two parties broke up, Badoglio was waiting for Holcombe. The duke caught hold of the latter, shook him and made threatening remarks. When Holcombe sought an explanation from the duke, the latter made off.

The incident having been reported to me by Colonel Eddy, I communicated at once with General Uriarte, delegate of the high commissioner in Tangier and, in giving him an account of it, I stated that I felt confident that he would take immediate steps to bring to light the perpetrators of this indignity offered a member of the staff of the legation and would take appropriate measures against those guilty.

General Uriarte was most apologetic about the occurrence, and the Spanish consul in Tangier, Rafael Soriano, called on me to express regret for it and to assure me the authorities were anxious to endeavor to arrange an amicable settlement.

After many exchanges back and forth, General Uriarte at length wrote me that "as a consequence of the steps that were taken both in writing and verbally with the Italian representation, I have received a letter from the Duke of Badoglio in which, referring to the assurance that I gave him that there were no gestures or attitudes against the Italian flag on the part of any of the American citizens that were in the group which he considered aggressors, he believes it is his duty to assure me that neither he nor any of his collaborators had the intention of offending Lieutenant Holcombe."

A no less extraordinary incident arose out of a request made of me in 1941, before our entrance into the war, by a British official, who shall remain nameless, that I convey explosive material by one of our control vice consuls to Casablanca. The material, it was represented, was needed for the blowing up of a quantity of rubber which had been unloaded in Casablanca for, it was believed, ultimate shipment to Germany via France.

I informed the British official who made the request that while I was wholly in sympathy with the purpose he had in view—that of providing much-needed rubber from falling into the hands of the Axis—I could not accede to his proposal. However important it was to deny rubber to the Axis, the work being performed by our control vice consuls in Morocco was, in my view, even more important. Any implication by them in the destruction of the rubber might hopelessly compromise all of them and lead to a demand for their withdrawal.

My interlocutor became visibly annoyed. "I suppose you know," he said, "the British Government has means of dealing with American officials lukewarm in aiding our war effort. A word from the Foreign Office to the State Department and your position may not be too comfortable."

I arose from my chair. "Let me make myself altogether plain.

Neither you nor the British Government can influence me, by threats or otherwise, to deviate from the course which I consider best serves American interests. Do I make myself clear?

"I have no authority," I continued, "to undertake what you suggest. My government may consider the risk worth taking and may order me to accede to your request. If I receive such an order, it will be executed faithfully, but until that time comes, neither you nor your government, despite your threats, will budge me." I nodded to the door and indicated that, so far as I was concerned, our conversation was at an end.

Some four or five days later, before my letter reporting the incident could have reached Washington, I received a cryptic message by telegraph that I should accede to the British request.

I picked up the telephone and informed the interested British official that I was prepared, on the basis of orders from Washington, to accept his package and forward it to Casablanca. He hurried down to the legation.

"Let me reemphasize," I said to him, "I am taking this action, not as a result of any menaces, but purely in fulfillment of orders." I added that I had written out a full account of our previous interview which I had transmitted to Washington by mail and that my government might have something to say on the subject when my report was received.

He shrugged his shoulders. "I don't understand at all. I can assure you there was not the least threat or menace on my part. It was a simple request and, if you have reported otherwise to Washington, you misinterpreted my remarks."

That was too much. I looked at him steadily as he sought to avert my gaze, and for the first and only time in my life, I gave the lie to another, unequivocally and unadorned: "You are a goddamned liar, and you know it."

I thought he would put on a great show in indignation and would feelingly resent the accusation. On the contrary, he sat mumbling a few feeble words of protestation.

When my letter reached the Department, the fur began to fly. Wallace Murray went to bat, as I knew he would, and the British were left, in no uncertain terms, with a knowledge of the Department's displeasure.

In the summer of 1941, months before Pearl Harbor, we instituted a Joint Anglo-American Intelligence Committee. Because of the large staff we had in French North Africa, and the absence of any British staff there, we gave, of course, a great deal more than we received. When Murphy passed through Tangier on one occasion and inquired whether I had any specific authority to exchange information with the British, my reply was that the Atlantic Charter, in my opinion, was a sufficient basis. British intelligence officers from Gibraltar, belonging to the staff of Lord

Gort, then British governor, were periodic visitors to Tangier. One of these, Captain Holland of the Royal Navy, who had presented the British demands to the French Fleet at Mers-el-Kébir in 1940, requested, in August 1941, on behalf of Lord Gort, my aid in transmitting to General Noguès the desire of the governor of Gibraltar to establish direct liaison with him. I did so, but General Noguès rejected the suggestion.

Relations between ourselves and the British in intelligence and other matters were so close that we were informed, at the end of December 1941, of British intentions to sabotage a secret German wireless station erected in Tangier for communication with German submarines infesting the Straits. Early in the morning of January 12, 1942, the station was put out of commission.

In reporting this development to Washington, I expressed the view that we might look for reprisals on the part of the Axis, against either the British, which was the more probable, or even against us, which was possible. In reply, the Department suggested that I should give up reading E. Phillips Oppenheim.

The sequel was what I had anticipated. On the afternoon of February 6, 1942, almost immediately after the arrival of the Gibraltar tug transporting the British courier and British official mail, a time bomb exploded on the quay in Tangier, killing a messenger of the British consulate, destroying the mail sacks and killing and wounding more than twenty persons. The bomb was obviously a German plant.

German intelligence in Tangier displayed considerable ability in its espionage activities. Although it even succeeded in placing an agent in our legation before the landings, the Germans in Morocco were caught completely by surprise by the event. It is owing to the precautions which we took that, notwithstanding their ability to introduce among our custodial employees a person in their service, they obtained no intimation of when the landing would take place. But we did not discover the wolf in sheep's clothing in our midst for a considerable time.

In the summer of 1942, when Malta was under severe siege and it looked for a time as if it might fall through lack of provisioning, the naval attaché's office was asked by the British to communicate with its contacts in Tunisia by telegraph with a view to mobilizing small boats in Tunisia to be sent with foodstuffs to Malta. Not being able to establish contact through its own communication facilities, the naval attaché's office appealed to me to send the message for them through our consulate in Tunis.

The message was duly sent. Several weeks later, friendly French intelligence sources informed the naval attaché's office that the French had intercepted and read a German code message reproducing the text of our message to Tunis.

This news, of course, created consternation among us. It was obvious to me that the Germans could not have abstracted the message from our chancery. My office, the file room and the code room were separated from the remainder of the legation by iron-grill doors, which were kept locked and were opened only for the admittance of American personnel.

Another investigation was conducted by one of the control officers whose imaginative gifts far exceeded his capacity for balanced judgment. In a report which Edgar Wallace would have repudiated for its fantastic suppositions, the finger of suspicion was leveled at one of our foreign clerks, a woman of mature years, the widow of a Foreign Service officer.

The report of the control vice consul, who was not subject to my jurisdiction but to that of Murphy, in Algiers, was forwarded to Washington. I received a communication indicating that serious consideration was being given to the dismissal of the accused. I replied giving substantial reasons for my complete confidence in her and my conviction of her innocence.

Many months later the mystery which had plagued our minds was finally solved in a most unexpected manner. The successor of Colonel Eddy as chief of the Office of Strategic Services, Wally Booth, informed me he had confirmation that the legation was harboring a German agent in its employ. A Spaniard who had been approached to work as an agent for our OSS and was actually serving at the same time in the German Secret Service in Tangier had stated that he would prefer to work for Americans, but he did not dare do so because his change of masters might become known. When pressed to explain, he stated that Germans had an agent planted in our legation.

We finally ascertained that the Germans had succeeded in introducing a Spanish charwoman who had been employed by the office of the naval attaché. She had been given instructions in the use of minuscule camera to photograph all documents left exposed. Further, she had been given a very special master key capable of opening locked file cabinets. Our previous inquiry had established that the telegram we had sent for the naval attaché's office, which had come into the possession of the Germans, had been left overnight in one of the locked filing cabinets of that office. It was by this means that they had gained possession of the text and not through the legation employee against whom accusations had been so unwarrantably made. The charwoman was promptly dismissed, of course, and the Spaniard entered our service, persuaded that our security was now protected.

Such was the atmosphere of intrigue with which we were surrounded in Tangier, from the moment of my arrival at the beginning of 1941 through the collapse of Italy in 1943 until the fall of Berlin in 1945.

That our lives were in some danger in this period was brought home to me by a conversation I had after the war with an American officer who had been stationed with our forces in French Morocco after the landings. When he was introduced to me at a cocktail party in New York, he remarked, to my great surprise, "Oh yes, I know Mr. Childs quite well."

"I am sorry," I said, "I don't recall we have ever met."

"We haven't, but I have good reason to know you."

"How is that?"

"Do you recall making a trip through Spanish Morocco, from Tangier to Tetuan, Kauen, Melilla, and thence through French Morocco by way of Oujda and Fez, back to Tangier?"

"Yes, in 1943."

"Correct. I was in French Morocco in intelligence and we were following your movements with a great deal of interest and, if I may say so, some apprehension."

"Really. Why this great interest?"

"It so happened that the Germans in Spanish Morocco were following your movements with even greater attention than our own. They were reporting your every movement and we were intercepting and reading their coded messages. It occurred to us that they must have designs on you and were preparing to bump you off at a given moment. There was great debate among us as to what we should do. If we notified you and warned you to take precautions, the Germans might have suspected we were breaking their codes. It was your life against our continued ability to read German messages passing out of Spanish Morocco. We decided the latter was the more important."

I laughed halfheartedly. Then I asked, jocularly, "Was this a general policy of the Army toward the State Department?" But, before I caught his answer, he had disappeared in the crowd.

In espionage activities we were enormously favored by the fact that the mass of the population of Morocco, whether French or Spanish, was pro-Allies. In Tangier, the Spanish population, which comprised the largest foreign element, was Republican Spanish; there was an important Jewish population, which was pro-Allies; and the French population, with exception of a few, was entirely with us. Apart from regularly employed agents, we were constantly receiving volunteered information.

After the collapse of Italy and the setting up of a neofascist republican government by Mussolini, the Italian consulate general, which had identified itself with the Badoglio government and was working in cooperation with us, was plagued by the local activities of the neofascists headed in Tangier by Judge Malmusi. Our agents had given us reports that a junior member of the staff of the Italian consulate was a neofascist reporting to the local group, but neither the Italian consulate nor we were able to obtain any conclusive evidence.

One day, a Jewish tailor came into the legation and said he had some information of possible value. While cleaning the suit of a member of the Italian consulate staff, he had found a letter from Judge Malmusi containing directions to his spy concerning the latter's activities, which our informant thought might be of interest to us. It was, indeed, for it was precisely the information we had been seeking.

I communicated with Berio, Badoglio's local successor, and furnished him the information without disclosing its source. Berio was visibly impressed.

An equally interesting case was that of a Swiss architect in Tangier who was employed in a professional capacity both by the German and the British consulates general. I had expressed some surprise to my British colleague that the British felt sufficiently sure of the Swiss national to employ him when he was in the employ of the Germans, but I had been assured that he had been investigated and that he was not a German agent.

We succeeded in getting hold of the passport of the Swiss, through an intermediary, and noted the frequent trips he was making into the French zone. Note was also taken of the dates of his visits to Casablanca. Sometime later, some papers of the German consulate general fell into our hands and, amongst these, were messages to Germany to the effect that the consulate general had succeeded in employing as an agent the "leading Swiss architect in Tangier" who had been of great assistance in turning in the names of Frenchmen working in French Morocco for the Allied cause. The German consul added that a condition of the Swiss national's willingness to work with the Germans had been a promise that his name would never be used in any communications. As there was only one Swiss in Tangier who was an architect, we did not have difficulty identifying him, but what made the evidence conclusive was that the dates in his passport corresponded exactly with the days when the German consul had interviewed him in the consulate to receive his reports.

The British were at last convinced and the Swiss national was included forthwith on the Anglo-American blacklist. He had been the representative in Tangier of the Swiss Red Cross, and one of the consequences of our action was the termination of his services in that capacity by the Swiss.

Our undercover organization was of enormous benefit to us both before and after the landings. It was something new for Americans, and mistakes were inevitably made in a work so foreign to us. Some of the young recruits were too much imbued with the romantic element attaching to espionage and suffered from an exaggerated cloak-and-dagger mentality. Considering our inexperience, I think the results, whatever the errors, were astonishingly fruitful, first under the direction of Colonel Eddy, then Waller Booth and, lastly, under Richard Bownass. While at some posts cooperation between the Foreign Service and the OSS left a great deal to be desired, there could not have been more effective working cooperation than we had between the two at Tangier. Had there been similar cooperation all along the line, the landings and their aftermath might have been attended with fewer casualties.

17
ATTITUDES TOWARD ALLIED INVASION

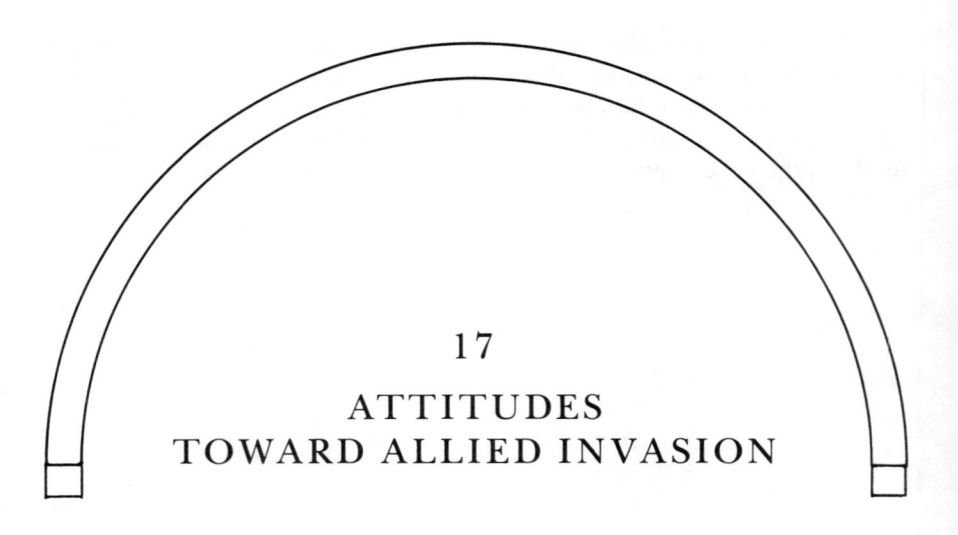

*O*ne of the momentous questions affecting the success of any Allied landings in French North Africa was, naturally, the action which Spain and Spanish Morocco would be impelled to take in such an event, acting either in protection of what it considered their own interests, or under pressure of the Axis. So far as the last-named contingency was concerned, Colonel Eddy, naval attaché of our legation, and I had received from General Orgaz the most unequivocal assurances in March (reported by telegram on March 13) that if Spanish Morocco were invaded by the Axis it would resist to the limit of its power. As to the first eventuality, I had formulated views and reported officially, as early as September 1, 1942, my evaluation of the probable attitude of Spanish Morocco in the event of an Allied landing in French North Africa:

> [In such an event] it may be expected that pressure would be exerted at once by the Axis upon Spain...
> The attitude of Spanish Morocco toward such demands would depend, of course, on the international situation at the moment and Spanish calculations concerning the respective chances for victory of the United Nations and the Axis. Since December, 1941, local Spanish sentiment has reflected a loss of faith in the possibility of a German victory, and since that time also Spanish disinclination to be involved in the war has steadily increased, it is believed that, in the face of German

demands for aid, every reasonable effort would be made to avoid acceding to them.

Spanish calculations would no doubt be based on the assumption that a yielding to German demands would probably entail inevitably the involvement of Spain and Spanish Morocco in war against the United Nations. On the other hand the Spanish would probably calculate that a refusal to grant such aid might not necessarily involve Spain in the war through the use of force by Germany. . . .

It is possible, though not altogether probable, that a decision on the part of the Madrid Government to yield to Axis demands might be met with refusal by the authorities of Spanish Morocco to execute orders of the Central Government. It is known that General Orgaz, Spanish High Commissioner, is strongly desirous of maintaining the neutral character of Spanish Morocco and, at a given moment, it is by no means improbable that General Orgaz might, under favorable circumstances, be induced to decline to agree to the use by the Axis of Spanish Morocco as a base of operations, even if permission therefor might be granted by the Madrid Government under pressure.

There can be little doubt that Spain's hesitance to embark upon other territorial adventures in North Africa has been due to a consideration of the risks involved. One very important consideration, which might curb the Spanish in undertaking a diversionary march into French Morocco from the north, or into Oran from Melilla, would be the realization that no single act would do more to solidify French sentiment against the Axis and in favor of the United Nations. It is on that account important that should an Allied landing at any time in the future be undertaken in French North Africa, the most explicit assurance should be given at once that the Allies entertain no territorial aspirations in North Africa. Such a declaration would do much to rally French assistance actively in behalf of the Allied landing for an attempt to occupy any territory in French North Africa.

On the eve of the Allied landings in French North Africa, persistent reports were received by me and by my British colleague, Gascoigne, then consul general and later ambassador to Russia, that Spanish forces in the Spanish zone would, under certain circumstances, move into French Morocco to the Sebou River. Clarac, who had just returned from Vichy and Paris, reported that, when he passed through Madrid, the French embassy there entertained forebodings that such a movement would take place in the event of an Allied attack on Dakar, an Allied landing in French Morocco or a major French political crisis. I could find no evidence in support of such apprehensions.

Gascoigne was so convinced that such apprehensions were well founded that, on October 26, thirteen days before the landings, he raised with me the character of the communication which should be recommended to our governments for transmittal to General Orgaz on the occasion of such landings. He expressed the view that we should be authorized both to assure Orgaz that our governments intended to respect the territorial integrity of Spanish Morocco, provided Spain maintained a neutral status toward our occupation, and that our governments would give the most sympathetic consideration to Spanish claims to certain territories in French Morocco.

I informed Gascoigne that, under the circumstances envisaged, in my view asssurances should be given to both the Spanish and French authorities in Morocco, disavowing any territorial aspirations on our part in respect of Moroccan territory. I expressed, however, serious misgivings as to the advisability of making any commitment to the Spanish authorities regarding the satisfaction of their territorial aspirations in French Morocco.

My British colleague suggested that, in the absence of such assurances, the Spanish military authorities might very well take matters into their own hands and proceed forthwith to the occupation of that part of French Morocco north of the Sebou line, to which they had laid claim for many years. The result might be a possible conflict between Spain and the powers occupying French Morocco.

I informed Gascoigne that I did not share his apprehension. I had just visited Spain and, from what I had gathered from both the American and British embassies there, Spain was further than ever removed from the prospect of involvement in the war. I thought the situation might be envisaged as presenting two alternative possibilities. In the event of a successful Allied landing in French Morocco, Spanish forces would at once cross the border from the Spanish zone or would maintain an attitude of reserve while awaiting developments. It was to be presumed that the Allies would not make the mistake of attempting an occupation of French Morocco with insufficient forces. Assuming, therefore, that such forces would be adequate for their task, it was to my mind extremely doubtful, provided the Spanish Army did not act at once, that it would decide to act after a successful landing and occupation of French Morocco by our forces.

Accordingly, since an action which the Spanish Army might be expected to take would, in all probability, be coincident with the landings, it appeared a reasonable hypothesis, I argued, that such action would have been decided upon well in advance. It seemed extremely unlikely, therefore, that any assurances we might offer to General Orgaz would alter the scales of Spanish calculations. The Spanish themselves had already carefully weighed the risks involved. They would doubtless have taken into account that any attempt on their part to advance in French Morocco to the Sebou line for the purpose of staking their claim to that territory would involve them in the risks of a belligerency which they had shown themselves, in the highest degree, anxious to avoid. I argued that, while not minimizing the possibility of Spanish action, we should not overestimate that possibility or fail to take into due account natural Spanish hesitation to make any overt move on the occasion of an Allied landing, which might provoke incalculable consequences for them.

Moreover, I contended, there was a further consideration of some weight so far as the French were concerned. It was presumed that, at the same time that our governments were conveying to the Spanish Government evidence of our intentions to respect the territorial integrity of Spanish Morocco, similar assurances would be given by us to the French. Any assurances of our readiness to give sympathetic consideration to Spanish pretensions in French Morocco would tend to vitiate the assurances given the French. Any sweeping assurances given the Spanish would certainly become known and would do more than anything else to alienate popular French support essential to the success of an Allied landing.

I concluded that any assurances to the Spanish authorities which extended beyond a disavowal of any territorial aspirations with respect to Morocco would be inadvisable for the reason that they would be inexpedient, both morally and practically, and could serve no useful purpose.

Complete concurrence in these views was conveyed to me by the State Department, I was informed that neither the United States nor British governments had any intention of supporting Spanish claims to French Morocco.

I had an interview with General Orgaz on October 28, a few days before the landings. In reply to my inquiry concerning his view of the international situation, he answered that it was clear no decision to support the Axis was possible in 1942. He added that we had thus gained a year, which was greatly to our advantage. I informed him I had just returned from Portugal and Spain, where I had observed a considerable shift of opinion in our favor and where it was considered the war had taken a more favorable turn for us. Orgaz nodded his head in agreement and said he found this shift only logical.

With the triumphal progress of the British Eighth Army in Libya during the days preceding the landings, I telegraphed the Department on November 6 that the success of Allied arms in Egypt had naturally produced a pronounced reaction in Morocco, most strikingly evidenced by the sharp shift in the Spanish press, now beginning to feature the news in a manner more favorable to us. It was added that the successful continuance of the Allied offensive in the Western Desert might be expected to have two important consequences in relation to any Allied operation in French North Africa:

1. It should have a deterrent effect on any Spanish plans which may have been contemplated for the occupation of any part of French North Africa and, further, it should stiffen notably Spanish resistance to any German pressure to that end.

2. It was already powerfully bolstering French morale favorably to the Allied cause and it would sensibly reduce such will to resistance to an Allied landing as may have existed among the waiverers, such as Noguès, who were no doubt debating in their minds the course of action they should pursue in the face of any Allied operations in French North Africa.

I had become convinced, on the basis of all the information available to the legation in Tangier, that the Spanish would not move from Spanish Morocco into French Morocco in the event of an invasion by us of the French zone. This belief had been conveyed on more than one occasion to the Department.

There was always the eventuality, of course, that the Germans would either bring sufficient pressure to bear upon the Spanish to move or that they would act alone. While discounting the first contingency, no one outside the German General Staff could have any worthwhile opinion on the second. We could report, however, as we did, that there were no visible signs of any German preparations for such a move.

The opposition which our Western Task Force encountered from French land and sea forces in Morocco in the landings of November 8, 1942, came as a great shock to millions of Americans who had counted upon our troops being welcomed with open arms as deliverers.

We had had, however, ample warning of what we might expect from those French authorities most in sympathy with us and not least from General Noguès, the supreme French authority in Morocco.

As early as March 1941, two French officials informed me that French North Africa would defend itself against an attack from whatever quarter it might come. It was true that, during April 1941, a year and a half before the landings, Noguès intimated to me that the time might come when French North Africa would have a useful role to play for the Allied cause, but this was the only occasion during my long association with him that he went that far. He said to me in April that, if French North Africa could be kept going through 1941, the time might come when it could have a part to play in the war, but he added that it was folly for the British to think that anything could be attempted at that time. Noguès' comments were doubtless directed to the overtures which the British were then making to Weygand. He never again, in his many conversations with me, held out the least promise that we might count upon the unopposed reception of Allied troops in Morocco; on the contrary, he many times emphasized that it was his intention to defend Morocco from attack from whatever source it might emanate.

I knew in Morocco no warmer supporter of the Allied cause than my friend Clarac. On May 30, he echoed independently the viewpoint expressed to me by Noguès. Clarac thought it was absurd for the British to expect that French North Africa was in a position to take active measures against the Germans for the present or to do more than was being done by Noguès and Weygand, in the face of all the difficulties confronting them.

At this time, one heard considerable private discussion in Morocco concerning the possibililty of the landing of American troops in the country or the possible display of American naval power by the visit of vessels of the United States Navy to Dakar, Casablanca and Tangier. The President's statement of May 15 about Franco-American relations and the declarations of prominent American personalities concerning American interest in northwest Africa had provoked widespread comment in Morocco and had led to the conclusion that we were contemplating some concrete manifestation of that interest. Moreover, from my contacts with members of Lord Gort's staff in Gibraltar, I gathered the impression that the British were pressing us for a display of naval strength in the area. I considered it desirable, in the light of these circumstances, to present my views to the State Department:

> The French are demoralized, and they have little stomach for anything but their personal security. The overwhelming majority are sympathetic to the United States, but they are no longer willing to pay a price in support of their convictions.
>
> A visit of American naval vessels would be received with the utmost enthusiasm by the French people in Morocco. The reaction of officials would probably be one of concern over possible German counter-measures.
>
> However, the visit of a few vessels of our fleet, unless we were ready and willing, in case of necessity, to undertake decisive action, would in all probability have consequences which we should seek to avoid than to provoke.
>
> Accordingly, until we may be prepared to prevent, by the deployment as well as by the display of power, the use of French Northwest Africa as a base for an attack against the Western Hemisphere, it would be most desirable to avoid provoking counter-measures which we may not be prepared to contest. French feeling in Morocco needs no artificial stimulus at present. Its stiffening prematurely might lead to subsequent disillusionment.

After thirty years, I do not find a word in this appraisal which I would change.

Pierre Lyautey, on September 5, gave me an extended expression of his views on a possible Allied military operation in northwest Africa. Considering his close contacts with the residency in Morocco, his opinions could be interpreted as a reflection of official French opinion in Morocco.

Lyautey opined it would be a great mistake for either the United States or Great Britain, together or separately, to undertake a military or naval operation in Morocco in the absence of an appeal from the French. My visitor recalled that General Weygand had stated he would defend North Africa against an attack from whatever quarter. There were a number of possible contingencies:

1. The British might launch an attack against Axis forces in the Western Desert of Libya and those forces might be pushed back to Tunisia. If forced to choose between surrender and entry into Tunisia, the Axis forces might attempt the latter. Weygand would probably be inclined to resist any entry of Italian forces into Tunisia and, at such time, he might well appeal for British and American aid.

2. The Spanish might be persuaded by the Germans to attack French Morocco from the Spanish zone, or the Germans might make a sudden move to acquire bases in North Africa. Under such circumstances, General Weygand could justify an appeal for, or the acceptance of, an offer of British or American aid, or both.

3. The Free Zone in France might be occupied by the Germans, and General Weygand, in consequence, released by Marshal Pétain from all obligations to him.

Lyautey stated that in December, 1940, it had been touch and go whether French North Africa might not go on its own. Upon his arrival in Rabat on December 26, 1940, General Noguès had informed him that it looked very much as if French North Africa might declare itself independent of the German and Italian armistice conditions, if the threatened occupation of all France by the Germans materialized.

My interlocutor observed that perhaps two thirds of the French officers in North Africa looked forward to the time when they would be actively engaged alongside British or American troops in North Africa. The most important question, in connection with the use of Allied troops in that area, was that of timing. He thought a propitious moment might be in six months.

Lyautey emphasized that Weygand and Noguès would have no other recourse than to defend French North Africa against a British or American landing if this were undertaken independently, without an appeal from, or an understanding with, the French. He thought Weygand was heart and soul for the Allied cause, notwithstanding the necessity that he was under to conceal his sympathies in his public utterances. As for Noguès, the view was expressed that he would follow the stronger side.

Already, on June 8, 1941, General Noguès had observed to me that neither Britain nor the United States was in a position to assist French North Africa militarily and that, in consequence, both he and Weygand were thrown upon their own resources. He added that, although they had little on which to depend, they were determined to defend French North Africa from any attack. On November 30, in making a plea for the continuance of our economic accord, Noguès expressed the view that it was in the French interest, as well as our own, to keep Morocco outside the war area. The advent of the war to Morocco would be disastrous. He insisted again that Morocco would defend itself from any menace.

Lyautey, on the other hand, was more optimistic. He argued that the disappearance of Weygand from Algiers did not modify the essential and fundamental fact that the Atlantic shores of Africa represented an economic vanguard and tomorrow would be a military fortress for operations which would permit the driving of the Germans from Africa, Italy and France.

Lyautey, of course, was a journalist. Noguès was the French administrator responsible for Morocco, whose sole preoccupation was the safeguarding of French interests there. This will help to explain the difference in their respective outlooks.

The even more conservative attitude of the French Navy was presented to Colonel Bentley, our military attaché, and Consul Stanton in Casablanca on November 24 by Admiral d'Harcourt, commanding French naval forces there. Admiral d'Harcourt stated that he had received no orders from Vichy indicating that bases in North Africa and units of the French Fleet were to be turned over to the Germans. He intimated, however, that he would follow Vichy's orders if Vichy ordered the peaceful turning over of the bases to anyone. He expressed the personal view that it was extremely unlikely the French Navy would ever fight for the Germans. He regretted that Americans continually drew a distinction between Vichy and French North Africa, emphasizing that both should be considered as an entity, and that they would always act together as an entity.

He added that, as a French admiral, he would act against the British, should they use force in an operation against the French, in precisely the same manner he would expect an American admiral to act against an attempted British landing at Savannah with the declared purpose of protecting Bermuda. He expressed the conviction that he or any other French naval officer would resist immediately any attempt which might be made to forcibly occupy a French base.

Other testimony came to us regarding the point of view of other high-ranking French officers in North Africa. At the beginning of February 1942, a high French military authority informed our military attaché, Colonel Bentley, that General Juin, addressing a meeting of officers the month previous, had stated in substance: "I know and you know we all wait and hope for one thing, the defeat of Germany. I must, however, impress on you the necessity of not discussing or expressing such feelings for, as yet, we can do nothing. Any reports of such remarks which reach the Germans can do us irreparable harm."

Whatever the view of General Juin, or of other officers, the attitude of General Noguès, the principal French authority in Morocco, was for us the fundamental factor. On June 5, 1942, the French resident general went at some length into a definition of his position in such a way as to make it unequivocal. He said, and these are actually a translation of his words: "Morocco is very favorably disposed toward the United States but we shall resist any effort which may be made to attack us, and I hope you will emphasize this to your government."

Noguès added that in his opinion nothing would draw the Germans more quickly to North Africa than a belief that there was a serious likelihood of an Anglo-American landing. He informed me that the Germans were already much disturbed on this score because of widespread reports that the British had been pressed by the Russians to create a diversion in French North Africa, on the Continent or in Norway.

I remarked to Noguès that we had not taken any aggressive action against any French possession during the war, and I expressed the view that it was extremely unlikely we should take action in Morocco in opposition to French desires.

Noguès answered that he had a great deal of confidence in us and he did not think we would do so, but he was afraid the British might.

I answered that we were acting in such concert that it was not possible to foresee one of the partners taking action independent of the other.

I then asked Noguès if he had any reason to believe the Germans had recently become particularly anxious over a possible Allied landing and whether they had begun any special plans in anticipation of such an invasion. Noguès' reply was that the Germans were a very methodical people and, since the arrival of the German Armistice Commission, they had presumably made plans for taking action under every possible circumstance.

On August 18, Clarac confirmed the attitude which Noguès might be expected to take toward an Allied landing. He recounted a conversation with a member of the German consulate in Tangier, who had refered to Noguès "as an enemy of the Germans." Clarac had endeavored to rebut this description by remarking that Noguès would react strongly against an American landing and that, in this respect, he could not be viewed as an enemy of Germany.

In September I visited Rabat. In reporting the impressions I had gained on the occasion of that visit, I stated that it appeared the French military authorities in Morocco did not anticipate an Allied landing in Morocco before 1943. In contrast to the concern which had been expressed to me by Noguès and others in June, 1942, over a possible Allied landing, the subject had not been raised by anyone. It was added, however, that the German Armistice Commission, which in June had been very nervous over such a possibility, had become extremely concerned over the subject again. I was told that the Germans were not disposed to rely on French support in the event of an Allied landing but were counting on taking such measures as might be available without French assistance. It was suggested that the Germans would endeavor, under such circumstances, to tempt Spanish cooperation by the offer of French Morocco, but it was not thought the Spanish would yield to the temptation.

Ten days before the landings, I reported the categoric opinion expressed to me by a French official source in Tangier regarding the French intention to resist an Allied landing. My Tangier source stated that, in the event of a German occupation of all of France, the dissident movement in French North Africa would be universal. He added the view that, unless an Allied landing in French North Africa coincided with a political crisis in France, bringing about a sharp cleavage of opinion, an Allied landing would meet with determined French resistance from the Army and the Air Force as well as the Navy.

Analyzing the attitude of Noguès toward an American landing, then and long after the event, it can be perceived that he was on the horns of a very real dilemna. He had before him the fiasco of De Gaulle's attempt to occupy Dakar in what was little more than a commando raid. He also had in mind the commando raids executed by the British in France, during which they had landed only to retire. At that stage of the war, in November 1942, no French military leader believed it conceivable that the Allies, with their efforts spread out on so many fronts, could launch a primary operation in French North Africa.

Noguès was a keen student of the war and he had followed its grand strategy closely. An Allied landing in insufficient force, in the nature of a commando raid or something but little better, was certain to provoke instant countermeasures on the part of the Germans. Although, in the event these did not take place in Morocco but only in Tunisia, it is almost certain the German measures in defense of Tunisia would have been taken in Morocco if the landings had been confined to that area. Noguès did not know, on the night of November 7–8, 1942, that the landings extended beyond Morocco and were on a large scale, for which lack of knowledge we alone were responsible.

If the landings were on a small scale, and of this Noguès was convinced, and if he failed to put up resistance, the Germans, in their countermeasures, would seize Morocco, and the country whose tie with France had been so carefully nurtured by Lyautey and Noguès would fall irretrievably to Germany, with certainly no advantage to the Allies.

There was also a further consideration, and that was the peculiarly French attachment to logic and the *droit administratif*, which exercise so great a fascination for the French national character. The freedom of maneuver of the logical French is governed strictly by the legality inherent in an action. General Noguès had taken his oath as an officer to obey orders from the constituted legal authority. As long as Marshal Pétain was chief of state, any order or instruction issued by him must be obeyed, irrespective of the character of the order. If such orders appeared to be in the interest of the Axis, it was not the concern of the officer called upon to execute them; they were legal orders and had to be fulfilled.

These must have been some of the considerations which were revolving in Noguès' mind on that fateful night. If we had adopted the measures which were available to us to convince Noguès that our landings were on a large enough scale to ensure their success and to make resistance useless and a needless waste of French lives, it is believed he might have been content to offer only token resistance. This would have upheld his honor and the obligations, as he conceived them, of a French military commander.

We failed, however, to take the measures with Noguès which the situation so obviously called for, with the result that our forces encountered in Morocco a resistance not equaled anywhere else in French North Africa.

It might be said that, in essence, General Noguès, in acting as he did, was conforming to the national characteristics of a Frenchman. It is no sin to be French. However incongruous his action in resisting appeared to us, not his enemies but his friends, he should be judged not on the basis of our standards of conduct but on his own.

We have already anticipated events. There must be reserved for subsequent examination the major error, committed not by the French but by us, which was of such tragic consequences to both ourselves and the French, as well as to General Noguès.

18
OPERATION TORCH

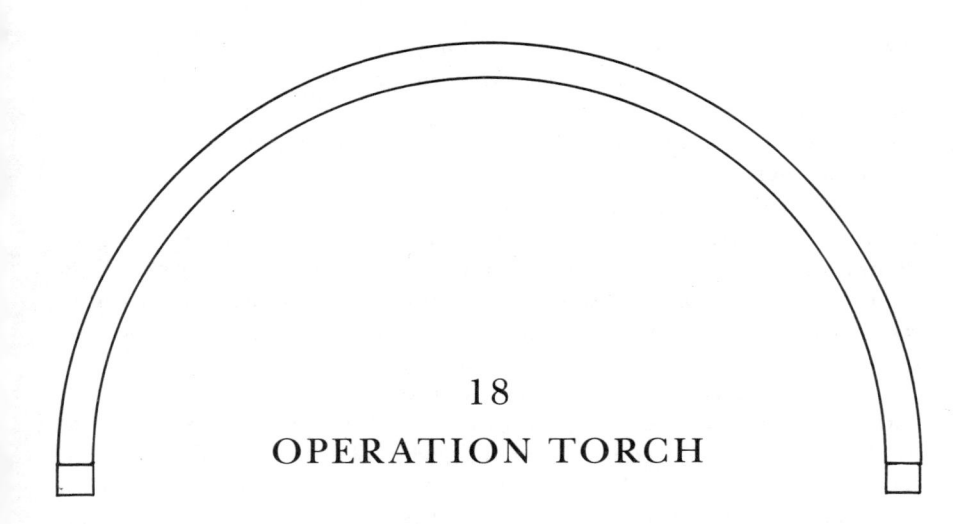

*W*hen Colonel Eddy arrived in Tangier on January 26, 1942, it was with the expectation that American landings on the French North African coast would materialize within a few months. He was bitterly disappointed and almost inclined to give up when he received news from General William Donovan that the campaign in the Pacific had compelled postponement of Allied plans for French North Africa.

The first word which the legation had of the operation, afterwards known as "Torch," came early in June 1942, with the arrival in Tangier of Colonel Robert A. Solborg, military attaché in Lisbon. Colonel Solborg, who had been previously in North Africa as a civilian with the OSS, showed me in greatest confidence a directive from the Joint Chiefs of Staff authorizing him to sound out the situation in North Africa to determine the French officer of high rank, whether in France or in North Africa, who was able and willing to rally the French forces to us if we should land in that area.

I informed Solborg I knew of no one in Morocco who answered that description. While Noguès was favorably disposed to us, I expressed the view he was not the man to take the lead. I counseled him against even sounding out Noguès. I did, however, offer to put him in touch with the chief of staff of the French air force in Morocco, who, both to me and to Colonel Bentley, had not concealed his hopes of an Allied landing.

Solborg and I drove to Rabat. There I called on Du Gardier, chief of the diplomatic cabinet, who was extremely friendly to us, and asked him if he could telephone to Colonel Koeglin-Schwartz and inquire if the latter could receive us that evening after dinner. I remarked that I hesitated to telephone him myself as I knew telephone conversations from our hotel were tapped.

Du Gardier grimaced. "And you don't suppose ours are?" he asked. He readily agreed, however, to send a messenger to Colonel Koeglin-Schwartz with my request for an appointment. Word came back a little later that he would be glad to receive me and my friend but admonishing me to leave my car some distance from his house and enter on foot so as to avoid any identification of the legation car with him.

We had a lengthy conversation with the chief of staff of the air force, without in any way disclosing the purpose behind our visit. Solborg did ask him, after a long general discussion, whom he considered most capable and willing to appeal to the French forces to throw in their lot with the Allies, should an occasion present itself in the future.

Without any hesitation, Colonel Koeglin-Schwartz answered that, in his opinion, there was one man to whom the forces in French North Africa would readily respond—General Giraud, who had lately escaped as a prisoner of war of the Germans.

As we left, at the end of our interview, Solborg said to me: "It is curious he should have mentioned Giraud. I have an appointment tomorrow in Casablanca with a Frenchman named Lemaigre-Debreuil, who is in touch with Giraud. From all I have been able to learn, Giraud seems to be the man for us."

Solborg asked that, upon my return to Tangier, I send the following telegram for him to military intelligence: "I have established contact leading to one remaining French general whose leadership would be unquestioned. Am planning to leave for Algiers this week for further exploratory talks. If successful, staff talks may begin forthwith. Will state general's name later. He is in France."

This telegram was sent on June 10. Solborg proceeded to Casablanca, where he met Lemaigre-Debreuil, who went to France, obtained Giraud's agreement and returned to acquaint Solborg with the results.

About ten days later, Solborg reappeared in Tangier from Algiers and acquainted me with what had been arranged. He added that, among the Americans, only he, Murphy and I were in on the secret. He asked me to send another message to the effect that the willingness of Giraud to assume the leadership had been obtained.

"Bob," I said, "this is too important and too dangerous to put on the air. My advice to you is to cable and ask for orders to proceed to the United States to discuss matters of the highest importance."

I asked him when the landings were projected. He said that it was expected they would take place in about three months. I expressed the view that it would be almost impossible to keep them a secret for so long, but I was mistaken. The secret was kept not three but five months.

I was correct, however, in the advice I gave him. He persuaded the military attaché to send his message and they both received a rap over the knuckles for transmitting the information, even by secret code, when so many eyes could view the contents.

The next concrete news of the planned landings came on September 5, 1942, with the return to Tangier of Colonel Eddy, who had gone to Washington to confer with our military and naval authorities on the subject. Colonel Eddy came immediately from the boat to the legation and disclosed to me the entire plan.

I asked him if a date had been fixed. He said the event would occur, if all went well, the latter part of October or early in November. I would be able to tell by the great convoys which would pass through the Straits two or three days before the landings. Moreover, he would take his departure four or five days in advance to join General Eisenhower at Gibraltar. He would be replaced as naval attaché at the legation to permit him to join Eisenhower's staff.

"Bill, it seems to me," I observed, "it would be an excellent idea for me to go on leave in a few days and remain absent until the eve of the landings. This would have the effect of throwing the Germans around here off their guard."

Colonel Eddy agreed with me and I accordingly telegraphed the Department on September 17 expressing my intention, in the absence of any objection, to absent myself on leave in Spain and Portugal from September 26 for two weeks or so. I learned later that my telegram had caused considerable discussion. For security reasons I had not thought it wise to explain the reasons behind my taking leave at such a time, but those in the Department read between the lines and concluded that it might be a useful tactic. I returned to Tangier on October 20.

I think it was on November 2 that Eddy took off for Gibraltar. A day or two later, the vantage points in Tangier were crowded with spectators craning their necks to observe the immense line of ships entering the Straits and speculating as to their destination. When questions were asked us, we shrugged our shoulders and suggested they might be headed for Malta.

November 7 was a Saturday. Gascoigne, British consul general, informed me that morning he had received news of a very important development which was to take place the following day but he had been enjoined not to disclose it. He did not need to, for I had instructions from the Department of State that, while it had been agreed with the British Government, Gascoigne was to give the Spanish high commissioner assurances of our peaceful intentions so far as Spanish Morocco was concerned, on the occasion of the landings in French Morocco, I was authorized, in my discretion, to give similar assurances following upon his.

The great question about which I realized the Department would be anxious to be informed was what the Spanish would do.

At 6 A.M. on Sunday, November 8, I telegraphed the Department, after listening to the radio the entire night, that news of the landings had been received in the early hours of the morning and that the situation in Tangier was entirely normal.

Gascoigne called at 9 A.M. to inform me he had delivered to General Mugica at two that morning, in the absence of General Orgaz who was in Madrid, the assurances he had been instructed to give. Immediately after Gascoigne's call, I decided to proceed to Tetuan to speak with General Mugica and to obtain the lay of the land.

I reached Tetuan, an hour's drive from Tangier, about eleven o'clock and lost an hour at the high commisariat in a vain endeavor to find someone in authority. I managed to track down one of the custodial employees, who directed me to the home of the acting high commissioner.

General Mugica received me most pleasantly. I conveyed to him the statement I had been authorized to make that the United States understood and appreciated the desire of the Spanish Government and people to remain neutral and that there was nothing in the policy of the United States that would necessitate any departure by the Spanish Government from their neutral purposes. Mugica said he had received comparable assurances from the British consul general that morning and that General Orgaz, with whom he had been in telephone communication in Madrid, had received similar assurances from Sir Samuel Hoare, British ambassador. Mugica added that Orgaz was returning to Tetuan by plane that afternoon.

Mugica was constantly called during our conversation to answer the telephone to receive reports on the North African situation coming from Melilla and other points in Spanish North Africa.

I found no appreciable traffic on the road to Tetuan, either going or coming. Tetuan was entirely calm, the streets being filled with the usual throngs of Sunday promenaders.

In presenting the situation in Tetuan to the Department, I added this unequivocal conclusion: "Unless I am badly deceived, the Spanish will not stir from the Spanish zone. They appear to have been caught quite unprepared by our action, they seem very much impressed by the rapidity and effectiveness of it, and they appear anything but displeased by it."

While these events were taking place, developments of even greater moment were occurring in the French zone, where our forces were endeavoring to effectuate landings at Safi, Casablanca and Fedala.

A week or ten days before the landings, there began to arise in my mind concern whether I had completely fulfilled my duties to the Department so far as Noguès was concerned. The fact that began to trouble me was that, notwithstanding the closeness of the relations between the legation in Tangier and the French resident general, we had never been consulted by the planners of Torch concerning Nogues' probable reaction (although, as this record will show, these had been conveyed at various times at some length to Washington). Nor had the legation been consulted as to how he might best be approached to persuade him to throw in his lot with us, including the argument that the resistance we were confident he would offer would be useless. What troubled me more and more was that we had not taken the initiative to express our views to those in authority. Such reluctance had ensued from the belief that, if the judgment of the legation in Morocco had been desired, it would have been sought. It was now resolved to repair this omission, even at the risk of the charge of presumption or of interference in a question which was the immediate concern of the White House and the War Department.

When, in June 1942, I had called on General Noguès to present Colonel Johnson, the new military attaché in succession to Colonel Bentley, Du Gardier, chief of the diplomatic cabinet, very pointedly had made the observation to the new military attaché as we emerged: "Colonel, we in the residency here would like to have you know that the American chargé d'affaires in Tangier and his legation have the singular confidence of General Noguès. General Noguès has said to me that there is no American in whom he has ever had such confidence as in your chief."

It was reasonable to suppose that Colonel Johnson would consider this statement of sufficient importance to report it to the War Department. Not only was there an error made on my part in not suggesting to the military attaché the desirability of reporting this significant comment home, but a further error was committed, through false modesty, in not myself reporting it to the Department of State. A diplomat has no right to suffer from a sense of false modesty when the matter concerns information of which his government may have need for its guidance.

On the eve of the landings, an effort was made to repair these sins of omission. A telegram to the Department was drafted expressing the legation's view that an American officer of general rank should be assigned to the legation for the express purpose of being in Rabat to talk with Noguès on the night of Operation Torch. It was suggested that, considering the close relations of confidence existing between the legation and Noguès, the American officer might convey a personal message from me to the resident general assuring him that Torch was a major operation and appealing to him to effect a reconciliation between the French forces and our own.

After the telegram was drafted, the military attaché and special assistant David Williamson were sent for to obtain their views. To a long succession of mistakes, I added another, that of allowing them to discourage me from sending it. Their argument was that plans had long ago been made and that the message, therefore, could serve no possible useful purpose.

It is not known who made the tragic decision to appoint, as intermediary between the United States Government and General Noguès, a junior vice consul from Casablanca. Consul General H. Earle Russell has assured me the decision was not his. It was certainly not that of the legation, for it was never privy with the planners of Torch.

However that may be, the most junior American representative in Morocco was charged with the responsible task of acquainting General Noguès, on the evening of November 7, with the landings. To add to the tragedy, the officer was one who was unfavorably regarded by Noguès.

It is not maintained by me that, had the approach outlined been followed, the decision taken by Noguès to resist us would have been different. It is a fact that, since the event, a number of Frenchmen prominent in French political life who were aware of the legation's close association with Noguès have asked me why such an approach was not made. I think it a reasonable statement to make that one could not possibly have chosen a less promising method of approach to Noguès than the one that was made.

Bear in mind that Noguès was a very high-ranking French officer, with a strict hierarchical view. No inference could have been more reasonable than that he was bound to judge the importance of a message sent to him by the rank of the messenger. To send a junior officer with a message of such momentous importance as that of our imminent landings in Morocco was not to enhance the effect which the message was presumably intended to make upon him. The method used to acquaint Noguès with our purposes has always been an inexplicable mystery. It could not possibly have produced worse results.

Here is the balance sheet:

American casualties in Morocco:
Killed 531
Wounded 1054
Missing 237

French casualties in Morocco:

Killed	651
Wounded	553
Total	3026

The only conclusion possible is that the planners of the operation had decided to ignore Noguès and had counted on his being immobilized by General Bethouart, who had been expected to seize the residency and to take command. The attempt was a fiasco. Noguès declined with some asperity to receive the American vice consul sent to apprise him of the landings in the early evening of November 7. He consented to receive the latter's message only through Du Gardier, his aide.

Du Gardier later stated that, when he presented to Noguès the letter from President Roosevelt and one addressed to the Sultan[1] concerning the purpose behind the landings, General Noguès' comment was: "It is nothing but a bluff. The Americans do not possess the ships necessary for a serious operation."

Du Gardier transmitted this comment to the young vice consul, who emphasized that it was no bluff. When this was conveyed to the resident general, he remarked that the denial was only a part of the bluff. Certainly, his attitude would have been far different if he had been dealing with an American general officer of rank comparable to his own.

Noguès communicated with the French admiral at Casablanca. The last-named assured Noguès that no important forces had been sighted off the coast. Noguès, concluding that he had to cope with nothing more than a commando raid, gave the orders to resist, having in mind his responsibility to maintain Morocco intact, whether against the Allies or the Germans, as he had so repeatedly assured me.

The most tragic decision in Noguès' long and honorable career as a French soldier and thorough patriot had been taken. I feel it my responsibility, for the confidence which he always showed me, to express my view that we ourselves bear a grave contributing share for the character of his decision.

Meanwhile, we were wholly without news of what was happening in the French zone, as the members of the consulate general at Casablanca were immediately interned. The little we knew was confined to the news published on November 9. This included the text of a message sent by Laval to Noguès: "I send you herewith a telegram which the Marshal has just sent President Roosevelt. Your duty is clear and the Government counts on you. You should repress energetically all dissident tendencies which have appeared or may appear."

To this, Noguès was quoted as having replied: "Thanks to the loyalism of most of the troops the dissidents have been reduced without any bloodshed after several difficult hours. I ask you to tell the Marshal he may count on us. The struggle may be expected to be severe but all French, as well as Moroccans, will make the necessary sacrifices, without distinction, for the future unity of the Government."

At the same time the press announced that the sultan of Morocco had issued a proclamation inviting the Moroccans to cooperate with the French authorities in operations to repel "the American aggression against certain of the Imperial ports."

Late in the afternoon of Monday, November 9, I had a most welcome visitor. Clarac, who had found himself in Rabat at the moment of the landings, had left Rabat on Sunday afternoon and had reached Tetuan Monday morning. He brought with him a message from the residency to Orgaz that French troops were being moved to the Spanish frontier, but without any aggressive intentions and only as a measure of security. Clarac informed me that the first evidence of anything unusual in Rabat was the blowing of factory whistles about 5:30 A.M. and at 8:30 A.M. some ten aircraft had flown over the city.

Clarac was not aware that the landings had occurred until he was informed at 11 A.M. by the Comte de Paris; he proceeded to the residency, where Du Gardier informed him he had learned of the landings about 3 A.M. He had dressed hurriedly to go to the residency but, on his way, he had been taken prisoner by supporters of the dissident General Bethouart and had been conducted to the offices of the chief of staff at the residency, where Bethouart and his supporters were assembled. Du Gardier had found, as prisoners with him in the same room, General Lahoulle, chief of aviation, and General Lascroux, commander of French military forces in Morocco. Du Gardier was subsequently released as "small fry." Clarac had only hearsay information of what had subsequently occurred. From what had been told him, Bethouart had been indecisive and, after holding the headquarters of the general staff for five hours, he and his supporters were taken prisoner by the protectorate authorities.

The day had been completely calm in Rabat, according to Clarac. The people were going about their business as if nothing unusual was happening. They appeared incredibly indifferent to events. It seemed to him they had only one wish: that whatever was happening should be gotten over quickly. The great majority undoubtedly hoped our efforts would be successful, provided no scarifices were demanded of them. Or such was his interpretation of their attitude. The protectorate administration was functioning normally.

When Clarac appeared in my office, his first words were: "You have kept me for these many months from leaving the service of Vichy but, now that Giraud has issued his proclamation in Algiers, you are not going to stand in my way any longer. I ask you to transmit both my own adherence and that of Gaire [his assistant] to Giraud."

In the afternoon of November 11, I received word from the French consul general in Tangier that General Noguès had communicated that morning an expression of his desire to see me in Rabat the following day. A little later I had a telephone call from Hardion, Noguès' chief of civil cabinet, informing me there had been a suspension of arms that afternoon, but that no armistice had as yet been signed. He repeated the urgent wish of Noguès that I call on him in Rabat on the twelfth.

While I was seeking permission from Washington to meet Noguès, who, it was believed, desired to use me as his intermediary with the American military authorities, another telephone call was received from the residency on the twelfth asking me to postpone my visit until the thirteenth, as Noguès had been called to Algiers to assist in a conference there.

This was the situation during those days of November 7–12, 1942. The Spanish, as we had anticipated, had not moved. The French, under General Noguès, as he had repeatedly assured me he would do and as I had reported to Washington, had resisted our landings by force of arms.[2]

We had committed a terrible blunder not only in failing to take Noguès' warnings into account but in failing to adopt measures which were readily available to us to persuade him of the seriousness of Operation Torch.

NOTES

[1]It is not known who drafted the President's letter to the sultan, but it can be stated that it was not someone versed in Moroccan affairs. The letter spoke of "our common interest, buttressed as it is by a long tradition of friendship, dating from the time of George Washington . . . to whom your noble predecessor gave as a mark of personal affection the building which houses the American legation at Tangier . . ."

The first legation building which this government acquired abroad was at Tangier, Morocco. This was in 1821. George Washington died on December 14, 1799.

This is cited as an example of the lack of coordination of Torch with the State Department.

One of the most persistent mysteries is why President Roosevelt placed such a strict ban on divulging any classified information concerning Torch. This restriction was even applicable to me, the acting chief of mission of the American legation in Tangier, responsible for American diplomatic relations with the

French authorities in Morocco. It was I who should have been responsible for the delivery of President Roosevelt's letter to the sultan through the intermediary of General Noguès, French resident general. The question has been raised with me innumerable times by French diplomatic and military authorities in Morocco as to the reason for such an extraordinary departure from accepted practice, the more particularly as it was public knowledge that I enjoyed the confidence of General Noguès as no other American. I have been informed by one of the senior French military authorities that, had I been the intermediary, the casualties suffered by French and American forces alike at the time of the landings would have been reduced from the thousands involved to zero or, at most, a mere handful.

Here is an interesting sidelight, never before made public, of an incident affecting Robert Murphy on his passage through Tangier en route to Algiers as Roosevelt's liaison officer with the French authorities in North Africa. I drove to the airport to meet Murphy. When we were returning to the legation, Murphy suddenly put his hand to his forehead in a gesture of dismay, exclaiming, "My God, I left my briefcase on the plane with top-secret documents."

We returned to the airport but the Spanish authorities disclaimed any knowledge of a briefcase having been off-loaded. We asked that a telegram be sent to the Spanish authorities in Melilla requesting return of the case.

It was some days before it was received.

Three or four years later, the Spanish consul general confided to me that, when the briefcase had been received, it had been opened and examined before being restored to Murphy through me. News of the projected landings had been read, but had *never been communicated to the Germans*.

This is the first disclosure of that incident.

[2]This and the foregoing chapters may be compared with the following excerpt from Robert Sherwood's *Roosevelt and Hopkins* (pp. 652–53):

"Roosevelt attached great importance to Eisenhower's confession of astonishment at the situation as he found it in North Africa; it did not 'even remotely resemble prior calculations.' When the supreme commander of a major military operation makes an admission like that it indicates that there must have been something wrong with his Intelligence Service. That is all the more surprising since North Africa had not been enemy territory, into which secret agents could be introduced only with the utmost difficulty and at their own extreme peril, but was friendly territory with which the U.S. maintained diplomatic relations. Therefore, the headquarters of Robert Murphy in Algiers and all the American consulates in that area and in Spanish Morocco [We had no consulate in Spanish Morocco but a legation in Tangier] were centers of Intelligence with large staffs which included observers of undoubted competence as well as courage. Yet Eisenhower was astonished when the local French failed to hail Giraud as a conquering hero. This led to a display of political crudity which made the U.S. Government look ridiculously amateurish."

19
DARLAN, GIRAUD, DE GAULLE

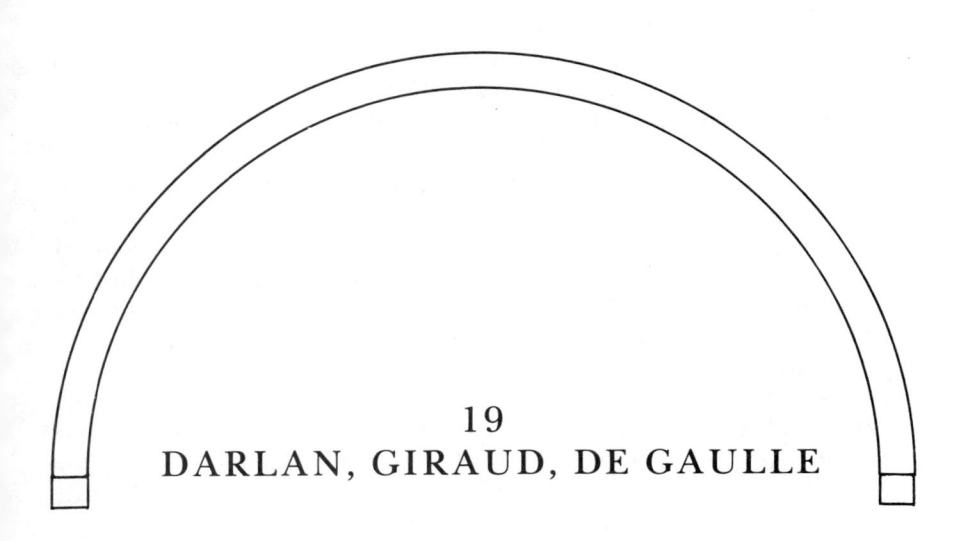

*W*hen the landings took place in French North Africa on November 7–8, 1942, a witches' brew resulted with the unexpected presence in Algiers of Admiral Darlan, "dauphin" of Marshal Pétain. Like Banquo's ghost, he took his seat at the deliberations, presided over first by General Mark Clark and later by General Eisenhower, at which it was determined that Darlan should be recognized as the supreme French authority in North Africa, after the refusal of the French to accept Giraud in that capacity, as had been contemplated by us.

In the meanwhile, I was awaiting an answer to the several telegrams sent to the Department concerning the desire of General Noguès to confer with me. On November 12, I was informed by Washington that, as General George S. Patton, Jr., had become responsible for all political as well as military relations with the French protectorate authorities, any meeting by me with Noguès must be with General Patton's concurrence.

With that obtained in a hurried visit to Casablanca, I proceeded to Rabat, where General Noguès received me in the late afternoon.

General Noguès was his old accustomed self, as cordial and friendly as he had always shown himself to me. He made no allusion, as I had expected he might, to the reasons actuating the resistance offered by him to our forces. Perhaps the principle which guided him in this respect was the precept of Disraeli: "Never complain; never explain." On my own initiative I found the occasion to put to him the specific question as to why French forces had fired upon their American friends in Morocco and Algeria, while failing to defend Tunisia against their enemies, the Germans. Noguès replied that such action had been taken in accordance with the "order of the Marshal."

The resident general observed that our Western Task Force in Morocco had been greatly favored by an unusual absence of surf and an extraordinarily quiet sea, as well as by a light fog which had obscured observation of our ships. He thought his resistance had been indirectly of some advantage to us. Vichy, he said, had telegraphed him on Sunday morning, November 8, that the Germans wished to send troops by air to Morocco to assist in its defense. He had replied that he could not answer for the loyalty of the French forces under his command in such an event.

General Noguès observed that, when the difficulties of the past few days had arisen, he had asked Hardion, chief of his cabinet, to send for me. He felt, from our close association over an appreciable period of time, he was able to speak to me with a confidence and freedom he might not be able to employ with others. He expressed his regret that he had been obliged to ask me to postpone my visit because his presence in Algiers on November 12 had been urgently sought.

The resident general detailed for me the conversations which had taken place in Algiers among the French and American authorities assembled there, from which he had only returned at noon that day.

General Noguès stated that, at his first interview with General Clark, whom he referred to as most difficult to deal with, he had, he thought, convinced the latter of the necessity of refraining from recognizing General Giraud as commander-in-chief of French forces in North Africa.

"When I encountered General Giraud at the conference," General Noguès remarked, "I refused to take his hand. In violating his oath as a French officer when becoming a dissident, he had committed treason to the French State. I was unable to take his hand under such circumstances."

Noguès said that, between his first conference with General Clark on the twelfth and the following day, Giraud had been able to persuade Clark to reverse his decision. There had then been a full meeting of the conferees, attended by General Eisenhower, Admiral Cunningham, General Clark, Admiral Darlan, General Noguès, General Giraud and Mr. Murphy. At this meeting, Noguès contended, Clark's decision to approve Giraud's appointment as commander-in-chief had again been reversed. At this meeting, also, a proposal had been approved by all those present that General Noguès should issue a proclamation remitting to Admiral Darlan the full powers delegated to the French resident general in Morocco by Marshal Pétain on November 19 when Darlan was in American custody, upon which Darlan should issue a proclamation, in the name of the marshal, assuming responsibility for French interests in French North Africa.

The French, Noguès assured me, would resist any aggression against North Africa. While nothing was known definitely of the attitude of Governor General Boisson, at Dakar in French West Africa, it was confidently expected he would adhere to the decisions taken.

Noguès remarked that Robert Murphy had been of great assistance at Algiers in facilitating an understanding and in helping interpret the views of one to the other.

I asked Noguès about the situation of the French fleet at Toulon. He said he had received private information from Admiral Alphand that the fleet would not move under Axis orders. When I inquired why the fleet had not responded to Darlan's appeal to proceed to North Africa, Noguès gave as an explanation the absence of orders to that effect from the marshal.

General Noguès was asked what role Giraud would fill. He answered vaguely that Giraud would doubtless command a mixed American force, probably in Tunisia. He added: "We are now wholly with you. The decision will not be announced in public, but our alliance will continue progressively as you are able to give us arms."

He stressed that the decisions reached would tend to maintain French unity and would make France and North Africa as one in the struggle. He emphasized that there had been no "dissidence and that the authority conferred upon Darlan had been "legitimate." It had been reported at the Algiers Conference that De Gaulle might attend. This possibility had been bitterly resented by the French there, as De Gaulle had broken his oath as an officer when creating a French dissident element in London.

By this emphasis upon "legitimacy," and blind adherence to the oath taken by officers, General Noguès and many others like him found themselves hopelessly entangled in the web which their logic had woven. In becoming the victims of a blind attachment to words, they tended to lose all sight of principles. French logic had come to imprison them inextricably and to reduce their actions in many ways to the absurd.

However strange Anglo-Saxons, with their pragmatic turn of mind and readiness to compromise, may find this, it is impossible to understand and appreciate the motives behind the actions of such men as General Noguès unless these considerations are taken unto account.

An even more striking example than that of Noguès was given me upon emerging from my long talk with the resident general. Hardion, Noguès' chief of civil cabinet, took me aside and exhibited to me a most extraordinary ultra-secret telegram which had just been received from Vichy. The telegram, according to a note made by me at the time, expressed the agreement of both Marshal Pétain and Laval with the decisions reached at Algiers and stated that, in view of the German occupation, they were unable to express their approbation publicly. So far as I know, there has never been any public reference to this message.

I returned to Casablanca that same evening and sought out General Patton to report on the results of my mission. He was understandably in excellent spirits over the success which had attended the invasion.

When I had seen him a few hours previous, he had complained about being completely in the dark as to what had happened in Algiers. He now informed me that he had meanwhile received by courier from General Eisenhower a full account of the Algiers decisions. General Patton remarked that General Giraud, instead of being relegated to a subordinate rank as General Noguès had suggested he would be, was to be named commander-in-chief of all French forces in North Africa.

General Patton had asked me to arrange with Noguès for the former's presentation to the sultan. I informed him that he would be presented either on November 16 or 18, as he might desire. Patton had also asked me to intercede with Noguès on behalf of General Bethouart, who had been confined by the resident general after Bethouart's abortive coup. I stated that I had pressed very strongly for Bethouart's release and had been informed that the case would be dealt with to the satisfaction of General Eisenhower and General Patton. In expressing his pleasure with what I had to report, General Patton desired me to continue my normal relations with the residency general.

I dined that evening with the general; his chief of staff, General Wilbur; my friend Du Gardier, chief of the diplomatic cabinet of Noguès who had been assigned to Patton as liaison officer with the French residency; and a few others of Patton's staff. About halfway through the dinner, General Patton suggested we leave the table momentarily to seek privacy for a more intimate exchange. We sought a toilet for the purpose and, once inside, he raised the question which was preoccupying him in a head-on assault.

"How much will it cost me to put Du Gardier in my pocket?"

"I don't understand."

"To put it brutally, I want to buy him."

"But—but—General, I don't know any better way of alienating him. Du Gardier is from a most aristocratic French Family . . ."

"You State Department people are all the same. You don't know the facts of life." With that, he turned on his heel and returned to the dinner table, mumbling unintelligibly.

I don't think I have ever met anyone more repellent, of such overwhelming vanity and with no consideration for anyone but himself. His political notions of North Africa were those of a neophyte. His one obsession was war. He did not pretend to any political *savoir faire,* and I think he was genuinely relieved when, some months later, he was replaced by General Mark Clark.

General Patton saw no incongruity in our deal with Darlan. His sole preoccupation, which one could appreciate, was to get on with the war. I perceived very quickly that I was wasting both my time and his in voicing forebodings over the arrangements which had been made at Algiers.

Later, I discussed the political situation with Consul General Russell and Consul Brooks in Casablanca. They shared fully my grave misgivings at the turn of events. Moreover, Russell and Brooks informed me that the afternoon papers, which I had not had time to read, had reported the news, which the public had received as I, with astonishment bordering on disbelief, that Admiral Darlan had assumed authority over French interests in French North Africa "with the consent of the American authorities."

Upon my return to Tangier on November 16, I telegraphed the Department that it would be difficult to exaggerate the consternation with which our friends in Morocco had received the recognition by us of Darlan as the supreme French authority in North Africa. I cited the comments of M. Clinchant, a former French ambassador, at the time living in retirement in Tangier. Clinchant remarked that it was inconceivable to him that power should have been permitted to pass into the hands of a man who, notwithstanding his position as admiral of the fleet, had found no commander at Toulon to heed his appeal to proceed to North Africa. Clinchant informed me also that feeling in Morocco was bitter against Noguès for having failed to order a suspension of arms on November 9, when he knew a similar suspension had occurred in Algeria. According to Clinchant, combat between French and American forces in Morocco had not ceased until November 11.

I was not in Algeria and, therefore, am not in a position to take into account all the complicated factors which entered into the difficult decision which General Clark and General Eisenhower had to make. General Eisenhower has given us, in his *Crusade in Europe,* a most persuasive account of the reasons for the decision. Churchill, in his memoirs, has offered justification for it. It came to be sustained by President Roosevelt and by Marshal Stalin.

In the face of the storm of criticism evoked in the United States and in other parts of the world when the Darlan deal became known, an official statement was issued in Washington:

> The present temporary arrangement in North and West Africa is only a temporary expedient, justified solely by the stress of battle. . .
> The present temporary arrangement has accomplished two mili-

tary objectives. The first was to save American and British lives, and French lives on the other hand.

The second was the vital factor of time. The temporary arrangement has made it possible to avoid a "mopping up" period in Algiers, Algeria and Morocco which might have taken a month or two to consummate. . . ."

Any private opinion formed of the Darlan deal, as here presented, must necessarily be based on that situation as seen from Morocco. This afforded a very limited perspective and, consequently, any commentary on it is submitted in all due humility and recognition of its incompleteness and possible incorrectness. In the judgment, however, of the legation at Tangier, the reaction of the American people to the deal, which it may be said, was identical with that of every Foreign Service officer in Morocco, was both justified and based on sound, if intuitive, considerations. The instinctive reaction of the American people was long ago reflected in the words of a great American, Robert E. Lee, who wrote: "Private and public life are subject to the same rules; and truth and manliness are two qualities that will carry you far through this world much better than *policy*, or *tact*, or *expediency*, or any other word that was ever devised to conceal or mystify a deviation from a straight line."

It is suggested, from hind- and not from foresight, that there was a way out of the dilemma confronting us which would have achieved all the President had in mind and would have accomplished the same objectives, namely, the saving of lives and the avoidance of any "mopping-up" period in Morocco and Algeria.

At Rabat, General Noguès had given me the texts of the proclamations which he and Admiral Darlan were issuing. The first, published in the official bulletin on November 13, read in part:

> General Noguès has had, during the afternoon of November 11, a first and long conversation with the American military authorities. The basis for an arrangement have been established. . .
> The Resident General retains full responsibility for the maintenance of order in the country.

The next, signed by General Noguès and published on November 14, read:

> The Marshal appointed me on November 19, 1942, before the entry of German troops in the non-occupied Zone his delegate in Algeria in the belief that Admiral Darlan was no longer free.
> Having come to Algeria, I have ascertained that Admiral Darlan had resumed complete possession of his liberty.

I have noted that we were in complete agreement on the course to be followed.

Consequently, in the name of the Marshal and with his approval, I return to Admiral Darlan the powers that he gave to me and I place myself under his orders.

The proclamation issued by Admiral Darlan and published at the same time read:

> The Marshal appointed General Noguès on November 10, 1942, before the entry of German troops in the unoccupied Zone, as his representative in Africa in the belief that I had been deprived of my liberty.
>
> General Noguès arrived yesterday, November 12, in Algeria. In complete liberty and in full accord with him and at his request, I assume full responsibility for French interests in Africa.
>
> I have the approval of the American authorities, with whom I count on assuring the defense of North Africa.
>
> French and Moslems:
>
> I count on your complete discipline. Everyone at his post. Long live the Marshal. Long live France.

For the purpose of this exposition it is important to bear in mind the following dates:

November 8	"Torch" launched in the early morning hours.
	Darlan is taken in custody by the Americans in Algiers, and on the same day he telegraphs to Noguès ordering him to cease resistance.
	Noguès refuses an offer of German troops from Pétain.
November 9	Marshal Pétain telegraphs to Darlan in Algiers affirming confidence in him.
	Giraud arrives in Algiers from Gibraltar.
	Suspension of arms in Algeria.
November 10	Marshal Pétain delegates powers to General Noguès to represent him in North Africa.
	Pétain dismisses Darlan.
November 11	In the morning, Noguès communicates with the French consul general in Tangier expressing a wish to confer with me.
	Sometime during this day, Darlan again orders Noguès to suspend hostilities.

	Germans march into unoccupied France.
	Suspension of fighting in Morocco.
	In the afternoon, Noguès meets with American military authorities.
November 12	Noguès flies to Algiers to confer with General Clark and Admiral Darlan.
	Darlan is recognized by the Americans and French as the supreme French authority in North Africa.
	Pétain approves North African decisions.

It is clear that Noguès had already decided, in the morning of November 11, to come to terms with us. It is possible he may have reached this decision on the evening of November 10, by which time he must have been convinced that Torch was no commando raid. He knew of the suspension of arms in Algeria on November 9. He had been given, by Marshal Pétain, full powers on November 10.

The great problem of "legitimacy," which had tortured the logical minds of the French, had been solved.

Of this, General Eisenhower has the following comment in his book:

> But we had another and more pressing reason for attempting to utilize Darlan's position. In dealing with French soldiers and officials General Clark quickly ran afoul of the traditional French demand for a cloak of legality over any action they might take...
> Without exception every French commander with whom General Clark held exhaustive conversation declined to make any move toward bringing his forces to the side of the Allies unless he could get a legal order to do so. Each of them had sworn an oath of personal fealty to Marshal Pétain..."

There is no question that the situation as General Eisenhower sets it forth is an eminently faithful reflection of the facts.

But, as Clarac had observed, Darlan was a man tainted with the brush of Franco-German collaboration. Noguès was not. Noguès, apart from Darlan, was the senior French officer in North Africa. He had had a long and honorable record. He had skillfully protected Morocco from German infiltration. He might have been ready to find accommodation with us on the night of November 7 had we played our cards more intelligently. And, last but not least, it was he who held the delegation of power from Marshal Pétain.

Had Darlan been thrust aside and Noguès confirmed by us in the authority conferred upon him by Pétain, there need never have been any deal with Darlan, any question of expediency to throw confusion among our friends and disunity among the French.

Noguès would have been relished with far greater taste by French officers in North Africa than was Darlan. There could have been no question of Noguès' legitimacy, for that had been conferred upon him by Pétain.

The President states that the deal with Darlan was made to save lives and to gain time which might have been consumed in a "mopping-up" period in Algeria and Morocco. However, a suspension of arms had taken place already in Algeria, on November 9, before the deal was made, and, in Morocco, on November 11, before the arrangement with Darlan was concluded on November 13. As early as the morning of November 11, General Noguès had sent for me. He would hardly have desired to see me if he had not wished to reach accommodation with us.

The assumption may be entirely wrong that the deal with Darlan was unnecessary. There may be other unknown factors, not brought out here, which have not been taken into account.

It has been said that the deal was unnecessary. It is not believed there will be any disputing the fact that it did great damage to the Allied cause.

It would be impossible to exaggerate the confusion and dismay created among the French people in Morocco by the deal with Darlan. The conclusion drawn by officials and by the rank and file alike was that we had thereby put our seal of approval on the Vichy regime and had repudiated those Frenchmen outside that regime who had thrown themselves into the struggle before the landings. Statements and explanations made after the event that the decision had been taken solely on military grounds and as a temporary expediency did something to calm public opinion, but not altogether to reassure it.

The immediate and inescapable effect was the strengthening of all Vichy elements and the weakening and disillusionment of all those who had risked their lives to work with us before the landings. Many of these last remained in prison, while the most reactionary French elements, including former Cagoulards, the most notorious collaborationists and many who had openly collaborated with the Germans, found themselves in positions of preferment.

A striking example of this was the case of a French journalist who had edited a collaborationist newspaper in Tangier, and, after the landings, fled to Algiers, where he became one of the principal propagandist spokesmen of the "new order" in French North Africa. He had been so notorious in his activities against the Allies before the landings that we were instrumental in having the Peruvian Government revoke his commission as honorary Peruvian consul. No patriotic Frenchman in Tangier would be seen in his company. Yet here he was, quoted over the Algiers and Rabat radios as the new spokesman of Allied purposes. I telegraphed in expostulation several times to Algiers, only to receive in reply word that, whatever his past might have been, he was proving useful in his present work. He could not possibly have done more damage to our cause in Morocco than by his identification with us, which only reinforced the prevailing opinion that we had repudiated our friends and were taking our former enemies to our bosom.

Those in authority, such as General Noguès, judged, from our apparent incapacity to make any distinctions between the past and the present and from our stress upon military objectives, that the political aspect of Morocco was a matter of indifference to us, and they proceeded accordingly.

Six weeks after the landings, during a visit to Casablanca, I found a propaganda center of the "National Revolution" still open to the public in the main street of that city, engaged in the continued distribution of collaborationist and violently anti-Allied pamphlets.

I telegraphed the Department on November 16 that there was uneasiness and disappointment over the indecisive turn of events in relation to the French administration in North Africa. Two currents of thought were observable: one looking for a new deal and new approach, the other represented by the so-called legitimists who gave their loyalty to Pétain and Darlan.

Noguès had contended with me that, by our acceptance of the *status quo*, we avoided possible disorders and civil strife. This undoubtedly was one of the motives behind the deal with Darlan, and it was a persuasive one. If we had made the deal with Noguès rather than Darlan, as had been suggested, this would have accomplished the same purpose and would have relieved us of some, if not all, the odium of our identification with one of the partisans of collaboration with Germany, something Noguès had never been. We might well have attached to the resident general in Morocco at once a political adviser with authority to assure that the political direction of affairs was in conformity with Allied aims. This was a very serious omission and one that might have avoided the cross-purposes which characterized the protectorate administration, its indecisiveness and its equivocal twists and turns. We failed to give Noguès the lead he would willingly have accepted.

In my telegram to Washington I recalled that Noguès had fought admirably during the past two and a half years against Axis influence in Morocco, noting that he was sympathetically disposed to us. But he and the followers of Pétain appeared to be endeavoring, with considerable skill, to maneuver us into committing ourselves to them and alienating our supporters who had run so many risks.

Early in December, a friendly official French contact reported that the attitude of Noguès was disturbing to him. He informed me that Olivier de Sardan, former chief of cabinet of Laval, had passed through

Tangier (before any border control had been established) en route to Madrid and Vichy. Sardan was said to have disclosed his confidential mission as that of establishing liaison on behalf of Noguès with the French ambassador in Madrid, a notorious Vichyite, and with Pétain in Vichy. My informant also referred to the extremely tepid attitude of the Rabat radio toward the Allies.

A comprehensive and understanding analysis of the state of mind of the French at this period was given me by Clarac in a letter of December 11: "It was unhappily significant that an event (the American landing) so greatly awaited has not brought that liberation of spirit which we looked for as a day of resurrection after two years of suffocation. The fog continues to hang heavier and blacker than ever. . . . The most recent reports from the French Zone show the people there in general suffering from the same anxiety and uneasiness as I."

Clarac recalled that he had entertained hopes early in November that, despite his misgivings regarding Noguès, the latter might effect that hoped-for rapprochment between the Gaullists and North Africa. Instead of this, subtle sabotage had been seen in all domains. He cited the resolve of Noguès not to break off relations with Vichy, the better to preserve the unity of France. He suggested this was a strange manner of defining unity, when, at the same time, De Gaulle and his followers were prescribed. Clarac added:

> The policy of President Roosevelt consists, I believe, in waiting for the end of hostilities in North Africa to bring about the establishment of a French government in Algiers on a really sound basis. The idea in principle is excellent but its application is extremely dangerous. We do not know if the military operation does not hold surprises for us. Perhaps we shall have to stiffen ourselves physically and morally in a hard form of resistance. . . Defeatist elements, free to act, can exercise their demoralizing influence. . . The longer you wait to clean the abscess the more difficult will be the operation.
>
> I urgently ask you to consider suggesting to your government, without the least delay, to examine well the risks which this state of affairs offers. Think also that the differences of views between Washington and London on Darlan, Noguès and De Gaulle are played up by our enemies.
>
> The initial solution of President Roosevelt was good. A Giraud government uniting by its side the De Gaullists and the less dangerous of the Vichyites in an effective and loyal collaboration without reserve with the Allies was a healthy formula for national unity. . ."

The legation telegraphed again to Washington, on December 13, that so long as the equivocal political situation in French North Africa continued, discouragement and doubt were deepening on the part of our friends and supporters, and great moral damage was being done our cause. Our French friends saw with astonishment little quislings, such as the French journalist to whom reference has been made, quoted daily in the Moroccan press. These were men who, a few months previous, were attacking us vitriolically and who had been in league with notorious German agents in Tangier. They saw Mas, who had figured in the Anglo-American blacklist, put forward by the residency as the spokesman for Moroccan journalism with our journalists. French friends of ours in official positions, such as Clarac, who had proved their loyalty to our cause were being persuaded, with great difficulty, to continue to carry on in their posts as French consular officers. There was deep concern on their part regarding the situation. A French diplomatic officer at Rabat, recently mobilized, was said to have been informed when he approached a superior and expressed the desire of the younger officers to receive instructions from the Americans as soon as possible, that he "should not be overzealous in cooperating with the Americans."

I was fully aware that the information I was telegraphing to Washington was not likely to be pleasant reading. I was not kept long in the dark.

The Department, I was informed on December 13, was concerned with my recent telegrams regarding political matters in North Africa and, in particular, the role Admiral Darlan was playing. I was enjoined to bear in mind the statement made by the President on November 17 that the association of Darlan with the forces of the United Nations was a temporary expedient brought about by the exigencies of war. The primary concern of the government "was not repeat not" with political problems but with winning the war as quickly as possible.

It was obvious, the telegram continued, that distrust of our arrangements with Darlan and attacks on the propriety of the assistance which he had been rendering to the Allied cause closely followed the Axis propaganda lines. The Department expressed its conviction that such sentiments were inspired by the Axis with a view to creating dissidence and dissatisfaction in the ranks of the United Nations. It followed that, by allowing such an attitude to spread, the aims of the Axis were substantially furthered.

I was instructed to endeavor actively to combat the development of those political attitudes which were resulting in the undermining of confidence in the arrangements with Darlan. I was to emphasize especially the desirability of a united front in the urgent task of prosecuting the war.

I replied that there was no disposition on the part of any of the French officials with whom we were in touch to question the desirability of all Frenchmen presenting a united front for the purpose of winning the war as quickly as possible. It was precisely for that reason that practically all our French official contacts in Spanish North Africa were deeply disturbed by evidence of lack of support for those aims on the part of those in important positions of responsibility in French Morocco who professed to be working with us. Our French contacts, I stated, were not unwilling to work with any who were sincerely desirous of prosecuting the war against the Axis, but they were disturbed that many in authority were displaying an unaccountable passiveness in working with us. All of us in Morocco were convinced that there existed solid ground for this anxiety.

The Department was assured that all Frenchmen who had expressed to us doubts about the situation had been referred to the President's statement. It was pointed out that we had not presumed and were not competent to comment upon the role being played by Admiral Darlan. The observations which had been made, it was emphasized, related only to French Morocco. Finally it was stated:

> Failure to establish an effective control over our new supporters jeopardizes our situation and undermines confidence in us. Our foreign friends, while appreciating the realism of a policy of temporary accommodation with Darlan and Noguès, consider that we have a right to insist, in the application of such a policy, that the suppport given us by the French should be wholehearted and without reserve, and that if the former pro-Vichy French are to be accepted as working partners they should cease persecuting our friends and leading even indirect aid to our enemies.

Toward the end of December, I had a lengthy discussion with Noguès. Hardion informed me the residency was disturbed with what he described as "malaise" in its relations with the American military authorities. He thought the atmosphere much better in Algeria than in Morocco. He said Noguès was disturbed about the situation.

I remarked to Noguès that the period following our operations had necessarily to be one of adjustment following two years during which a poisonous atmosphere had been engendered. There were many lesser officials who were probably not giving themselves loyally and wholeheartedly to cooperation with us, and this occasioned distrust and suspicion on our part. I referred to the continued activity of the propaganda center of the "National Revolution" in Casablanca. He promised me to have it closed at once and stated he thought it had already been done.

I expressed the belief that many of the present difficulties had arisen from rectifiable misunderstandings. I hesitated to make any suggestions about the Moroccan situation to one who knew Morocco so much better than I. He interrupted to say that he had greater confidence in my understanding of Moroccan problems than any American with whom he was acquainted.

I said I appreciated his confidence and would make a suggestion. Our paramount aim was that of defeating the Axis. If he could make this plain, by a personal appeal to the people in Morocco, urging them to bury their factional differences and stating that he was not concerned with whether Frenchmen belonged to parties of the Right or the Left so long as they were united in a common cause, this would give a lead to French officials who were misinterpreting the character of the residency's cooperation with us.

Noguès thought the suggestion an excellent one and said that he would probably choose the occasion of the New Year to do so. He observed that this was not the time to settle the political destiny of France and that French North Africa was, moreover, only a small part of France and not competent to undertake this task.

In reporting this interview, I suggested that the struggle going on in French North Africa was a political one, divided roughly between those of the Right, including former collaborationists and Vichyites, and those of the Left, who comprised the Gaullists and those who identified the cause of the common man with the Allies. The leaders in Morocco were generally in the former group.

Noguès did issue a New Year appeal, but it was so innocuous and watered down from what I had in mind that it might as well not have been issued.

Early in 1943, it was suggested to the Department that Noguès was playing rather clumsily at the game of divide and rule. He appeared to be intent on maintaining himself in power as the sole repository of legitimate French authority in North Africa, with a view to handing it back at some future time to Pétain or his successors, to insure that the Vichyphile generals and not the democratic politicians and the Gaullists—so much despised by those generals—should determine the future destiny of France. It was concluded that we did not probably sufficiently appreciate the extent to which the fascist virus had entered into the thinking of the Vichyphile general officers in Morocco.

I endeavored, on January 29, 1943, to sum up in an official dispatch the equivocal attitude which Noguès had displayed after the landings and to endeavor to account for it, while admitting the difficulty of doing so, considering his previous very cooperative attitude toward us. It was suggested that the many books written on the fall of France had been fairly unanimous in crediting the older French generals, including in particular Pétain and Weygand, with having been persuaded to seek an armistice and collaboration with Germany more by fear of a social upheaval in France than any other one factor. A wit had remarked that the only difference in this respect between the Spanish and French generals, in their efforts to stay revolutionary forces which they both alike feared, had been that, in Spain, the generals had invited the Axis in by the front door and, in France, by the back. When the accounting came in a liberated France for a policy of collaboration, much would depend, it was suggested, on the extent to which the Vichy group might bring its influence to bear. The opinion was offered that the Vichyites must, for this reason, fear above all an unequivocal victory of the United Nations, as such a victory would spell the doom of Vichy's influence on a future government of France.

These views tended to be confirmed some two months later by a high official of the Moroccan administration, M. Bolifraud. He assured me there was a very general desire among the people of Morocco for unity between the partisans of General Giraud and those of General De Gaulle, with Giraud taking the leadership in military matters and De Gaulle in political affairs. There was need of a political housecleaning, particularly in Morocco, and the elimination of such men as Noguès, Admiral Michelier, General Lascroux, Governor General Boisson in West Africa, and others. Some of these men desired a military dictatorship in France and saw their hopes for such a dictatorship thwarted by a United Nations victory. It was his understanding that the greatest obstacle which stood in the way of a Giraud–De Gaulle agreement was the latter's insistence on sweeping clean these men who were an obstacle to French unity.

Considerable skepticism was expressed by other American political authorities in North Africa at our analyses of the situation in Morocco with particular reference to our reports that the French protectorate authorities were but halfhearted in their support of our aims and were still secretly in league with Vichy. Through our undercover services, it was discovered, in May, that the State Bank of Morocco in Tangier, on orders of the State Bank at Rabat, and in conformity with instructions of the Bank of France in Paris, had shipped to Paris via Lisbon, in February 1942, 614 kilograms of fine gold. This was a case of trading with the enemy which was not only against Allied interests but was in violation of even French North African regulations issued after the landings. The excuse proffered was that the transaction was in discharge of an obligation of the State Bank of Morocco incurred before the landings! Those responsible found themselves in prison, after a searching investigation conducted by Raines of the U.S. Treasury and a French treasury expert sent from Algiers.

Finally, on June 4, 1943, when evidence for the need of a thorough housecleaning in Morocco admitted no longer of any doubt, the resignation of General Noguès as French resident general was announced, and Ambassador Gabriel Puaux was appointed in his stead.

General Noguès afterward called on me in Tangier on his way out of Morocco to exile in Portugal. I had only a deep feeling of regret and pity for a splendid career which had ended in virtual disgrace. No man could have opposed more effectually and skillfully German infiltration and influence in Morocco from 1940 until our landings. His courage and patriotism had been fully evidenced in the lead he took in June 1940, in favor of carrying on the struggle against Germany even after the collapse of France. I have always felt that had we persuaded him of the strength of our forces and the deadly seriousness of our purpose, the result might have been different.

M. Puaux effected the housecleaning which was badly needed in Morocco. He was not a politician but a career ambassador in the French civil service, with no ties to Vichy. His broom swept clean, with the result that the dust of Vichy, which had hung like a poisonous fog over Morocco, began to be dissipated.

In a published declaration on July 25, 1943, the new French resident general stated:

> It would be futile to conceal the fact that a political problem exists in Morocco at the present time. This problem is more acute and complex than I had imagined upon my arrival...
>
> Every Frenchman has the right to have his opinion concerning the future regime of France on condition that he does not pretend to impose it by force upon his fellow citizens... We shall safeguard liberty in spite of those who may be tempted to abuse it. Vichy had organized a kind of white terror. We shall stage no system of this kind.... Those only shall be struck at who are promoters of civil war, and servants of the enemy...

A little while before, De Gaulle had been allowed to come to Algiers, where, on May 31, 1943, agreement was reached for the establishment of an executive committee including Giraud and De Gaulle. For a time, he shared power with Giraud; a short while later, he was recognized by the French in North Africa as the supreme authority.

We persisted for long, however, in declining to recognize his Committee of National Liberation. When I returned to the United States for consultation, from March to May 1944, I was so deeply disturbed by the situation that I spoke on the subject to everyone in the Department who would listen to me. My theme was that, in espousing the cause of Giraud in the struggle for power between him and De Gaulle, we had reinforced the prestige of De Gaulle. If the situation had been reversed and France had adopted some American general as its protété at the expense of an

American around whom Americans had rallied, no matter what the prestige of the former might have been, the mere fact that he was championed by a foreign state would have been sufficient to undermine his influence. Whether we liked De Gaulle or not, irrespective of De Gaulle's virtues or faults, the inescapable fact was that he had become a symbol for the French people and was the temporary authority *they* recognized.

It is dangerous for a nation to allow its foreign policy to be determined by emotional considerations. Fortunately, we had not allowed emotional factors to influence our continued recognition of Vichy after the armistice in 1940. Such continued recognition served a definite American interest. Unhappily, the American public has come to confound *recognition* of a government with *approval* of a government. The two were never intended, in the intercourse between states, to have anything to do with one another.

Our recognition of De Gaulle was bound, by the logic of the situation, to come sooner or later; unfortunately, it came later than it should have, as was recognized generally at the time.

20

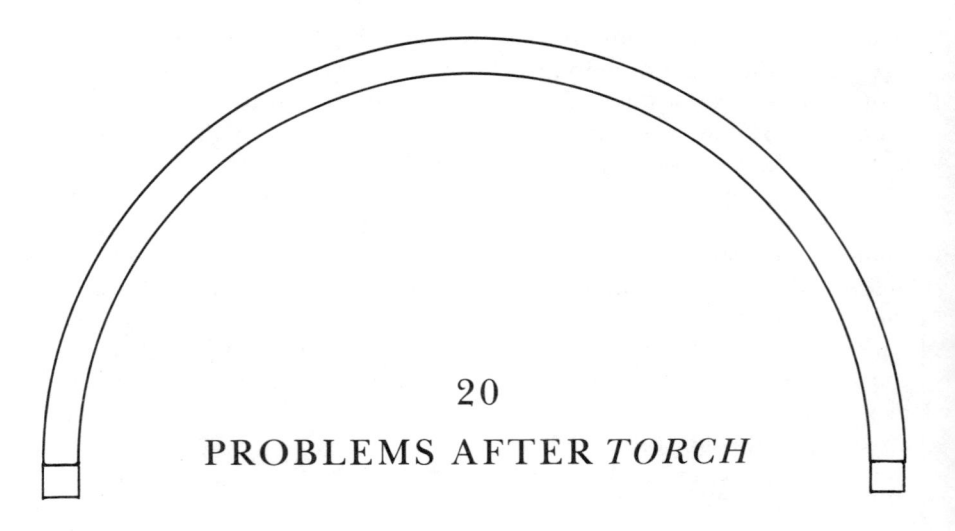

PROBLEMS AFTER *TORCH*

The Allied landings in French North Africa brought home to the Spanish the mounting strength of the Allies. Consequently, they reinforced the necessity for Spain to observe the greatest prudence to avoid being involved in the war and, at the same time, to move from a status of nonbelligerency to one of true neutrality.

The first move in that direction came, as might have been expected, in Spanish North Africa. General Orgaz, on November 10, upon his return from Madrid, very candidly stated to me, "I need the backing of your government and of yourself in my intention to maintain a correct and strict neutrality in Spanish North Africa."

Operation Torch thus marked a turning point in our relations with the Spanish authorities. Before that time, the Spanish authorities had shown a marked leaning toward the Axis; after November 8, there was a firm endeavor, in which the Spanish high commissioner took the lead, to introduce and maintain an attitude of neutrality as between the Allies and the Axis.

The transition could be neither easy nor abrupt. Until the very end of the war, the Falange, for example, and Falangist elements in the Spanish administration never concealed their sympathy for the Axis.

I recall a visit paid to authorities in Morocco. Almost immediately after the landings, it became apparent that no arrangements had been made by our military authorities for any effective control of the border separating the French zone from the Spanish zone of Morocco. Collaborationist French were fleeing like rats from French North Africa for France, while, at the same time, extremely dubious characters, including possible German and Spanish agents, were passing unmolested into French Morocco.

The War Department, as well as General Patton, had, of course, perhaps many more serious problems to deal with than this, and it was not until December 14 and after repeated telegrams that the legation received word authorizing me, on behalf of both the War and State departments, to proceed to General Patton's headquarters to discuss the question with him and to work out a satisfactory arrangement.

I drew up proposals which provided that travelers proceeding to French North Africa from Tangier should receive their visas from the French consulate general in Tangier, with the joint concurrence of the American legation and the British consulate general, and after proper investigation, where necessary, by our several security services. Travelers leaving French Morocco should be subject to a joint control by the French and American services.

When General Patton received me on December 18, he stated that the question of border control was outside his competence and could only be dealt with by General Eisenhower. I showed him the instructions I had received, but he reiterated his inability to act. I thereupon left with him, in what I considered to be the discharge of my duties, the proposals for border control which had been drafted before my departure from Tangier. These were introduced later, with the concurrence of Algiers, and made highly effective. So effective, in fact, that in a report of February 15, 1943, made to Berlin by the German consulate general in Tangier, it was plaintively remarked, as an excuse for the failure of the Germans to do more in French Morocco, that "the frontier between the zones is hermetically closed."

General Patton had expressed considerable skepticism before the introduction of any control that there was any movement of undesirable persons across the border. I was able to show him, in support of the legation's concern over the absence of any border control, a secret report by a Spanish agent (who, incidentally, was on our blacklist) which had been obtained by our security services after the Spaniard's return from a visit to French Morocco. It read in part:

> The attitude of the French towards the American landings is incomprehensible... It cannot be said that there is any enthusiasm and for the moment French collaboration appears rather passive.
>
> The curious situation has arisen in which the principal collaborators of the Americans, who are accepted by the latter with the greatest confidence, are precisely the military authorities who put up

defense against them. On the other hand, it appears that several of the French officers, who collaborated with the Americans from the first, are languishing in prison.

The portrait of Marshal Pétain continues to be seen in the streets and public buildings.

I lunched with General Patton at the splendid Villa Mas, where he had established himself, afterward an air force hotel for important visitors. At the conclusion of the lunch, I brought up the question of supplying us with information regarding the names and disposition of the German armistice commissioners who had been captured by American troops at the time of the landings.

Much to my surprise, when I broached the subject to Patton, he was as uncooperative with me as his staff had been with Consul General Russell. When I pressed our desire for the data, he finally remarked, in a tone of finality, "If the State Department wants the information so badly, have them apply for it to the Quartermaster's Department in Philadelphia."

Shortly after my return to Tangier, a telegram was received from the State Department, taking the legation to task for not having furnished a complete report to Washington with the names and whereabouts of the armistice commissioners and the disposition which had been made of those captured by the American military forces. The Department explained that the German Government had made it known that the treatment of the American diplomatic personnel at Vichy, interned by German authorities upon the German occupation of the whole of France, would depend upon the treatment accorded by us to the German armistice commissioners.

General Patton had lost no prisoners and he was not thinking of any possible retaliation upon his own men. I had an intuitive feeling that the information, involving as it did foreign nationals with whom we had concerned ourselves, would at some time be needed by the State Department.

Without mentioning General Patton's name, I telegraphed that we had been seeking for days to obtain from our military authorities the information requested and that further efforts would be made. Once I had explained the purpose for which it was desired, General Patton finally gave orders that it was to be supplied us.

During the period in which American military forces were in Morocco and responsible for our political relations with that country—which was to say from November 1942, under General Patton, until the later part of 1943, with the transfer of General Clark's headquarters from Morocco to Italy—the legation was sedulous in making available to the headquarters of those officers copies of every telegram and report which related in any way to political or economic conditions in Morocco. During that period, the legation never received copies of any reports which they were sending to the War Department, but was left in ignorance, except by General Clark, both of the military policies decided upon and of information which the army intelligence services gained of that area. Unfortunately, the responsible officers of the War Department apparently never appreciated the desirability or the need, if the United States Government's purposes were to be served with full effectiveness, of keeping the legation informed to promote the mission for which we had been responsible and would be responsible after the departure of the Army. When the Truman Committee later made an investigation in Morocco, Senators Burton and Tennell found most anomalous the disclosure by the military authorities that the legation, which by then had resumed its responsibility for the political relations of the United States with Morocco, had never been supplied with any information regarding American air and naval bases in Morocco, as regarded the sites themselves or the terms under which they had been acquired.

I have no doubt that this state of affairs could have found its parallel in the relations between the diplomatic and military authorities of Germany, Italy and many other countries. Happily for our government, I believe that we have since profited by the mistakes of that period.

It would not be fair to the Army if acknowledgment were not made that the position of the legation in Tangier was a very anomalous one. With responsibility which had accrued to General Patton for political relations with French Morocco, the consulate general in Casablanca, situated as it was within the area controlled by the United States military forces, fell under the political jurisdiction of the American military authorities and was thereby stopped from submitting political reports directly to the Secretary of State but rather was required to channel them through the military authorities. Copies, however, could still be forwarded to Washington and to the legation. As Tangier, however, was in an area controlled by the Spanish, we were not subject to American military jurisdiction and, consequently, were completely free to submit reports on the Moroccan situation directly to the State Department.

The deal with Darlan had the effect of introducing the greatest confusion in the political situation in Morocco. One principal effect was the prestige given all Vichyites by our recognition of Darlan and the implicit repudiation of all anti-Vichyites and Gaullists. Consequently, many of those Frenchmen who had been most active in the assistance given us prior to the landings found themselves in jail as "dissidents" or "traitors."

During this extremely confused period, I had occasion to call on

General Patton. He remarked with great asperity: "You are giving me a great deal of trouble. You are constantly sending in reports to the State Department which are being passed to the War Department and I am having to spend several hours every day investigating them and preparing my comments for transmittal to the War Department."

"I am sorry, General, to hear that I am causing you trouble," I replied. "As an officer of the State Department, I am under obligation to report to it the situation as I see it, just as you are answerable to the War Department. Let me assure you that I send no report affecting Morocco of which I do not send you directly a copy. Furthermore, if you will read my reports carefully, you will see that I am at great pains to give the source of my information and to distinguish meticulously between reports which I regard as authentic and those which must be accepted with caution. I don't think I could possibly be more careful than I am."

The general brought his fist down on his desk with a resounding crash. "Yes, damn you, that's the trouble, you are too damned careful."

There had been a suggestion by Foreign Minister Jordana in Madrid that it would contribute to the improvement of American-Spanish relations if a meeting were arranged between General Orgaz, high commissioner in Spanish Morocco, and General Patton. The latter asked me if I would undertake to make the arrangements and expressed his desire that I be present. As it was I and not he who was responsible for political realtions with Spanish Morocco, I thought his suggestion somewhat supererogatory, but I expressed my appreciation nonetheless. When I returned to Tangier and before I had had the opportunity to see General Orgaz, I received a telegram from Patton stating he had changed his mind and wished the meeting with Orgaz to be confined strictly to military personnel.

When I saw Orgaz on December 30 to discuss the arrangements, it was agreed that he would meet Patton at the frontier at Araouna on January 4 and would conduct him to Larache in Spanish Morocco, where he would entertain him and his staff at luncheon. Orgaz added that he, of course, expected that I would be present as his guest.

I said that it was my understanding the meeting was a purely military one. Orgaz was insistent, however, and pointing his finger at me in the dictatorial manner to which he was accustomed, he jovially remarked, "I expect you to be present; there is nothing more to be said."

The goodwill of General Orgaz was more important in my official capacity than that of Patton. Besides, it was Orgaz who was the host and the meeting was taking place in Spanish Morocco, where Patton had no authority. At the same time, I did not care to give needless offense to Patton. I was nonplussed for a while until the happy inspiration suddenly came to me to place the decision up to the Department. Back came a telegram with official instructions to attend.

I should have acquainted General Patton in advance with my instructions but it was overlooked in the press of work. I might have anticipated General Patton's wrath. The only thing he did not do was lift his hand against me.

At the frontier, General Orgaz and his staff assembled a hundred yards or so from the barrier. Orgaz suggested that I go to the French side of the frontier and escort Patton and his staff and make the presentations.

Patton was half an hour late in arriving and, when he caught sight of me, lightning began to flash from his eyes. If looks could have killed, I would have been stricken on the spot. He strode past me without so much as a greeting. I caught up with him and faced him boldly. "General, I would have you know I am not here out of caprice or of my own volition, but under specific orders of the Department of State."

He shook my hand and the lightning in his eyes disappeared. "I am glad you could come," he said. "It is nice to have you." I knew that he did not mean one word of what he said.

At the luncheon which followed, we discovered we were very distant cousins through the James River Harrisons. The knowledge did not add to his equanimity.

General Patton was a soldier and a very capable one, or so I have been told. He was, however, lacking in political acumen; for that matter, I never heard him make any pretense in that direction. In all my experience, I never met anyone more of a brute who professed to be of good breeding. He left Morocco in the early part of 1943 and was replaced by General Mark Clark. The last-named was astute enough to remove his headquarters from Casablanca to the remote confines of Oujda near the Algerian border, far removed from the political intrigues of the coast. General Clark sent me an invitation, shortly after the establishment of his headquarters, to visit him for a day or two to discuss Moroccan problems. The letter read in part, "I shall be happy to have you come to Oujda." When the letter was received, there was carefully clipped from it by the military censor the word "Oujda." As everyone in Morocco knew where General Clark was, I had no difficulty finding it.

The atmosphere at General Clark's headquarters was entirely different from that at Patton's. There was a desire to be informed on the political situation as seen from Tangier, and much closer cooperation was established between headquarters at Oujda and the legation at Tangier than had ever existed with General Patton. I later assisted at a meeting at Tauima in Spanish Morocco between General Clark and General Orgaz and, some weeks later, when General Clark received General Orgaz at Oujda. At the luncheon which followed, there were seventeen American generals at the table, plus General Orgaz, General Noguès and one or two other French and Spanish generals. I was seated next to General Omar Bradley, who had just returned from Tunisia, where he had distinguished himself. He greatly impressed me.

A curious instance of the crossed wires which we found in our work in Tangier in the period immediately following the landings came to my knowledge in a very casual manner. One of the control vice consuls assigned to the legation came in one day with a report which he asked if I might have typed for him. He asked that no copies be made. Naturally I read the report, which was a political one concerned with Spanish Morocco. To my astonishment, it contained recommendations which might have seriously affected the relations of the legation with the Spanish authorities, for which I was responsible. I therefore instructed the typist to make an extra copy. When I handed one of the two copies to the vice consul, he upbraided me for having an additional copy made. I let him know in no uncertain terms that decisions affecting the legation, so long as I was in charge, were my responsibility and not his.

He thereupon calmly informed me that he was not subject to my orders but to those of General Mark Clark. I told him that I was guided by the biblical principle that man cannot serve two masters and that it seemed to me an intolerable situation for me to have as a member of my staff a man who was subject to another's orders. When this situation was brought to the Department's attention, he was transferred within twenty-four hours.

In the spring of 1943, in an attempt to reduce the independent reporting of the legation, as well as the consulates in Rabat Casablanca, should be "screened" before transmission to the Department. suggestion was made at Allied Force Headquarters at Algiers that all reporting of the legation, as well as the consulates in Rabat and Casablanca, should be "screened" before transmission to the Department. The word "screened," of course, was a euphemism for "censored." The authorities in Algiers understandably desired that Washington should receive a picture of what was happening in North Africa which was in conformity with their views.

I communicated with the Department of State opposing the proposal, remarking that if such "screening" were applied, it should, in fairness, be applicable also to British Foreign Office establishments. I suggested that the British Foreign Office might take a rather jaundiced view of the censoring in Algiers of the reports of British diplomatic and consular officers. It was added that there had already been a popular outcry in the American and British press against the deal with Darlan and subsequent political developments. This killed it.

In addition to these problems, we had many others of an unprecedented character. In the days immediately following the landings, three American airplanes bearing paratroopers headed for Algeria were forced down in Spanish Morocco. The airplanes were sequestrated by the

Spanish and the crew temporarily interned. The troops had landed with practically nothing but the clothes in which they stood. An officer from the legation was sent to the eastern corner of the Spanish zone, where they were lodged, in order to minister to their wants. We expended some five thousand dollars in their behalf and then tried to collect it from the military attaché. Army regulations had never contemplated the relief of aviators forced to land in foreign countries and we were left, for the time being, "holding the bag." The American Red Cross at length came to our relief and reimbursed us. Later, the military attaché received instructions authorizing him to make expenditures under similar circumstances.

I was enjoying a nap in the legation one Sunday afternoon when the Spanish authorities notified me that an American plane had landed at the Tangier airport. I was informed that if I would take custody of the aviator and agree that he would not endeavor to escape, he would be released to me. A car was sent to the field and I never encountered a more chagrined officer than the one who shortly presented himself.

Fighter planes had been so desperately needed in Tunisia that a plan had been improvised in England for a number to be sent out, escorted and guided by long-range bombers. As the fighters had only a single pilot, no navigating instruments and no radio operators, the bombers were each to escort some dozen fighters. Off the coast of Portugal a storm drove a number of the fighters, including my unexpected visitor, away from their escort and they were forced to shift for themselves. This one had reached the Straits and had seen from his map that Morocco, which he understood to be in Allied hands, was underneath him. He was almost out of gasoline and he had to land at once. He espied the field in Tangier and made for it, only to find, to his great surprise, that he was in Spanish-occupied territory.

I asked him to show me his maps but he demurred, stating he was not authorized to do so. I sent for the military attaché, explained the situation, and suggested to the pilot that if he wished to save those who were coming after him from a like predicament he had better comply with my request. He finally reluctantly agreed when the military attaché assured him the legation was an American establishment and that I was an officer of the United States Government.

His map showed Morocco with no division between the French and Spanish zones and no indication that Tangier and the Spanish zone were under Spanish occupation.

I asked him why he had not landed at Gibraltar, which was just across the way. He said he did not know Gibraltar was in British hands!

We telegraphed the embassy in London suggesting that fighter pilots be equipped with better maps and be better briefed.

With time, we effected a high degree of cooperation between the armed services and the legation. In 1944, after the transfer of General Clark's headquarters, the legation suggested to the naval, air and army commanding officers at Casablanca that a roundtable conference of two or three days' duration be convened for an exchange of views to better understand each other's objectives. The army commander was somewhat skeptical of the value of such a conference, but it was held to the profit of us all. At the end, our most skeptical participant rose to his feet and stated fraeinkly he had doubted if such a conference would serve any useful purpose, but he wanted to admit publicly that he had been entirely wrong, as the conference had demonstrated convincingly to him its constructive achievements.

Commodore McCandlish, commanding American naval forces in Morocco, asked the help of the legation in dealing with the extremely delicate situation which had arisen between his forces and the Spanish forces in Spanish Morocco. German submarines had been very active in the waters around the Straits, and on several occasion navy blimps based at Fort Lyautey and navy planes had been fired upon by Spanish batteries when our blimps or planes had pursued German submarines which sought to escape by fleeing into Spanish Moroccan territorial waters.

The problem was a new one in international law. The principle of "hot pursuit" was recognized so far as surface vessels were concerned, but it had never been recognized, so far as I knew, in respect of airplanes or blimps.

My relations with General Orgaz had by then developed so cordially that I was convinced I could obtain from him recognition of the right of our planes to pursue German submarines and attack them when taking advantage of Spanish Moroccan waters.

I telegraphed the Department on a Friday and stated that in the absence of any objections I proposed to discuss the question with Orgaz on the following Monday.

A copy of the legation's telegram was sent to Algiers, which replied, in a telegram to Washington, repeated to us in Tangier, that as the problem was one which involved Spanish metropolitan territorial waters as well, the question should more properly be raised by Ambassador Hayes with the central Spanish Government in Madrid. I was of a contrary opinion, as I considered it highly likely that Orgaz would be more favorably disposed than Madrid and that any concessions which might be obtained from Orgaz would subsequently serve as a useful lever by Ambassador Hayes with the central authorities.

On Monday morning I was getting into my car to proceed to Tetuan when the legation's code clerk, Mack Henderson, came running out with a telegram in his hand. "You are not to go," he said. "The Department has agreed with Algiers."

This was the only order I have ever disobeyed, but I was so sure of my ground that I decided to do so in this instance. "Mack," I said, "take that telegram back and forget you ever showed it to me."

I had no difficulty explaining the situation to Orgaz. When I finished my exposition, he said: "We are neutral, as I have assured you previously. I shall give immediate orders to my shore batteries to refrain from firing on any of your planes or blimps which pursue submarines violating our neutrality by coming into our waters."

When I returned to Tangier and drafted the telegram reporting the successful results of the interview, I could not resist adding: *"Unfortunately* the Department's instructions directing me not to raise the issue were only received upon my return from Tetuan."

Ambassador Hayes has pointed out in his *Wartime Mission in Spain* that the decision taken by Orgaz was helpful and instrumental in obtaining a like decision on the part of Madrid.

The most striking example of perfect cooperation between the United States Navy, the OSS and the Foreign Service was achieved under most dramatic circumstances.

On February 18, 1944, Lieutenant Commander Wright and Major Hooker of the OSS flew unexpectedly to Tangier from Casablanca and presented to me a problem which was giving the Navy great anxiety. There had been a recrudescence of German submarine warfare in the Straits, with heavy losses to Allied shipping. A convoy of the highest importance was passing through the Straits within the next few days and it was desired at all costs to take all available measures against any attack on it. It was known that the Germans had possessed throughout the war secret radio stations which were still functioning in Spanish territory in North Africa. Would it be possible, as one means of safeguarding the convoy, for all available personnel of the legation, particularly the service attachés, to spend the next few days moving ostentatiously up and down the coast in their cars with a view to "flushing" any Spanish elements who might be cooperating with the Axis in submarine warfare?

I replied that I would do more than that. I would seek out General Orgaz on the following day with the naval attaché, Commander Robert Gilmore, and present to the former an official communication on the subject, if this were agreeable to the Navy. This measure being concurred in, steps were taken to obtain an appointment with the Spanish high commissioner for the next day.

General Orgaz received us at noon on February 19. I recalled his attachment since 1942 to the preservation of the neutrality of Spanish Morocco. It was pointed out that Allied losses in the Straits from enemy submarines had been exceedingly heavy. It was alleged that the German authorities were continuing to obtain prompt information from Spanish North Africa concerning the movements of Allied convoys. There was strong reason to believe that contact continued between elements of the Spanish intelligence service and Axis intelligence. In the opinion of the United States naval authorities, it was not to be excluded that contact existed between the shores of Spanish North Africa and enemy submarines. In view of these circumstances, the Spanish authorities were asked to institute at once a patrol of the shores and to permit the naval attaché to make such observations as he might consider desirable to detect any possible evidence of the improper activities we had in mind.

The high commissioner repudiated the suggestion of Spanish unneutrality with great indignation. As evidence of Spanish good faith, he offered to permit Commander Gilmore access to the entire coast, including Spanish military installations at Ceuta, in company with an officer of the Spanish general staff who would report to the legation on the following day.

We returned to Tangier thoroughly satisfied. At a staff conference at the legation I outlined the problem. The head of OSS, Dick Bownass, interjected: "We have some information which has come to us in the last few hours which fits like a jigsaw puzzle into the picture. We have learned from an informer that an Axis radio station staffed with Spanish and Germans is operating at Calle Teniente Pacheo 16 in Ceuta for communication with Axis submarines. The radio is kept concealed, when not in use, in a large flower box. I can't vouch for the information, as the informer is new to us."

Our search, which had been hitherto indefinite, now had a precise objective. A careful plan was made to avoid any tipping of our hands; on a number of previous occasions, when efforts had been made to run down such secret German stations, the birds had flown when entry was made with search warrants issued by the Spanish authorities.

Gilmore, accompanied by the Spanish officer and another member of our staff, Edward Brenes, was directed to proceed to Ceuta, and only there to reveal the destination of the party. Once arrived at the house, if objections were made to their entering, Gilmore was to make a most vigorous protest against the nonfulfillment of General Orgaz's commitment to me. If Gilmore were called away with the Spanish officer to seek instructions from Orgaz by telephone, Brenes was to stand guard over the premises.

. Events developed as we foresaw. The Spanish officer objected strenuously to our entering a private dwelling. Gilmore protested. Recourse was had to a telephone and, at length, the Spanish officer was ordered by Orgaz to allow Gilmore and Brenes to enter and make their investigations.

While Gilmore was absent, Brenes was able to observe a number of persons making a hurried exit from the rear of the house.

Upon the return of Gilmore and the Spanish officer, they entered the house, where the occupant, a certain Frau Meyer, was found in great agitation. From the left side of the house there was a clear view of the Straits, and two sets of binoculars in the room indicated the use which was being made of the premises. Wires were observed running from the room to a small room on the roof, where there was a crate on which rested two big flowerpots. Upon removal of the flowerpots and the raising of the lid of the crate, a black suitcase was found. This proved to be the radio transmitter, and there were found enclosed with it papers with code symbols. Upon inquiry, Frau Meyer admitted the suitcase had been introduced into the house by the German consul at Tetuan, Herr Seydel.

General Orgaz, when indignantly spurning any suggestion that unneutral acts were taking place in Spanish North Africa, had asked that I give him precise details. I was now in a position to do so. I thereupon wrote him:

> A Spanish national by the name of Manuel Centeno is employed by the German Intelligence Service as the Chief of all German observation services in the Ceuta area. As such, Centeno receives 3,000 pesetas in monthly salary and 5,000 pesetas for expenses. He employs officers and radio operators of ships touching at Ceuta as informers and couriers. His code name with German intelligence is Antonio.
>
> Centeno has three observatories at Ceuta; one known as the Madrid bar in the Villa Javita was operated until December, 1943. Another post was maintained in the Recinto district, and a third, that visited this morning, at 16 Teniente Pacheco contained a radio transmitter and receiver for communicating secretly with Axis submarines. The radio was delivered to this house on January 27 by Hans Seydel of the German Consulate in Tetuan. The radio operator is the son of a Spanish police inspector in Ceuta.

I do not believe General Orgaz had any knowledge of the existence of this station. I am convinced he was sincere in his belief that no unneutral acts were being committed in Spanish North Africa.

The station was closed, and this was the end of radio communications between the Spanish-controlled Moroccan shore and Axis submarines in the Straits.

The convoy about which the Navy was so concerned was the one escorting President Roosevelt on his return from Yalta to the United States.

The operation of closing this Axis station was a striking example of the most perfect coordination between different services of the United States Government.

The United States Navy set forth the problem and inspired the action. The intelligence services of OSS furnished information which made the action possible. The Foreign Service was the executor of the action.

If cooperation between members of the different departments of our government at the time of Torch had left much to be desired, we had all profited subsequently and, in the end, had evolved a cooperation with could not have been more closely knit.

21

FOUR YEARS IN SAUDI ARABIA

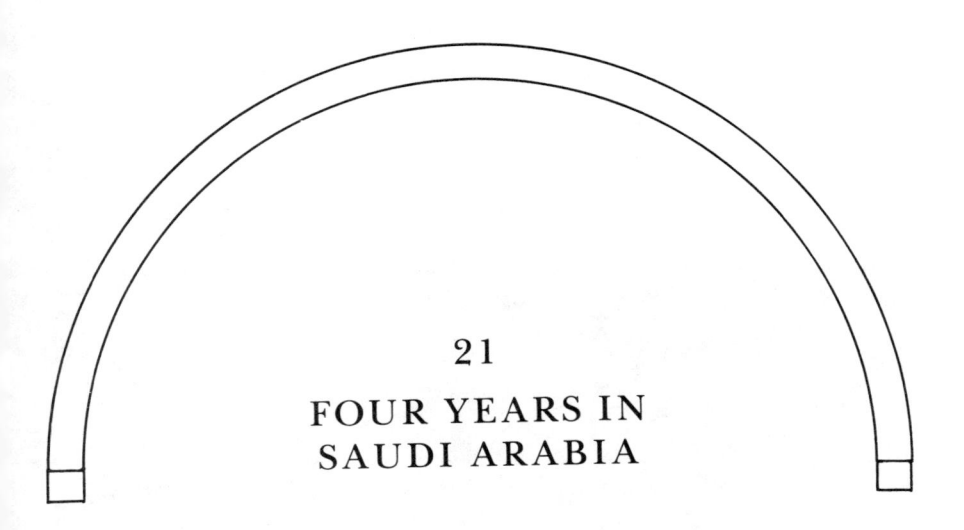

On June 23, 1946, a U.S. Army plane deposited me on a primitive airstrip at Jidda in Saudi Arabia, where I had been assigned as U.S. minister.

I was to spend four years there. It rained once a year, and then only for a few minutes. The temperature rose at times to 135 degrees, with prickly heat so disfiguring our bodies that my wife was able to spend only a few weeks there during the winter. It was only after the lapse of a year or two that I was able to persuade Washington to install air conditioning for some modicum of comfort. I had agreed to stay for two years, but once installed and in the light of the exceptionally close relations I was able to develop with the remarkable King Ibn Saud and the appeals made to me, I was persuaded to remain. The decisive factor was a telegram sent me by Admiral Richard Conolly, commanding U.S. naval forces in Europe. On reading it, I blushed the colors of the rainbow and decided that anyone who thought as much of me as he should not be let down.

I once inquired of the Persian minister, my neighbor in Cairo when I was assigned to the legation in Tehran, how I might best make friends with Persians. He smiled and stated without hesitation, "You have only to be yourself." It was impossible for me to be otherwise, happily, and so it was that I found myself gaining the confidence of acquaintances wherever I was assigned.

Ambassador Childs dining with King Ibn Saud of Saudi Arabia, 1947 (from the University of Virginia Library).

With my natural candor and adaptability I seemed to be accepted in Saudi Arabia by everyone from the lowest to the highest. Of no one was this more true than King Ibn Saud himself. During the four years that I enjoyed his friendship, I never witnessed any coolness or discourtesy on his part. At the end of two years, I decided to bring with me to Riyadh an excellent photograph of him which I desired him to autograph as a memento of our association. When I took it with me to an audience one morning and explained the purpose, he asked me to leave it with one of the attendants and he would return it duly signed the following day.

The next morning, to my bewilderment, the king received me with marked reserve which contrasted strikingly with his invariable affability. While I was wondering of what I had been guilty and wracking my brains to recall how I might have offended him, his face relaxed in a smile and his eyes twinkled as if deriving pleasure from my discomfiture.

"I have no intention of signing the picture you left with me," he said gruffly.

"I am sorry," I said, completely nonplussed.

After seeming to squeeze the last ounce from my embarrassment, his face relaxed in a broad smile. "My wife cautioned me not to sign it, as there were several gray hairs to be seen in my head."

When he had exhausted the scenario, his face broke into a broad smile. "Never mind; I have another photograph, in which there are no gray hairs, which I shall sign and give you."

He was the soul of delicacy. The autumn of my arrival in 1946, I had gone to the Jidda airport preparatory to flying to France for a much-needed change of climate. As my wife had only just arrived with her mother to spend a few weeks, there was no thought on their part to leave. The minister of finance had come to see me off and held in his hand a parcel enclosed in a greasy newspaper. My interpreter explained that the minister had a gift from the king intended for my wife. I offered to accompany him to her presence, where she was chatting with friends. Nothing could have been quite so incongruous than the spectacle of the minister of finance being conducted by me and presented to my wife with the greasy package in his hand. Once we were assembled, he made known to Georgina that he had been commissioned by the king to present her with a small gift. The "small gift" proved to be a string of resplendent pearls. I was in a quandary, which could not be resolved until my return from leave.

On my return, I drafted a dispatch to the State Department explaining that it would have been impolite on the part of my wife to decline the gift and inquiring what course we should follow. It proved to be an insoluble problem for the State Department; we never had any acknowledgment.

The first telegram sent from Jidda, seat of the U.S. legation, elevated shortly after to an embassy, one of the most prophetic ever sent by me, rests framed in my study. It may be found in *Foreign Relations of the United States, 1946,* volume VII, *The Near East and Africa.*

Secret

Jidda, July 1, 1946—5 P.M.

207. Department's 173, June 26. Following presentation letter of credence Prince Faisal offered customary dinner to staff and leading members American community and I had opportunity to inform him that reply to King's letter might be expected soon, that overall Palestine policy not yet determined but being considered by Cabinet Committee.

In long discussion which followed, and which full report being made by dispatch, Viceroy [also Minister for Foreign Affairs] expressed considerable gratification that no final decision reached and expressed most earnest hope that decision would be a just one which would not prejudice the greatly valued friendship of the United States by Saudi Arabia. He added Palestine question was matter of life and death to Arabs who viewed Zionist aspirations Palestine as having ultimate end of swallowing up Arab world. His statements were temperate but firm. He reiterated that Saudi Arabia and Arab world were placing great store in sense of justice of United States.

In this initial talk with mouthpiece of King, I am convinced that unless we proceed with utmost circumspection in considering all phases of possible repercussions of Palestine question, we may raise difficulties for ourselves in this most strategic area of vital national interest which will plague United States constantly in years to come.

Pursuant to a message from the king at his palace in Riyadh of his urgent desire to confer with me, I flew there on December 1, 1947, from my residence at Jidda. The next morning I was received in audience at the royal palace. As evidence of the importance attached by His Majesty to our meeting, he broke all precedents by dismissing my personal interpreter, Mohammed Effendi, who accompanied me to Riyadh, as well as the palace interpreter. Instead, he requested Fuad Bey Hamza, minister of state, to serve as interpreter. Moreoever, while the first audience with His Majesty after arriving in Riyadh is one limited normally to an exchange of courtesies, on this occasion His Majesty, soon after mutual inquiries re our respective healths, at once broached the purpose for which he had requested me to come to Riyadh.

His Majesty began by stating that he knew I was a sincere friend of the Arabs. My government had taken a decision with respect to Palestine which was most distasteful to the Arab world. We did not intend to speak, however, of that. That was past and the Arabs would take such measures as they deemed necessary for the defense of their interests.

What would come out of it would be the will of God. He added, "Although we differ enormously on the question of Palestine, we still have our own mutual interests and friendship to safeguard."

His Majesty stated that he was much concerned by two problems; one, the question of Russian influence and Communist propaganda; and two, the menace which might be offered by the Shereefian family of Jordan.

The king stated that he wished to speak in the frankest possible way with me. For that reason he would define the position of Saudi Arabia in relation to other Arab states with respect to the Palestine question as it presented itself now in consequence of the decision taken by the United Nations.

His Majesty stated; "I occupy a position of preeminence in the Arab world. In the case of Palestine, I have to take common cause with other Arab states. Although the other Arab states may bring pressure to bear on me, I do not anticipate that a situation will arise whereby I shall be drawn into conflict with friendly Western powers over this question."

His Majesty remarked that, apart from Palestine, his relations with the United States were of the closest. He considered that, aside from Palestine, there were no points of conflict between the two countries, whose interests were complementary to one another.

For the above reasons, His Majesty wished to inquire of the remaining three points on which he wished clear answers:

(1) Leaving aside wholly the question of Palestine, what was the attitude of the United States Government toward the government of Saudi Arabia? To put the question in another form, His Majesty wished to know how and in what manner he might rely upon the United States.

(2) Concerning the second point, His Majesty prefaced his question by remarking that a close British friend, who had been in his confidence since the days when Sir Percy Cox was high commissioner in Baghdad, had recently informed him that it made no difference what arrangements Saudi Arabia might make with the United States, as there was a secret understanding between the United States and Great Britain according to which the United States acknowledged this area as being within a British zone of political influence. His Majesty wished to know whether such an understanding existed between the United States and British governments by which the United States recognized Saudi Arabia as being within a British political zone of influence.

(3) His Majesty remarked that one of the most sensitive parts of his kingdom was the northern part (referring to the Saudi Arabian border with Iraq and Transjordan, Shereefian states) through which there would pass the trans-Arabian pipeline, which was of equal importance to the Saudi and United States governments. His Majesty wished to give

that portion of his kingdom the greatest possible protection. He had the troops but he was lacking arms.

There was the possibility of trouble being caused on that border through Communist propaganda or through the instigation of the Shereefian family. His Majesty cited a recent incident in Transjordan in which the offices and autos of Tapline had been attacked and mentioned also proclamations and speeches made by prominent Iraq leaders. It appeared to His Majesty that Saudi troops should be sufficiently supplied and trained to cope with such a situation. He desired to ascertain therefore whether the United States would supply the Saudi Arabian Government and Army with the necessary materials for that purpose and precisely to what extent might the Saudi Arabian Government count upon assistance from the United States Government in this respect, since the threat was one not only involving Saudi Arabia but also vital American interests.

His Majesty observed that he had originally instructed his son, Prince Faisal, to proceed from New York to Washington upon the conclusion of the session of the General Assembly of the United Nations in order to see the President and Secretary of State on His Majesty's behalf to obtain clear and direct answers to these three questions. However, tension had become so great in the Middle East owing to the Palestine decision that His Majesty felt it might arouse undue suspicion in the Arab world should Prince Faisal proceed to Washington for the purpose of conferring with President Truman and Secretary Marshall.

His Majesty said he had, therefore, instructed Prince Faisal not to go to Washington. His Majesty added that he had the fullest confidence in me and that he had asked me to come to Riyadh to present these very important questions to me instead. He wished to ask me to communicate with my government and to request that I be summoned to Washington to deliver his extremely important questions in person to the President and Secretary of State, to acquaint them personally with his attitude and to bring back to him the answers. It was too important a subject to commit to writing.

Finally, His Majesty stated that he did not expect me to attempt to supply any answers to the questions he had raised. He would only ask that I conform with his requests.

I replied to His Majesty that I would not fail to discharge faithfully the great confidence he had reposed in me, which I fully appreciated. In view of the importance of the subject, I asked His Majesty if he had any objections to my dictating an account of our conversation to my confidential secretary, Mr. Gleaton, who had accompanied me from Jidda. It was my thought that Khalid Bey and Fuad Bey Hamza could then review the memorandum which I might dictate and make any corrections they might consider necessary and, if His Majesty so desired, the corrected memorandum might be submitted to His Majesty tomorrow. His Majesty said he was entirely in accord and that he left the matter entirely to the discretion of Khalid Bey and Fuad Bey Hamza and me. He would receive us the following day.

I had a second audience with the king on December 3, reported from Jidda, to which I had returned. The king had reiterated that the crucial question for him was whether and to what extent he might count on United States aid in resisting incursions from Iraq and Transjordan.

The acting Secretary of State, in a top-secret urgent telegram of December 12, 1947, instructed me, in reply to the questions raised by the king, Hamza and Prince Saud, that I might inform the Saudi Arabian Government as follows:

"US appreciates spirit of friendship shown by King and his Govt. at this difficult time, agrees that our relations are of closest and that, apart from Palestine, there are no points of difference between two countries whose interests are complementary. Furthermore US is reassured that King does not anticipate situation will develop whereby he will be drawn into conflict with friendly Western Powers over Palestine question.

"US has in past and will continue in future assist nations of Near East in resisting Communist influence. This Govt. is not unmindful of the possible new aspect in this regard presented by developments relating to Palestine and is watching matter closely.

"This Govt. feels now as in the past that apprehensions regarding Middle East peace and position of Saudi family arising from feared intrigues of Hashemite family are primarily a matter for intra-Arab consideration, which is capable of solution by direct arrangement, by Arab League, or in last resort by UN. As King Ibn Saud has seen from events of the last nine months the US has been in communication with Govt. of Great Britain more than once on this subject and is convinced that British are not supporting Hashemite claims to Greater Syria and that they have actually used restraining influence on Hashemite circles desirous of expanding their control.

"You may assure King Ibn Saud there exists no understanding of any kind between US and Great Britain acknowledging all or any part of Saudi Arabia or any other Arab country as being a British zone of political or economic influence. Saudi Arabia is a sovereign kingdom and does not come within sphere influence of any Power. It is true US seeks to maintain friendly relations with Great Britain which like the US is interested in the preservation of peace and tranquility in the Near East. The two Governments, therefore, exchange views from time to time regarding various Middle Eastern problems of common interest. Such exchanges, however, do not include views and statements given in confidence to either Govt. by Saudi Arabia or any other country.

"This Govt. has noted with appreciation and satisfaction that there have been no disturbances within borders of Saudi Arabia, despite state of public feeling re Palestine question. Note has been taken of request of King Ibn Saud for arms and munitions of war, including equipment for motorized divisions and military airplanes to be used solely for defensive purposes of Saudi Arabia and never to be used either against US or so as to conflict with any of our interests. In particular, consideration has been given to statement of King regarding 'great pressure' being brought upon him by Hashemite states, and his feeling that his failure to come into open economic conflict with US by cancellation of the oil concessions may lead to incursion from Iraq or Transjordan into his domain.

"Govt. of US cannot conceive of situation arising under which Hashemite states would attack Saudi Arabia merely because King Ibn Saud continued to be friendly to United States and to private American companies doing business within borders of his country. This Govt., after careful consideration, recently decided that broad interests of peace can best be served if in existing circumstances US should for time being refrain from exporting arms and munitions to Palestine and neighboring countries.

"King Ibn Saud should be reminded that as previously indicated to him and Prince Saud inability on the part of US to provide him with military aid requested should not in any way be taken as an indication of any lessening of friendship on part of US towards Saudi Arabia. It should rather be considered as indication of US view that so long as Palestine situation remains acute, shipment of arms and munitions from US to Middle Eastern area should cease pending UN consideration of security aspects of that situation.

"As was pointed out by Secretary Byrnes to Crown Prince Saud when he was in Washington last January, one of the basic policies of United States in Near East is unqualifiedly to support territorial integrity and political independence of Saudi Arabia. If Saudi Arabia should therefore be attacked by another Power or be under threat of attack the US through medium of UN would take energetic measures to ward off such aggression.

"For Childs. You are commended for able way in which you conducted these difficult conversations with King."

Immediately on receipt of the Department's telegram, I communicated with Prince Saud in Mecca. He came to Jidda and received me the morning of the fifteenth, when I handed him the note to His Majesty embodying the replies. I remarked to Prince Saud that I was entirely gratified by the rapidity with which my government had answered and thought that this could be interpreted as evidence of the very friendly disposition entertained by the United States toward Saudi Arabia and the importance attached to any request of His Majesty. A translation of the note was then read by the legation interpreter.

On the morning of December 16, Prince Saud handed me the lengthy reply from King Ibn Saud which was sent in translation to Washington. In it, the king expressed his thanks for the explanations given to two of the three principal questions raised by the king with me in my audience with him.

Prince Saud followed a translation of the note with obvious gratification. He remarked that the Saudi Government fully appreciated explanation given by the United States *re* the shipment of arms to the Middle East at this time. He hoped, however, this policy would not continue indefinitely. His government was very grateful to the United States for assurances contained in the note. Relying implicitly on those assurances, it would formulate its policy in light of them, secure in belief in their strength and their fulfillment. Saudi Arabia did not credit the Hashemites with any substantial intrinsic strength. Its concern was with the power standing behind the Hashemites and the use which might be made of Hashemites by that power, an obvious reference to the British.

Prince Saud stated he would communicate to me certain information on a top-secret basis for my personal information alone. The previous day, in an Arab league meeting, the ministers of Iraq and Transjordan had requested that Saudi Arabia break relations with the United States and cancel oil concessions. The Saudi representative had replied it saw no reason to take such a measure; Saudi Arabia was at one with other Arab states in opposition to the establishment of a Jewish state but saw no reason to run counter to Saudi Arabia's own interests by severing relations with the United States. He added that, if Iraq and Transjordan insisted, Saudi Arabia would break relations not with the United States but with these two states.

In concluding the audience, the crown prince said the United States Government reply could not have been more timely. It would be forwarded by special plane to His Majesty and, if King Ibn Saud had any special observations to make, His Majesty would communicate back to me subsequently. He asked that very great thanks be conveyed to my government for the prompt and clear reply.

Thus King Ibn Saud had declared his thanks for the explanations given by the United States Government to two of the three principal questions discussed in my audience on December 2 and chiefly for the reiterated assurances of friendship for the Arabs, support of their independence and the intention to maintain the status quo.

On the other hand, the king could not conceal his disappointment concerning the response to the third question, namely, the request for American aid to enable Saudi Arabia to take the necessary measures to assure the protection of mutual interests in the event of any emergencies. In the remainder of his long message, the king took pains to make detailed observations which he hoped would remove any wrong impression concerning his purposes. He feared that there had been misinterpretation of Saudi Arabian attitudes, particularly in respect of the decision of the United States Government in preventing the export of arms to the Middle East, including Saudi Arabia. He declared that any military assistance would never be used against the United States or for aggressive attack against others. There was an extremely large difference between the position of Saudi Arabia and that of other countries, because there were vital mutual economic and strategic interests there, such as the protection of the oil fields and pipeline, which did not exist elsewhere.

King Ibn Saud reconfirmed his guarantee that any military aid would not be used for other than defensive purposes. He pleaded that his real purpose was to establish a modern, mechanized military force to be used only as a means of defense around the airfield at Dhahran and in the area of the pipeline. The king asserted that he intended to ask the United States for the assistance of a training mission to supervise the training of this force and the preparation of such bases as would be required. In the light of these assurances and explanations which he had frankly reiterated, King Ibn Saud hoped that the United States would review its position and, inspired by the existing situation, could work out a practical way which would lead to the realization and attainment of the king's purposes.

In a telegram of December 16, I reported that I had emphasized to Prince Saud that the attitude of the United States toward shipment of arms to the Middle East was not based on any doubt or reservation regarding the friendly intentions and disposition of the king and his government. The decision to embargo arms shipments had been adopted in the light of general considerations involving the peace and security of the area.

And on December 22, I suggested that the sending of a military mission to Saudi Arabia would materially enhance the possibility of extending American occupancy of the Dhahran air base beyond March 1949. In a telegram of January 23, 1948, the Department informed me that the Departments of State, Army and Air Force were giving careful consideration to the sending of such a mission.

On January 13, 1948, I telegraphed the Department:

"We may be approaching, if we have not already passed, a decisive stage in our relations with Saudi Arabia. Until Palestine partition decision we have not had a firmer friend in Arab world than Ibn Saud.

"Although no official intimation has been given me to such effect, it is suggested King may be influenced to abandon hope of close political relations with US and return to his previous policy of relying more particularly upon his political relations with Great Britain by Faisal's recent report to him and reluctance displayed by US to give positive form to his overtures, namely:

"1. Middle East settlement suggested by King in June.

"2. Raising our respective Legations to Embassies; reported information from Saudi Deputy Minister for Foreign Affairs that the British had raised their Legation at Jidda to that of Embassy and expressed the hope that US would take similar action.

"3. Sending military mission Dhahran.

"It would appear reasonable infer our reluctance in respect 1 and 2 above may have persuaded him to raise question attitude toward Saudi Arabian Government of US Government.

"Our support of Palestine partition has no doubt accentuated King's doubt whether he could find in US a stable political partner in substitution for his old ally, the British. What must have however intensified King's doubts has been contrast between British refusal to be drawn into an imposed Palestine settlement and reports brought to him by Faisal of what last named described to me yesterday (Jan. 12. 1948) as American delegates to UN General Assembly acting as spokesmen of Zionists, one of parties to dispute, and pressure brought by American Delegation on other foreign delegations to vote for partition after assurances given Faisal by Department no such pressure would be exerted.

"Above coupled with readiness with which British accepted Saudi Arabian Government proposal raising Legations to Embassies and our generally negative attitude toward this and other specific Saudi Arabian Government's proposals closer political relations, incline King reexamination his former policy moving away from British and basing his foreign policy on development closest political relations with US."

Two months later, this top-secret telegram of April 17, 1948, went to the Secretary of State:

"In accordance request His Majesty that I go urgently Riyadh, I flew there fifteenth and sixteenth returned. I saw His Majesty twice and conferred at length with Shaikh Yusuf Yassin (Deputy Foreign Minister).

"In long discussion, I presented following essential points: We had granted aid to Turkey when international situation was far from as threatening as at present. Turks had basis trained army. Today situation was such we could not improvise or hope to gain time for preparations as we had been able in first two world wars. We and British had planes and ships and motorized equipment. Arab states had very little. First brunt of defense would fall on those powers now in state of preparation. It might take several years to bring forces of Saudi Arabia and other Arab states to point where they would share burden of defense. First and most important task confronting problem of defense measures was providing adequate facilities to those powers capable of taking immediately defensive measures. I expressed also strong hope that insistence upon question of sovereignty or of freedom of territories from occupation did not necessarily mean that in elaboration of any plans necessary facilities for adoption defensive measures would be denied. I cited fact repossessed bases in British and Portuguese sovereign territories, amongst others, which did not detract from sovereignty of those countries, and were not considered a servitude.

"I expressed strong personal hope His Majesty would use his influence with Arab League induce League pass resolution along lines mentioned in British memorandum. His Majesty stated he was prepared conclude treaty with both US and Great Britain, and added in consideration very close relations with US our treaty should contain supplementary protocol providing special circumstances incident to our close relations. Shaikh Yusuf added that His Majesty would be prepared use his influence along line suggested. Shaikh Yusuf, who appeared impressed by my arguments, stated fundamental principles set forth in last paragraph of British memorandum quoted above are, of course, subject to discussion and interpretation. He said 'We are ready to accept any suggested amendments from you.'"

In a top-secret telegram from Jidda, April 19, 1948, I reported:

"His Majesty desires views US Government regarding above and his reply to British memo.

"Shaikh Yusuf outside audience satisfactory settlement Palestine and Egyptian questions were necessary to achieve unity between Arabs and US and Great Britain. I replied I thought Arabs should be convinced we are making every effort in UN to bring about Palestine settlement which would attain peace in that country, while British were in our opinion sincerely desirous reaching Egyptian settlement which was most conducive security objectives we all shared."

With the arrival of Major General Robert Harper, commanding general of the Air Transport Command; Richard Sanger of the Department of State, Colonel Richard J. O'Keefe, designated successor to Colonel Seeds as commandant at the Dhahran airfield, and Colonel Harry R. Snyder, chief of the air training mission at that field, I informed the Department we had spent April 21 to 23 at Riyadh and had had several audiences with His Majesty and long exchanges of views with Shaikh Yusuf Yassin. In my top-secret telegram of April 24, following our return to Jidda from Riyadh, I reported:

"General Harper outlined at length what Department of Air Force was able to offer in way of funds and training at Dhahran air base. (On

April 6 the Department has informed me that $15,000,000 had been allocated to recondition that base.) His Majesty listened most attentively and asked pointedly, 'Is that all?' When General Harper assented, His Majesty expressed great disappointment and said he was going to speak frankly as one friend to another. He then said he had requested US Government some months ago for concrete military aid. With present acute situation, he stated Saudi Arabian needs as consisting of four Saudi Arabian groups of 20,000 men each, fully equipped and trained in mechanized warfare. Implicitly he recognized that he would rely on US for any defense against a major power but emphasized Saudi Arabian forces he had in mind would not only assist our defense plans but would be available to him for use in developing defense his borders against Hashemites whom British were arming. It was stated in event attack by Russia, there was no doubt in His Majesty's mind but what we would come immediately his defense but suppose, by way of example, Saudi Arabia were attacked by Bahrein. We would probably be content to refer matter to UN.

"King stated 'Truly and actually, I never believed US Government would give me this kind of reply to my request for aid. What General Harper has to offer is satisfactory for a time of civilization and peace but it is not for today. There are hostilities all around us. War may be with us very soon. If the Americans are to arrange to give such training as offered at Dhahran, at Nejd, and elsewhere in Saudi Arabia, that would not be useful in such critical circumstances. I do not know of any other government except the British from which I can get help. In the past, British have been my friends and have given me considerable assistance but since discovery of oil and granting oil concessions to Americans, British have changed in their attitude. They are now supporting Hashemites. Truly I am in a critical situation. British themselves will not harm me but Hashemite groups will. My enemies are saying I have turned Saudi Arabia over to the Americans. My enemies in Islamic countries spread rumors I have even permitted Americans to occupy holy places. If the Americans are really my friends, they must change the offer that General Harper has brought. America must help me at least as the British are helping the Hashemites.'

"As reported previously, His Majesty is averse to treating question continuance our occupancy Dhahran air base apart from broad general question Saudi Arabian defense. One of the reasons for this and perhaps controlling one is that if we furnish him specific military aid he has in mind he can then justify to Arab world facilities he is prepared and entirely ready to grant to US at Dhahran as well as elsewhere. Such an agreement, it is believed, would satisfy His Majesty's request for mutual defense pact and would have other obvious advantages.

"Attitude His Majesty may best be summed up in statement 'do something concrete now or tell us that you are going to do nothing.' Under these circumstances we suggest the various studies now being carried on in Washington regarding US defense plans in Saudi Arabia be pushed to a rapid conclusion. If decision these studies is negative King should be so informed as quickly as possible. If on other hand it is decided we will take active steps to defend the Arabian Peninsula we suggest that a party of American technicians under auspices Department Defense come to Saudi Arabia and confer with King and his advisers, and be prepared submit cost program to SAG which they would be expected to bear. It is opion His Majesty and our opinion the time for talk has passed and it is imperative group which is sent to Saudi Arabia should be empowered to make commitments which might be incorporated in agreement referred to above."

To summarize in the words of Shaikh Yusuf: "If the United States should offer adequate military aid, the United States Government may ask what help it may need and His Majesty will grant it. In fact, His Majesty will not wait for you to make requests. He will make the offers to you when needed."

The finance minister sent for me at Jidda on July 6, following his return from Riyadh. He referred to an inquiry made by the State Department of the Saudi Arabian Government legation in Washington as to whether Saudi Arabian Government intended to take up a balance of $15,000,000 from the Export-Import Bank. The finance minister stated the question had been considered by His Majesty two days before and it decided that no part of the remaining loan available would be taken up. He added that the decision had been reached in view of the attitude taken at this time by the United States Government. No specific reference was made to Palestine but the meaning was obvious. The finance minister said he had been instructed by the king to acquaint me with the foregoing.

We shall probably never know the true facts which conspired to bring about creation of the State of Israel. The British Government, under constant harassment in discharging its duties as the mandatory power in Palestine, was moved at length to announce its intention to withdraw from that country on May 14, 1948. Previously, the United States announced, on October 11, 1947, its support of the partition of the country which had been approved on November 29 by the bare two-thirds majority of the General Assembly required. This resolution had no binding force until implemented. The storm unleashed by its adoption gave pause both to the United Nations and the United States. It had one result: the British announcement of its intention to withdraw from Palestine. On May 14, 1948, the Zionists proclaimed the creation of the

State of Israel, which was at once recognized by the United States, unleashing the disorders and bloodshed which have followed almost without cessation ever since.

In the period immediately following, this introduced an impasse to any fruitful understanding with Ibn Saud, and it was only by slow and deliberate steps that we gradually worked our way out of what at first seemed to represent almost insurmountable obstacles to the reestablishment of productive relations.

Something of this dilemma emerges from the consideration given in the latter part of 1948 to the extension of the Dhahran air base agreement, one of our principal concerns.

On January 7, 1949, the British ambassador and I were received together in Jidda by the king to discuss political problems in an unprecedented dual confrontation. His Majesty cited the use being made of the Jews by the Russians and the disorders which were bound to ensue unless effective measures were taken by his friends and by him. He recalled the strong ties which united him with Britain and the United States. He observed that the former had recently reaffirmed treaty obligations to Egypt, Transjordan and Iraq. This left only Lebanon, Syria and Saudi Arabia as Arab states whose friendship had not been publicly acknowledged by either Britain or the United States. He had repeatedly approached the United States Government for some assurances regarding its attitude toward him but had not obtained anything. He could not be left in this fashion and he had therefore taken this step of calling together with him both British and United States representatives to express his viewpoints and request them to bring these before their governments.

On January 24, I telegraphed the Department that the deputy foreign minister had called late on the twenty-second and told me he discussed Dhahran with the king and Prince Faisal. My message said:

"From this conciliatory manner I am convinced King has intervened to exercise a moderating influence on Faisal. Yusuf began by repeating a statement he has frequently used recently that His Majesty did not set any term or limits on friendship with US. He expressed strong desire to reach Dhahran agreement without any arguments. 'I realize,' he said, 'importance Dhahran to US and its defense needs in present international situation. It is our wish however stay of US in Dhahran will not have appearance of occupying that area. For outward appearance, we propose new agreement on a nominal lease basis.' Compensation for lease would be *pro forma* and character of compensation would be left to conscience of US. SAG recognizes arms embargo precludes military equipment as compensation and are thinking in terms such items as airplane engines of which there is great need. Yusuf said SAG recognized difficulty would be encountered in obtaining from Congress funds under short-term lease. Ability to obtain funds would be measure of US confidence in SAG. He emphasized it was in our mutual interest renewal be in form new agreement to (a) include such provisions of existing agreement which it might be mutually desirable to retain and (b) certain general provisions which he would outline."

In a top-secret telegram of February 27, I reported to the Secretary of State that all members of the Saudi Arabian Government had been in Riyadh some days where a discussion took place on Saudi Arabia–United States relations:

"Following return of Prince Faisal and Acting Foreign Minister to Jidda I spent three hours at the Foreign Office with latter. Yusuf said HM had instructed him to discuss SAG–US relations based on latest developments. He said: 'International situation is as momentous as it was. Sole problem which US has had in connection Arab states in general, and SAG in particular, is Palestine. HM would like to know view US Government of US–SAG relations.

" 'Is US Government still of opinion present situation does not permit any modification previously expressed view time not propitious discussion military and other aid SAG, including tripartite agreement between US, UK and SAG. Whenever questions raised with US Government, it always referred SAG to United Nations.

" 'His Majesty says US Government ought to reconsider its attitude re SA, because its common interest with SAG are not as those with any other country, so its attitude toward US would differ from that toward other countries. If US Government believes has interests in SA vital and fundamental, and if US Government would like to develop and strengthen such interests with SAG, we would be pleased to receive either special US delegation with US Minister Jidda or send SAG delegation to US to be headed by one of Princes to discuss existing mutual interests between two countries. Such delegation should not be appointed unless we are sure US Government prepared to reconsider its attitude and is ready to do so.'

"I said HM's observations would be studied with great care, interest and attention, by US Government. I assured Acting Foreign Minister that purpose and desire of US Government was to strengthen our relations with SAG. I added principal difference between points of view US Government and SAG was as to time and means of achieving an aim shared by both. I mentioned attention US Government now largely concerned conclusion Atlantic Pact and if there was any delay in making known by my Government to HM of our comments on his observations, this should not be attributed to any indifference our part or any lack of realization of the importance HM's remarks."

Yusuf said he himself felt the principal difference separating us on this question was a matter of time, and he added that the king had said, "Time has come."

Later on, the acting foreign minister mentioned that the king had expressed hope that a reply might be had within ten days or so, as apparently he has other decisions awaiting a reply to my telegram.

In view of our previous Palestine policy, the king found it particularly difficult to renew to us openly privileges at Dhahran which might have been interpreted by other Arab states as indifference on the part of His Majesty to the Arab cause. The position of the Saudi Arabian Government was represented as desirous of continuing to grant us in effect the same privileges but of making it appear to the world in the written instrument that Saudi Arabia was in fact the master to Dhahran.

After deep reflection, it appeared to me that the most desirable course was to trust the sincerity of the Saudi Arabian position by endeavoring to work out the terms of an agreement with them which would give us the privileges which we desired while preserving the *amour propre* of the Saudi Arabian Government of which it was justifiably jealous. I sought O'Keefe's counsel and he concurred wholeheartedly. We therefore threw ourselves into the task of reformulating the Saudi Arabian counterproposals in a manner which would be acceptable to us as affording a practical working basis for our air forces at Dhahran while preserving the necessary appearances to the world of the Saudi Arabian Government. The services rendered by O'Keefe and Elkins were invaluable. It was O'Keefe and Elkins, assisted from time to time by me, who were principally responsible for the skillful manner in which the Saudi Arabian counterproposals were transformed to give Colonel O'Keefe and the air force the necessary operative working control at Dhahran.

The evening of March 21 was a crisis point in our negotiations. I found it difficult to determine the purpose of Fuad Bey's obduracy that evening. I was so confused by his change of attitude that I even entertained as a reasonable suspicion that Saudi Arabia was endeavoring to compel us to take the initiative in withdrawing from the negotiations by raising impossible conditions. I was at a loss to account for Fuad Bey's attitude in view of the completely changed and conciliatory position he subsequently assumed when I threatened to take my difficulties directly to the king.

In consideration of all that I had reported, it was hoped the Department would agreee that no other course was left open to us than the one outlined. An important factor in the decision taken was the goodwill opened to us in our endeavor to meet the Saudi Arabian desires halfway. I felt strongly that hesitation on our part might well have produced suspicion as to our motives, and I felt that the results achieved by our spirit of accommodation exceeded the most optimistic hopes of Colonel O'Keefe and me.

The widespread disorder in Saudi Arabian finances had been for some time a subject of great concern to me. After taking counsel with a few trusty acquaintances, I determined to broach the subject with the crown prince and to sound him out as to the propriety of my raising the question with the king himself. I considered the advisability of seeking instruction on the subject from the Department of State and rejected that move. What I proposed was quite contrary to all protocol and it was certain that the Department, unacquainted with the background, would hesitate long before authorizing such a demarche on my part.

I enjoyed the confidence of the king to a very unusual degree. He had assured me of this himself. It was my duty to act, and that was enough to motivate me. When my first telegram was received by the Department reporting my action, there was, as I was to learn, something like consternation, soon mollified by reports of the reactions, one and all favorable locally.

My first telegram on the subject was one of February 13, 1950, reporting an initial discussion on the subject, "at great length, but in very general terms," with Crown Prince Saud on February 8 at Dhahran. Upon the conclusion of my remarks, Saud said: "I wish to thank you from the bottom my heart for the friendliness which has inspired your comments. I wish you to know that I will always welcome the expression of any opinion from you which you may feel disposed to express on any matter.

"I am fully aware of the situation you have mentioned, which has been a source of deep disturbance to me for some time past. The situation is one by no means confined to the Ministry of Finance but extends to almost every administration of government.

"There is only one person in Saudi Arabia to whom I am unalterably attached and that is my father. I will do nothing to hurt him or prejudice his state of mind or his health. I shall act decisively when I have power and I shall spare no one in taking necessary measures I recognize to be necessary for the well-being of my country, whose interests I place above everything else in life except my religion."

The crown prince informed me also that his father's advisers, referring particularly to the finance minister, had his ear and confidence to such an extent that anything he, the crown prince, or his brothers might say might so severely react on him and his brothers as to prejudice their position.

Saud then confided to me he had spies throughout the administration who were reporting to him personally on everything happening. For some time past, he had been studying constitutional and budgetary practices of neighboring Arab states as well as Turkey, and he directed his private secretary to show me a draft decree he had prepared providing for a new constitution setting up a cabinet, legislature and senate along an Egyptian model.

He was deeply appreciative of my comments and requested me to repeat them to the king without reference to the fact that I had made them previously to him or that this suggestion had come from him.

As I anticipated, it was extremely difficult to make the king understand the situation. First of all, I felt his health had failed considerably during recent months, and the crown prince was also concerned with this phase of the situation. I emphasized that my remarks were not directed at the manner in which he disposed of his revenues but at their proper conservation and their orderly expenditure. I also said I was not criticizing any individuals but I likened the situation to that of a once small store whose accounts might first have been kept in the head of the owner but which were now too complex for any one man.

In March of that year, George C. McGhee, then assistant secretary of state for Near Eastern affairs visited Saudi Arabia. McGhee had extended talks on March 22 with Shaikh Yusuf Yassin in Riyadh during which McGhee touched upon Israeli relations with Arab states. McGhee made a plea for the use of moderating influences in the Arab League to remove points of difference among Arab states and to assure cooperation as far as those states were concerned. He emphasized that United States policy was one of complete objectivity and impartiality as between Israel and the Arab states.

Yusuf said he warmly welcomed this. Saudi Arabia had never sought a pro-Arab policy from the United States Government; all it asked was that the United States should weigh the scales between Israel and the Arabs in a spirit of complete impartiality tempered by a sense of justice and right.

McGhee wondered whether something could be done by the Arab states themselves to normalize their relations with Israel and achieve some kind of working relationship, pointing out that present Arab policies were likely to produce the aggressive Israeli reaction most feared by Arab states.

Yusuf stated very politely, but emphatically, that this was not possible and that Arab states would never agree to any working relations with Israel. He added that Arabs considered Israel a great menace and without any limits whatever to its territorial ambitions. The Arabs believed Israel had every intention of expanding beyond Israel to include Syria, Jordan, etc. Arabs had no aggressive designs against Israel, but intended to treat that state as if a wall surrounded it. If Israel wished to expand beyond that wall, it could put its people on vessels and send them overseas to London and Paris.

In the course of the conversation, Yusuf said, "We shall never admit a Jew in Saudi Arabia and we shall never admit anyone traveling with an Israeli visa."

That afternoon, Mr. McGhee and I were received by the king, at which time McGhee reviewed in summary manner the problem of meeting Saudi Arabia's security requirements. He said that, if the independence or integrity of Saudi Arabia were threatened, the United States would take immediate action. The king would understand, however, that in the light of the complexities of the situation which might exist at any future time, that it was not possible to state in precise terms what action might be taken.

His Majesty referred at some length to his problem with the Hashemites, with which he was obviously preoccupied. He said the two Hashemite rulers had been imposed on their respective countries and had never been accepted wholeheartedly by the people. Their military power was entirely derived from British support, without which they would represent no threat. Saudi Arabia, on the other hand, had no such outside support.

The king said that he had at one time offered the oil concession in Saudi Arabia to the British but they had refused it, although he himself was well aware, on the basis of information given him by the Turks, which they had obtained from the Germans, before the First World War, that Saudi Arabia was potentially one of the richest countries in the world so far as oil was concerned. Although the British had been given first refusal of the oil, they had always resented the fact that the concession had finally been given to the United States, and his difficulties with the British had begun from that time. Accordingly, Saudi Arabia had every right to expect that we would approach its needs in security requirements with sympathy.

The king referred to his boundary difficulties and described the British position as very unreasonable. He said that the British were a people of "but." They made statements and gave you assurances but always at the end said, "but." He asked us to meet with Shaikh Yusuf Yassin and Fuad Bey Hamza, at which time the discussion could be continued and amplified.

That evening, there was a state banquet. Dinner was served in complete Western style, except to the king himself, a very recent innovation at Riyadh.

At my request, His Majesty recounted the capture of Riyadh, which represented the first stage of the establishment of the king's power in the Arabian peninsula. McGhee inquired if any Arab rulers had previously controlled the peninsula as the king did. His Majesty replied that a member of his family, coincidentally with the same name, had established such control over the Arab peninsula some two-hundred and fifty years before. This consituted the only previous union of Saudi Arabia. Subsequently, his family had ruled only over minor villages.

Ibn Saud was assisted in his conquest of Riyadh by some forty followers. They proceeded to the vicinity of Riyadh on camels, from which they descended and then walked some four hours to Riyadh, arriving after dusk. The king knocked at the door of a house at the edge of the village, which constituted a part of its outer fortifications, and was received by a woman who refused him addmittance. He advised her, however, that he was a servant of the amir and that, if she did not admit him, he would see that her husband was killed by the amir, whereupon she acceded. When he entered the house, she immediately recognized him because he was apparently well known, but when his identity became known to the other members of her family, they acclaimed him and agreed to support him. To prevent the woman from disclosing his presence, he locked her in her room and he and his followers proceeded over rooftops to an adjoining house, where he found a man and his wife sleeping in bed. He also locked them in a room so that they would not give an alarm.

They then proceeded to the home of one of the amir's wives, whom they found sleeping with her sister. She, when awakened, advised that the amir was in his palace but warned Ibn Saud that he could not overcome the amir, whereupon he locked them up. It was still a long time before morning, so he and his followers prepared coffee and slept until dawn.

At dawn, as was his custom, the amir emerged from the palace, which was well defended, along with some seven of his guards. The gate was opened and they came into the open courtyard in front. Ibn Saud and his followers, who had been lying in wait, attacked them and the seven guards fled back into the palace with the amir behind. Ibn Saud grabbed the amir and arrested his flight. The amir in turn kicked Ibn Saud and pushed him down, whereupon Abdullah Saud bin Jelui hurled a spear at the amir and killed him.

The group then attacked the palace, which was defended by some two-hundred soldiers, and took it with the loss of only two killed and fourteen wounded after inflicting a loss of fifteen men on the defenders. Within two days, some four-thousand men had rallied to Ibn Saud's support.

He said that the Riyadh conquest was a difficult one, especially because it was the first, but not the most difficult one. On two occasions all of his followers, aggregating some eight-hundred or nine-hundred people, were killed and he alone escaped to recruit more support.

McGhee questioned the king as to any conversation he might have had with the king of Afghanistan, who had departed several days before, after visiting His Majesty, with respect to the dispute with Pakistan over the northwest territory. His Majesty said he had spoken with the king urging upon him every effort to reach agreement with Pakistan over the issues between them involving the Pushtoon tribes of the northwest territory. The king had promised to do so.

In response to a passing remark from McGhee about the relations between Saudi Arabia and Ethiopia, the king said Saudi Arabia had friendly but never close relations with Ethiopia and did not, in fact, have a representative in Ethiopia, although it did have one at one time. He had, he considered, close relations with Pakistan.

His Majesty complained that European-style dinners were too long-drawn-out to suit him.

After dinner, Fuad Bey Hamza and Shaikh Yusuf Yassin came to our quarters for a further discussion. In the course of an extended conversation, Fuad Bey, who acted as Arab spokesman, set forth at considerable length the desire of the king for the closest possible treaty relations with the United States, preferably in the form of an alliance which would assure Saudi Arabia of its security.

Saudi Arabia needed to be assured that the United States had more than friendship for Saudi Arabia, that is, had vital interests, because American support would flow from such interest. Fuad Bey questioned whether or not Americans had sufficient incentive to protect Saudi Arabia's oil interests and those of American companies in Saudi Arabia because there were adjoining countries, such as Kuwait and Bahrein, where American companies also had interests. He was assured that the United States did consider it had vital interests in Saudi Arabia both from the standpoint of its oil and from the standpoint of the strategic importance of its stability and independence. He was assured that the United States would take all appropriate steps to protect legitimate Saudi Arabia interests.

It was explained that the United States had not traditionally entered into treaties of alliance such as those entered into by the British and others, but that it was believed that the United States' record for assisting friendly states and those where it had vital interests was sufficiently clear to give assurances to the Saudis.

McGhee said that, despite the fact that we could not envisage the conclusion of an old-style treaty of alliance, he thought that there were several measures open to the United States which would not only give evidence of our great desire to assist Saudi Arabia but which might also serve the practical purposes of a treaty of alliance. These measures he summarized as: (1) the conclusion of a treaty of friendship, commerce and navigation which might symbolize and serve as notice to all concerned of the closeness of our relations; (2) the making available of such technicians as Saudi Arabia might desire under the Point Four program; (3) the making of loans such as the Export-Import Bank loan under discussion; and (4) the conclusion of a long-term Dhahran air base agreement which would include or follow (5) a possible program of military aid to carry out these recommendations, including the making of arms available on a cash reimbursable basis and the sending of an appropriate military mission to aid in the training of Saudi Arabia forces.

Fuad Bey was disposed to question at first whether the granting of a loan might be claimed as a real service inasmuch as Saudi Arabia could obtain loans from others. McGhee pointed out that such loans were not easily obtained and it seemed doubtful if a loan such as Saudi Arabia desired might be available from ordinary banking sources. McGhee added that he did not know of any other government which was in a position to make a loan to Saudi Arabia.

Fuad Bey asked whether Saudi Arabia might obtain the arms it needed through commercial sources. McGhee stated that the arms available through commercial channels in the United States were rather limited, but he said other common items, such as trucks and transport aircraft, which would be a part of the Saudi Arabia defense requirement, would be available. Most modern purely military items could be obtained only by purchase from the United States armed forces and this required congressional authorization. When Fuad Bey suggested that Israel had been obtaining arms in the United States, it was pointed out that the arms which Israel had obtained were those limited quantities available through ordinary commercial channels and that they were equally open to Saudi Arabia. It was added that Israel had obtained no authorization to purchase arms from the United States armed forces.

Faud Bey stated that Saudi Arabia by this time appreciated some of the difficulties in the way of the fulfillment of its complete desires. It could be most unfortunate if it were suddenly to be confronted with an adverse decision by the United States and he hoped Saudi Arabia might be kept informed of the progress of the United States' purposes with respect to Saudi Arabia to avoid the shock of some sudden unexpected reverse to the plan. McGhee reassured him on this.

At the end, Shaikh Yusuf raised the question of why, if we professed such friendship for Saudi Arabia, we could not make available military aid on a grant basis, such as we had made available to other countries, including, in particular, Greece and Turkey. McGhee replied that this was not a matter of friendship and pointed out that the resources of the United States were not unlimited, that we already were suffering from a budgetary deficit that year of approximately five-billion dollars and that it was essential for us to confine our grants of military aid to those countries whose economy did not permit them to sustain such a burden. Our National Advisory Council, which made policy in such matters, required countries who were in a position to pay, such as Saudi Arabia, to obtain assistance on a reimbursable basis. Greece and Turkey were not able to repay.

Shaikh Yusuf said, in conclusion, that there were two things which the king really desired: (1) arms on a grant basis and (2) conclusion of a military alliance. However, we had discussed with him the possible alternatives. He realized that Saudi Arabia desired more than we could fulfill, whereas the United States had offered less than Saudi Arabia desired. It was agreed that our purpose would be to reach a common ground between these two.

The next morning, word was sent to us that the king was somewhat fatigued and would not be able to receive us as planned but that, instead, we would be received by Crown Prince Saud.

The crown prince welcomed us very cordially and stated what a great satisfaction it was to have the visit of Mr. McGhee and the opportunity for such frank exchanges of views. He added that Fuad Bey Hamza had reported him and to the king at great length the conversation of the previous evening. The crown prince said that, while Saudi Arabia desired a treaty of alliance, it fully appreciated the difficulties which stood in the way of the conclusion of such an agreement, as had been explained by Mr. McGhee.

McGhee remarked that it was very gratifying to know that our warm friend Saudi Arabia had understood our difficulties and that it was a mark of the closeness and friendliness of our relations if we endeavored to understand and appreciate the problems of the other in connection with our mutual interest. Our friendship was certain to be founded on fundamentally strong and lasting ground when we took the pains to understand one another's point of view in solving our common problems.

The crown prince stated he very much hoped this would not be the last visit which Mr. McGhee paid to Saudi Arabia but only the first. That afternoon, on our way to another audience with the king, Faud Bey Hamza met us and told us that, after an explanation of the conversation of the previous evening to the king and the crown prince, His Majesty had been persuaded to accept the basis outlined by Mr. McGhee for our relations. Fuad Bey suggested that McGhee summarize the points briefly for His Majesty and emphasize that Saudi Arabia would be kept advised on the progress toward the realization of a military program.

When we were received by His Majesty, Mr. McGhee went over the points briefly and gave the suggested assurances to the king, who stated that he welcomed them and that he wished it to be understood that he considered the United States and Saudi Arabia as one state. He said that he hoped, when final plans for military aid had veen worked out, someone such as Mr. McGhee might be sent to Saudi Arabia to review them before final decision for their execution.

Later in the afternoon, we were received by the crown prince at his summer palace and were offered tea followed by dinner. During dinner, the crown prince was asked his views concerning the development of Yemen. He stated he could best answer by recounting the conversation he had in Cairo a few days previous with the Yemen delegate to the Arab League who had called on him. The crown prince said he had expressed the hope that Yemen would open itself to greater development and contact with the outside world. He pointed out that Saudi Arabia had welcomed an American oil company and had benefited greatly by this enterprise without any prejudice to its sovereignty and that the only way Yemen could raise the standard of living of its people was by welcoming outside assistance. According to all the information of the Saudi Arabia Government, conditions in Yemen were anything but stable and he hoped that, when I visited Yemen, I would urge the same views on the Yemen Goverment.

There intruded upon us at this time a particularly sensitive subject in the light of the strongly Moslem character of the Saudi Arabian state, which withheld approval of public activities of any other religion.

In a telegram of April 3, 1950, to the Secretary of State, I reported the reaction of the Saudi Government to the holding of public Christian religious services on the Dhahran air base or anywhere else in Saudi Arabia.

During a call at the Saudi Foreign Office, Khairradin Bey, temporarily in charge, told me that they had received a report that an American "missionary," a Captain Sloan, was holding public religious services on the Dhahran air base attended not only by United States Air Force officers and men but also by people from Aramco. In a long discussion which followed, Khairradin Bey emphasized that Saudi Arabia was unique among Arab and Moslem states in that it included the Moslem holy places and that not since the time of Mohammed had any Christian activities ever been permitted in the country.

I informed Khairradin Bey that this was an extremely delicate question and that I hoped the Saudi Arabian Government would not bring it up in a way to make it difficult for us. I said very frankly that to press us unduly might have extremely unfortunate consequences. In my discussion, I emphasized that we fully appreciated the delicacy of the question for the Saudi Arabian Government but said we expected the Saudi Arabian Government to show as great an understanding of our difficulties as we were disposed to show of theirs. Both I and Aramco had been pressed for an active pursuit of the matter with the Saudi Arabian Government, but we felt that the situation would work itself out if the matter were handled with appropriate delicacy and if neither side were precipitate. I assured Khairradin Bey that, so far as I was aware, there were no American Christian missionaries in Saudi Arabia nor were there any regularly established churches, and I could assure him further that there were no public Christian religious services held so far as I knew. I requested him earnestly not to press me for any further assurances beyond these. I said that I could not believe the king would object to the private assembly of officers and men of our air base for the saying of prayers.

Khairradin said, after considerable argument, that the objections of the Saudi Arabian Government were not to what occurred in the privacy of the homes or quarters of the officers and men but to public gatherings for the holding of public services in a fixed place and at fixed times. He said it had come to the Saudi Arabian Government's attention that Captain Sloan was a religous leader who was conducting these services and he wondered if Captain Sloan could be transferred.

I replied that, if the Saudi authorities could present me with facts establishing that Captain Sloan had conducted public services at which Moslems were present or could establish the fact that he had engaged in religious discussions with Moslems, I would be glad to bring the facts to the attention of General O'Keefe, the commandant, with a recommendation for his transfer. I could not admit a complaint against Captain Sloan, however, for discussing religious matters with the officers and men of the USAF at Dhahran, as this was a purely internal administrative question which solely concerned General O'Keefe and the internal organization of the air base.

Khairradin's conversation was extremely conciliatory but, at the same time, he sought by every means to obtain more specific assurances from me that no regular services which were open to the public would be held in a specific place at regular times. I avoided giving any such assurances and made it plain to him as diplomatically as possible that I could not and would not interfere with private devotional exercises at Dhahran for American officers and men, but I stated I would take steps to see that such gatherings were restricted exclusively to those officers and men and that there were no public gatherings to which outsiders might have access. I did everything possible to impress on Khairradin Bey the necessity of letting sleeping dogs lie as quietly as possible. He said he realized that I had a very great appreciation of the Saudi Arabian Government's position in this matter. I replied that I did but, if we were to keep this question from reaching a very dangerous impasse, it would be well to show as much understanding and appreciation of our situation as we had been disposed until now to show of theirs.

Later, our very able Arab secretary, Mohammed Effendi, told me that a Colonel Nagshabandi of the Saudi Arabian Army had informed him that, when a party of Saudi officials had visited the airport on a Sunday, their attention had been attracted by the numerous cars and visitors outside the base's Character Guidance Center and that he had been obliged to disclose the nature of what was taking place in answer to their inquiries. Mohammed said he believed this was the occasion for the démarche on the part of the Foreign Office.

The situation rapidly worsened and, two months later, I recommended to Washington that such services be held in a building other than the Guidance Center, to which Saudi Arabian visitors would not have access, and that Captain Sloan be replaced by an officer who would show more discretion. I summed up the situation in my next cable to the subject:

"FonOff asked me meet Prince Faisal late yesterday for further exchange views re extremely delicate religious services Dhahran. I had one and half hour talk with Faisal whose statements and conciliatory attitude impressed me greatly as indicating SAG as deeply desirous as we to find some satisfactory formula which would enable matter to be kept within bounds. Briefly Faisal stated:

"SA as Holy Land Islam made situation here different from other Arab countries and made it essential King have regard not only for extremely strong feeling existing interior re protection character this Holy Land but also possible criticism from abroad by other Arab or Moslem states.

"Prohibition existed against holding any public religious services by any other of four orthodox Sunni sects and this prohibition extended not only the Christian religion but even to Shia Moslem rites as well. King under very great pressure in this respect and Faisal did not believe we realized extent feeling in many parts kingdom. HM was already proceeding much too far in his accommodation Americans. But for great personal prestige of HM, SA would never have been able to go as far as it has in way innovation.

"I repeated many arguments I have already used. I stated FonOff had informed me that morning Christian religous leaders not permitted in Saudi Arabia. I knew for fact SAG had invited members Dutch Reformed Mission Bahrein to SA as doctors who had same holy character as Sloan and furthermore assignment chaplains at air base no new development. I repeated neither I nor General O'Keefe nor USAF could accept deprivation by USAF personnel spiritual counsellors.

"I replied I regretted not have had any comment so far from General O'Keefe but I could state frankly I had recommended assemblies cease at Guidance Center and prayer services be transferred to more private premises. I could also state Sloan would be transferred but I emphasized this would not necessarily be tomorrow and SAG must give us time both to avoid any possibility appearance his transfer at instigation SAG and in order to effect his replacement. Faisal stated services in private premises not as conspicuously identified as place of worship. Althought I had stated Guidance Center not a church, Saudis did not know what a church was and accordingly had come to identify Guidance Center as church...

"In light of all facts it is very evident desire of SAG to find accommodation US which will not make difficult HM's position with religious leaders. It is my considered judgment foregoing represents most satisfactory solution this very difficult question which has troubled me more than any problem I have had in SA since Palestine partition.

"I wish emphasize Sloan's transfer would not be made at suggestion SAG as Faisal assured me there was no suggestion whatsoever of his expulsion. It is my view his transfer would contribute much to relieve situation and it was on this account I proposed it although no immediate urgency.

"In face extremely explosive elements confronting King I believe SAG has displayed considerable goodwill and appreciation our own position in closing its eyes to question religious services Dhahran until we by our own imprudence and excessive zeal forced SAG raise issue. I strongly feel we should take measures now proposed which represent real concessions on part SAG even though some concessions on our part but which when balanced with need protecting King's position, conform with our own interests.

"It was agreed interim reply would be made to King while awaiting comments from O'Keefe."

General O'Keefe finally sent a message that he would convert the Guidance Center to a base library, hold worship services in the base theater and request the transfer of Sloan.

George McGhee's visit was followed shortly thereafter by one from General Lawton Collins, then chief of staff of the United States Army. We held meetings with the king, the crown prince, Minister of Defense Prince Mansur and Fuad Bey Hamza on the question of military aid. The Saudis were shocked by the enormous costs of their requirements and again raised the question of grants of military aid. I reiterated the statements made a week earlier by McGhee to the effect that grants were made only to those countries unable to bear these costs and the Saudis did not fall into this category. General Collins supported my arguments strongly.

On May 20, 1950, I reported by telegram from Jidda that Shaikh Yusuf had asked me to meet him at the Foreign Office to meet the Syrian prime minister. We had a discussion lasting one hour and a half. Yusuf Yassin said the Syrian prime minister had on his own request sought an audience with Ibn Saud to discuss the general situation in the Middle East and what could be done to improve general feeling in the Middle East toward the United States.

The prime minister said it was his desire do everything possible to remove factors which stood in the way of closest possible relations between Syria and the United States and between Arabs generally and the United States. He had learned this was also Saudi policy. There was widespread public feeling in the Middle East against the United States because of the conviction that the United States constantly favored Israel against Arabs. The United States was withholding arms from Syria but granting them to Israel and was doing nothing to obtain compliance by Israel with UN resolutions, while constantly exerting its influence with Arab states to make peace with Israel. Neither Syria nor any other Arab state had any aggressive intentions against any country in the Middle East, and the Arab states would be glad to give positive assurances to this effect and urged that similar assurances be sought in Israel. Syria and the Arab states generally were obsessed by fear of Israeli aggression and, while they were willing to give assurances against aggression, they were doubtful if Israel would give similar assurances, particularly as Israel had indicated it could adopt any policy it chose toward Arab states without any United States interference while it could count on immediate United States support re any Arab action vis-à-vis Israel.

I stated that I greatly welcomed this opportunity to have such frank, friendly discussion with the prime minister, of whom I had heard many favorable things from our very able minister in Damascus, Keeley. I stressed that Keeley deserved the fullest possible support of the Syrian Government and intimated he had had very rough treatment recently. I emphasized we would do well to turn our faces to the present and the future rather than the past and that I thought the objectives we sought, namely peace and stability in the Middle East, were shared by all concerned, although we might differ as to the means of obtaining this objective. The Syrian prime minister interrupted to remark he agreed except re Israel's objectives.

I recalled a brilliant analysis, by Minister Keeley at the State Department's Istanbul Conference, of Arab public feeling and stated he had doubtless heard from Keeley that one of the most important decisions reached at Istanbul was the unanimous view that chiefs of mission of the United States Government should maintain an impartial attitude as between Arabs and Israel. I did not believe we had deviated from this.

Shaikh Yusuf said he would like to sum up Saudi Arabia's views: Introducing peace and stability in the Middle East had been discussed by the Syrian prime minister at length with the king at Riyadh. This was a subject of deep concern to all Arab states. Facts were that the United States Government had imposed Israel upon the Middle East and a situation had been created which had been the source of great disturbance and unsettlement. No effort had been made by the United States Government to obtain the compliance of Israel with UN resolutions. Arab states had gained the impression that the Saudis had great influence with the United States Government, but facts were that the king's representations re Israel had proved of no avail. It was important that we all make strenuous efforts to bring about the cessation of uncertainty and disturbed conditions in the Middle East. Arab states had no aggressive intentions and accepted the fact of Israel but had the greatest concern re Israel's intentions. The king had thought of asking me to join them in Riyadh, but considered it best the discussion take place in Jidda and, after a report of this initial conversation had been made to the United States Government, he would discuss the United States Government's observations.

The Syrian prime minister said he would like to add that he and responsible officials in Arab states were strongly opposed to Communism and wished to see the Middle East a source of strength to the United States rather than weakness. Unless we pursued a policy designed to attract Arab states to us rather than against us, the aid we were giving Turkey would be nullified.

I said I thought our very frank and cordial exchange of views had been most fruitful as it was evident to me we were all earnestly seeking the same objectives. I knew my government would welcome and take particular note of assurances that Syria had no aggressive intentions against other states in the Middle East. I asked if he had made a similar statement to Keeley.

He replied he had not, but had said arms furnished Syria would be used only for defensive purposes. At my suggestion, he agreed to reiterate his assurances to Keeley on his return to Damascus and he took the initiative stating he would urge Egypt and Lebanon to give similar assurances.

I said my government had been greatly impressed by assurances given in 1947 by Crown Prince Saud on behalf of Saudi Arabia to the United States Government in this regard and that I felt certain we would consider assurances given by Saudi Arabia, Syria and other Arab states as steps forward toward the goal we were seeking.

At one moment in our conversation, the prime minister said, unless there was the same willingness on the part of Israel as there was on the part of Arab states to reach a just and equitable settlement, any peace treaty would mean nothing.

I said his statement closely conformed with Secretary Acheson's words re a peace treaty with Russia, to the effect that treaties and agreements are only of use when they reflect existing situations of fact.

I asked if the Arab states had formulated any reply to a recent invitation to Israel and the Arab states to send delegations to Geneva. I remarked I understood Israel had agreed to send a delegation without conditions. Yusuf Yassin said the decision had been taken at the Arab League to send a delegation only if Israel would agree to execute United Nations resolutions. Arab states were adamant in this regard. Yassin concluded by saying they had always used the utmost frankness with the United States Government in view of their close friendly relations. He had stated the problem and it was up to the United States to take cognizance of this situation.

A further exchange of views with Shaikh Yusuf on May 21 was telegraphed to the Secretary of State that day. He had said to me at the Foreign Office that he wished to add, under instruction from the king, certain information to that given me the day before.

The Egyptian foreign minister had told Yusuf in Cairo that the Arab states were disappointed because King Ibn Saud had not been able to exert greater influence on the United States to obtain Arab rights. Both the United States and the United Kingdom were making difficulties about arms shipments needed for defense purposes and were doing nothing to accede to the Egyptian Government's desire for the evacuation of British troops from Suez. Russia was buying Egyptian cotton and selling Egypt wheat and, if United States and United Kingdom cooperation was unobtainable, Egypt would have no difficulty in obtaining arms from Russia or in concluding a nonaggression pact with Russia which would make the presence of British troops unnecessary.

The Egyptian foreign minister emphasized that no responsible leader in the Arab world wished Communism in their country but the United States and the United Kingdom had cooperated recently during the war to defeat Germany; the Arab states might be forced to make such a diplomatic alliance if the United States and the United Kingdom remained deaf to Arab pleas for justice and if the United States continued its all-out support for Israel at the expense of Arab states.

I remarked I had too great a respect for Shaikh Yusuf's intelligence to be under the necessity of pointing out to him fallacies in these arguments. Dawalibi had stated that Arabs preferred a Soviet to a Zionist regime. Yusuf would agree that by no stretch of imagination could any United States policy be interpreted as directed toward the Zionisation of the Arab world. One had only to look to Eastern Europe to see what would happen to Arabs under a Soviet regime.

Yusuf said what Dawalibi said was not so important as the causes behind it and the fact that it symbolized widespread resentment and bitterness on the part of both people and responsible leaders against the manner in which Arab states had been treated. It was most important to endeavor to remove these causes, although he had no suggestions or proposals to offer but left this for us. He hoped we would treat this information as confidential because the Egyptian Government might not welcome their divulging to another government secret conversations between them and Saudi Arabia.

On May 24, the British ambassador and I paid a visit to Riyadh to inform the king of a tripartite declaration by the United States, British and French governments concerning security in the Near East. We met separately with the king in the afternoon to present the declaration. He appeared visibly pleased and emphasized that Saudi Arabia's great interest was to combat Communism and to take measures with the United States to that end.

The tripartite declaration regarding security in the Near East was issued after a meeting of the foreign ministers of the United States, United Kingdom and France in London in May 1950.

At the end of July, I had a very extended conversation with Abdullah Effendi, private secretary of Crown Prince Saud, in which he stated that the crown prince had asked him to inquire of me what I thought of Saudi Arabia's general financial situation, particularly in view of the king's refusal to approve the budget as submitted by Shaikh Abdullah Sulaiman, minister of finance, and Najib Bey Salha, assistant deputy minister of finance.

I told Abdullah Effendi he might tell Saud I was very deeply disturbed about the financial situation and that he might recall that I had informed the king, when I discussed the subject with him that, while the Saud dynasty was at the present time secure, the time might come when, if the pressent situation were allowed to continue, no one could prophesy what might happen. I added to Abdullah that I was even more concerned at the present time than I was when I had discussed the situation with the king.

Abdullah stated he was also concerned and that he had discussed the situation repeatedly with the crown prince. He had urged upon the crown prince his responsibility in the matter and the necessity for him to press the need of reforms to the king. The crown prince had stated he feared the king's anger and displeasure and that the king might even go so far as to pass him over in favor of one of his other sons. Abdullah had remarked that, knowing the king's character, he would probably admire the crown prince's action and take it as indicating that he was following in his father's footsteps.

Abdullah said the truth was that the king did not in fact have too high an opinion of the crown prince and the crown prince did not enjoy the cooperation of his brothers. There was certainly a gathering discontent in the country. He thought that the crown prince should go to Prince Faisal and Prince Mansour and persuade them to accompany him to the king to press upon the king the need for thoroughgoing financial and other reforms. Even if the crown prince's brothers refused to act, he should take it upon himself to do so, as it was definitely his responsibility. Abdullah asked what I thought. I said it was hardly appropriate for me as an ambassador to make any comment but, personally and in view of the deep interest I had in Saudi Arabia and the Saud family, I thought his advice could not have been sounder. History was full of examples of disaster attending those who let matters drift until the situation became so aggravated that it was incapable of normal and orderly correction. If I were the crown prince, I would not hesitate. I would first of all endeavor to enlist the cooperation of my brothers in proposing a voluntary cut in budgetary allocations. I would then go to the king and present the need for drastic reforms and indicate the disinterestedness of those proposing them by the voluntary offer to accept a substantial reduction in present personal allocations from the budget.

Shortly after this conversation, having been United States ambassador to Saudi Arabia and minister to Yemen since 1946, I submitted my resignation for those posts on July 7, 1950. I left Jidda on July 21 for leave in Europe before returning to the United States, and Heyward G. Hill assumed charge of the embassy until the arrival of the new ambassador.

President Truman approved my resignation on August 1. In the early days of September 1950, I received the following letter:

THE WHITE HOUSE
WASHINGTON

August 28, 1950

My dear Mr. Childs:

    I have your letters of July seventh, in which you submit your resignation as Ambassador to the Kingdom of Saudi Arabia and Minister to the Kingdom of Yemen.

    You have carried out the duties of these positions during the past four years in a manner highly creditable to our Government. Because of health considerations and your exceptionally long period of assignment at Jidda, I am accepting your resignation in both capacities, effective on a date to be established after your return to the United States.

I recognize that the close friendship and good working relationship which you enjoy with officials of Saudi Arabia and Yemen are due to your interest in, and excellent understanding of, the people and problems of those two countries.

I commend you for your splendid record as Chief of Mission and wish you the very best of good fortune in your future endeavors in the Foreign Service.

Very sincerely yours,
Harry S. Truman

22

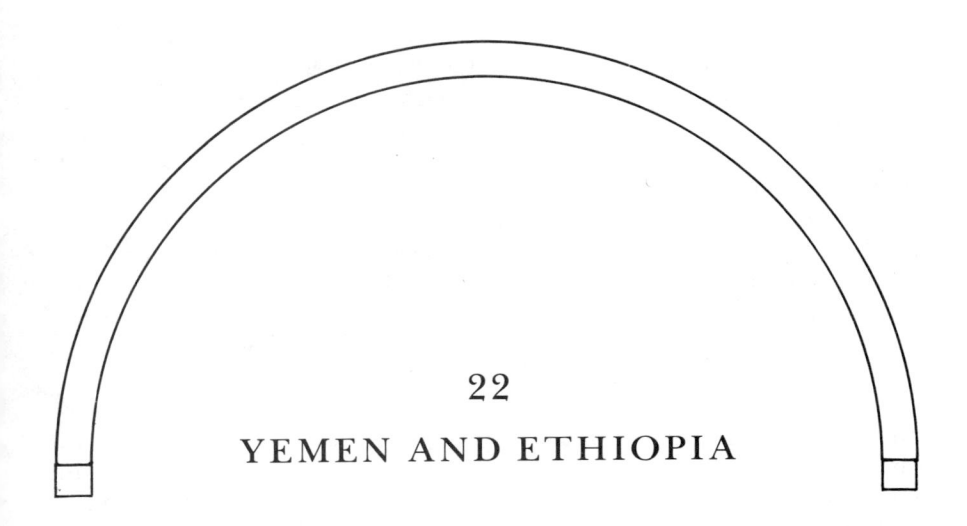

YEMEN AND ETHIOPIA

*I*n 1946, I had been appointed to serve as first American minister to Yemen concurrently with my duties at Jidda. The ancient land of Yemen, Saba of the Bible, once seat of the Queen of Sheba, lies in the southern part of the Arabian peninsula. It was ruled in 1946 by Imam Yahya, some eighty years of age, despotic successor in a dynastic line which had endured a thousand years but was destined to disappear shortly from life's increasingly uncertain stage. The isolation of the country was such that probably fewer than a hundred Christians had set foot in its capital, San'a, situated in the mountains at a height of some seven thousand feet.

The first Western diplomatic representative, my French colleague in Jidda, had been admitted only a few months previous to the presentation of my own letter of credence. The country has been aptly described as "rushing headlong into the Middle Ages." By comparison, Saudi Arabia was a modern state. The subsequent revolution in Yemen, with the declaration of a republic, according to reports, has done little to alter its feudal character.

To reach it was in itself an adventure. I flew to Kamaran Island, then administered by Britain, in the Red Sea, whence a British launch conducted me to the three-mile limit of its offshore waters. There native skiffs were awaiting me. On approaching the shore, I had to be conveyed to land on the backs of porters because of the shallowness of the waters.

A waiting truck was our means of conveyance to a government rest house in Hodeida for an overnight stay. From there, a car of especially high clearance made the fantastic ascent to the highlands by way of a river-bed, in the absence of a proper road, to the foothills and thence along what passed for a road to the plateau. A journey of one hundred and twenty miles took us two days.

Before reaching San'a, a government representative accompanying me had to telephone for the Imam's permission for us to enter the capital. The sight of foreigners was, in 1946, so unusual that our progress attracted hundreds crowding the way. In the city itself, I was never able to quit the comfortable guesthouse provided for our accommodation without being followed by crowds of the curious.

No city I know of has so distinctive an appearance as Yemen's capital. From afar, the many stone buildings, rising to a height of from six to eight stories, present a modern skyline. On closer inspection, the modernity disappears. Yet no place could be more attractive than San'a, with the rich vegetation surrounding it springing from the heavy seasonal precipitation swept in from the Indian Ocean. The thick forests of the interior offer striking contrasts with the utter barrenness of Saudi Arabia.

Only a few hours in San'a sufficed to make me aware of the cat-and-mouse game Yemenis delighted in playing with foreigners. I was first assured the Iman was ill and that it was doubtful if he would be able to receive my letters of credence. After a day or two of delay to exhaust my patience, it was suggested in a note from the foreign minister that the diplomatic secretary of my mission, Harlan Clark, who, as consul at Aden, had made an earlier visit to San'a, should be deputed to meet with a Yemeni representative to transact any business we had to propose.

I refused to fall into that trap. Once the Yemenis learned we had nothing concrete to offer, there would have been no inducement for the Imam to receive me and I did not relish returning to Jidda and having to report failure in my mission to be received officially by the Imam. When I replied that the formula was unacceptable because I alone was authorized to deal with the government, the Iman's health took a suspicious turn for the better. Soon afterward, I had word that I would be received by the sovereign at his palace on the following day.

At the audience, less impressive than those of King Ibn Saud, the Imam announced that, because of his age and infirmities, he would depute his son, Prince Hussein, to serve as his spokesman with me.

Imam Yahya's fate was that of many Near Eastern monarchs. A year and a half later, in a short-lived insurrection, both he and Prince Hussein were assassinated, along with many of the notables I had met. Upon succeeding to the throne, Crown Prince Ahmad, who owed his life to his residence in Ta'izz in the south, refused to move to San'a.

During the best part of a week, I conferred with Prince Hussein at his home. During this time I outlined what the United States had in view in Yemen. His Highness was attentive but quite uncommunicative, offering not the slightest comment. When I had finished my exposition, the prince informed me that he would give the imam a full account of my remarks and that answers to the various questions raised would be forthcoming on the day preceding that fixed for my departure.

When I called on that day at the appointed time in the morning, the foreign minister received me and we waited for the prince. An hour elapsed, and then a second, with no sign of Prince Hussein. I took my leave, leaving the foreign minister in considerable confusion. An hour later, the minister called at the guesthouse to present Prince Hussein's excuses: he had been summoned by his father to the palace. No explanation was forthcoming of his failure to inform me of the fact sooner. I was assured that, if I would be good enough to return at three o'clock that afternoon, he would be awaiting me. As a measure of reparation, I was offered access to the royal library of Arabic manuscripts, which no foreign visitor had ever previously been permitted to view.

At three, I returned to Prince Hussein's home, where I found the foreign minister, but not His Highness. When he had not appeared after fifteen minutes, I informed the foreign minister that I had an appointment with a Lebanese delegation in San'a and that I would never contemplate being so altogether lacking in courtesy as to keep the head of that mission waiting for so much as a minute. My appointment actually was two hours later. The foreign minister was embarrassed and unable to offer other than a vague explanation of the prince's absence. If I had been in Yemen longer, I would have better appreciated that his conduct was entirely in keeping with Yemeni character.

I strolled about the town until it was time for my call on the Lebanese and, that concluded, I paid a visit to one of the two European residents of the city, an Italian doctor. While we were having tea, an excited messenger from the prince, who had learned my whereabouts, appeared to state that his master wished to pay me a visit at the guesthouse, an unheard-of departure from Yemeni protocol. I answered with studied indifference that it would be at least another hour before I would be there. To emphasize my lack of eagerness to receive the prince, I lingered beyond the hour and then, instead of returning in my car, made my way back on foot. The servants at the guesthouse presumably had instructions to give notification of my arrival, for it was not long thereafter before the prince made his appearance. He was not alone but was accompanied by the entire Yemeni Cabinet. It was handsome acknowledgment of the lesson I had conveyed by indirection. Prince Hussein lingered so late in the evening that it was close to midnight before he took leave with his deputation.

To acquire a more thorough knowledge of the country, I proposed to return to Jidda by proceeding overland south to Ta'izz, where Crown Prince Ahmad resided, and thence to Aden. There was a road only to the foothills of the central mountain range. A car conducted us there, where a convoy of pack mules had been provided to transport us across the mountains into a rich, populous valley. After an overnight stop in a village at the foot of the mountains we had traversed, we continued to the eastern extremity of the valley of Ibb, where we were received at lunch by Prince Hassan, the local governor. The only radio in this entire region was in his possession. There was not a newspaper in the country and the introduction of those published in Aden was discouraged by the government. The situation with respect to the press was thus far more draconian than in Saudi Arabia, where the king permitted publication of at least one weekly newspaper devoted to official news, although he rarely allowed foreign journalists to enter the country.

In Ta'izz, which lay in the coastal tropical fringe of Yemen, we were accommodated in a guesthouse provided by the crown prince. A chamberlain called to announce that I would be received promptly the next morning at nine because I had given notice of my intention to leave by eleven in order to reach Aden that same day. As nothing ever goes according to schedule in Yemen, I was not astonished when the hour of nine passed the next day with no sign of anyone to conduct me to the crown prince's palace. When nine-thirty came, I determined to lend myself no longer to the perpetual Yemeni game of cat-and-mouse. Accordingly, I asked an attendant to inform His Royal Highness of my regret that I would be denied the pleasure of being received by him and asked that I be sent the police pass permitting my departure. I was not altogether surprised to be informed that the crown prince was waiting my pleasure to grant me audience.

Following my first visit to Yemen, I was asked by a colleague what I considered my most notable accomplishment as minister to that country. I replied that the answer could not be simpler: six months after my return to Jidda and after a protracted exchange of notes, I had succeeded in obtaining an official receipt for a truck which the United States Government had presented as a gift to Yemen a year before the presentation of my credentials.

Happily, I was able to count much more substantial and less farcical achievements later. Thus, I eventually persuaded the Yemen Government to permit the official visit to the United States of Prince Abdullah, the first ever paid by a Yemeni official. I also succeeded in inducing Yemen to make application for admission to the United Nations and to appoint a minister to Washington, as well as concluding other accords. My mission as first American minister to Yemen thus resulted in an important breach in the century-old isolation of that country.

During the four years I was accredited to Yemen, I repeatedly endeavored to visit Marib, the ancient capital of the Queen of Sheba, lying on the edge of the desert in the northeast, close by Saudi Arabia. Only two Europeans, archaeologists, had ever set eyes on it, in the second half of the nineteenth century. Whenever I raised the subject of Marib with the Yemeni authorities, I was met with evasive replies.

The opportunity I had so long sought came in 1950. After patient overtures, I obtained permission, in connection with an official visit to Imam Ahmad at Ta'izz. It was something of a risk, as the primitive airstrip had been constructed on the sloping crest of a small hill in a narrow valley enclosed on every side by peaks rising several thousand feet high. I had, however, implicit confidence in my pilot, Jack Womack. We landed safely, but when we prepared to take off at the end of our stay of ten days, Jack was not altogether happy.

The flight plan disclosed to the Yemenis was to fly north in a very short hop to San'a, where we were to stop for a few hours. I proposed to Jack that, en route, we make a diversion northeastward in the direction where we conjectured Marib to be and, if we found the ruins, to circle as low as possible for a good view and then to proceed to San'a. The delay should be no more than an hour; we could always claim we had lost our way after quitting Ta'izz. Such an explanation was the more plausible in that no proper aerial maps of Yemen existed.

When Jack again surveyed the airstrip for our takeoff on the morning of our departure, he shook his head. We were ten in the party with the crew, the runway was alarmingly short with a precipice at either end, and there was a crosswind. It seemed prudent to him to offload several hundred gallons of gasoline and to keep only the bare minimum needed to take us to Marib and San'a. The latter was close to Kamaran Island, where we could refuel. We held our breath until airborne and until we had surmounted the peaks which encompassed the primitive airport.

Soon our search for Marib began. Wide circling sweeps were made over an extensive area for an hour or more with no sign of our objective. We had but little to go on except the meager accounts of the city and its ancient ruins in the desert which were said to have been alongside an ancient river course and dam, the breaking of which had inundated the Queen of Sheba's capital.

After a vain search of more than an hour, Jack announced that our gasoline supply was running so low that it was imperative we head west for San'a. There was no identifiable landmark by which our position might be fixed. However, the Red Sea was due west of us and, once there, we would be able to obtain our bearings. Accordingly, we reluctantly relinquished our quest of Marib and proceeded on a due westerly course. We had hardly done so when there was a shout from a member of our party. Scanning the horizon, he had espied an ancient site in the far distance slightly to the left of our course.

There was no mistaking it once we had arrived in its vicinity. A walled enclave on an eminence was evidently the comparatively modern town of Marib. Alongside it was a dry riverbed across which could still be discerned the remains of the great dam which had served to store water for the area in antiquity. Spread out in the desert were the marble columns of the palaces of the Queen of Sheba, making identification unquestionable.

So short was our fuel by this time that we were unable to descend but had to content ourselves with one circle of the area from the height at which we were flying. During that time, our photographer was busy taking the first pictures ever snapped of the historic and inaccessible site.[1] There could be no thought of landing at San'a before replenishing our fuel supply at Kamaran, to which we could practically coast. When we made our landing, there was hardly a cup of gasoline remaining.

On hastily making our way back to San'a, which we reached at two o'clock, we found still assembled at the airport the Yemeni officials who had been awaiting for us since early morning. They were far too intelligent to be taken in by our lame explanation that winds had diverted us off our course. They confided that reports had been received of our having been sighted at various points in the east. It was quite impossible, however, to draw from them any specific identification of the towns and villages over which we had passed; Yemenis prefer to mystify rather than enlighten a foreigner about their country.

If dealing with the people of Yemen required the exercise of more patience than was needed at any other time in my career, it was not without its entertaining side. Whether the Arabs concerned are Yemenis or Saudis, a foreigner needs to have infinite patience and a sense of humor and to avoid any least display of temper.

On the flight back, when stopping at Asmara, I was received by one of the king's sons residing there temporarily for his health. When I was presented to him, he failed to rise. Later, when I expressed to one of his suite my distress that His Highness was suffering from an inflammation of his limbs, he was quite positive in his assurances that he suffered from no such disability. "You must be mistaken," I told him. "When I was introduced to the prince this morning, he remained seated in his chair, although his father, the king, a much older man, rose when receiving me in audience."

If one of the essential traits of a diplomat when dealing with the Arabs is imperturbability, equally important is that of administering a merited rebuke without giving offense. I was once about to take off in my plane from Jidda to keep an appointment with the king in Riyadh when I was halted by the Saudi airport authorities. They objected that they had received no clearance from the king for my visit. Instead of exhibiting any trace of annoyance, I calmly left the plane with my staff and returned to the embassy.

My first act was to send a telegram to the principal minister at the palace asking that he convey my regrets to the king for failing to keep my appointment. I was confident that the underling in charge at the foreign ministry would be expecting a vigorous protest on my part and that, after reading a copy of my telegram, which would be relayed to him, he would be on the telephone offering me every facility.

That seemed to me too easy an out under the circumstances. Accordingly, I gave orders that I was not accepting any telephone calls. I then ordered the embassy launch to be readied and announced that I was going fishing for that day.

On my return, late that afternoon, I was informed that the foreign ministry had been endeavoring to telephone me ever since my departure and that I had been asked to call back urgently. There was no hurry; I would let the pot simmer and wait until the ranking official telephoned again. When he did so, he informed me that a most regrettable mistake had been made. No one in Jidda had been informed of my appointment with His Majesty; an urgent telegram had been received from the king inquiring when I might be expected. "It depends on you," I calmly answered.

"May we say that you intend to leave tomorrow morning?"

"You may, provided you intend to place no obstruction in my way," I observed in my mildest voice.

Upon termination of my four years as ambassador to Saudi Arabia and minister to Yemen, I was named ambassador to Ethiopia.

From remote times, even before the Christian Era, Ethiopia was linked with Yemen and Egypt. It was actually a province of Egypt under the eighteenth dynasty. About the eleventh century B.C., it became independent and eventually, through a turn of fortune's wheel, it gained the mastery of Egypt, over which it exercised sway for some four centuries. It was from the ancient Coptic church of Egypt that Christianity was introduced into Ethiopia in the fourth century, and it was this church which, until recent years, asserted its right to name the Ethiopian archbishop, known as abuna.

The fortunes of the two countries are inextricably linked by nature. It is the heavy precipitation of the Ethiopian highlands every summer which feeds Lake Tana and the Blue Nile; in turn, this unites with the

White Nile near Khartoum to form the river whose waters sustain Egyptian agriculture. So fixed is the schedule of rainfall that, so long as the emperor reigned, he would issue a proclamation announcing the day the rains would end and fixing a time for the celebration of its cessation.

From Yemen, Ethiopia derived part of its population, an immigration which took place in crossing the Red Sea from Asia to Africa from remote antiquity. According to a deeply rooted tradition, the late emperor was represented as descending from a son of King Solomon and a Queen of Sheba (Saba). One of the most popular souvenirs offered to visitors in the past was a succession of scenes painted on a canvas roll depicting the nuptial ceremony of King Solomon's son and the Queen of Sheba. Their naïveté renders them more comic than serious.

I have long entertained the view that the worst possible introduction to a country is by airplane. It was for this reason that my wife and I chose to make the journey of 436 miles from the coast at Djibouti on the Red Sea to Addis Ababa, capital of Ethiopia.

We left by a comfortable sleeping car on the evening train from Djibouti which reached Diredawa the following morning. There, we had breakfast and changed to a diesel-powered coach which slowly ascended the lowlands to Addis Ababa at eight thousand feet on a high plateau. The train passed through typical scrub bush of the African landscape with heavily forested mountains looming in the distance. An added attraction was the wildlife scampering for cover at the noise of the train. So rich is the fauna that, when I was accorded permission by the emperor to shoot in his game preserve, the sight of hundreds of dik-diks, gazelles, oryxes, elands and many other species of antlered game with which the country abounds took from me all desire to shoot game which was so tame as to render its killing sheer massacre.

Addis Ababa, the capital of Ethiopia, lying spread out in the saddle of a mountain, resembles in some respects the site of Darjeeling in the Himalayas. The climate was in sharp contrast with the trying heat from which we had suffered for four years in Saudi Arabia, where I had rarely been free of prickly heat until the introduction of air conditioning. A very comfortable and commodious embassy, set in a large park of eucalyptus trees, one of the distinguishing features of central Ethiopia, afforded us an existence far less primitive and stark than that of Jidda. If the natives of the interior pursued a way of life quite as simple and patriarchal as Saudi Arabians, there were numerous highly refined Ethiopians in Addis to make life agreeable.

The capital was an extraordinary contrast of the old and new. Even the most cultivated Ethiopians were addicted to raw meat, as well as to the choicest dishes of the West. Tukels, or round thatched conical huts, resembling the rondavels of central Africa, in which natives made their homes, were ranged alongside the most modern buildings. In the center of the city, which was undergoing rapid modernization, aged lions were maintained as symbols of the emperor's title of "conquering lion of Judah," while at night hyenas roamed the streets and served as natural garbage collectors.

Archaeological remains at Aksum, of Yemeni origin, reflected the close ties which had once existed between Yemen and Ethiopia. At Gondar, imposing castles resembling the medieval fortresses of Europe offered relics of Prester John, who had appealed, in the sixteenth century, for aid against the Moslems when Portuguese influence extended over a large part of the coastline of Africa and Asia. Italian roads, on which Mussolini had expended some two hundred million dollars, remained as evidence of fascist Italy's folly in invading the country in 1935 and occupying it until 1941. Curiously, the Italians, even in their brief sojourn, had left such an impress that their language remained the *lingua franca* even in the most remote regions.

I was privileged to have interesting exchanges of views with the emperor during my two years' sojourn. He was much more formal than King Ibn Saud and markedly more reserved. I cannot recall that I ever saw him smile. His passion was the education of his country's youth. I visited some of the schools and was impressed by the ability of the schoolchildren to acquire at an early age a knowledge of English, then an official language of the country, along with Amharic, the indigenous tongue of Ethiopia. In a discussion of education with the emperor he remarked: "I am more interested for the moment in providing my people with technical training than with purely cultural knowledge. What we need most of all to begin with are technicians. We have no place at present for a plethora of college graduates incapable of using their hands."

In Egypt I had observed the illogic of an overemphasis on higher education with the turning out of college graduates in such numbers that insufficient jobs were available for them. The emperor seemed determined that, if possible, Ethiopia should be spared the imbalance with which many countries were being increasingly plagued.

Unfortunately for Ethiopia, the emperor's sons were not of his stature and proved an early disappointment to him by reason of either ill health or the strength of character required as his successors. That was his tragedy and that of Ethiopia.

My work proved anticlimactic after the challenging five years in Tangier and four in Saudi Arabia. In many respects, Ethiopia was a diplomatic backwater. Relations with the United States were so friendly as to present few problems. The emperor had very astutely avoided overreliance on any one power. For educators, he had turned to the

Ambassador Childs presenting a visiting academic delegation to Emperor Haile Selassie of Ethiopia, 1952 *(from the University of Virginia Library)*.

British; for organization of the police and air force, to Sweden; to the Dutch for financial advice; and to the French for maintenance of the one railway line. He relied on us for personnel to operate the Ethiopian Air Lines and our public roads people for improvement of the highway system. During my stay I prepared the ground for a military agreement, including a training program, the negotiation of a treaty of friendship and a Point Four program. To familiarize myself with the country I traveled as much as the main roads permitted. Beyond these communications were difficult and dangerous because of the presence of unfriendly primitive tribes, especially in the south in the vicinity of the Sudan and Kenya borders. On a trip through Sodda, a member of the embassy staff had encountered naked tribes, armed only with spears, pagans who worshiped trees, waterfalls and even snakes. Those most held in reverence were pythons. The Borani kept the snakes in a cave where they were fed sheep and goats. Once a year, they were transported in baskets, by camel, to a remote area in lava fields south of Moga on the Kenya border where live children were fed them. The families of the children deemed such sacrifice a great honor.

In the variety of its people and their distinctive customs, Ethiopia is, in a sense, an ethnological museum. It is also rich in archaeological remains of a primitive character. Travelers have reported the presence near Neghelli of a series of oblong monoliths about two feet square by eight feet high, the tops of which are pointed. They are spaced at fairly even intervals of about one thousand yards. Another series, of dressed red granite, about four feet wide, have been found between Neghelli and Adola, center of the gold-mining industry. There is every indication that they had once been erect and had fallen, each breaking into four roughly equal segments. No inscriptions or designs are observable on the exposed parts. In the rear of the American embassy in Addis Ababa, within the garden, was a series of stone monoliths which appear to have been cut to a uniform size and half-buried in the earth in strict alignment, the exposed parts measuring roughly some ten feet in length. Neither these nor the other monoliths to which reference has been made seem to be the product of any geological process. Several hundred, lying in a line, have been reported between Uondo and the northern shore of Lake Abaya. These bear carvings believed to be symbols of fertility. The stones themselves are said to be of a phallic nature, although no remnant of phallic worship is now practiced by natives in the area. These details were communicated to me by Charles Reynolds, after a 1952 journey made at considerable risk. Some of the monoliths described may have a certain analogy with the ancient menhirs found in Brittany.

Aside from Gondar and Aksum, which are among the most interesting cities historically in Ethiopia, I was interested in paying a visit to

Harar in the southwest. This city had only been a part of Ethiopia since 1887. In outward appearance it is far more Arabian than Ethiopian, having been settled by Arabs from Yemen. It was long a terra incognita to foreigners. The translator of *The Arabian Nights* and great explorer, Sir Richard Francis Burton, was the first European to enter Harar, in 1854, disguised as an Arab, as he made his way to Mecca.

Harar seems to have offered a romantic appeal out of the ordinary to European adventurers, so much so as to have attracted that extraordinary figure Arthur Rimbaud to take up his residence there from 1880 to 1891. At the age of nineteen, after dazzling the European literary world with his genius as a poet, he had renounced his precocious gifts and set out for Aden and Ethiopia as a trader in coffee, ivory, gold and even slaves. Upon leaving Ethiopia, he came to an untimely end in Marseilles in 1891 at the age of thirty-seven, destined to world fame as a poet, although he never published a line after nineteen. In 1952, I was unable to find any person in Harar who had known him or who had ever heard his name mentioned.

Ethiopians are a highly conservative people and they looked askance at certain of the unceremonious ways of Americans and other foreigners in their midst. The embassy compound comprised a series of attractive bungolows for the housing of the senior personnel and their wives. On arriving in Ethiopia, the wives often appeared in the compound in slacks and even shorts, to the scandal of the Ethiopians to whom they were visible. As soon as this came to my attention, I published a notice forbidding the use of such garb outside the home. The next day I was waited on by a deputation of American wives. Their spokeswoman found it difficult to conceal her indignation that an American male should dare to dictate to American women what they should wear.

"I am charged," I replied, "with the responsibility of safeguarding American interests in this country and of conserving our prestige and good name. Addis Ababa is not a suburban town in the United States. Here a woman who wears slacks or shorts or pants demeans herself in the eyes of the Ethiopians as well as of other foreigners. They are the attire of a common prostitute. You may wear what you like when you are in your home, but I must have something to say when the name of the United States and the reputation of its citizens are at stake."

"Suppose we refuse to conform?" one of the women asked.

"In that case I shall see that the husband of the recalcitrant wife is recalled, which will mean her departure also. Any other question?"

And that was the last of the slacks and shorts issue.

My troubles were not confined to the gentler sex.

When Eritrea, once an Italian possession on the Red Sea, became a part of Ethiopia in 1952, I recommended that we send a warship to

YEMEN AND ETHIOPIA

Massawa as a courtesy to the emperor in honor of the occasion. On the appearance of the admiral, he readily fell in with my suggestion that he invite the emperor and empress to a luncheon aboard his ship.

In Addis Ababa we made up a caravan to proceed overland to Asmara to assist at the ceremony, to which the diplomatic corps had been invited. In the absence of suitable hotels en route, we took our own camping equipment. The trip offered an excellent opportunity to view the grandiose mountain scenery with which the plateau abounds and to test the superb road built by the Italians to connect the Ethiopian capital and the former capital of Eritrea. The supendous labor expended by the Italians on this road which traversed one mountain after another evidenced the degree of permanence which the Italians ascribed to their conquest of the country.

In Asmara my military attaché and I called in the admiral's aide to discuss the arrangements for the luncheon. I stated that, of course, the emperor and empress would act as host and hostess on board the American vessel. The aide was quite outraged by the idea. I explained patiently that, in accordance with universal protocol, when an ambassador received a sovereign the latter was given the place of host even though an embassy was as much national territory as a naval vessel.

The aide would have none of it. "The admiral will never agree," he repeated stubbornly.

"How long have you been in the Navy?" the military attaché inquired sharply.

"Three years."

"I have been in the Army for twenty and an ambassador in the Foreign Service for almost thirty. My advice to you is to listen and to report to the admiral with no further comment on your part."

At the luncheon, the admiral was seated on the right of the empress and the admiral's wife on the right of the emperor.

Happily, not all of my work was as inconsequential as this. By a curious quirk of fate, a problem which had concerned me from the outset of my career in 1923, in Palestine, continued to be with me until the end, thirty years later.

In common with other missions in the Near East, I was requested in 1952 by the Department of State to comment on the lack of support accorded the United States by the Arab states during the sixth session of the General Assembly of the United Nations. In my reply I stated:

> United States support of Israel has undermined the confidence and trust which we once enjoyed in the Arab world. Pious and platitudinous professions of interest in that world are not likely to change the distrust in which we are now held by the majority of Arabs.

The Arabs cannot forget that on the eve of the creation of the State of Israel the most explicit assurances were given their governments of our intentions to take Arab interests into account, assurances which were shortly thereafter disregarded. Nor can they forget the assurances given by President Roosevelt to King Ibn Saud that no measures would be taken affecting Arab interests without consultation. Such consultations in most instances have taken the form of the presentation to them of *faits accomplis*.

The Arabs are told that we intend to treat henceforth the Arabs and Jews alike, but this equality is interpreted by us as an equal division of grants between the Israeli and Arab world when there is no comparable proportion in either the number of states involved nor in the number of peoples concerned. They hear the Vice President declaring that Israel is an island of democracy in a sea of despotism and they learn through their own experience that there is no equality in the treatment of news by the American press in matters relating to Israel and those relating to the Arabs. Until the United States treats Arabs and Israelis officially and unofficially on a footing of real and not professed equality, we have little likelihood of restoring even a modicum of the trust and confidence in us which was at one time universal in the Arab world.

In a way, it was my swan song. I was highly gratified by numerous expressions of concurrence in the conclusion on the part of colleagues to whom it was sent; I would have been more gratified if it had struck a responsive chord in Washington.

In 1952, at the age of fifty-nine and with some six years still remaining before involuntary retirement, I came, after long thought, to the decision to take the initiative in bringing my diplomatic career to a close. In this I was moved by many motives.

On leaving Saudi Arabia, I had hoped for a European assignment. When I wrote to George McGhee and made the suggestion, he replied that he, in his capacity then as Assistant Secretary of State for Near Eastern Affairs, would not oppose my use of any political influence I might have to that end. I answered that, after more than twenty-five years in the service, I did not intend to resort for the first time to such means in obtaining an assignment.

When my request was not acted upon and I was assigned as ambassador to Ethiopia, I indulged in no self-pity nor did I entertain any feeling of grievance. I had long since recognized that I was far from being an ideal diplomatic agent. I know of no better summary of the qualities befitting a diplomat than that once offered by the sometime Italian diplomat Jacques Casanova de Seingalt:

> In general, the real superiority of the mind, study, science, simple

and quiet tastes are qualities little esteemed in a diplomat. They only serve to close the door to the discharge of his duties. I know more than one of high rank who had owed his disgrace entirely to his merit. Governments always prefer to have under their hands blind and docile instruments.[2]

I was anything but a "blind and docile instrument." I had never hesitated to express my point of view. An officer who gains a reputation for persistence in making his views known, particularly on measures the lines of which have already been formulated, comes inevitably in the end to make a nuisance of himself. I was aware that I fell within that category. Independence of mind—and I write without any intended irony—is a quality which detracts seriously from the value of a diplomat. His not to reason why; what is essential is that, with no interposition of his own personality, he carry out blindly the instructions of his government. That is the guiding principle of the ideal officers. There are none who come closer to the ideal than Soviet diplomats. It may be only a question of time before American Foreign Service officers are equally self-effacing and obedient. My temperament was such that I was incapable of assuming such a role.

There were yet other considerations which persuaded me to retire. I had made a balance sheet of my career. From 1923 to 1941, I had practically marked time. True, I had built up a certain amount of goodwill for the United States, but goodwill is as evanescent as smoke.

In Morocco, in 1942, I might have made an important contribution by averting some three thousand casualties there on the occasion of our landings. That opportunity was denied me.

In the Near East, where I had spent much of my life and where I, along with all other chiefs of mission to Arab states, had warned against the partiality we had shown to Israel, there had been a progressive deterioration in our relations with the Arab world as well as in Arab-Israeli relations. Our warnings had counted for nothing.

My conclusion was that I was more competent to direct my own activities in constructive pursuits than was the United States Government. A casual incident tipped my hand. I telegraphed Washington suggesting that it would be useful for me to go to Rome to confer with Ambassador James C. Dunn on a problem in which we were both involved. He concurred, but the State Department thought otherwise. That settled it for me. If my judgment carried so little weight, it was more than clear that every day I spent in office was a waste of my time and a quite useless expenditure by the government in paying my salary.

There was one final contributing factor. I had enjoyed a life of relative pomp and power. To me there was a deep moral satisfaction in

Ambassador Childs at the close of his diplomatic career, 1953.

voluntarily renouncing it. That I was correct in this estimate was proved abundantly in the inner strength I acquired after my return to private life.

So it was that I offered my resignation to become effective at the close of President Truman's last term in office. Early in 1953, I took leave of Ethiopia and of the Foreign Service. It was a painful moment to bid farewell to my staff and to a lifetime of service in government.

But, for the first time in thirty years, I was free to do and write and speak as I pleased. And that I have done ever since.

NOTES

[1] André Malraux has claimed to have flown over Marib in 1934 and to have taken aerial photographs of the site (*Antimémoires*, Paris: Gallimard, 1967), but the claims have been disputed. The descriptions he gives of both the flight and of Marib are vague. A review of the book in the *Times Literary Supplement* (London) of January 11, 1968, found it in part fictional, with "high spots of mystification."

[2] *Memoires* (Paris: Flammarion n.d., VI, 317)

23

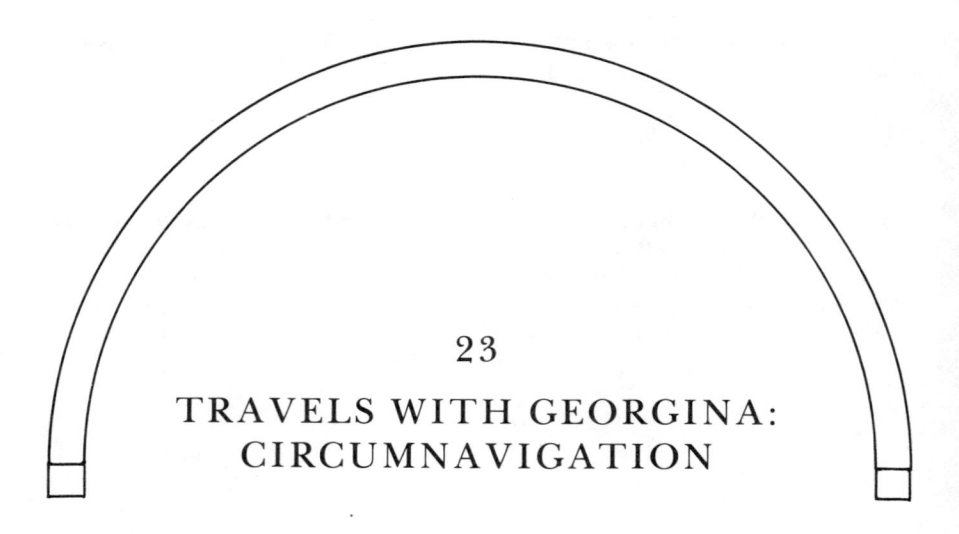

TRAVELS WITH GEORGINA: CIRCUMNAVIGATION

*W*e had no children and no close relatives when I decided to retire after thirty years in the Foreign Service. Georgina's French mother had married a Russian naval officer and, after the Russian Revolution, had chosen to purchase a small attractive home at Èze-sur-Mer on the French Riviera. To be near her, we had decided to seek an apartment at Nice close by and had no more than made the decision when she died. The house in Èze was sold, but we were fortunate in finding for sale a small commodious apartment in a building known as Château des Baumettes. From it, we had an undisturbed view of the Mediterranean.

Early in 1956, after we had been three years in Nice, Georgina remarked one morning over breakfast: "If we are ever to do any more traveling, we had better start. We are not getting any younger, you know."

We determined to visit countries we did not know and to pursue our travels leisurely by freighter. A first objective would be the circumnavigation of the world by way of the Far East and the Pacific.

We were scheduled to leave Marseilles for Japan via Suez.

Three days before our anticipated departure came the Israeli attack on Egypt. Upon reaching Genoa, it was announced that, as Suez was now closed, we would have to reverse our course and proceed around Africa by the Cape of Good Hope. We embraced the diverion, free as we were.

Our first stop was Dakar and then Penang, Malaya. In our passage, we sighted Cape Town, Reunion, Madagascar and Sumatra in their tropical splendor. At Penang, where we disembarked to regain our ship at Singapore, we had our introduction to the East. An excellent air-conditioned train made the day's journey from Penang to Kuala Lumpur, capital of Malaya.

We might have been seated in a movie theater from the swift succession of tin mines and rubber plantations exposed to our avid view, interspersed with thick jungle. To our keen disappointment, no wildlife obtruded. The danger of travel, we learned, was not from wildlife, but from man; in consequence, once darkness had fallen, our train was preceded by an armored one to Kuala Lumpur, our destination for the night. We rejoined our ship the next day at nearby Port Swettenham, from which we proceeded downriver amid sampans and junks to Singapore.

Thailand was our next stop; we anchored below Bangkok to offload part of our cargo. Passengers were transported by launch to shore where a bus transported us to the capital, seventy miles distant, through rice fields and canals. Bangkok, one of the great cities of the East, was overrun with American cars as well as Americans, presenting an air of prosperity. From there, we arranged to proceed on a three-day excursion to Angkor Wat, Cambodia. At the frontier, the Cambodian authorities insisted on placing two armed police in each car to accompany us.

We visited the colossal temple-tombs of Angkor Wat on the edge of enormous jungles, more imposing than Persepolis or Karnak. To form an idea of the whole, picture a hundred palaces of Versailles in the forest of Fontainebleau, but more ornate, with elaborate friezes, portals and colonnades. On our return to Bangkok, the people at our embassy expressed surprise that we had been so bold as to venture the side trip to Cambodia, in view of the general insecurity.

On a previous voyage, our ship had been fired on when entering Saigon; now it was peaceful—for the time being. From there, we left for Hong Kong, where we arrived two days later.

Six days later, we were in Manilla. Our most striking impression of Manilla was its imposing buildings, cheek by jowl with shacks. Manilla was uncomfortably hot. Our next halt, the port of Pusan, Korea, was cold and overrun with war refugees. We thought, with sinking hearts, of what must have been the reaction of American troops when landing on these bleak shores. From Pusan, our way took us through an entrancingly beautiful inland sea to Kobe, where we reluctantly disembarked after seventy-two memorable days aboard.

It had been Georgina's urgings which had brought us to Japan. The prejudices aroused by Japan's conduct in the war had poisoned my mind against that country and people. I was now to find these prejudices compounded of errors. With France, Persia and Morocco, Japan was to make on me the most profound impression of any of the fifty-odd countries previously visited, not excepting any of the sixty or more which remained to fall within our subsequent ken. Both France and Japan have developed the art of living to a supreme degree, reflected in almost every manifestation of life, their art, their food, their culture, and general level of education. Everything in Japan reflects the artistic sense of its people: their homes, their temples, their gardens, their manner of eating, their tea drinking, their attire, their arrangement of flowers. By the time we had made the brief journey by car from Kobe to Osaka, the impressions made by the country and its people were not slow in inducing in us a state of exhilaration. We seemed to be denizens of a different world and civilization, marked by exquisite courtesy encountered on every hand and the transformation of the simplest objects into things of beauty. The country creates an ineffaceable impression.

We visited Nara, the ancient capital of Japan, seeing en route the Horyuji temple and, in Nara itself, Yakushiji and Toshadaiji temples and the Kasuga shrine with its giant statue of Buddha. The quiet precincts of these temples and shrines with their graceful architecture induce meditation on man's destiny. Spiritual illumination came later with the sight of the unforgettable Buddha of Kamakura, as moving as any statue ever seen, comparable with that of Lincoln in Washington.

We continued to Kyoto, also a former capital of the country. Both Nara and Kyoto were spared American bombing owing to their sacred character, a solicitude, so far as I am aware, not extended by us to Vietnam. But Vietnam never represented the power of Japan.

Kyoto contains more than a thousand temples, the most important of which are Heian shrine, Nijo castle, and the temple of Moss, one of the most famous rock gardens in Japan. Here are also the detached palaces of Syagakuin and Katsura, where the Emperor is traditionally crowned.

Finally, we arrived in Tokyo, second largest city in the world. Of world centers, Tokyo for me ranked for charm below Paris but alongside Vienna, Madrid, San Francisco and Hong Kong.

Unexpected were the prevailing courtesy and kindness of the Japanese. We saw no evidence or resentment of the havoc wrought by our atomic bombings. On their surrender, the Japanese had anticipated terrible American reprisals and were so warned by their military. An officer of the Japanese merchant marine confided to me that, when American troops first appeared, his wife had daubed her face with charcoal to escape ravishment. He had gone into hiding. On appearance of the first American jeeps, people had rushed to take cover like partridges, expecting to be slaughtered. Everyone was dumbfounded when, instead, they were asked, "What do you need?" Two members of Japan's Cabinet living outside Tokyo had been summoned to meet the emperor the day after our troops had landed. When their car was stopped by an American soldier hitchhiking to Tokyo, they thought their last hour had come. In the car, the American had reached in his pocket for his cigarettes, which he had offered to his Good Samaritans. Their initial reaction had been to reach for their revolvers. When the car entered the outskirts of Tokyo and the soldier requested to be let out, they thought, "This is it," and were astounded when he shook their hands and thanked them for their assistance.

Few people are more philosophic than the Japanese. Burtt, in his *Teaching of the Compassionate Buddha*, considers that Buddhism is the only one of the world's great relgions consciously based on a rational analysis of the problems of life and ways for their solution. Pauline doctrine equating sex and sin finds no adherents in Japan. This may explain the reputed general refinement of Japanese prostitutes.

We could not quit Japan without visiting Kamakura for a sight of Buddha's reowned statue there. The statue rests larger than life-size in the open air with a serene, impassive countenance, oblivious of time. The eyes are drooped in meditation as if ruminating upon the world's supreme enigma, man's origin and destiny. As the moments passed, I was spellbound by the Buddha's expressionless face, immobile in its absorption of man's fate. As my gaze rested fixed under the hold of one of the world's most majestic figures, I felt a veil lifted from my eyes with the sloughing off of the inanities and pettinesses of existence which receded from me. I felt elevated above the earth and floating high above life's strife. The constricted, hitherto veiled view of existence opened as the petals of a flower. Beauties of nature hitherto ignored leaped into consciousness. I felt merged with the world and my fellow men. Daily vexations and problems which had been magnified out of all proportion now disappeared. Had I captured something of the serenity and supreme calmness of the Buddha of Kamakura?

I believe so; life has never since presented the same appearance.

24

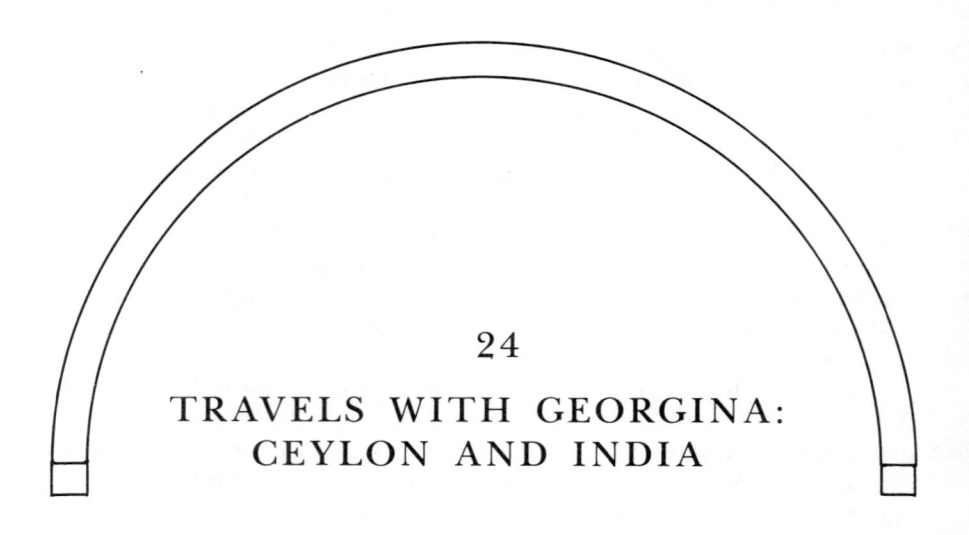

TRAVELS WITH GEORGINA: CEYLON AND INDIA

For 1958, we planned to visit Ceylon, Burma and India. We engaged passage from Marseilles to Calcutta by way of Colombo, Madras, Rangoon and Chittagong, and arranged a forty-day tour of India.

Our first stop was Port Said, where we were provided with a car to Cairo and later to Suez to reboard our ship. We encountered singularly little traffic on the familiar palm-lined desert road to Cairo where we had spent, with an interlude of two years in Persia, five unforgettable years in an atmosphere not far removed from that of the *Arabian Nights*.

From an early age, I had been an avid reader of the *Nights*. While at Harvard, I had had the good fortune of acquring in a Boston bookstore two sets of a remaindered edition in seventeen volumes, the scholarly text annotated and translated by Sir Richard Francis Burton, for the sum of $17.50 each. I was satisfied that I could dispose of the extra set and I was not deceived. That same evening, I had no difficulty in auctioning the extra set for twenty-five dollars, which reduced the cost of my own to ten dollars. In time, the volumes became as familiar to me as any English classic. Thanks to my absorption in this fundamental classic of Arabian literature, I acquired a knowledge of Arab psychology to which I owed my subsequent understanding of Arab character.

There had been few countries where our stay had proved happier than the years in Egypt. We now sped into Cairo on a splendid new road which brought us to a new hotel near the Nile. I had the feeling now that there were more plainclothes police circulating inside than guests.

We had last left Cairo in 1953 on our way through it from Addis Ababa. Prices now were high; there was an uneasiness such as that prevalent in Russia at the time of Stalin. Georgina tried to telephone her childhoood schoolmate, Sherifa of the royal family, without success. We were counseled to avoid entering into contact with old Egyptian friends, who might be compromised as a result. The superficial impression gained was that Egypt had become a Russian satellite country. Street banners announced a Soviet film festival and a Russian circus. In Suez, we were to find a welcoming banner in Russian, English, French and German. After conversation with Egyptians we encountered, we concluded that Russian influence was more apparent than real. Nasser was up to the age-old Egyptian bazaar-merchant maneuver of playing off the Russians against the West. One could not but be impressed by what he had accomplished. Great buildings in the center of the city, some built with Saudi funds, gave an appearance of strength not previously apparent. Noticeable also was the absence of luxury cars and loungers in cafés, such as formerly distinguished Cairo. Life now possessed an unaccustomed grim aspect.

Our drive the next day to Suez was saddened and subdued. There was no longer the festive, joyous atmosphere which had characterized the country even under the previously existing widespread poverty, alongside blatantly conspicuous wealth.

Reboarding our ship, we reached dirty, dull and dismal Aden. On account of labor troubles at the port of Colombo, Ceylon, it was so congested that, upon our arrival, we were delayed being put ashore for three days. As the docking of our vessel was likely to be indefinite, we arranged for a tour of the island and headed north in the midst of coconut plantations along the sea. After a hundred miles, we turned inland into the jungle for twenty-four miles to Anuradhapura, the most ancient capital of Ceylon, with its dagobas and brick shrines of the fourth century B.C.

From there, we visited the second capital, Polonnaruwa, with ruins of the eleventh century A.D. and extensive artificial lakes. The most interesting site in the country was the remains of the palace of Sigiriya, built on the summit of an immense rock cone four hundred feet high. Halfway up the side of the rock cliff were colored frescoes of twenty-one ladies in a state of undress with their bosoms exposed. Access to the frescoes was by a spiral stairway. I alone ventured the climb in hope of seeing something new. It proved to be old hat—expurgated Follies of A.D. 1100.

Back at Colombo, we were immobilized on our ship for nine days before sailing.

Upon leaving Colombo, we stopped in Madras for two days, which gave us time for a quick visit to Mahabalipuram, with elephants carved in the solid rock in the seventh century A.D. Three days later, we arrived at the mouth of the Rangoon River. That port proved to be as crowded as Colombo had been. It was three days before we could go ashore to visit the city. Although the Burmese Government was making progress in the pacification of the country, the American ambassador advised against a railway trip to Mandalay, where the flying fishes play and the old Moulmein Pagoda echoes its presence immortalized by Kipling in verse. We had to be content with local sights, notably the Schwedagon Pagoda, one of the most interesting religious shrines in Asia. Originally only sixty-eight feet high, it was elevated in the fifteenth century to a height of three hundred feet, dominating the city. It is surrounded at its base by sixty-four smaller pagodas outstanding for the great beauty of their rich decorations. They were thronged by worshipers in varied costumes, adding color to the scene.

To keep our carefully planned travel schedule in India, we were obliged, to Georgina's annoyance, to fly to Calcutta rather than continue by ship via Chittagong. A plane brought us in two and a half hours the thousand miles which separated us from Calcutta, long the capital of India. We were impressed by the continued presence of most of the statues erected by the British during their occupation. When I expressed surprise that they had not been removed, as in Egypt, an Indian made the sensible remark: "Why should they be removed? They are a part of our history."

As a Virginian, I find it to our credit that the names of English sovereigns given to many of our counties were left unchanged after our Revolution. There could have been no better evidence of our maturity and good sense, as in India for following a like policy. It may explain the goodwill for Britain which is widely expressed by Indians.

When I asked a guide to conduct us to the Tiretta Bazaar, I was astonished to learn he had never heard of it. I explained that Tiretta, an Italian, occupies a fairly prominent place in the *Memoirs* of Giacomo Casanova (1725–98), whose classic work first came to my notice about 1932 when I was stationed in Egypt and of whom I had made a lifelong study, culminating in a standard bibliography and a biography first published in England and later translated into French, Italian, Japanese and German.

Casanova occupies a large place in the European academic world as a leading mathematician of his time and author of one of the earliest works of science fiction (*Icosameron*, five volumes), a man who was acquainted with most of the crowned heads and leading men of letters of his time. The German scholar, Barthold, wrote that, if everything printed in Europe in the eighteenth century were to perish, Casanova's

History of My Life would suffice to recreate the life of his time. It is a measure of American provincialism that he is virtually unknown here except for his amorous adventures.

Tiretta, Casanova's friend, emigrated to Bengal in the eighteenth century, made a fortune, and was so well reputed that a bazaar was named for him in Calcutta and his name was thus perpetuated after being accorded world fame by Casanova. We found it on many shops in the bazaar. To crown my good fortune, our guide turned up in a local bookstore a Bengal translation of Casanova's *Memoirs*.

After journeying to Darjeeling to see Mt. Everest, New and Old Delhi and Benares, we visited the magnificent Vale of Kashmir, eighty-four miles in extent, encircled by the lofty snow-covered Himalayas, indubitably one of the most beautiful and overpowering landscapes I had ever looked upon.

Seventy-five percent of the Kashmiris are of the Moslem faith, and consequently their attachment is not to the Hindus of India but to the Pakistanis. The former have adamantly refused to accept a plebiscite of the population of Kashmir, proposed by the UN, as to whether they would prefer Pakistani or Indian rule. Not one but desires union with Pakistan, which is why India refuses a plebiscite. India has been a consistently strong advocate of the UN except where that organization cuts across Indian interests, resembling Israel in this respect.

We bade farewell to Kashmir with deep regret to go on to Amritsar, center of the Sikh population. We found there a number of American and British journalists stationed in India, who had been drawn to Amritsar by a Communist conference as well as by observance of the sixtieth anniversary of the firing on an Indian assembly by British troops in 1919. I can still recall when I was an AP reporter in Washington and news of the occurrence came over the wires, and Eddie Hood, senior of our staff, remarked presciently, "The British will come to rue this day."

I questioned some of the journalists about the situation. One thought that India would be Communist within ten years, a conclusion not shared by cultivated Indians I met. Nehru was admired but was said to be surrounded by too many scheming, venal politicians, a phenomenon not peculiar to India. The Congress Party was the only one of any influence. The general opinion was that it should have split when independence was achieved, as Gandhi had proposed. Now it was held together only by Nehru. Socialists were ineffectual, and Communists, while small in number, were active and growing and had already gained power in one state. India was filled with idealists comparable in many ways to those in Russia before 1914. There was industrial progress, but the population problem was quite acute and growing with no apparent practical solution.

Before leaving, we visited the site of the massacre, now preserved as a memorial, and, in the heart of the city, the Golden Temple, one of the great monuments of India, a place of pilgrimage for the Sikhs. The building, covered with gilded copper in simulation of gold with interior walls of marble, rests alongside a great pool. It was thronged with bearded Sikhs, the handsomest of Indians.

I left India with a conception of the Indian as deeply spiritual and tolerant. Our greeting card that holiday season expressed the hope: "Christ, Allah, Buddha, or Siva abide with you. Let's stop trying to find utopias; if we do it's possible we may end by molding a better world."

25
TRAVELS WITH GEORGINA: SOUTH AMERICA

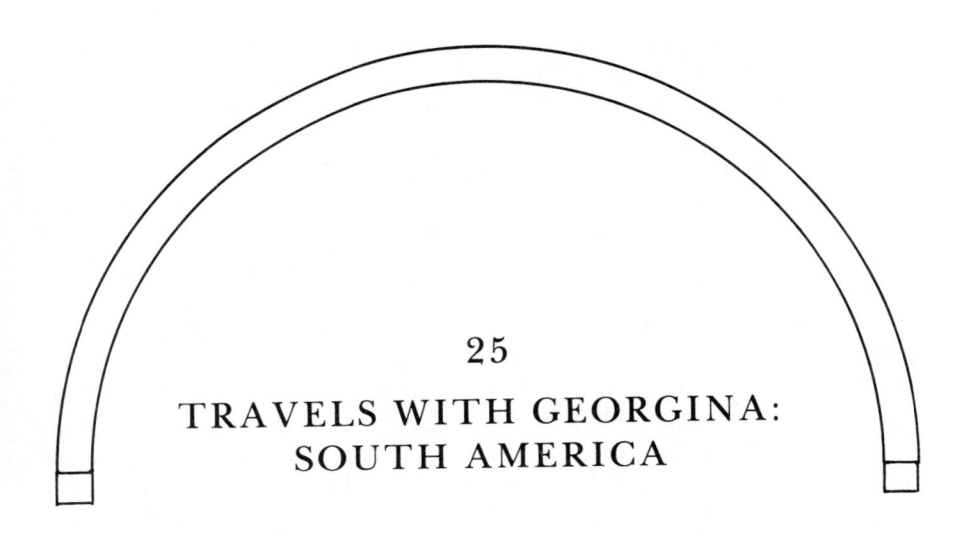

Our travel agency in Nice told us that no one ever made the journey overland from Colombia to Argentina. When we announced our intention of doing that, they looked at us askance. But we made arrangements to go to Colombia by way of Panama.

We found Bogotá agreeably chilly at its altitude of eight thousand five hundred feet after the sticky heat of Panama. With skyscrapers and a population exceeding a million, the capital of Colombia presented a modern aspect except for the appearance of Indian men in ponchos and Indian women in what looked like men's felt hats and robes of many hues.

The key to an understanding of South America is the conquistadors, for the most part of incomparable bravery alongside complete unscrupulousness. In 1532, Pizarro, with but 167 followers, made his epic way from the interior of Peru to Cajamarca. Surrounded by the Inca Army, he invited the ruler, Atahualpa, to dine. On Atahualpa's arrival, Pizarro fell upon his guest, taking him prisoner. The Inca ruler offered to fill the room with gold as a ransom. When this was done and some weeks had elapsed, Atahualpa was informed he was to be executed by burning at the stake. As an alternative, out of Christian charity, he would only be strangled if he adjured worship of the Sun God. On agreeing, he was baptized by the bishop and, after strangulation, the Spanish cynically attended a mass for the repose of his soul. There followed a ruthless pillaging of the remaining gold and silver of the Incas and the razing of Inca temples for the construction of churches, with the consequent near-eradication of the most interesting local culture.

Pizarro's rapacity and that of other conquistadors set a tone threading Latin American history, culminating in such disreputable regimes as those of Perón in Argentina, Batista in Cuba, Pérez Jiménez in Venezuela, and many others who despoiled those countries for personal gain with the dominant motive of self-aggrandizement.

While, in the United States, gangsters seek to control municipal governments and labor unions, in South America they are more covetous in aiming at control of national governments. Pizarro sent his gold to Spain for security; modern gangster-dictators send their spoils to numbered accounts in Swiss banks. Politically, most of South America gives off the smell of a corpse awaiting decent burial. Of Pizarro's original followers, all came to a violent end; only two left families surviving in Peru. It was perhaps poetic justice that the bishop who assisted in the execution of the Inca ruler himself was later eaten by Indian cannibals.

In Ecuador, Quito, perched on one side of a valley, is one of the most rewarding cities in South America. It would merit that title if for nothing else than its S. Francisco church, built on the ruins of an Inca palace, and Cesena, with a solid gold altar; the interiors of both are ablaze with solid gold leaf. The gold was stolen from the Indians for the glory of God (always the dispossessors' God), while the Indians' culture was destroyed in the name of Christianity. What a succession of crimes in the name of religion! I asked myself if the Indians were any better men and women for having substituted the Trinity for the Sun God. Certainly, in one respect, the answer is negative; the Indian religion rigorously proscribed thievery, which is now rampant.

We found Peruvians the least sympathetic people in South America. Yet the country had once had the richest indigenous culture on the South American continent. Its destruction by the Spanish left a cultural vacuum.

Lima was founded by Pizarro. Its center comprised stately avenues. Its Plaza des Armes and St. Martin were impressive, but its churches were less rich than those of Bogotá and Quito. Pizarro was buried in the cathedral there after his assassination. But the most interesting memorial is the pre-Inca museum, with relics of pre-Inca civilizations dating back six thousand years. Well-preserved textiles of great beauty of design were found in tombs. The museum also contains a collection of erotic figurines, described to me by the late Dr. Kinsey as one of the most remarkable in the world, but, unfortunately, it was not open to the public.

We made a slow journey by narrow-gauge train to La Paz. Our way traversed an arid, barren plateau, to which color was given by the snow-capped Royal Cordilleras rising in savage splendor 19,000 feet to our left. Three hours later, from the crest of a hill 13,500 feet high, the train made its slow serpentine way down the face of a natural bowl 1,000 feet below, where the Bolivian capital was spread out over hillsides and declivities. Its height and situation made it unique among the world's capitals. Numerous modern high buildings on broad avenues were interspersed with humbler dwellings in narrow streets.

We left La Paz in a sleeping car of ancient vintage. Once we had reascended the rim of the natural bowl in which La Paz is situated, we continued along a high plateau of 13,000 feet. The country was bleak and arid. The night was bitterly cold despite two blankets in which we were each enveloped. At the Chilean frontier, we were held up four hours for protracted formalities exceeding any found elsewhere, even in the Soviet Union.

Once in Chile, the landscape became more interesting, comprising extensive salt lakes, borax and sulphur deposits, and several active volcanoes. Though bleak, it was wild and grandiose. The appearance of more substantial dwellings indicated that Chile was more advanced and less primitive than Bolivia.

In Argentina, we found Buenos Aires a lovely metropolis faintly reminiscent of Paris. We left there by ship, calling at Santos in Brazil. We took a bus excursion over the mountains to São Paulo, fastest growing city in the world at this time, second largest in South America, pulsing with energy, four million population and incredible industrial development. Skyscrapers and modernistic apartment buildings attested its dynamism. I have since seen only in Soviet Russia these last years evidence of such vibrant inner strength.

We found Rio incomparably the most beautiful city in South America. A fog obscured the view from Corcovado, where the towering image of Christ was hidden in mist. A taxi swept us all too hurriedly along famed Copacabana beach, lined with apartment buildings and hotels of a uniform height. The absence of restaurants along the beach and of bathing cabins along the sea added a stateliness and dignity lacking sadly on the Promenade des Anglais in Nice or the beach in Cannes. Rio and Brazil entrance me; they are so far in advance of other South American cities and countries as to make comparison superfluous.

26

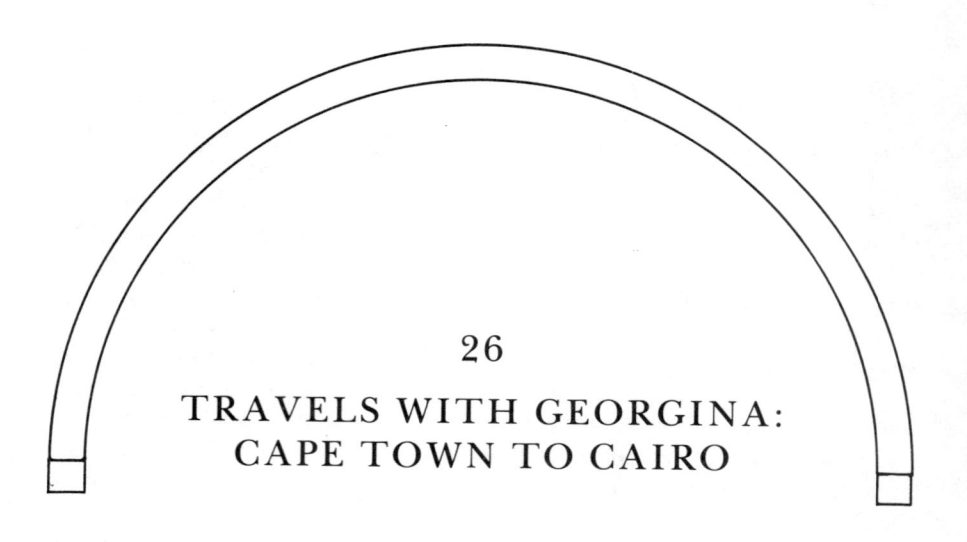

TRAVELS WITH GEORGINA: CAPE TOWN TO CAIRO

To fulfill one of life's dreams, we embarked in the early fall of 1960 for Cape Town, from where we planned to take off overland for Cairo. I had been working until the eve of departure on a brief biography of Casanova for the German publisher Rowohlt, to be followed by a more extensive text for Allen & Unwin in London.

We made a brief stop at Dakar, Senegal, where a marked development was evident since our last visit in 1956 en route to Japan. Here, relations between the former French colonists and natives were founded on mutual respect and confidence, a reflection of a state of native development in advance of that of most of black Africa, as well as French goodwill.

At our next port, Pointe Noire, the recent unsettled state of the Belgian Congo was evident in the accumulation of cars abandoned by Belgian refugees fleeing the country, as observed also later at Juba in the Sudan, close by the Congo. Four Belgians, with half their trucks salvaged, embarked for Cape Town, where the South African Government was granting freedom of the port to Belgian refugees. A French official of the local postal service reported that, for two years before the Congo crisis, the most violent inflammatory propaganda had been mailed to local agitators from Chinese, Czech and Russian sources. Yet the Belgians who boarded our ship had left behind relatives in Leopoldville who entertained the belief the situation might work itself out.

We finally put in at Cape Town, finding it an amalgam of modernity and Old World charm, reflecting evidences of the earliest Dutch settlement in Africa. Elsewhere, many of the towns bore a strong resemblance to those of our Far West.

At this time, the population of South Africa comprised nine million Bantus, three million whites and one and a half million of mixed blood. It was the whites, first Dutch and later British, who wrested a largely unpopulated region from the wilderness. The South African Government has created extensive reserves of some of the richest land for the native Bantus, many only recently emerged from savagery, in the belief that segregation of whites and blacks best ensures the development of two such widely different cultures.

For a better understanding of Africa, it is important to distinguish among the multiracial groups. The most primitive are the bushmen, unable to count beyond three, doomed to extinction owing to their unadaptability to so-called civilization. The bushmen are still living in the Stone Age after twenty thousand years, identical with those prehistoric men whose traces are found in the prehistoric caves of southern France and northern Spain. Second are the pygmies on the Uganda-Congo border, gay and friendly but with repulsive features and of retarded development. Third are the negroes in the tropical forests of the Congo, with thick lips and flat noses, the principal victims of the slave trade. Last is a group comprising the Bantus, Hamites and Berbers, the last two north of the Equator, all finer-featured and more developed than the three previously named.

Going north we visited Rhodesia and, from Lusaka, traveled by the Rift Valley to Iringa, with a detour to Isimila, one of the most important paleolithic sites in the world. On a dry riverbed we picked up two 100,000-year-old well-fashioned axe heads and many artifacts, which were later presented to the Museé de l'Homme in Paris. Where, until comparatively recently, the age of prehistoric man was reckoned a few hundred thousand years, discoveries made in Africa, by the Leakeys in particular, have extended this calculation to no less than four and perhaps even five million years. It pulls one up short when reference is made to my Oxford University Press Bible of 1917, where the date of "B.C. 4004," *ne quid nimis*, is attributed in a commentary on Genesis, Chapter I, to "the original creation." Quite a difference from the calculations of archaeologists of the present day!

We went on to visit Serengeti, the Congo area, Treetops, the Sudan, and, finally, Egypt, before returning to Nice. We had traveled by 8 ships and 7 trains, and stayed at 41 hotels; we covered 8,644 miles by ship, 8,469 miles by car, and 2,798 miles by train, or a total of 19,911 miles, representing by far the most unusual of all our odysseys.

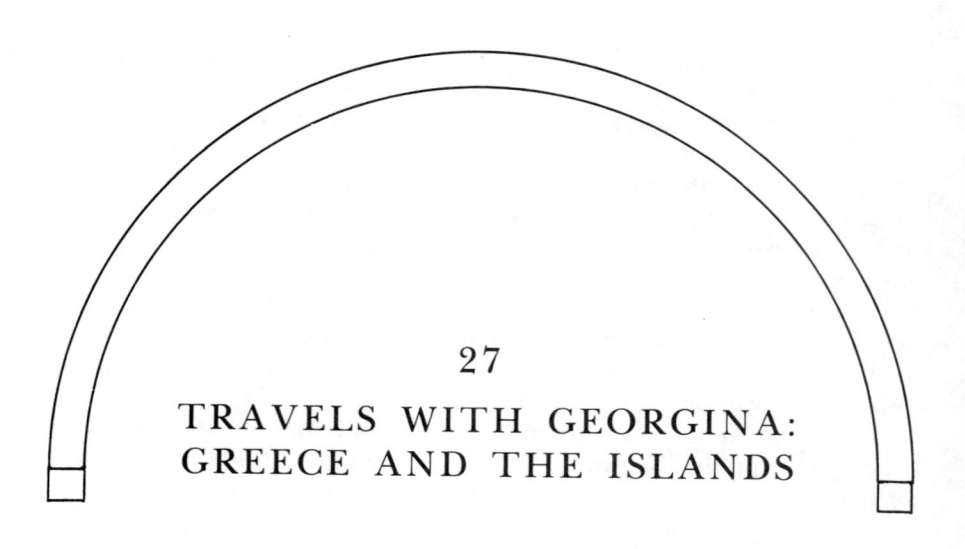

27
TRAVELS WITH GEORGINA: GREECE AND THE ISLANDS

A year later, near the end of September 1961, some two weeks late considering the Greek climate, we visited Greece, breaking the journey for two days in Corfu, a veritable terrestrial paradise.

Corfu was a possession of Venice from 1386 to 1864. Casanova had visited it twice, first in 1741 and again in 1745. We retraced his footsteps in visiting the Venetian fort and its picturesque streets, which had changed little since the eighteenth century. In 1958, Dionysus Romas, a Greek deputy and writer, in a comedy entitled *Casanova at Corfu,* borrowed from Casanova's account of his visit, as recorded in the latter's *History of My Life.*

Old residents meet in the evenings, as they did in years past, under the arcades at the Astoria Café, alongside the promenade, where formerly only the nobility and local officials had access. It is still known as "La Lista," from the list established in Venetian days of those persons who were permitted to use it.

During the Second World War, Germans occupied the island and, as a mark of their presence, wantonly destroyed the city's archives and fifty thousand volumes of the local library. Today, it is difficult to find anywhere in the world a more delightful and peaceful spot.

From Corfu, we went on to Athens, from where we embarked on a cruise of the islands.

Our first stop was Crete. At Knossos, site of the Minoan civilization of 2,000 B.C., we saw extensive remains of a palace uncovered by Arthur Evans in the last century. The artistic development of the Minoans four thousand years ago is breathtaking in its impact when viewed at Heraklion in the second most important museum in Greece.

We continued to Rhodes, a medieval walled city occupied by the Knights of St. John in the fifteenth century and restored in 1912–45 by the Italians during their occupancy of the island. Ten kilometers away, we visited Lindos to view a temple to Athena and an ancient acropolis on a peak overlooking the bay where St. Paul had landed.

Here, and on other Greek islands, the whitewashed walls of the buildings, under the rays of a radiant blue sky, imparted a captivating gaiety and charm quite enthralling. Lord Byron's tribute leaped to mind:

The isles of Greece, the isles of Greece!
Where burning Sappho loved and sung,
Where grew the arts of war and peace,
Where Delos rose, and Phoebus sprung!
Eternal summer gilds them yet,
But all, except their sun, is set.

We put in at Halicarnasus, in Turkey, birthplace of the father of history, Herodotus. Then we went on foot to the castle fortress of the Knights of St. John. Opposite, there once stood one of the seven wonders of the world, the Mausoleum of King Mausolus. An hour away by the sea, we saw Cos in Greece, site of Aesculapeum, in a partial state of restoration, where Hippocrates elaborated the principles of medicine in the fifth century B.C. That afternoon, we got to Patmos and went by donkey to the Greek monastery, atop a steep hill, with a world-famous library and the grotto where St. John is reputed to have composed his Revelation.

Delos, the Pompei of Greece, sacred in antiquity to Apollo and now uninhabited, was our next stop. The small island was dotted with many well-preserved stone homes with mosaic floors, with temples, a theater and a row of seven stone lions dating from the seventh century B.C. Thence to Mykonos; to Santorini, perched on a hill, which we reached by donkey; and to Paros, birthplace of the great sculptor Praxiteles, where an abundance of marble is found. At Paros, we visited a fourth-century church erected on the foundations of an ancient temple.

Returning to Athens, we began a classical tour, beginning with Daphne and a Byzantine church of the eleventh century on the site of an ancient temple to Apollo. Then Eleusis, Megara and across the Corinth Canal to old Corinth, with important ruins and an interesting museum.

From there, we passed to Mycenae, where Agamemnon reigned in the twelfth century B.C. It was Schliemann, the discoverer of Troy, who found in the last century the remains of this great civilization described by Homer and commemorated in the tragedies of Aeschylus, Euripides and Sophocles. Nearby rested a cupola tomb, of astonishing size, dug in the earth. Then we went through Argos for a sight of a theater and acropolis, to Tiryns for its Cyclopean walls, and to Epidaurus for its uniquely preserved theater accommodating fourteen thousand spectators.

The day following took us on a spectacular drive of twelve miles over a breathtaking serpentine mountain road, unsuitable for the weak-hearted, by Tripolis and Langadhia to Olympia. Here, visible from our hotel window, were extensive ruins of temples and a stadium in a pine-studded valley, which we later visited afoot, including a museum containing the sculptured Hermes of Praxiteles. The scenery, here as elsewhere in Greece, afforded an appropriate backdrop to the remains of its glories. Via Patras and Aigion, we reached the ferry that would transport us from the Peloponnesus to the mainland. We visited on foot the ruins of ancient Delphi, overspreading a hillside from where the solemn pronouncements of the Delphic oracle spread throughout ancient Greece. Late the same day, we regained Athens, deeply moved by the echoes of Greece's glorious past.

Shortly thereafter, we were off again on a small yacht for a cruise of unvisited islands. Our first landing was at Aegina Marina to visit the temple Aphaea; then to Hydra, now a popular resort. The harbor was picturesque and impressive, words which one exhausts in Greece. Then we touched at Spetsais and Poros. We would have done better to visit the islands by comfortable Greek vessels plying daily from Piraeus and disembarking on those islands which took our fancy to remain overnight. On our return to Athens, we made a final excursion from Athens to Cape Sounion, a magnificent coastal drive to the incomparable Poseidon temple by the sea.

Back in Athens, Georgina and I parted company to go our separate ways for some days. She went by ship to Egypt to visit a childhood school friend, and I took an excursion to Mt. Athos. There I proposed to visit four monasteries, built in Byzantine times, which once numbered forty thousand monks but were now reduced to two thousand. These are unique in that women are excluded and, until recently, even hens. The monasteries are situated on the summits of cliffs facing the sea and contain incomparable manuscripts and icons, although not so old as those to be found in the monasteries of St. Catherine and St. Anthony in Egypt. If Athos' monasteries are not so impressive in age, their wild, rugged situation is of surpassing drama.

On returning to Athens, I took occasion to repair an oversight, perpetuated the innumerable times I had visited Athens, by inspecting the Agora museum and particularly those objects illustrative of the daily life of antiquity. A potsherd bore the inscription: "Cleon handsome boy," with underneath the notation, "Sappho pretty girl." I had rarely if ever found in any museum such a revivification of the past as this echo of two voices across twenty or more centuries.

The best handy summary of the character of ancient Greece is to be found in Kitto's *The Greeks*. Its incomparable attainments during the brief period of two hundred years, the fifth and fourth centuries B.C., give pause to the measure of progress in our own era. Where today are men of the stature of Socrates, Plato, Aeschylus, Sophocles, Euripides, Herodotus and Hippocrates, to whom the small city-states of antiquity gave birth in this brief time?

28

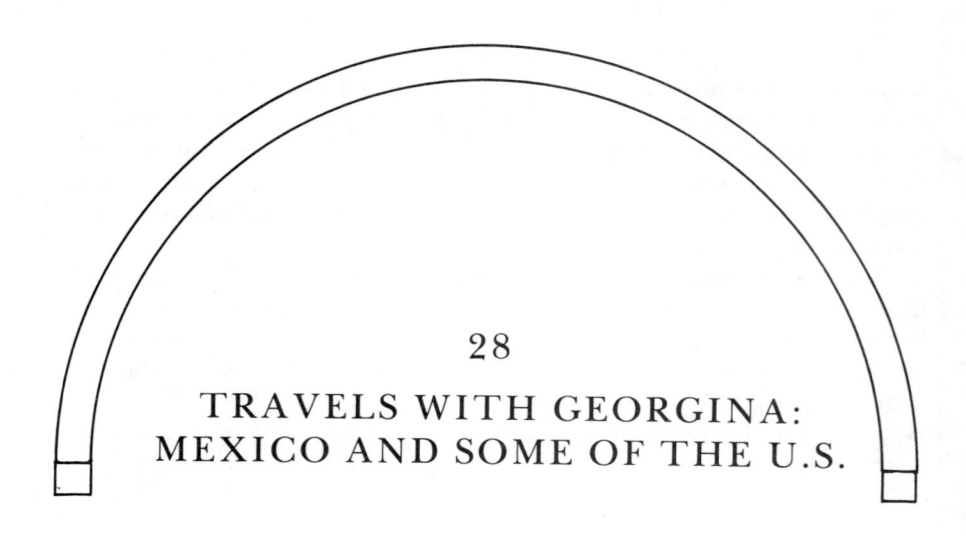

TRAVELS WITH GEORGINA: MEXICO AND SOME OF THE U.S.

*I*t had been our original intention to make our way by sea from Nice to Costa Rica and thence north overland through Central America to Mexico in 1962. Unable to obtain information about the feasibility of such an enterprise, we were obliged to settle for Mexico.

We went by way of Lisbon, where we encountered my right hand in Tangier, Burke Elbrick, then ambassador to Portugal and Elfie, his charming wife and helpmate. I remembered an earlier visit.

In 1941, Georgina and I had landed in Lisbon on our way to our new post in charge of the legation in Tangier, Morocco, and were met by Burke, a recently arrived young secretary at the legation in Portugal. I was most unfavorably impressed, so much so that when, some months later, I received word from the State Department that he was being assigned to Tangier as my principal assistant, I impulsively drafted a telegram in reply that I did not care to accept him.

On reflection, I decided that I could not compromise his career by any ill-considered action on my part. I recollected that we had on duty in Tangier a young woman staff member recently assigned from Lisbon. I sent for her.

"Did you know Mr. Elbrick well in Lisbon?"

"Yes, sir."

"What was your judgment of him?"

"One of the best officers we had, respected by everyone."

That set me back on my heels and I dismissed her and proceeded to tear up my telegram. It was not long after he reported for duty that I recognized him as one of the ablest young officers assigned us. My efficiency reports of him were so enthusiastic that the Department concluded that one of his talents was more needed in Washington than in Tangier. He was transferred to the Department and given a double promotion. In 1949, when I was serving temporarily on the senior promotion board at the Department of State, Burke, as an officer of Class II, was eligible for promotion to Class I.

It was I who sponsored him; the other members of the board objected that he was too young. When I inquired if any of them had had him for a subordinate officer, none had. I observed that I had and that I considered him one of the most outstanding officers in our service. It was a tradition on the board to respect the opinion of a member who had personal knowledge of a candidate, and so he was passed and confirmed and was soon thereafter appointed a career ambassador.

We sailed from Lisbon to La Guaira. There we took a taxi over the mountains, twenty-five kilometers by an excelent autostrade to the Venezuelan capital, Caracas. The modern buildings we observed alongside miserable shacks were characteristic of like contrasts we had seen in 1959 throughout South America. Admirable here was the extended network of cloverleaf boulevards uniting Caracas, sprawling in a valley, with Independence Plaza serving as dramatic capstone.

We arrived in Mexico at pleasant, palm-studded Vera Cruz. From there we left by comfortable bus, with reclining seats well adapted for sleep, for Mérida. A young Japanese was the only other foreigner; Mexicans were friendly and helpful. Modern bus stations at frequent intervals compared favorably with American ones. The chief inconvenience was the necessity of dismounting for safety reasons at five ferry crossings during the night. An entrancing dawn appeared over the ocean, along which our way had led for many hours through coconut groves. Thatched huts in the wooded area were suggestive of Malaya. At Campeche, we left the sea for the interior. After twenty-two and a half hours of travel, we drew into Mérida, Yucatan.

The next day we left by car over a good road for a drive of seventy-five miles through a flat country of hemp plantations to Chichén Itzá, seat of the Mayan civilization of the fifth century A.D. Stone temples were visible over a wide area. Most imposing was a pyramid, with ninety-one steps on each of its four sides representing the days of the four seasons, and with a step at its base on all four sides representing the 365th day of the year.

Equally important was an area with two high stone walls on either side and seats for the king and nobles at either extremity. Here popular games were played, as depicted on a stone mural. The objective was the projection of a rubber ball through stone rings projecting from the wall. The captain of the losing team was decapitated.

In a nearby natural pool, a virgin was annually flung as a propitiation to the rain god, after being stupefied with tequila. Times are little changed. Today virgins are stupefied with champagne to propitiate contemporary satyrs.

In a nearby temple to warriors stood stone columns, suggestive of the Doric, and stone murals of snakes, jaguars and warriors.

The day following we drove sixty miles to Uxmal, with a conglomeration of lofty pyramids and temples. In the afternoon we continued to a temple and museum at Dzibilchaltun. These Mayan sites are as impressive as Angkor Wat in Cambodia, Persepolis in Persia and Karnak in Egypt, and even more so than Machu Picchu in Peru. In comparison with the Aztec relics outside Mexico City, the Mayan remains in Yucatan and Guatemala reflect a distinctly higher culture. The forebears of these ancient civilizations, who emigrated some thousands of years ago from Asia across the Bering Straits, developed a calendar superior to the Julian and utilized the zero before the Arabs.

From Mérida, we went on to Mexico City. On a tour of the city we saw Chapultepec Castle and the most lifelike murals of Diego Rivera at the National Palace. At the Palace of Fine Arts we found reproductions of murals depicting Lenin and revolutionary themes. The originals, after being commissioned from the artist for Rockefeller Center, were ordered destroyed by the Rockefellers. A useful example of American tolerance would have been offered if they had been preserved undisturbed. One of the quirks of American character is the pathological reaction, bordering on mental disorder, toward anything touching the Russian Revolution or Communism.

In 1934, when stationed in Persia, I had received a letter from a Senor Rubio Mañé of Mérida. He wrote that he had learned from a member of the Carnegie Institute in Mérida of my authorship of the recently published *Reliques of the Ryves*. He said he was descended from a branch of the family established in the Canary Islands in the seventeenth century, which he believed belonged to the English family of Damory Court, Dorset, and solicited my aid in establishing the connection. In replying, I suggested that, as it was known Sir Richard Ryves, grandson of Thomas, had engaged in Spanish trade, my correspondent was most probably descended from either Valentine or Benjamin, sons of Thomas. As I heard no more, I concluded that the leads given had been unproductive.

However, before setting out for Mexico, I bethought me of my hypothetical Mexican cousin; on the off chance that he was still alive, I wrote him at the address he had given me in Mérida. I had an early reply stating that he was now professor of history at the University of Mexico and director of the Mexican National Archives. Upon arriving in Mexico City, I had the pleasure of meeting him and learning that, through his independent researches, he had confirmed in part my conjecture. The documents he kindly furnished me offered a unique proven example of an English family which had projected one branch in colonial Virginia and another in the Canary Islands. This last had become Catholic and Spanish and had changed the name to Rivas, with one line represented by a governor of Yucatan and another by a member who changed the name to Ribas and emigrated to Venezuela, where he took part with Bolívar in the war for that country's independence. Many webs are woven by family displacements, but few are as traceable as in these instances, involving five distinct nationalities widely separated.

In Mexico we began a systematic survey of the important sites around Mexico City, beginning with Teotihuacán's ancient sacred city with its Sun and Moon pyramids. From there we took a short drive to the Quetzalcóatl Temple, the Highway of the Dead, and a local museum. We journeyed by car through the valley of Toluca, with a visit to its colorful weekly market and moved through rolling valleys and mountains to Cuernavaca and Taxco. This last was the most picturesque town visited in Mexico, reminiscent of the hill towns in Spain. Georgina's exemplary patience throughout all our travels was rewarded by the abundance of inexpensive, attractive silver work. The road which had brought us to Taxco was breathtaking. And the Cortez palace with Rivera murals and the cathedral of 1529 in Cuernavaca alone made the day more than worthwhile.

We found Mexico one of the most picturesque of Spanish-American countries, of an archaeological interest comparable with, if not surpassing, Peru and Bolivia, and possessing a dynamism rivaling that of Brazil. In the course of our stay in Mexico City, while traversing the large square fronting the cathedral, we were so shaken by an earthquake that we were obliged to cling desperately to a convenient flagpole to maintain our equilibrium. We felt later a less violent recurrence on regaining our hotel room. I believe the most violent earthquake in all our travels was in Bucharest, Romania; I cannot now recall the many to which we have been subject.

We left Mexico City by bus over an excellent road via Monterey to Laredo. We continued through San Antonio and Houston to New Orleans.

New Orleans is one of the few places in the United States where drinkable coffee and superior food are generally available, even in the cafeterias. I write not as a chauvinistic Southerner but in the interest of truth when remarking that food in the South, as a general rule, is superior to that in the North. I am thinking of Brunswick stew, Smithfield ham, beaten and soda biscuit, Sally Lunn, fried chicken, barbecue, chess pies and fruit cobblers.

We went from New Orleans to Franklin, Tennessee, to visit my cousin Margaret Wyatt, as absorbed by racing horses as I am by books, and were conducted to Wyatt Hall, an old southern mansion over which a Confederate flag is raised every morning. A reporter for the Nashville Tennessean, born in the Dakotas, was deputed to interview her, and one of the first questions he asked her was why she flew a Confederate flag over her home. "A while back," she answered, "we had a little dispute with the Yankees; if we ever have another I wanted to make sure there was no mistaking where I stood."

Margaret drove us to Nashville, where we took a bus for Washington via Knoxville. The Tennessee Valley was studded with cloverleaf networks of modern highways and public works of the Tennessee Valley Authority, striking testimonials of one of the most outstanding accomplishments of the federal government in our generation, largely owing to the consecration of Senator George Norris. The TVA provided electric current in 1962 at a cost of one cent a kilowatt hour, or the lowest rate in the United States—compared with a rate of twelve cents we paid in France! Yet, for his pains, Norris was vilified at the time as a Communist, America's conception of the lowest rung of humanity.

We were heading for Washington and Dacor House, where we saw many dear Foreign Service friends, and thence to Baltimore, where we were entertained by bibliophilic friends: Curtis Carroll Davis and the Douglas Gordons. These last drove us to Washington to board a private railway coach offered at their instance by the president of the R.F. & P. Railroad to transport us to Ashland, Virginia, where I was scheduled to inaugurate the new Walter Hines Page Library at Randolph-Macon College. The last journey Georgina and I had made in a private railway car was that provided us by the Tartar Soviet Republic when serving with the American Relief Administration in Kazan, 1921-23.

My address, given the next day, was entitled "The Rewards of Book Collecting," with emphasis on Shakespeare, Restif de la Bretonne, Casanova and Henry Miller, with whom I had occupied myself as a collector. The Richmond newspapers, with an eye to the sensational, headlined the talk R-M SPEAKER DEFENDS CASANOVA, MILLER. CASANOVA CALLED NOT A BAD GUY BY R-M COLLEGE SPEAKER. Naturally, nothing was said of my attachment to Shakespeare; to compliment that writer was not news.

An unexpected reaction to my platform appearance was an invitation to take up residence in Ashland to give four lectures between April 15 and May 15 at weekly intervals. The emolument proffered was four thousand dollars. I protested that the sum was so far in excess of my deserts that I could not possibly accept it, even though the larger part would come out of the pockets of a cousin and former classmate.

More judicial comment was Phil Scruggs' editorial in the Lynchburg *News:* "... his comments justly make laughable and hypocritical those bitter critics of Miller who have so nearly created in the public mind the idea that Miller is an obscene writer.... What Mr. Childs said would be above their heads, but to truly literate readers he will make such appeal as to compel them to read Miller and discover for themselves that he is a great writer."

In Richmond, Director John Jennings conducted us over the stately new premises of the Virginia Historical Society and called my attention to a portrait of my great-grandfather I had never seen, presented by Mrs. Randolph Fairfax.

We paid several visits to my birthplace in Lynchburg, Virginia, then set out through enchanting Blue Ridge mountain scenery to Charleston, West Virginia, and Plymouth, Ohio. On our way we passed through the country of the Amish who, turning their backs on the modern world, dress in the garb of their ancestors and, for transportation, revert to the horse and buggy.

During our stay in Plymouth, we were taken to Lake Erie where, at Put-in-Bay, we visited the monument to Perry's victory in a naval engagement with the British in the War of 1812. If, as we profess, we are devoted to peace, why should we not end these depressing memorials to men's foolish acts of destructiveness?

En route to Jacksonville to embark for Marseilles, we passed a sign: WE BUY MODEL WRECKS.

Our impression of Florida was that it was more honky-tonk than ever, but one may say this is true of most of the world. The only part of Florida with any touch of the South is the northern section.

29

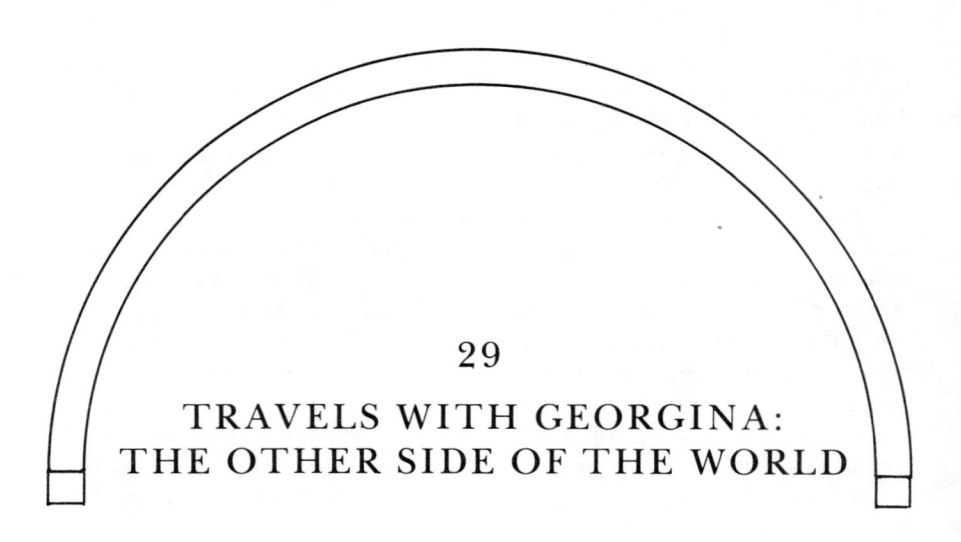

TRAVELS WITH GEORGINA: THE OTHER SIDE OF THE WORLD

*W*e returned to the United States again in March of 1963 and, in May, we embarked for the Antipodes from San Francisco.

On our ninth day, we touched at Bora Bora, an enchanting isle—from a distance. A launch transported us ashore where a typical Tahitian lunch had been prepared over bakestones and was served around open-air tables under a thatched roof. Singing and dancing natives were provided for our distraction. We quickly concluded, somewhat cavalierly, that a little went a long way, while guarding this exclusively for ourselves.

We spent two days at Papeete, capital of Tahiti, which was quite enough, as the bloom which had once distinguished it had long since disappeared in the relentless standardization of the world. A tour of the island gave us a view of its lush vegetation and thatched native huts lining the sea. Afterward, seated in a waterfront café, we saw Gauguin's ne'er-do-well son, monstrously fat, hawking his pitiful daubs, travesties of his famous father's paintings, to naïve visitors. The famous Quinn's bar nearby was thronged with prostitutes, unknown in Tahiti until the increasing influx of tourists. Tahiti's former charm as an island paradise is now drab and faded. Western commercialization marches on. Upon taking leave of Tahiti, we lay offshore of Cook Island at Rarotonga for a visit of native singers and dancers, an entertainment beginning to cloy with repetition.

Five days later we disembarked at Auckland; it was the start of a twenty-one-day, two-thousand-mile tour of New Zealand in midwinter. Despite the cold and some insufficiently heated hotels, any discomfort was mitigated by the scenic splendors of New Zealand's South Isle. It proved to be a little England, of dull uniformity except for its natural scenic beauties not subject to standardization. The people were more friendly and affable than the Australians, whose rough-and-ready manners were reminiscent of some Westerners. The best hotels were government operated.

We were bused to Waitomo for a sight of the justly famous glowworm caves and thence by private car through a rolling countryside of sheep farms to Rotorua, a Maori settlement with nearby geysers and boiling mud pools. The bitter outside temperature contrasted sharply with invigorating natural thermal baths.

We rode through rain to Wairakei, an excellent government hotel. This was one of the most impressive areas in the country, including spectacular geysers and a blowhole of escaping steam with the world's second largest geothermal power station. We continued in a pouring rain to Wellington, capital of the country.

The next day, we made a three-hour ferry crossing of Cook Strait, with an attractive view of the harbor, through Queen Charlotte Sound to a whaling station and stately fiords to Picton, South Isle.

The following day, we were interested to observe en route the strict ritual, observed alike by Kiwis (New Zealanders) and Aussies, of taking time out for tea morning and afternoon.

The next day, we went by diesel train across Arthur Pass, 2,500 feet high, affording us the most spectacular scenery observed so far in New Zealand. Christchurch, where we spent two nights, was reputed to be the most English town outside of England. We visited its excellent museum and university with a tour of the North Summit, a lofty ridge overlooking the city with a superb view of Lyttleton Harbor.

The next day, to Dunedin, peopled by Scottish and quite attractive, but much too cold to appreciate. We were obliged to stuff a jammed hotel window with towels, an indication that New Zealand is home of the world's most ardent fresh-air fiends.

Another bus transported us along snowcapped mountain ranges to Lake Te Anau. Inclement weather prevented our visit to the nearby world-famous Milford Sound, but did not cause an abandonment of the projected tour of the lake by launch along lofty fiords. A succession of lakes revived memories of the lakes in southern Chile. An indifferent hotel could not mar the superb mountain scenery surrounding us.

After two days, we continued by bus to the foot of the glaciers of Mount Cook at 13,000 feet. Here we spent three days at the Hotel Hermitage, one of the world's most attractive caravanserais, with a suite facing the peak, under whose spell we remained throughout our stay; it was a perfect climax to a most memorable tour of a charming, friendly land. We would have lingered willingly had we not been faced by the exigencies of an inexorable schedule. So it was that we returned by bus to Christchurch and, after dinner, embarked by the overnight ferry to Wellington.

Here we spent two days, prior to departure for Australia, beginning with a tour of the city and its heights in a spectacular drive. On the summit is a monument to the Virginia explorer of the Antarctic, Admiral Richard Evelyn Byrd. British Robert Falcon Scott is similarly commemorated both at Christchurch and Queenstown, as it was from New Zealand that both expeditions set out. We did not overlook a visit to the Turnbull Library to see the momentos and notebooks of Katherine Mansfield, whose gifted life was cut off so prematurely. In the afternoon we traveled by a river launch along depressingly uniform homes to a koala bear sanctuary and other peculiarly Australian fauna.

That night we boarded a crack Sunlander Express for the 675-mile journey to Proserpine, North Queensland, which took twenty-six hours. The French Mistral covers the same distance in eleven hours. The third day we traveled by bus and launch for an unwisely chosen twelve-day stay to view the Great Barrier Reef, our main objective in visiting Australia.

To our discomfort, it was piercingly cold, with no heat in our cabin. The wooded island was lovely, but once the five miles of the island were circuited afoot, the local distractions were practically exhausted except for a nightclub with good music in the evenings and cockatoo watching in the day. We took one all-day launch trip over the Great Barrier Reef to inspect this natural wonder of exquisitely colored coral, giant crabs and other sea life exposed at low tide on the coral strand. We would have done better to see the reef from Cairns, Lindeman or South Mole Island.

For our impatiently awaited return to Brisbane, we journeyed along interminable rows of eucalyptus trees and intermittent homes resembling those of our Far West a hundred years ago. There was a marked dearth of population except along the coast, with few towns or cities. We spent another day in Brisbane awaiting an overnight Sydney express. There we passed five of our most interesting days in Australia, with good food for a change. We went one day to the zoo for further acquaintance with unique examples of Australian fauna, particularly birdlife, and made a second daytime excursion to the Blue Mountains, whose gorges bear some resemblance to our Grand Canyon. We traveled another day to Berowra Waters and the Hawkesbury River, with a koala sanctuary, passing by Palm Beach. And one day we ferried to Manly Beach and returned by bus. Then we took an all-day bus trip, 191 miles each way, to

Canberra, the capital and the most attractive Australian city, with its unique war memorial.

We went by ship to Melbourne, not so attractive as Sidney, and then to Adelaide. At Freemantle we took a train which transported us in thirty-five minutes to Perth, with spacious streets and a remarkable collection of gaily plumed Australian birds in the zoo. At Perth we enjoyed our last Australian oysters, among the best in the world. It is noteworthy that, during our three-week stay in Australia, we saw no kangaroos or koala bears except in captivity.

We reached Djakarta, capital of Indonesia, a few days later. It was a filthy city, reeking in misery. We were assailed by hawkers bartering native wares for our personal possessions and exchanged a packet of cigarettes for a hand-carved statuette. Evidence obtruded everywhere of the presence of a police state. Our tour bus hostess did not hesitate to express regret at the departure of the Dutch. Docks were piled high with unused and rusting machinery received from abroad. To us, the country appeared rushing headlong to ruin. The people now possessed freedom—to starve.

On leaving Djakarta, we touched for a day in Singapore, which we had last visited in 1957. Then we took a taxi eighteen miles to Johore across the causeway the Japanese had used to capture the city from its undefended rear during World War II. The prosperity of Singapore, then part of Malaysia, was in striking contrast to that of Djakarta. We stopped briefly at Bombay, last visited in 1959. Uncollected garbage lay strewn in the streets owing to a strike of municipal workers. India also had its troubles, along with the rest of the world.

We encountered monsoon weather between Bombay and Aden. Here, I discussed with a knowledgeable vice consul the situation at my old post of Yemen. He was unable to account for our recognition of the Republic of Yemen.

Then we went through the Suez Canal; Port Said appeared remarkably clean compared with our last visit. We touched at Messina and Naples and finally reached Genoa. An hour after landing, we caught a train for Nice, returning after an absence of five months. We returned so exhausted that Georgina announced categorically, "No more long trips."

Perhaps she would reconsider. Perhaps? From 1956 to 1963, we had traversed several continents overland. Our galloping ages dictated rest.

30

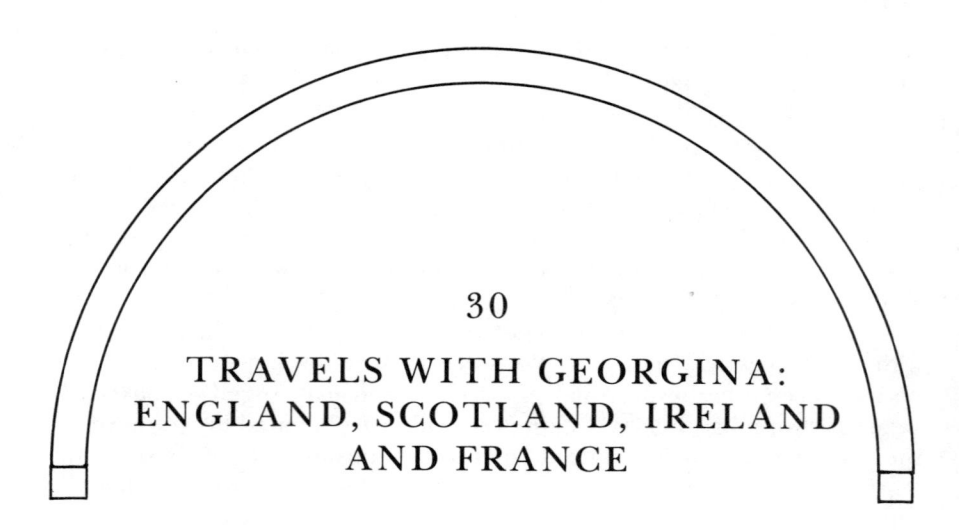

TRAVELS WITH GEORGINA: ENGLAND, SCOTLAND, IRELAND AND FRANCE

*I*n the face of Georgina's disinclination to undertake our long projected trip up the Amazon, we decided to visit more accessible countries in 1964, such as the British Isles, more particularly because my forebears had migrated thence to Virginia some three hundred and fifty years previous.

We headed for Calais via Grenoble and Dijon, continuing via Chaumont, where I had spent ten months in 1918 on the general staff deciphering German ciphers. Thence to Flornoy, south of Reims, whence a Huguenot ancestor, Laurent Flornoy, fled following a massacre in nearby Wassy. An inscription in French on a building there (here translated) recounted the story:

> FIRST OF MAY 1562 FRANÇOIS DE GUISE, EN ROUTE TO PARIS, HALTED AT WASSY UNDER PRETEXT OF REMONSTRATING WITH THE CALVINISTS, GATHERED IN A BARN BUILT ON THIS SITE. A BRAWL ENSUED IN WHICH HIS ARMED FORCES KILLED AND WOUNDED SOME 250 PERSONS. THIS DAY, CALLED THE MASSACRE OF WASSY, USHERED IN AN ERA KNOWN AS THE WARS OF RELIGION.

They were just whetting their knives then. Laurent, not choosing to abjure his Calvinist faith but fearful of the troubled times, sought safety in Lyons. The St. Bartholomew massacre, ten years later, raised the insurance rates on French Protestants, forcing Laurent to seek refuge with his wife and son Jean in nearby Geneva. The latter's grandson Jacob emigrated with his family in 1700 to Manakintown, Virginia. This accounts in part for the entrance of the present writer on the stage seven generations later.

Having pigeonholed that particular bit of history, let us turn to the Pommery champagne caves in Reims and from there to Compiègne, first visited in 1915 with the American Ambulance Corps. Undesirous of committing suicide by driving on the left side of the highway in accordance with a quaint British custom, we garaged our car at Calais, from whence we proceeded by ship and train to London. The evening of our arrival we rushed to see the Abbey Players in Sean O'Casey's *The Plough and the Stars*, and the next night went to see a superb actress in Chekhov's *The Sea Gull*. We spent the days at Stratford-on-Avon to see *Richard II* and parts 1 and 2 of *Henry IV*. Anyone who fails to attend the theater in London or Stratford needs psychiatric attention.

We made an excursion to Warwick Castle and to Coventry. Coventry's rebuilt cathedral we found as hideous as an abstract painting, and its restored tapestry seemed a colored rag.

A car and driver picked us up at Oxford for a three-week tour of England, Scotland and Wales. Under the conviction that we were blooming idiots of a class he had previously escorted, he outlined a trip whose emphasis was on scenery, with no provision for Stonehenge or Burns' birthplace or the great cathedral at York. After returning his itinerary, upon gaining our composure, we set out on our own improvised routing and headed for Newbury, Whitechurch, to lunch at the White Hart Inn, and thence to Winchester to view its thirteenth-century cathedral and to Salisbury for its fourteenth-century cathedral. We made a diversion to Stonehenge the next day, where boulders shaped to catch the summer solstice resembled those we had seen fulfilling a like function near Lake Titicaca in Bolivia. We spent two days at the Crown Hotel for a sight of the charming, restful Blandford Forum, from whence my line of Ryves emigrated to Virginia via Oxford. At nearby Shroton, the rector showed us family relics. Later, we lunched in London with Philip Ryves Harding, a fourteenth cousin, the first of the English family encountered.

We drove to Dorchester in Exeter, then over the moors to Carlyon Bay in Cornwall and along a wild picturesque seacoast to Lynton to the ruins of the first English church at Glastonbury and the great Gothic cathedral at Wells. We passed two nights at Bath, a pure Georgian gem, with visits to the Pump Room, the Circle and The Royal Crescent, and delightful strolls about the town. From Bath, we went to impressive cathedrals at Gloucester and Hereford and thence to Wales through a lovely rolling countryside abounding with charming Old World courtesy. We spent a dreary evening at Llandrindod Wells owing to a misdirection; thence northeast via Machynlleth, with an ancient Welsh church, along Cardigan Bay through Aberdovey, Dolgellan, Ruthin and Mold, all with old churches well repaying visits, to stately Roman Chester, dating from A.D. 100.

We spent two days in Chester walking atop the ancient Roman wall for an intimate view of the city, followed by visits to the cathedral and cursory examinations of those houses surviving from the Middle Ages. It was a fitting prelude to Roman York and Lincoln and their majestic cathedrals, not omitting the White Hart Inn in Lincoln dating from 1460, most noteworthy inn in England outside of London. We stopped at Selby for a sight of the Washington coat of arms on a stained-glass window in the abbey, with a pedigree on the wall showing the descent of Queen Elizabeth II from Robert Porteus of Virginia, whose wife had a common ancestor with Washington. Altogether the cities of York, Chester, and Lincoln proved to be quite *sui generis.*

Our route took us to curious menhirs in Bidborough and thence to Ripon. In the cathedral, we came upon a memorial tablet to Thomas Binns (1835–96) of nearby Sawley Hall. I recalled that the first Binns in Virginia was probably Dr. Thomas Binns, residing at Jamestown in 1624. While the name is a most uncommon one today in Virginia, apart from Richmond, the family appears most prolific in the English county of Yorkshire, which we traversed. The brick homes and the gentle rolling countryside appeared to both of us strikingly reminiscent of southside Virginia. On reaching Carlisle on the Yorkshire border of Scotland, I examined, as was my wont, the local telephone directory for Binns. On finding a Reverend Mr. Binns, I telephoned him to seek information about the family. When I informed him I could trace my descent from the immigrant in the early seventeenth century, he laughed and remarked that Americans appeared to be more interested in their ancestry than the British, adding that his own information about the Binns did not extend beyond his grandfather. To cap our exchange, he stated that if I found anything interesting about the English Binns, he would appreciate being informed!

We passed into Scotland at Gretna, pausing at Dumfries to visit the Burns museum and the monument to Burns in an adjacent cemetery. There we found confirmation of Burns' dictum that "A man's a man for a' that" in the presence of tombs to the memory of masons, joiners, innkeepers and others of comparable social rank. Curiously enough, our driver confessed, when we requested that our itinerary include a visit to Burns' birthplace, that we were the first Americans to express interest in visiting Burns' birthplace, Alloway. A museum there housed a collection of every available edition of Burns' poems, whatever the translation. On the cottage wall we found this tribute to Burns by the well-known American orator and freethinker Robert Ingersoll, written in Burns' cottage on August 19, 1878:

> Though Scotland boasts a thousand names
> Of patriot, king and peer,
> The noblest, grandest of them all
> Was loved and cradled here.
> Here lived the gentle peasant prince,
> The loving cottar king,
> Compared with whom the greatest lord
> Is but a titled thing.
> 'Tis but a cot roofed in with straw,
> A hovel made of clay.
> One door shuts out the snow and storm;
> One window greets the day;
> And yet I stand within this room
> And hold all thrones in scorn,
> For here beneath this lowly thatch
> Love's sweetest bard was born.
> Within this hallowed hut I feel
> Like one who clasps a shrine,
> When the glad lips at last have touched
> The something seemed divine.
> And here the world through all the years,
> As long as day returns,
> The tribute of its love and tears
> Will pay to Robert Burns.

We reached Edinburgh in the late afternoon. Happily, a nearby mist failed to obscure the castle area, towering majestically over this outstanding city and people who have contributed so notably to the Scottish name. The next day we crossed the bight by ferry en route to Perth, with a detour at Falkland Castle to Braemar. Skirting Balmoral, we headed north into the heart of the wild highlands, much resembling the New Zealand sheep country, with majestic scenery as we passed Tomintoul, Grantshouse and Inverness; as a climax, in the valley beneath, we beheld the towering ruins of Macbeth's castle.

We drove along the western shore of Loch Ness to Fort William, facing the sea and spent the next day in a spectacular scenic trip by a vista-dome train, eighty-three miles along the sea and across the hills to Mallaig and return. From Fort William, we went via Carmach, Tyndrum, Crianlarich, and fishing villages on the western shore of Loch Lomond through Balloch, Dryhem, and Aberfoyle; lunched at Lake

Trossachs, then Callender to the Golden Lion Hotel in Stirling, redolent of Scottish history in which I was steeped when a child, thanks to the Scottish inheritance of my mother. An imposing monument to William Wallace on the outskirts of an eminence overlooking an ancient battlefield commemorated "SCOTS WHO HAE WITH WALLACE BLED." I had a rush of memories poetic and historical; these journeys put flesh on the dead bones of the past. We visited the abbey, a castle, the John Knox church, a statue to Burns and old homes. En route to Edinburgh via Falkirk, we halted at Linlithgow Castle, imposing despite its decay.

We spent five captivating days in stately Edinburgh, with visits by rubberneck bus to St. Giles Cathedral, Thistle Chapel, the museum, the Law Courts, the Royal Mile, Arthur's seat, the National Gallery, and the National Library, with a superb exhibition of Shakespeare quartos recently acquired from Falkland Castle. We left regretfully by train for Glasgow and thence by overnight ship to Belfast in northern Ireland. A quick tour of Belfast environs, including the impressive Parliament, followed the next day as part of an all-day bus tour of the northern coast via Antrim, Kilrea, Coleraine, Port Rush, the Giant's Causeway, Cushendun, and Ballgally Castle.

We went by train to Dublin, a visit prompted by an invitation from an old friend and fellow bibliophile, Sir Chester Beatty. We had first known him in Cairo, and the friendship had been renewed and much strengthened in Nice and Monte Carlo. The visit began most auspiciously, for, on emerging from the Royal Hibernian Hotel, my attention was happily attracted to an important bookstore opposite. A study of Casanova and the European eighteenth century had awakened my interest in one of Casanova's particular acquaintances, Ange Goudar, whose *Chinese Spy* in six volumes I had long been searching for unsuccessfully. Entering the bookstore, I was waited on by a young man to whom I confided my interest in Goudar. Instead of answering my question, he entered into a long examination of my collecting interests. Once he appeared satisfied with my *bona fides,* he asked to be excused and, a few minutes later, reentered the room triumphantly holding over his head in his two hands the small-sized volumes. I had never seen a set previously and I had difficulty concealing my excitement.

"The price?" I finally managed to ask.

"Ten pounds," he replied.

I hastened to take the pound notes out of my pocket and place them in his hand before he might be tempted to change his mind.

Then I went with Georgina to call on Sir Chester, who had asked us to join him at lunch with Dr. R. J. Hayes, who not only headed the National Library in Dublin but also was conservator of Sir Chester's famous library of Oriental manuscripts and books. When I confessed that I had just made an important addition to my collection of a six-volume set, of which there was no copy in either the British Museum, the National Library in Dublin, or the library of Trinity College, Dr. Hayes accepted my purchase under his nose quite gracefully.

We parted regretfully from our host to embark the next evening by ship for Liverpool, where we entrained for London. That night we attended Chekhov's *Cherry Orchard* performed by the Moscow Art Theatre troupe. I had seen their production in Moscow of *Uncle Vanya* some forty years previous; it had left a lasting impression, however fragmentary my Russian was then. Chekhov is such a supreme artist that he projects his message by a magic touch over all language barriers.

We returned to Calais to pick up our car and drive to Bayeux to view the tapestries depicting the Norman Conquest, woven contemporaneously and preserved miraculously from that time. Then we drove to Aromanches on the coast to visit the well-organized museum consecrated to the Allied landings of 1944. A French guide delivered a masterly lecture, whose interest was enhanced by the large-scale maps accompanying it. We next proceeded along the coast to Omaha Beach, with interminable rows of crosses erected over the graves of our casualties. To remark that the sight was heartrending was a supreme understatement. I was reminded of the touching verses which serve as appropriate inscriptions to the dead at Arlington Cemetery:

ON FAME'S ETERNAL CAMPING GROUND THEIR SILENT TENTS ARE SPREAD,
AND GLORY GUARDS WITH SOLEMN ROUND THE BIVOUAC OF THE DEAD.

For my part, I am no longer stirred by these cemeteries nor by the sight of marching soldiers, with bands playing and flags flying, designed to arouse the patriotic emotions of the assembled. To what end?—the indefinite of mass murder. It would be more responsive to the sentiments of many of us if troops were paraded to Chopin's "Funeral March," with the colors draped in mourning of man's irrationality.

We made our way along the coast through Saint-Lô and Granville; experienced the moving sight of Mont-Saint-Michel rising like some strange mirage from the sea. We went on to Saint-Malo, with its old walls and such buildings as survive World War II, and then, by ferry, to Dinard. From there, we went on to Quiberon on the Brittany coast; continued to Carnac, encircled by dolmens and menhirs, charming Nantes and Fontenay-le-Comte.

Niort was our next stop and then through Old World Angoulême,

Périguex and Brantôme to Cahors. Under moonlight shadows, its fascinating old buildings and narrow streets came ghostlike to life. Adjacent Point Valentre proved of exceptional interest. At the old walled city of Albi we stopped to visit a Toulouse-Lautrec exhibition, thence drove through Castres to Montpellier, still preserving its Old World charm.

Seven days and eighteen hundred kilometers from Calais, we reached our home in Nice, quite exhausted and with dazed memories of the kaleidoscopic scenes which had flashed on our visions. Four months later, Georgina opted to remain behind while I returned to Stratford-on-Avon to attend the four concluding plays in Shakespeare's history cycle: *Henry V, Henry VI* and *Richard III*. I was held spellbound as the evils of the totalitarian regime unfolded.

What a man! Or was this Shakespeare half divine?

EPILOGUE

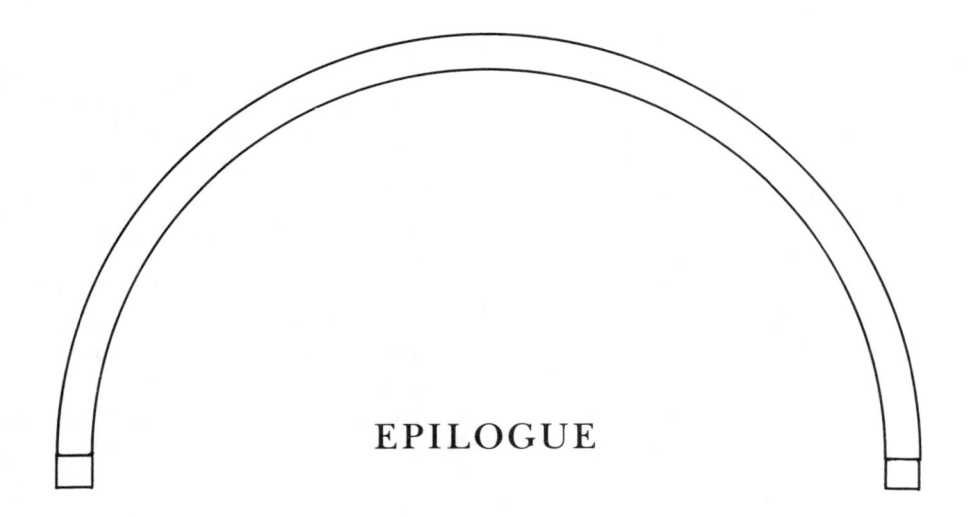

A few weeks later, my beloved companion, whom I had married on August 13, 1922, in St. Isaac's Cathedral in Leningrad, was suddenly taken from me on the morning of November 23, 1964, at our home in Nice.

As I wrote in a pamphlet, *In Memoriam,* in December 1964: "No one can be more deeply conscious than I of the part she played in contributing to whatever success I may have realized in my career. She was the personification of tact and possessed an instinctive sense of the art of diplomacy. She was the sweetest and most unselfish character I have ever known. As so many have written, to have known her was an inestimable privilege. As in women generally, she had a touch of divinity such as is lacking mostly in men. She radiated loving kindness and was ever more concerned with others than herself. What a wonderful legacy to have left!"

A few final words, by way of summing up some of the most important lessons I have drawn from the fleeting passage in the course of which I have endeavored to pierce the mystery of existence. A few of these I have touched upon in my two earliest books: *Before the Curtain Falls* (published anonymously in 1932) and *The Pageant of Persia* (1936, under my pen name of Henry Filmer).

Paul Jordan Smith, in the Los Angeles *Times,* termed the former "one of the most interesting human documents produced in this country since 1914." Of the latter, the New York *Herald Tribune* wrote: "His chapters on recent political and diplomatic history are fluent, precise and authoritative. His analysis of Soviet Russia's changing role in the East is especially informed. As regards the antiquities of Persia, he is encyclopedic and he brings [Lord] Curzon's work down to date."

The first appeared at the height of the Great Depression and sold only 3,500 copies. It was a profound cry of anguish, a reaction to what I had observed in the American Ambulance Service attached to the French Army in 1915 and in the war as I had rubbed shoulders with it in those tragic years from 1915 to 1923 in France, England, the Balkans and the Soviet Union.

The conviction was brought home of what a searing tragedy World War I had been, exceeding anything the world had theretofore known in the way of calamities and excluding the possibility that life might ever be the same again. It was a conclusion strengthened by the tragedies witnessed wherever I had been in Europe, Asia and Africa. In the light of such suffering, I was incredulous when doubt was voiced by newcomers from America as to whether the Treaty of Versailles, involving our adherence to the League of Nations, would ever be ratified by the United States Senate. It was unbelievable that the blood and treasure we had sacrificed would turn out to have been purposeless, especially if followed by a second World War, as seemed inevitable to those capable of reading signs and omens. One could but weep at the folly of mankind.

Happily for me, I had come to the conclusion some time previously that a negative conception of life led only to a dead end, that we must regard the world positively with eternal hope in our hearts and that, whatever the trials and tribulations we are faced with, these should be accepted as in the ordained order of things. As Goethe has so aptly written:

Who never ate his bread in sorrow
Who never spent the long night hours,
Weeping and waiting for the morrow,
He knows ye not, ye heavenly powers.

Life is a supreme test from which there is no escaping; we must accept it as such, firm in the resolve to pursue it without self-pity. Some years ago, I came across this pregnant observation of a British writer, F. G. Happold, in his *Adventures in Search of a Creed:*

> I was conscious of a lovely unexplained pattern in the whole texture of things, a pattern of which everyone and everything was a part, and weaving the pattern was a Power, and that Power was what we faintly call Love. I realized that we are not lonely atoms in a cold, unfriendly, indifferent universe, but that each of us is linked as in a rhythm, of which he may be unconscious, and which we can never really know, but to which we can submit ourselves trustfully and unreservedly.

EPILOGUE

There were certain periods in my life when I felt assured of being in tune with the infinite. One of these manifested itself during a period of some weeks in 1938, while we were residing in Alexandria, Virginia, under assignment for four years to the Division of Near Eastern Affairs of the Department of State. The telephone would ring in our home and, before taking the receiver from the hook, I was aware of who was calling and the subject of the call. Some years previous, in 1922, when stricken in Kazan with typhus and in a coma, oblivious for some days to the world, I had had two premonitory dreams of highly important events, one of crucial importance but which I left unheeded—to my misfortune.

During my first seventeen years in the Foreign Service, I was increasingly discouraged by the slowness of my progress with only four promotions. But, assigned in 1941 in charge of the legation in Tangier, followed by the American landings in Morocco in 1942, three promotions followed rapidly in four years, culminating in the rank of career minister and appointment as ambassador to Saudi Arabia soon afterward.

My appointment in 1930 as second secretary to the legation in Cairo had already marked the initial turn in my fortunes. In accordance with a resolution already formed, I had resolved to cultivate Egyptians, contrary to the practice of the resident diplomatic corps, which generally held aloof from mixing socially with the native population. Pursuant to this objective, I interrogated half a dozen Egyptian friends, requesting that they present me with a list of half a dozen youthful Egyptians who offered the greatest promise of distinction. The most frequently named was a young journalist, Abdul Rahman el Azzam. Ten or twelve years later, I found him Secretary General of the Arab League.

In 1946, en route to my new post as minister to Saudi Arabia, I stopped off in Cairo to dine with Azzam. It was a most fortunate meeting for me. The letter of introduction he gave me to his father-in-law, royal counselor of King Ibn Saud, served to cement the very close ties I formed with his majesty in Saudi Arabia.

It was some years later, after my retirement to Nice, that I discovered that my friend Georges Painvin had established a new home twenty minutes' drive from Nice at Monte Carlo. A French friend whom we had invited to lunch happened to mention the name of Painvin as residing there with his wife. As soon as our guests had parted, I lost no time in telephoning him. He was as astonished as I had been; our former warm friendship was quickly renewed.

When I returned to Virginia in 1973, I decided to live in Richmond at the charming old Jefferson Hotel—now, alas, closed and awaiting rehabilitation at some future date. I was barely established in my native country, where I felt almost a stranger after so many years abroad (I had not lived in America for more than four years at a time since 1918), when I was asked to address a meeting of the Virginia Writers Club.

As I stood talking to my cousin, Margaret Freeman Cabell, on the day of the lecture, I saw a young woman enter the room with her husband; for some reason she captured my gaze. I was not surprised when she came toward me, but when she told me who she was, I was stunned. She was a connection of my own from Lynchburg, Virginia, who had grown up across the street from my family home, her people and mine distant relatives and close friends for generations. I had forgotten her existence, for she had been a child when I saw her last, but she was a child no longer. She and her husband, Samuel T. Schroetter, Jr., made me so welcome that I soon felt at home.

Hilda Noel Schroetter and I shared a background but, as much to the point, we also had many tastes in common. Soon we became inseparable and, when the time came that my age made it seem unwise for me to travel alone, I threw myself upon Sam's charity and borrowed Hilda as a companion.

Together, we visited Paris, Venice, Vienna, Munich and London; together, we spent weeks each summer in Nice, my home for twenty years, where we found a new home at the Park Hotel. And I had the joy of seeing familiar scenes in a new light, through Hilda's eager, enthusiastic eyes. In the fall of 1976, we traveled to the Soviet Union, visiting Moscow; Leningrad, where I found that St. Isaac's Cathedral, where Georgina and I had been married in 1922, had become a state museum; Tbilisi, Georgia, which we both loved; Tashkent; Samarkand, where we saw the tomb of Tamerlane; Bukhara, of the drifting rose-gold dust; Penjikent and the Sogdiana fortress, where Alexander the Great met Roxane; Irkutsk, halfway across Siberia; and Lake Baikal, deepest lake in the world, a jewel among forests of birch and evergreen. And together we always found something amusing along the way. When I wrote *Vignettes,* I dedicated it simply, "For Hilda."

A year or two ago, a lady whose opinion I greatly respected wrote me a letter which deeply touched me. Here it is in part:

> You ask to be of service to me, but you have been in the most roundabout way. Because I had so recently read portions of your *Vignettes* to a friend, I reread those words about your wife and all of the book again, and then, my interest aroused, I read much of your other works too.... I am filled with admiration at your knowledge ... as well as the ability to make and express judgments and foresee cause and effect.... And I wondered, reading the last paragraph of *Before the Curtain Falls,* if you still had any hope or optimism about the future leadership of America in world affairs ... I went through my middle years truly believing that the Western World was leading the wicked

Old World into new and democratic paths . . . I think there is no change except for the worst, and fear even to think of the years ahead.

I replied that the questions raised demanded such reflection that I would have to take some time before answering. There intervened the congressional elections of November 1978. I was in the throes of writing this book and decided that I would try to introduce in it such answer as the development of events might dictate. I was in the midst of this when a commentator on the election results remarked with some dismay that no less than forty of those making up the new Senate were millionaires. One of the conclusions that imposed itself was that, until some limits are decreed on the sums permitted to be expended on political campaigns, the American people are destined to be ruled by Mammon rather than by principles of conduct based on integrity. It was inescapable that we are fast approaching a state of affairs similar to that which contributed to the fall of the Roman and other empires. When elections are purchasable, there is little reason why citizens should bother to enter a polling booth.

Shortly after I returned to the United States, after my many years abroad, I accepted, with some misgivings, an honorary post at Randolph-Macon College, of which one of the founders was my great-grandfather. The title, scholar in residence, was a pretentious one, which I was far from meriting. After an apparent failure to gain the confidence of the students, I was on the point of throwing in my hand. Then it occurred to me that a way might be found by eating in the cafeteria alongside the students. On entering it, I observed a student seated alone, the picture of dejection, staring into space. On a sudden impulse, I approached and took my seat alongside him.

"You look downcast," I ventured. "Why don't you tell me your troubles; it might afford you some relief."

He shifted his position to one more erect. This was followed by a series of disjointed phrases from which I learned that he had just been notified that his grades were insufficient to warrant his remaining in college and that he must pack and go home. It was all too much of a shock to enable him to make up his mind what to do.

"I will tell you," I said. "First you will go home and explain it manfully to your parents. Tell them you intend to look around for a college or a tutor near your home so that you might make up your grades to present to this college as warranting your readmittance."

He brightened considerably. "I will do it," he said, with a sense of renewed confidence. His changed demeanor convinced me that he would.

That autumn he was back at college, smiling and self-confident. "I made it," he assured me, "thanks to you."

"It was thanks to yourself. I gave you the necessary prod, that was all."

He remained on and I was present when he graduated the next year, receiving his diploma in the presence of his admiring parents. They could not have been prouder of him nor more grateful to me for the small part I had played. They seemed loath to accept my insistence that I was only an instrument in the denouement.

There have been few acts in my life which gave me greater satisfaction than helping students, which I at length discovered to be within my power.

In the evening of my life, as I review it, I find that it has been a succession of disappointments interspersed with some positive accomplishments. The essential was, as my mother was ever repeating, devoted as she was to aiding her fellows: "Never look back."

To that, I would add: "Never worry about what can't be remedied."

If I had learned this sooner, my life would have perhaps been calmer—but far less interesting.

Let us leave it at that.

Index

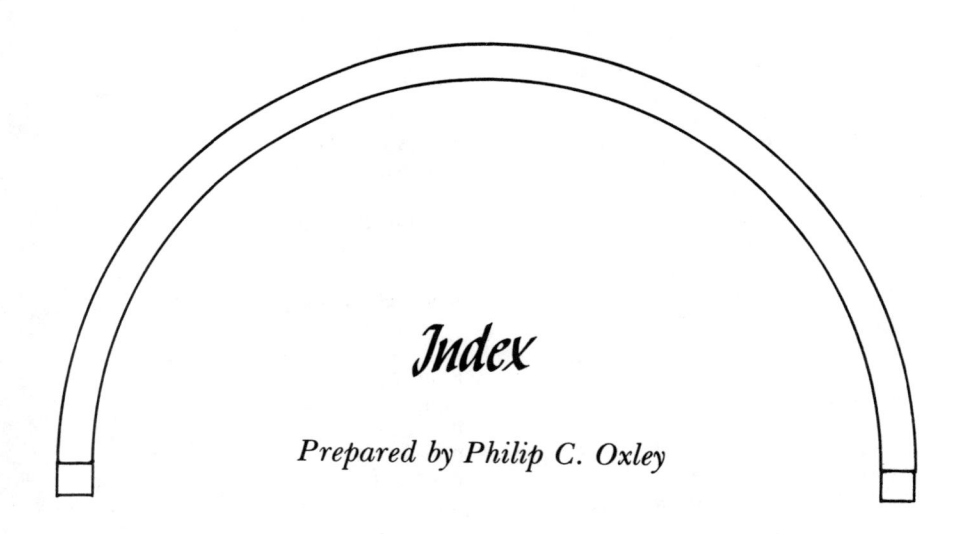

Prepared by Philip C. Oxley

Abdullah, Emir, 89
Abdullah, Prince (Yemen), 272–73
Abdullah Effendi, 266
Abdullah Saud bin Jelui, 255
Abdul Wahab Pasha, 110
Abrines, Mr., 139
Achaemenian rulers, 106
Acheson, Secretary Dean, 265
Addis Ababa: described, 276–77
ADFGX cipher, 30, 33–38, 50
Ahmad, Crown Prince (Yemen), 272, 273
Agora museum, 303
Aksum: archaeological remains, 277
Alexander the Great, 106, 324
Algeciras Conference (1906), 134, 136
Algiers Conference, 205–08
Allenby, High Commissioner Edmund, 90
Allen, Julian, 19
Allied landing in French N. Africa: killed, wounded and missing, 200–01; dates surrounding, 211–12—preliminary attitudes towards: Spanish Morroco, 184–88, 198; Gen. Nogues, 188–91, 192–94; French Navy, 191. *See also* Ch. 18
Alling, Paul, 123
Alton, Illinois, 19
American Ambulance Corps, 18–19, 315, 322. *See also* World War I
American Black Chamber, 38
American College, Beirut, 83

American Relief Administration, 43, 46–48; Soviet Union famine, 59–61, 143; Tartar Republic, 66–79, 308
American trench code, 30–31
American University, Cairo, 83, 99
Amish, 309
Amritsar, India: massacre, 293
Anarchism: in Barcelona, 115–17. *See also* Spanish Civil War
Angkor Wat, Cambodia, 287
Anglo-French accord (1904): Morocco, 134
Annradkapura, Ceylon, 291
Antifascist Militia, 116–17. *See also* Spanish Civil War
Antonius, George: *The Arab Awakening*, 88–89, 105
Apollo, 301
Arab: characterized, 153
Arabian American Oil Company, 105; religious services at Dhahran, 259–262
Arabian desert, 119
Arabian Nights, 104, 280, 290
Arabi Pasha, 99
Arab League, 241, 246, 259, 265, 323
Arab oil boycott, 85
Aramco. *see* Arabian American Oil Company
Arlington Cemetery, 319
Armistice Control Commission (North Africa), 145
Army War College, 26

327

Arnold, George, 92
Aromanches, France, 319
Arslan, Emir Adel, 89
Artaxerxes I, II and III, 106
Arthur Pass, New Zealand, 311
Asbury, Bishop, 1
Asmara, Yemen, 274
Asquith, Sir Herbert, 90
Associated Press, 51–58
Astoria Cafe, Corfu, 300
Atahualpa, 295–96
Atherton, Ray, 126
Atlantic Pact, 250
Australia: travels in, 312–13
Aztec relics: Mayan compared, 306

Babbitt, Irving, 15
Badajoz, Spain, 143
Badoglio, Duke of, 176–77
Bahrein, 256
Bajadere, The, 97
Balfour Declaration (1917), 81–82. See also Israel; Palestine
Baltimore *American*, 7–8, 51
Baltimore *Sun*, 7
Bangkok, Thailand, 287
Bantus, 299
Barcelona: in Spanish Civil War, 115–18. See also Spanish Civil War
Barnes, Capt., 24, 26
Batista, Fulgencio, 296
Battle of Britain, 123
Bayeux tapestries, 319
Bayh, Sen. Birch, 87
Beatty, Sir Chester, 318–19
Beaulac, Willard, 160
Before the Curtain Falls, 321–22
Behobie, France, 113–14
Beigbeder, Colonel, 142, 149
Belfast, Northern Ireland, 318
Belgian Congo, 298
Belleau Wood Memorial Association, 58
Ben-Gurion, David, 88. See also Israel
Bentley, Bill, 5
Bentley, Col. William C., 138, 147–48, 191–92
Berbers, 299
Berle, Adolph, 83, 126–131
Bernadoni, Capt. Bernard, 148
Berthold, Capt., 29
Besly, John, 100, 101
Bethouart, General, 202, 208

Bey, Alan, 47
Bey, Bakhoum, 98
Bible: and archaeology, 299
Bidassoa River, 113
Binns, Thomas, 316
Biratou, France, 113–14
Blackwell, Robert, 16
Blois, France, 27–28
Blue Mountains, Australia, 312
Blum, Leon, 155
Bode, Captain, 123
Bogota, Colombia, 295
Boisson, Governor General, 207
Bolifraud, M., 219
Bombay, India, 313
Booth, Waller, 182
Borani, 279
Borrow, George, 10
Boston *Transcript*, 19
Bownass, Richard, 182, 232
Boyd, John, 68, 78
Bradley, Gen. Omar, 228
Bragassa, Mrs., 3
Brenes, Edward, 232
British-French Moroccan clearing agreement, 124
British Purchasing Commission, 124
Broadmoor Hotel, 20
Brown, George Lyman, 59–60
Brown, James Leftwich (grandfather), 1
Brown, Lucy Howard (mother), 1–3, 109
Brylkine, Georgina de. *see* Childs, Georgina de Brylkine
Brylkine, Paul, 76
Bucharest, Romania, 49
Buckingham, Wheeler, 5
Buckingham Female Institute, 1
Buckingham Institute Guards, 2
Budenny, Gen. S.M., 60
Buenos Aires, Argentina, 297
Bullitt, William Christian, 129–131
Burgess, Ed, 14
Burns, Robert, 316–17
Burton, Sir Richard Francis, 280
Burtt's *Teaching of the Compassionate Buddha*, 289
Bushmen, 299
Byrd, Adm. Richard Evelyn, 312
Byron, Lord George, 301

Cabell, Margaret Freeman, 324
Cagoulards, 213

INDEX

329

Cairo: described, 291
Calcutta, 292
Canberra, Australia, 313
Candler's Mountain, 4
Caracas, Venezuela, 305
Carmen, 69
Carson, Pirie and Scott, 19
Carson, Warner, 19–20
Carvajal, Colonel, 154
Casanova de Seingalt, Jacques, 298, 318; diplomat's qualities, 282–83; *Icosameron*, 292; *History of My Life*, 293, 300; in Corfu, 300
Centeno, Manuel, 233
Champ Fleury, 18
Character Guidance Center, 261–62
Chateau des Baumettes, 286
Cheka: described, 78
Chekhov, Anton, 16; *The Sea Gull*, 315; *Cherry Orchard* and *Uncle Vanya*, 319
Chester, England, 316
Chicago *Tribune*, 19, 59, 67
Chichen Itza, Mexico, 305–06
Chicherin, G.V., 52–54, 65
Child, Gabriel, 1
Child, John, 1
Childs, Georgina de Brylkine (wife), 70, 76–77: death, 321
Childs, J. Rives: parents and grandparents, 1–3; Army Commission, 25–26; marriage, 76–77; U.S. Foreign Service appointment, 80; Saudi Arabian appointment, 85; resignation from Foreign Service, 282–85; wife's death, 321
Childs, Rev. John Wesley (grandfather), 1
Childs, John William (father), 1–3
Childs, Wesley (brother), 7
Chile, 297
Chopin, Frederick: "Funeral March," 319
Christchurch, New Zealand, 311
Christian, Jr., George B., 58
Christian Science Monitor, 80
Churchill, Gen. Marlborough, 40
Churchill, Winston, 123
Ciano, Galeazzo: *Journal*, 150
Cipher Bureau, British War Office, 31
Ciphers. *see* Cryptography
Circus Princess, The, 97
Clapper, Raymond, 54
Clarac, Claude, 146, 162, 172–73, 185, 189, 192, 202–03, 215

Clark, Gen. Mark, 159, 205–06, 209; Patton's headquarters contrasted, 227
Clark, Harlan, 270
Clayton, Sir Gilbert, 88
Clinchant, M., 209
Codes: ciphers distinguished, 32
Coins, Russian, 76
Colby, Sec. Bainbridge, 54, 61
Col de la Perche, 115
Cole, Felix, 64, 126
College of Juilly, 18
Collins, Gen. Lawton, 262
Colombo, Ceylon, 291
Colonial Dames of Virginia, 109
Colorado Springs, Colo., 19–20
Communism: Arab states views on, 239, 264–66; American pathological reactions to, 306, 308
Congressional Quarterly, 87
Congress Party (India), 293
Conolly, Adm. Richard, 235
Conquistadors: characterized, 295–96
Consolidated Railway Express Company, 2
Constantinople, 48
Control vice consuls, 174–75, 228
Convoys: in Straits of Gibraltar, 231–34
Coq d'Or, 28
Corcovado, 297
Corfu: described, 300
Corinth, Greece, 301
Cornell University, 2
Countess Maritza, 97
Coventry, England, 315
Cox, Sir Percy, 239
Crabites, Judge Pierre, 99
Crane, Charles R., 105
Crete, 301; German attack on, 149–50
Cristine Hotel, 143
Croix de Guerre, 37
Cryptography, 26, 29–39, 45
Cuernavaca, Mexico, 307
Cunningham, Admiral, 206
Current History, 63
Curzon, Lord, 321

Daily Advance, 4
Dakar, Senegal, 287, 298
"Dancings," 40–41
Darius the Great, 106
Darlan, Adm. Jean F., 145, 170–71; Algiers Conference, 205–07; Gen. Nogues contrasted. 212–13

—Darlan deal: reactions to, 209–221; effect of, 213, 225, 228
Davis, Curtis Carroll, 308
Dawalibi, 265–66
De Gaulle, Gen. Charles: Giraud-DeGaulle agreement, 219–21; Committee of National Liberation, 220–21
Delos, Greece, 301
Delphic oracle, 302
Democratic National Convention, 7
Dempster, Ernest, 153–54
Dennis, H. R., 17
Dhahran air base, 244–47, 249–50; religious services, 259–262
d'Harcourt, Admiral, 191
Diplomat: qualities befitting, 282–83
Djakarta, Indonesia, 313
Dr. Eliot's Five-Foot Shelf of Books, 16
Donovan, Gen. William, 195
Dracula, 97
Droit administratif, 194
Dublin, Ireland, 318
Du Gardier, M., 147, 195, 199–202, 208
Dulles, John Foster, 64
Dunedin, New Zealand, 311
Dunn, James C., 283
Duranty, Walter, 66, 67
Dzibilchaltun, Mexico, 306

Early, Bishop John (great-grandfather), 1
Early, Mary Virginia (grandmother), 1
Earthquakes, 307
Eccles, David, 123–24, 144
Eddy, Col. William A., 138, 148, 162–63, 175, 182, 195, 197
Edinburgh, Scotland, 317–18
Edwards, Maj. John W., 148
Egypt: population characterized, 99; Great Britain's influence on, 100; JRC's policy recommendations, 107; revolution (1952), 111–12; social inequalities described, 112; in Arabian desert, 119; monasteries, 119–20; JRC's *Escape to Cairo*, 120; Ethiopia linked with, 275–76; Israel's attack on (1956), 286
Egyptian Gazette, 101
Ehrhard, Jean, 114–19
Einstein, Albert, 57–59
Eisenhower, Gen. Dwight: Algiers Conference, 205; *Crusade in Europe*, 209–10, 212
Elbrick, Burke and Elfie, 304–05

England: travels in, 315–16
Eritrea, Ethiopia, 280–81
Escape to Cairo, 120
Espionage, 138, 148; control vice consuls, 174–75; chief pilot incident, 175–76; Joint Anglo-American Intelligence Committee, 178–79; Malta telegraph incident, 179–80; Malmusi incident, 181–82; Swiss architect, 182
Ethiopia: JRC named ambassador, 275; Egypt linked with, 275–76; Addis Ababa described, 276–77; Yemeni ties, 277; archaeological remains, 277, 279 Italian roads, 277, 281
Evans, Arthur, 301
Evanston Country Club, 20
Everyman Library, 10
Export-Import Bank, 248
Eze-sur-mer, 286

Fabyan, George, 26
Fairfax, Randolph, 309
Faisal, Prince, 240, 249, 250
Falange (Spain), 222
Farajollah Khan, 105
Farnsworth, Major Gen., 26
Farouk, King, 111, 112. *See also* Egypt
Farquar, Percival, 95
Fechin, Nicolai, 70–71, 77
Federation of Anarchists of Iberia, 116
Feis, Herbert, 124, 126, 128–29
Feisal, Prince Ibn al Saud, 85
Filmer, Henry (pen name). *see* Childs, J. Rives
Firdausi, 104
Florida: honky-tonk, 309
Flornoy, Laurent, 314–15
Foreign Relations of the United States, 162, 238
Foreign Service. *see* United States Foreign Service
Francis, David R.: described, 63–64
Franco-German Convention (1911): Morocco, 134–35
Franklin Literary Society, 1
Fraternities, 7, 14, 24–25
French logic: characterized, 194, 207
French Minstral, 312
Friedman, William, 26, 30
Fulbright, Sen. J. W., 87
Für God cipher, 31

INDEX
331

G2A6. *Cryptography*
Galitsch, Zena, 75
Gascoigne, Consul General, 185, 197–98
George, Lloyd: Mansion House speech, 135
German Armistice Commission, 169, 176; Moroccan aims, 145–46, 149; isolation of, 147; American aid to N. Africa, 149; Allied landing possibilities, 192–93; capture of during landings, 224
German Military Terms and Abbreviations, 30
German Port Commission, 145
Gezira Sporting Club, 101
Gibbons, Floyd, 67
Gibbs, Sir Philip: *The Middle of the road*, 67
Gilbert, Prentiss, 102
Gilmore, Robert, 26–30, 44
Gimore, Commander Robert, 231–33
Giraud, Gen. Henri H., 196; Algiers Conference, 206–07
Giraud-De Gaulle agreement, 219–21
Glass, Congressman Carter, 2, 5, 9, 22
Glass, Ned, 2–3
Gleaton, Mr., 240
Gneisenau, 170
Goeritz, Hermann, 173
Goethe, Johann Wolfgang von, 322
"Golden Rule" luncheon, 90
Golden Temple (India), 294
Gordon, Douglas, 308
Gort, Lord, 178–79, 189
Goudai, Ange: *Chinese Spy*, 318
Grady, Henry F., 126
Graham, John, 26, 44
Grandpre, A. de: *Cryptographique pratique*, 30
Gravel, Sen. Mike, 88
Grayson, Adm. C. T., 56
Great Barrier Reef, 312
Great Britain: Italo-Ethiopian war's effect on, 110–11
Greece: Persia compared, 106
Guise, Francois de, 314
Gulf of Kotor, 119
Gunther, John, 101
Gypsies, 97

Hackworth, Green, 83
Hafiz, 104, 106
Haile Selassie: King Ibn Saud contrasted, 277

Halicarnasus, Turkey, 301
Hamilton, Cosmo, 21
Hamites, 299
Hamza, Fuad Bey, 238–41, 251, 254, 256–59, 262
Happold, F.G., *Adventures in Search of a Creed*, 322
Harar: described, 280
Harding, Pres. Warren G., 55; described, 57–58
Hardion, M., 203, 206, 207–08
Haroun-al-Raschid, 104
Harper, Maj. Gen. Robert, 246
Harper's Ferry, Va., 5
Harrison, James River, 227
Harvard University, 13–17
Harzfeld, Dr. Ernst, 106
Hashemite family: British support of, 241, 243, 247, 254
Haskell, Colonel, 69
Hassan, Prince (Yemen), 272
Hawkins, Harry, 126
Hay, Major, 31–32, 34
Hayes, Ambassador C.J.H., 160; *Wartime Mission in Spain*, 230–31
Hayes, Dr. R.J., 318–19
Haynes, Capt. Garland, 2
Hebrew University, Jerusalem, 82
Heian shrine, 288
Heine, Heinrich, 18
Hendaye, France, 113
Henderson, Mack, 230
Heraklion, Greece, 301
Herodotus, 301
Herter, Christian, 76
Hewitt, Vice Adm., 164
Higginbottom, Joe, 4
Highway of the Dead, 307
Hill, Heyward G., 267
Hippocrates, 301
Hitler, Adolf, 55; N. African mistakes, 121, 150–51
Hitt, Parker: *Hitt's Manual*, 30
Hoare, Sir Samuel, 156, 198
Hodeida, Yemen, 270
Holcombe, Lt. Frank, 175–77
Holland, Captain, 179
Homer, 302
Hood, Eddie, 52, 133, 293
Hooker, Major, 231
Hoover, Calvin B.: *The Economic Life of Soviet Russia*, 101–02

Hoover, Herbert, 59, 61; Smoot-Hawley tariff, 95; public opinion of, 103 *See also* American Relief Administration
Horyuji temple, 288
Hotel Crillion, 40
Hotel de France, 27–28
Hotel Hermitage, 311
Hot pursuit, 230–31
Huguenots, 314
Hull, Secretary Cordell, 83; *Memoirs*, 129
Humphrey, Sen. Hubert, 88
Hurley, Patrick, 64
Hussein, Prince (Yemen): JRC's talks with, 271–72
Hutton, Barbara, 111
Hydra, Greece, 302

Ibn Saud, King, 14; JRC's relations with, 237; request for U.S. aid, 238–43; capture of Riyadh recounted, 254–55; family; Israel; Palestine; Saudi Arabia
Inca, 295–96
India: politics, 293
Ingersoll, Robert, 317
In Memoriam, 321
Intelligence. *see* Espionage: Office of Strategic Services
International Herald Tribune, 87
International News Service, 54
International Press Correspondence, 93
Iran. *see* Persia
Irun, Spain, 113–15. *See also* Spanish Civil War
Isfahan, Persia, 106
Isimila, 299
Israel: statehood, 86, 248–49; pro-Israeli Senators, 87–88; JRC's policy recommendations, 108; Arab states relations, 253–54; Syrian views of, 263; U.S. support of, effects, 281–82; attack on Egypt (1956), 286
Istanbul Conference, 263
Italian Armistice Commission, 146, 169
Italo-Ethiopian War, 109–111
Italy: Ethiopian roads, 277, 279. *See also* Italo-Ethiopian War

Jackson, Gen. Stonewall, 5
Jackson, Sen. Henry, 88
Jacqueline, 41–42
Japan: trip to described, 287–89
Jardine, William N., 99, 103, 104

Jefferson Hotel, 323
Jennings, Al, 17–18
Jennings, John, 309
Jigger Shop, 21
Jimenez, Perez, 296
Johnson, Colonel, 199
Jordana, Foreign Minister, 226
Jouvenal, Baroness Marcel de: *White, Brown and black*, 112–14
Juin, General, 192

Kalman, Emmerich, 97
Kamakura Buddha, 288–89
Kamaran Island, 269, 273
Kansas A. & M. College, 99
Kaplan, Rose, 75
Kashmir, India, 293
Kasuga shrine, 288
Katsura palace, 288
Kazan District: American Relief Administration in, 66–79. *See also* American Relief Administration
Keeley, Minister, 263, 264
Khairradin Bey, 259–60
Khalid Bey, 240–41
Kilpatrick, Emmett, 41, 43, 59–60
King-Crane Palestine mission, 105. *See also* Palestine
Kinsey, Dr. Albert C., 296
Kirkpatrick, Young, 5
Kitto, H., *The Greeks*, 303
Kittredge, George Lyman, 15
Knightley, Phillip, 63–64
Knights of St. John, 301
Koeglin-Schwartz, Colonel, 196
Kossovo, Battle of, 47
Kressenstein, Gen. Kress von, 33–34
Kreuger, Ivar, 94
Kuala Lumpur, Malaya, 287
Kun, Bela, 75
Kurhan, Sherifa, 98
Kuwait, 256
Kyoto, Japan, 288

Lahoulle, General, 202
Lahovary, Madame Simonne, 93–94
Lake, Kirsopp, 119–20
Lake Tana, 275
Lake Te Anau, 311
Lamb, Frank, 54
La Paz, Bolivia, 297
Lascroux, General, 202

INDEX

Laval, Pierre, 171
La Vie Parisienne, 44–45
Lawrence of Arabia, 21, 34, 140
Lawrenceville School, 20–21
League of Nations, 47, 322; Lodge's effect, 55–56; British Mandate in Palestine, 81–84. *See also* Balfour Declaration; Palestine
Leakey, Louis, Mary and Richard, 299
Lee, Gen. Robert E., 2, 5, 210
Legion of Honor, 37
Le Grand Vatel, 42
Lehar, Franz: *The Merry Widow*, 119
Lemaigre-Debrevil, M., 196
Lenin, V.I.: described, 61–63, 75, 102; Wilson's Fourteen Points, draft note, 65–66
Libya: British retreat, 169–70
Lima, Peru, 296
Lindbergh, Col. Charles: kidnapping, 111
Lindos, Greece, 301
Litvinov, Maxim, 60
Lockwood, Milt, 47–48, 119
Lodge, Sen. Henry Cabot, 55–56
London, Meyer, 22
London School of Economics, 92
Loraine, Sir Percy, 100
Los Angeles *Times*, 321
Los Caracoles, 118
Lubianka Prison, 60
Lyautey, Marshal L.H.G., 155, 156
Lyautey, Pierre, 168, 170, 172–73, 190–91
Lynch, Col. Arthur, 67
Lynchburg High School, 2
Lynchburg *News*, 86, 309

MacAndrews, Jack, 92
Macbeth's castle, 317
Mackensen, Gen. Von, 35–37
Madgearu, Virgile, 96
Magnes, Rabbi Judah, 82
Mahabalipuram, India, 292
Malmusi, Judge, 181–82
Malraux, Andre, 111, 285n1
Malta: siege, 179–80
Malval, Baron Henri de, 112
Manchester Guardian, 96, 101
Mane, Senor Rubio, 306–07
Manilla, Phillipines, 287
Maniu, Prime Minister Jules, 96
Mansfield, Katherine, 312

333

Marchal, Leon, 123–24
Marib, Yemen: JRC's flight over, 273–74
Marie, Queen (Romania), 93–94
Martin, Senator, 26
Mathews, Freeman, 123, 127, 129
Mausolus, King: Mausoleum of, 301
Maxim's, 42
Mayan civilization, 305–06
Mayne, Horace, 100
McCarthy, Joseph, 64
McCandlish, Commodore, 230
McGhee, George C., 253–59, 282
McNown, Colonel, 50
Medal of Freedom, 50
Medals, 37, 50
Merida, Yucatan, Mexico, 305–06
Mexico: characterized, 305, 307; Mexico City described, 306–07
Meyrier, M., 163, 165
Milford Sound, 311
Military aid: Saudi Arabia's request for, 239–242, 257–58, 262; Ethiopia, 279
Miller, Henry, 308–09
Minoan civilization, 301
Mohammed Ali, 99
Mohammed Effendi, 238, 261
Mohammed Mahmoud Pasha, 100
Mokattam, 89
Monasteries, 47, 119–20, 301, 302
Monastery of Detchani, 47
Monick, Emmanuel, 123–27, 157, 165–66
Monnet, Jean, 124
Monoliths: Ethiopian, 279
Montenegrin cap, 47
Montenegro, 47, 119
Moorish nationalism, 141–42
Moorman, Colonel, 29–32, 36–37, 50
Mormons, 10–11
Moroccan Institute of Culture, 142
Moroccan Unity Party, 141
Morocco: JRC's policy recommendations, 108; Hitler's mistakes in N. Africa, 121, 150–51; strategic importance of, 133; Franco-German Convention (1911), 134–35; French protectorate treaty, 135; Tangier's significance, 135–36; U.S. interests in, 136–37, 138–39, 152; Spanish protectorate, 137–38; Moorish nationalism, 141–42; German intentions towards, 144–47; Spanish threat to, 148–49; border control problems, 223–24. *See also* Allied landing in F.

334   INDEX

North Africa; Nogues, General; Orgaz, General; Tangier
Moscow: described, 61, 66
Moseley, Frank, 41
Moulmein Pagoda, 292
Mt. Athos monasteries, 302
Mount Cook, New Zealand, 311
Musee de l'Homme (Paris), 299
Mowrer, Edgar Scott, 101
Mugica, General, 198
Muktarov, 68–69
Muktarova: *Carmen*, 69
Mumm's party, 42–43
Murphy, Robert, 174–75, 178, 204; Weygand-Murphy accord, 126, 129–131, 155, 165; Algiers Conference, 206–07
Murray, Wallace, 123, 126–27, 130–31, 152, 178
Muskie, Sen. Edward, 88
Mycenae, 302

Nagshabandi, Colonel, 261
Najib Bey Salha, 266
Naksh-i-Rustam, 106
Nara, Japan, 288
National Advisory Council, 258
Nationalist Reform Party (Morocco), 141–42
Nationalists. *see* Spanish Civil War
National Reform Party (Morocco), 141–42
"National Revolution" center (Casablanca), 214, 217
Near East: U.S. policy in, 242; tripartite declaration on security in, 266. *See also* Israel; Palestine; Saudi Arabia
Neghelli monoliths, 279
Negroes, (Congo), 299
Nehru, Jawarlal, 293
Neiswanger, Don, 14
New Economic Policy, 63
New Orleans, La.: food, 307–08
New York *Herald Tribune*, 321
New York *Times*, 53, 123
New York *World*, 58
New Zealand: described, 311–12
Nice, France, 286, 324
Nicholas II, Czar, 79
Nichols, Leonora, 19–20
Nijo castle, 288
Nile river, 275–76
Nimr, Dr. Faris, 89
Nitchevo, 70

Noel, Burroughs, 7–8, 15
Nogues, General, 125, 127, 140–41, 168–73; German aims in Morocco, 145–47; Spanish threat to Morocco, 148–49; characterized, 155–56, 165; Gen. Orgaz meeting, 163; Allied landing, reaction, 188–91, 192–94; Operation torch, 199–203; Algiers Conference, 205–08; Darlan deal, 210–11; Darlan contrasted, 212–13; resignation, 219–20
Nokrassy Pasha, 110, 111
Norris, Sen. George, 308
No-Ruz, 106
North African economic accord: origins, 122–23; Weygand-Murphy accord, 126–131, 155, 165, 174
Numismatics, Russian, 76

O'Casey, Sean: *The Plough and the Stars*, 315
Office of Strategic Services, 148, 175; allied convoys, 231–34. *See also* Espionage
Ogpu. *see* Cheka
O'Keefe, Col. Richard J., 246, 251–52, 260–62
Olympia, Greece, 302
Olympic Games, 7–8
Omaha Beach, 319
Omar Khayyam, 104
"Open door" principle: Morocco, 134
Oppenheim, E. Phillips, 179
Orgaz, Lt. Gen. Luis, 149, 156–57; characterized, 158–60; interventionist attitudes, 161–62; Gen. Nogues meeting, 163; Axis invasion of Spanish Morocco, possibility, 184; Spain's neutrality after *Torch*, 222; Patton meeting, 226–27

Pageant of Persia, The, 321
Page's *British Poets of the Nineteenth Century*, 15
Painvin, Capt. Georges, 30, 32, 37–39, 50, 323
Palestine: British mandate over, 81–82; Jewish immigration to, 82–84; Roosevelt-Saud meeting, 84; UN Commission of Inquiry, 86; King-Crane mission, 105; Saudi Arabia's reaction to partition, 238–42, 244–45, 248–49, 250–51
Palmer, Eliot and Eno, 92
Paris, France, 18; restaurants, 42

INDEX   335

Paris Peace Conference, 40
Parker, Stanley, 101
Park Hotel, Nice, France, 324
Paros, Greece, 301
Patmos monastery, 301
Patton, Jr., Gen. George S., 205; described, 208–09, 227; Moroccan border control problems, 223–24; Orgaz meeting, 226–27; Gen. Clark's headquarters contrasted, 227
Pearl Harbor: effect in Spanish Morocco, 160–61
Peden, Mr., 43
Penang, Malaya, 287
Perdicaris, 133
Pere Lachaise, 18
Peron, Juan Domingo, 296
Persepolis, 106
Pershing, Gen. John J., 55
Persia: religions and literature of, 104; Greece compared, 106; described, 106–07; JRC's policy recommendations, 107; Soviet relations, 107
Perth, Australia, 313
Peru: Peruvians characterized, 296
Petain, Marshal Henri Philippe, 145, 168; Vichy-German collaboration, 166–67; and Pierre Laval, 171
Petch banquet, 48, 119
Petroleum accord: U.S./Spanish Morocco, 163–64
Phi Delta Theta, 14, 24–25
Philby, St. John, 34
Phillips, William, 110–11
Pizarro, Francisco, 295–96
Place de la concorde, 18
Point Four program, 257, 279
Political campaigns: financing, 325
Pollyana books, 57
Polonnaruwa, Ceylon, 291
Porteus, Robert, 316
Port Said, 313
Poseidon temple, 302
Potash and Perlmutter, 69
Powell, Captain, 31
Praxiteles, 301, 302
Prester John, 277
Prinz Eugen, 170
Probert, Dick, 51–54, 58
Promenade des Anglais, Nice, France, 297
Propper, Senor, 158
Proteges: in North Africa, 146–47

Protopopescu, Ionel and Nina, 94–95
Pryor, Arthur, 16
Puaux, Gabriel, 220
Puigcerda, Spain, 115
Pusan, Korea, 287
Pushtoon tribes, 256
Pygmies, 299

Queen of Sheba, 269, 273, 276
Quetzalcoatl Temple, 307
Quinn's bar, 310
Quito, Ecuador, 296

R.F. & P. Railroad, 308
Radek, Karl, 65
Rahman el Azzam, Abdul, 89, 110, 111, 323
Raisuli, 133
Ramblas, 118
Randolph-Macon College, 1, 5–6, 14, 16; JRC's and wife's portraits, 71, 77; Walter Hines Page Library, 308; scholar in residence, 325–26
Randolph-Macon Monthly, 7
Randolph-Macon Woman's College, 2
Rankin, Edith, 22–23
Red Cross: Ryan report on Soviet Russia, 52–54
Red Sea, 119
Reed, Arthur C., 124–27
Reed, John: *Ten Days that Shook the World*, 17
Reichmann, Mme. Renee, 159–60
Religious services: Dhahran air base, 259–262
Reliques of the Rives, 306
Republicans. see Spanish Civil War
Reston, James, 87
Reynolds, Charles, 279
Rhodes, 301
Riaz, Maria, 111
Richmond *Times-Dispatch*, 87
Riga Agreement, 59–60, 68
Rimbaud, Arthur, 280
Rio de Janeiro, Brazil, 297
Rivera, Diego, 306, 307
Rives, Elizabeth Browne (great-grandmother), 1
Riyadh: capture of recounted, 254–55
Rockefeller Center: Rivera murals, 306
Rogers Act (1924), 130
Romania: Queen Marie's U.S. visit, 93–94;

People's Democratic Republic of, 95; Soviet Union's export competition, 95–96; origins, 97
Romas, Dionysus: *Casanova at Corfu*, 300
Rommel, Field Marshal Erwin, 162–63, 172
Roosevelt, Pres. F.D.: King Ibn Saud meeting, 84
Royal Hibernian Hotel, 318
Rue Gustve Zede, 18, 41–42
Russell, H. Earle, 176, 200, 209
Ryan, Colonel, 59–60; Ryan report, 52–54
Ryves, Sir Richard, 306

S.S. *Luceric*, 18
S.S. *Rochambeau*, 19
Saba, 269
Sa'di, 104, 106
St. Anthony's monastery, 119
St. Bartholomew massacre, 315
St. Catherine's monastery, 119–20
St. Nazaire affair, 172
Salaries, 102, 130
Samuel, Sir Herbert, 88, 89
San'a, Yemen: described, 269, 270
Sanger, Richard, 246
Sao Paulo, Brazil, 297
Sardan, Olivier de, 214–15
Saud, 242–43
Saud, Ibn, King, 105; FDR meets with, 84; American Israeli policy, 88; *See also* Israel; Palestine; Saudi Arabia
Saud, Prince: Saudi Arabian finances, 252–53; U.S. treaty relations, 258–59
Saudi Arabia: JRC's appointment to, 85; as British zone of influence, 239–242; finances, 252–53, 266–67; Israeli relations, 253–54; Ethiopian relations, 256; treaty relations with U.S. desired, 256–59; JRC's resignation, 267–68; Yemen compared, 269
Scharnhorst, 170
Schliemann, Heinrich, 302
Schroetter, Hilda Noel and Samuel T., 324
Schwarz, Karl: Cheka, 78
Schwedagon Pagoda, 292
Scotland: travels in, 316–18
Scott, Robert Falcon, 312
Scruggs, Phil, 309
Seamen's Church Institute, 18
Sebou River, 185–86
Sellers, Lee, 26, 28, 35, 44

Sellers, Phil, 35
Serruys, Bud, 10
Sevki Pasha, 120
Shaikh Abdullah Sulaiman, 266
Shaker, Emir, 89
Shakespeare, William, 15–16; Francis Bacon controversy, 26; Stratford-on-Avon visited, 315, 320
Sheean, Vincent, 111
Sheehan, Edward: *The Arabs, Israelis and Henry Kissinger*, 84–85
Shereefian family, 239–40
Sherwood, Robert: *Roosevelt and Hopkins*, 129
Shia Moslem rites, 261
Shillock, John C., 154
Shiraz, Persia, 106
Shirer, William, 101
Sigiriya palace, Ceylon, 291
Sigma Upsilon, 7
Sikhs, 293, 294
Simpson, Deacon, 52–53
Simson, William, 70–72, 74–75
Sineky, Jevad Khan, 69
Singapore, 313
Skinner, Cornelia and Otis, 15
Skvartsov, 72–74
Slim, 10, 11
Sloan, Captain, 259–62
Smith, Paul Jordon, 321
Smith, Walter, 163–64
Smoot-Hawley tariff, 95
Snake worship, 279
Snyder, Col. Harry R., 246
Socony-Vacuum Oil Company, 124, 127
Solberg, Col. Robert A., 144, 195–97
Solomon, King, 276
Soong, T.V., 13–14
Soriano, Rafael, 177
South Africa: multiracial groups distinguished, 299
South America: Conquistadors, 295; politics, 296
Soviet Union: Ryan report on, 52–54; U.S. intervention in, 64; Romanian exports, 95–96; Persian relations, 107; German attack begun, 150; 1976 visit, 324
Spain: intervention (WW II) attitudes, 160–61; neutrality after *Torch*, 222
Spaniard: characterized, 153
Spanish Civil War: Irun battle, 113–15; Republicans and Nationalists

characterized, 115; Barcelona, 115–18; JRC's sympathies, 152–53
Spanish Morocco. *see* Morocco; Tangier
Stack, Sir Lee, 90, 110
Stalin, Joseph V., 63
Stanton, Willard Quincy, 147, 191
Stimmel, W.S., 70
Stone, Melville, 51
Storrs, Sir Ronald, 88
Straits of Gibraltar: Great Britain's concern for, 134, 136
Stratford-on-Avon, England, 315, 320
Strauss, Richard, 97
Suez Canal, 100
Suner, Serrano, 149, 161
Sunlander Express, 312
Sunni sects, 261
Sun Yat-sen, Madame, 13
Suzanne, 41
Swope Park, Kansas City, Mo., 16–17
Syagakuin palace, 288
Sydney, Australia, 312
Syria: views on U.S./Israeli relations, 263–64

Tahiti: described, 310
Tamerlane, 324
Tangier: JRC's assignment to, 131–32; international character of, 135; strategic significance of, 136; Tangier Convention (1923), 136–37; Spanish incorporation of, 137–38
Tapline. *see* Trans-Arabian pipeline
Tartar Republic: American Relief Administration in, 66–79, 308. *See also* American Relief Administration
Tatiesheff, General, 79
Taxco, Mexico, 307
Telephones, 99
Temple of Moss, 288
Tennessee Valley Authority, 308
Terry, Bland, 15
Tennyson, Alfred: *Ulysses*, 15
Thailand, 287
Thais, 106
Thomas, Lowell, 21, 34
Time magazine, 107
Tiretta Bazaar, 292–93
Tischendorf, Konstantin von, 119
Tokyo, Japan, 288
Toshadaiji temple, 288
Toulouse-Lautrec, Henri de, 320

Traders Bank, 2
Trans-Arabian pipeline, 239
Transylvania, 97
Treaty of Versailles, 46–47, 56, 322
Triat, M., 144
Trotskyites (P.O.U.M.), 116
Truman, Pres. Harry: Palestine policy, 84–85; JRC's resignation as Saudi Arabian Ambassador, 267–68. *See also* Palestine; Saudi Arabia
Tukels, 276
Tumulty, Joseph Patrick, 54, 55
Turner, Van Arsdale, 68
Twitchell, Karl, 105

Union of Proletarian Men, 113
Union of Socialists and Communists (P.S.U.C.), 116
United Nations Commission of Inquiry: Palestine, 86
United States Congress: World War I debates, 21–23
United States Dept. of State. International Economic Advisers Office, 124
United States Dept. of State. Near Eastern Division: North Africa study, 122–23
United States Dept. of State. Trade Agreements Division, 124
United States Foreign Service: JRC's appointment to, 80; salary cut, 102; described, 130; diplomat's qualities, 282–83
United States Geological Survey, 9
University of Virginia, 1, 7
Untermeyer, Sam, 42
Uriarte, General, 177
Uxmal, Mexico, 306

Vale of Kashmir, 293
Vann, Bryant King, 14–15, 35
Van Zealand, Paul: *Reflections on the Five-Year Plan*, 102
Vichy government: in North Africa, 123, 125; Weygand's attitude towards, 165–66; French attitudes to, 167; effect of Darlan deal, 213, 225, 228
Victoria High School, 8
Vignettes, 324
Villa Mas, 224
Villard, Harry, 123
Virginia House of Burgesses, 1, 109
Virginia Military Institute, 5–7

Virginia Writers Club, 324
Voisin, 42
Von Kluck, General, 18

Wadi Natrun monastery, 119
Wadsworth, George, 99, 104
Wahren, Ivar, 66, 68–69
Wairakei, New Zealand, 311
Waite, Aline, 16–17, 19, 20–21
Waitomo, New Zealand, 311
Wales: travels in, 315–16
Walker, Herschel, 76
Wallace, Edgar, 180
Wallace, William, 318
Washington College, 2
Washington *Post*, 52, 54, 87
Washington *Star*, 52, 54
Weddell, Alexander, 156
Wellington, New Zealand, 312
Weygand, Gen. Maxime, 89; in French N. Africa, 123, 125, 145; Weygand-Murphy accord, 126–131, 155, 165; Vichy attitudes, 165–66; recall, 166, 169; Allied landing, reaction, 190
White, Chief Justice Edward D., 55
White, J.C., 126, 131
White Hart Inn, 315, 316
Wilbur, General, 208
Williams, Jim, 54–55
Williamson, David, 200
Wilson, Pres. Woodrow, 46–48; illness of, 54–55; and Henry Cabot Lodge, 55–56; letter to C.J.R., 55–57
Womack, Jack, 273–74

Woods, Colonel, 36
World War I: effect, 17, 322; JRC in Ambulance Corps, 18–19; Congressional debates on, 21–23. *See also* Cryptography
Wrangel, Baron P.N.: White Army (Russia), 60
Wright, Lt. Commander, 231
Wyatt, Margaret, 308
Wythe, George, 59

Xerxes I, 106

Yahya, Imam, 269, 270–71
Yakushji temple, 288
Yardley, Capt. Herbert O., 26, 37–38, 41–43
Yassin, Shaikh Yusuf, 245–46, 248–50, 253–54, 256–59, 262–65
Yemen: Prince Saud's views of, 259; Saudi Arabia compared, 269; Yemeni character, 271, 274–75; JRC's accomplishments in, 271–73; Ethiopian ties, 277
Yencken, Arthur, 144
Yugoslavia: American Relief Administration, 43, 46–48; medal of, 50. *See also* American Relief Administration
Yuste, Colonel, 144

Zionism: lobbying of American Zionists, 82–84, 86–88. *See also* Israel; Palestine
Zogheb, Count Michel, 113
Zoroastrianism, 106